500 ESSENTIAL
CONTAINER PLANTS

Window Boxes • Balconies • Patios

500 ESSENTIAL
CONTAINER PLANTS

Window Boxes • Balconies • Patios

Edited by
Andrea Rausch and
Annette Timmermann

REBO
PUBLISHERS

© 2004 Rebo International b.v., Lisse, The Netherlands

This 2nd edition reprinted in 2006

Edited: Andrea Rausch and Annette Timmermann

With texts by Wolfgang Beuchelt (Scriptorium Köln): Achillea millefolium – Kniphofia
(Perennial), Regine Ermert: Beta vulgaris – Raphanus sativus / Fragaria x ananassa –
Vaccinium corymbosum / Ocimum basilicum – Allium schoenoprasum (Herbs, Vegetables,
Fruit), Ralph Henry Fisher: Pennisetum setaceum – Zinnia (Plants for as single season),
Alexander Kerkhoff: Dendranthema Indicum hybrids – Melampodium paludosum (Plants
for a single season), Sonja Leyers: Bidens ferulifolia – Dahlia (Plants for a single season),
Samuel Liebe: Acalypha hispida – Bellis perennis / Mesembryanthemum
crystallinum – Pelargonium (Plants for a single season), Brigitte Lots: Climbing plants,
Roses (Rosa "Alba Meidiland" to "Meidiland"), Andrea Rausch: Roses ("Muttertag"
to "Zwergkönig") and all other texts, Brigitte Rüssmann (Scriptorium Köln):
Pernettya – Viola cornuta (Perennials)

Photographs: © Annette Timmermann, Stolpe

Translation and typesetting: Rosetta International, London, UK and A. R. Garamond s. r. o.,
Prague, The Czech Republic

ISBN 90 366 1703 0

Contents

Introduction

What is still stopping you from turning your balcony or terrace into a "green room"? Even the smallest space can be converted into a green oasis where you can find peace and relaxation and give free rein to your passion for gardening. We shall help you achieve this. We shall make suggestions and give you tips on selecting the most beautiful and most suitable plants for balconies and terraces, which you will easily find in any well-stocked nursery or garden center.

Many popular balcony flowers, container plants and herbs are native to the Mediterranean and the tropics. Without their magnificent array of flowers your balcony or terrace would lose much of its attraction throughout the year. This is true even though many of these plants are not frost-resistant, but there are ways of protecting them in the winter. Recently the range of plants for balconies and terraces has vastly increased and now includes many hardy ornamental plants and herbaceous perennials that until now were only found in gardens. Even fruit and vegetables are no longer restricted to the fruit and vegetable garden.

It is important to discover as much as possible about the plants you will be choosing for your balcony or terrace. You need to know whether the plants require full sun or shade; whether they are annuals or perennials; whether they can remain outdoors for winter or whether they should be protected against frost. How large should the container be and what kind of material should it be made of? What kind of compost should you use? How often should the plant be watered? Can you propagate it yourself? And particularly important for terraces and balconies above ground level – do the plants tolerate wind and draught? You will find the answer to all these questions and many others in the introductory chapters and detailed plant descriptions.

The plants have been grouped into categories thus making it easy for you to locate the right plant for the right purpose. Within the categories, the plants are arranged alphabetically according to their Latin botanical name. The English common name is also included. If the plant is also known under another name, this is indicated in the text.

The editors Annette Timmermann and Andrea Rausch are qualified horticulturists and have selected the plants most suitable for your balcony or terrace. Andrea Rausch, who works as a freelance writer and lecturer, is responsible for the practical sections on the cultivation and care of plants as well as for the chapter on with container plants. Annette Timmermann works for a wholesale nursery in northern Germany. She is responsible for the beautiful color photographs in this book.

You will find the most important information about each plant at a glance in the small boxes next to the descriptions. The symbols shown below have the following meanings:

💧 water freely   ₒ°ₒ propagate by seed
○ water sparingly   propagate by cuttings
                    ✄ propagate by division

☼ prefers sun
☀ tolerates shade   ❀ flowering plant
☼ prefers partial shade   ❧ foliage plant
                    ❦ climbing rose

⊔ tolerates being waterlogged
△ sensitive to rain   ❄ frost hardy
⚠ needs sheltered position   ⌂ cover
                    ❅ cool greenhouse
✖ poisonous or can   🌡 temperate house
  cause allergies   ❆ heated greenhouse

⊙ annual
∞ perennial

Cool greenhouse: light, 41–50° F. Conditions suitable for most container plants, which can also be found in cool conservatories or small greenhouses, unheated stairwells and entrance halls.
Moderate: light, 50–59° F. For sub-tropical plants. These conditions can be found in lightly heated conservatories, greenhouses, stairwells or cool living rooms.
Heated house: light, 59–68° F. Tropical plants need warmth, which can be found in heated conservatories, greenhouses and living Hareas.

Please note:
Poisonous and allergenic plants are indicated by the symbol ✖. People with young children, who are often attracted by colorful flowers and fruits, should steer clear of such plants. Also heed the warnings about allergenic plants. The choice of plants is so large that it is always possible to find an alternative to your original choice.

The question of location

The question of location

Before choosing plants for your balcony or terrace, you must first establish the kind of micro-climate on your balcony or terrace. Does your terrace get full sun all day long? Or does it overlook a shady courtyard? Or is it a roof garden exposed to all Kinds of weather, including strong wind?

You must also take the regional weather conditions of your area into account. These include for instance the numbers of hours of sun, the amount of rainfall, humidity of the air as well as, perhaps most important, the length and severity of the winters. Naturally, it is best to select plants whose natural growing conditions such as light, temperature, humidity and soil correspond to the conditions on your balcony or terrace. For instance, in a cool to temperate climate it is best to choose native plants or plants that are native to regions with similar climatic conditions. Plants which in warmer regions are used to big differences in day and night-time temperature are also suitable.

By careful breeding, horticultural growers have created many varieties that are much more tolerant regarding their growing conditions than in their wild form. Find out about the best location for each plant in the section "What thrives where" towards the end of the book.

Full sun

Most summer-flowering plants grow best in the sun. The ideal location is a south-facing balcony or terrace where they get the sun all day long. Marigolds, asters, lemon and orange trees and michaelmas daisies as well as most herbs are among those plants that prefer a south-facing balcony or terrace. In fact, marigolds and Livingstone daisies only open in full sun. Some plants with silvery-blue or gray-green leaves, such as olive trees, eucalyptus, cistus and lunaria are ideally suited for south-facing balconies and terraces. Because of their composition, these leaves heat up less and evaporate less water. Also leathery leaves such as laurel leaves transpire very little, as do the small, needle-like leaves of myrtle and rosemary. But the plants that are best equipped to survive long periods of drought are succulents such as agaves and sedums, whose fleshy leaves are able to store water when it is available.

Sun with midday protection

Some sun-loving plants, especially those with large, tender leaves, need protection from the strong midday sun in summer. Plants such as angel's trumpets and mallows will lose too much water through transpiration if directly subjected to the sun's heat and will wilt. They therefore need a location that is shaded from the heat of the midday sun. This protection could be in the shape of an awning, a sunshade or the moving shade provided by a wall or tree.

Sun to partial shade

Plants that grow in full sun and partial shade usually cause few problems. Southeast or south-west facing balconies or terraces are usually ideal for these types of plants, which include Ageratum, trailing geranium, loosestrife, Grass-of-Parnassus, violets and grasses such as sedge, quaking grass, fescue and moor grass. Plants with variegated leaves also prefer this type of location. They contain less chlorophyll than green-leaved plants and therefore need more light.

Partial shade

It is fortunate that there are also many plants which do not like like too much light. They are ideally suited for partially shady areas because all they need are a few hours of sun in the morning or in the evening on the east or west side of the building. If they stand in full sun, the roots are not able to transport water fast enough to the upper parts of the plant. This shortage of water results in scorched leaves and dried up plants. Plants that grow best in partial shade include burning bushes, fuchsias, begonias, hydrangeas, busy lizzies and clematis.

Shade

The plants most suited for growing on cool, shady, north-west or north-east facing balconies or terraces include ivy, Japanese hop, spotted laurel, camellias, periwinkles, coleus and most ferns, which in nature grow mostly under trees where they get little light.

A shady location is particularly important for these plants during summer when the large soft leaves would heat up too much in the sun and become scorched as a result. They would also lose too much water. On the other hand, variegated species and varieties revert to green again in the shade.

Temperature

Temperature depends not only on location but also on regional climate. Plants that thrive in warmth are happiest in regions where the number of hours of sun is very high and the winters are very mild – wine-growing regions in fact.

Plants of tropical origin such as bougainvillea, cassia and myrtle only grow and flower in relatively high temperatures, while plants native to coastal regions will grow happily in a cooler climate. Dwarf palms, fuchsias and laurel are more robust.

Wind and storms

In coastal regions there is always a stiff breeze on exposed terraces, high balconies and roof terraces. In this case you must choose robust plants such as juniper, broom or gingko that do not require warm conditions. In places exposed to the wind, plants dry out much more quickly. For instance, bamboo transpires so much water that it is very difficult to keep up with watering. Plants with fragile stems or large, soft leaves such as cottonweed, aralias and willow would not be happy in such exposed locations.

In any windy location, it is also advisable to choose large containers for the plants so that they can store enough water in the soil. Large container-grown plants should be arranged in such a way that they cannot be blown over. Walls and hedges will protect the plants from the wind and provide a warmer microclimate in their vicinity. Roofed-over areas are ideal for plants that are particularly sensitive to rain such as smoke

trees, oleanders, leadwort and many types of palms. Succulents, which are native to regions where it rains very little, prefer excessively dry conditions to wet ones. Camellias and fuchsias on the other hand come from regions of the world with fairly high humidity and are therefore very happy during humid, cool summers.

Good manners
Usually a tenant is allowed to decorate a balcony or terrace according to own taste as long as it does not disturb his neighbours. If window boxes are hung on the outside of a balcony or building it is essential to secure them properly. Also, make sure that when watering the plants the water does not run down the facade, onto other people's gardens or property, or onto the pavement. The latter can be particularly dangerous in winter when it freezes. Before undertaking any building work on your balcony or terrace, such as a mini-greenhouse for instance, it may be necessary to first come to some arrangement with your landlord or co-proprietors.

The right container

When choosing a container, it is important to be guided not only by personal taste but also to make sure that it fits in with the environment and that it is large enough for the plant. Remember too that plants with shallow roots are more suitable for growing in containers than plants with deep roots.

Remember to take weight into consideration when selecting plants and containers for your balcony or terrace. A balcony should not be overloaded with plants and garden furniture, an approximate standard being 50 lb per sq ft. However, this is also depends on the size of the balcony and the type of building.

There is a wide choice of shapes and materials available on the market and the guidelines below will help you make the right choice.

Models

Balcony window boxes: These are usually plastic and come in colors ranging from brown, green, white to terracotta and standard lengths of 16, 24, 32 and 40 in. For annuals plants, herbaceous perennials and

dwarf woody plants, we recommend large window boxes at least 8 in wide and deep so that the plants have enough space for the roots to grow. For larger herbaceous perennials and woody plants larger containers will be needed. Boxes with water-tanks are very practical because they will save a lot time in summer when the plants need a lot of water.

Hanging flower pots: These are available in various sizes and are usually made of plastic, their diameter ranging between 8 and 20 in. Do not choose too small a pot because plants can grow very quickly when well looked after. It is important that they hang securely because they can become quite heavy after watering. Preferably they should be sheltered from the wind. There are also hanging flower pots with water-tanks. This will spare you the problem of watering "over your head."

Pots and trays: The good old flower-pot still has its place on balconies and terraces today. Besides the tried and tested clay flower pots, there are now also plastic pots and trays that come in a variety of designs and colors. Imitation terracotta pots are very popular, one of their advantages being that they are very light and do not evaporate water so quickly. Pots are ideally suited for temporary or alternating arrangements because you can just place the pot where you want at the time.

Box or container: These come in a variety of materials such as plastic , stoneware, clay, terracotta or wood. In the case of

larger containers, it is not only appearance which should be taken into account but also weight, especially if they are to placed on balconies and roof terraces. And do not forget that you must be able to move them even when they are full.

Milk churns and the like: You can also use your imagination and be creative. In every household there will be objects such as old milk churns, cast-iron cooking pots, a wheelbarrow or wicker baskets that can easily be converted into containers for plants. So as not to damage the inside of the container, it should first be lined with foil with holes for drainage. If you cannot make any drainage holes in the bottom of

the container, use clay shards or expanded clay to provide a layer of drainage. Wicker baskets should only be used for short-term planting.

Materials

Clay and terracotta: Clay and terracotta containers immediately conjure up images of Mediterranean gardens. Terracotta refers to all unglazed clay pots. They allow good ventilation of the soil but this also means that it will dry out relatively quickly. This material meets the requirements of natural water-balance but is not so good for plants that need a lot of water.

Quality varies enormously especially as far as frost-resistance is concerned. The harder the clay has been fired, the less water it will absorb and therefore the more frost-resistant it will be. In machine-made

containers, there is often a deposit of chalk along the edge because the lime contained in the clay has not been completely burnt out. On the other hand, the development of a patina is a sign of good quality. The high price of hand-made clay pots as opposed to machine-made ones is therefore usually quite justified. Clay pots are heavy but at the same time their weight makes them very stable. Unfortunately, they are quite fragile.

Plastic: The advantage is that they are light in weight and comparatively cheap. The water evaporates very slowly, which is why plastic pots are recommended for moisture-loving plants. The soil warms up quickly but the plastic offers little insulation against frost. Their durability depends mostly on the quality.

Wood: A timeless material with a long tradition – think of "Versailles containers". Wooden containers can be very robust and durable, depending on the type of wood. Oak, for instance, is very long-lasting. They are lighter than terracotta and provide good insulation. However, they are not weatherproof so they should be varnished or painted, and lined inside with foil.

Stoneware: Fired stoneware containers come in various qualities. They are often made in Asia. These glazed containers are both decorative and practical because they extremely weatherproof and easy to wipe clean. They do not develop chalky deposits on the sides. They are frost-resistant but are very heavy and not cheap. There are also containers made from "artificial stone" that are cheaper.

Natural stone: Marble, sand or limestone can be used to make troughs, bowls, vases, urns and much else. But they are heavy and relatively expensive.

Concrete: This is wind-proof and heat-resistant but very cold in winter and very heavy so it is not ideal for balconies. Concrete containers should be washed thoroughly and left outdoors for a long time before planting.

Fibrous concrete containers: These containers come in a great variety of colors and shapes and even include terracotta reproductions. They are made from a mixture consisting of glass fibre, cement and other substances. They have several advantages since they are relatively light, resistant to frost and they "breathe."

Important points you should remember:
- All containers must have an drainage hole at the bottom so that the plants do not become waterlogged.
- Never place the container directly on the soil but arrange it so that the water can drain away. Wooden containers will rot otherwise. Raise the container on wooden battens, bricks, terracotta or ceramic supports.
- Cylindrical shaped containers are best because they combine stability and manageability.
- Before using an unglazed clay container, soak it in a large container of water until no more bubbles rise from it, or leave in the rain for a few days.
- Medium-sized plants such as container plants , small trees or shrubs such as Christmas trees need a container at least 20 x 20 x 20 in.

Propagating plants yourself

There are many reasons for propagating plants yourself. True, you can always buy young plants from nurseries and garden centres, and these may have the advantage of developing and flowering more quickly. But it is more exciting to grow your favorite plants yourself. A further bonus is that propagation from seed, cuttings or division is considerably less expensive than buying plants. If you have large areas to cover this is an important consideration. Finally, it is a fact that some exotic plants, herbs and vegetables are only available as seed, so propagating them yourself is the only way to grow these plants.

Generative propagation

This term refers to the propagation of plants from seed. Balcony gardeners with little space available for propagation trays should restrict themselves to plants that develop quickly from seedling to the flowering stage. This is the case with many summer-flowering annuals, climbers, herbs and vegetables, and even for some herbaceous perennials and grasses.

On the other hand, biennials such as daisies or pansies take much longer by definition: sown in summer, they form a leaf rosette in the first year and only flower the following spring or summer.

Seeds: When buying seeds check the sell-by date and make sure that the sealed packaging has not been damaged. Avoid faded seed packets, since this is an unmistakable sign that they been left too long in the sun and the seeds' ability to germinate may already have diminished. Seeds should always be stored in a dry, well-ventilated place so as not to reduce their germination potential.

Calibrated seeds have been graded according to size, while coated or pelleted seeds have been coated with a protective covering that also makes them easier to handle because they are larger. Vegetable, herb and flower seeds are also frequently sold in the form of seed tape, which automatically places the seeds the correct planting distance from each other.

Seedlings raised from seeds you have harvested yourself will vary to a greater or lesser degree. They can surprise you every year with their variety, while bought seed from F1-hybrids produce plants that are very true to type.

The explanation for this phenomenon is as follows. In the case of F1-hybrids, these are the first generation of a crossing between two homozygous parent plants whose positive properties are combined. But their descendants do not remain uniform, which means that for consistency you must buy seeds every year.

You can harvest your own seeds from a large number of plants very easily. Pick the ripe seed pods, put them in a bowl or box and leave them to dry for a few days in a well-ventilated place.

As soon as the pods have dried out, gently shake the seeds out of the pods and store them in screw-top glass jars or paper bags until the following spring. Remember to label the containers!

Germination containers: You can use ordinary plastic bowls, polystyrene boxes or clay or plastic flower-pots. Nurseries and garden centres sell seed trays with transparent covers as well as heated mini-greenhouses with temperature control for more exotic plants. Multi-pot flats have the advantage that the seedlings quickly develop a firm root ball. Pots made from compressed peat, which swells up when watered, can be planted as they are with the seedlings inside them; they are of course also biologically degradable.

Compost: Compost used for propagation must not be too rich in nutrients because these would "burn" the still fragile roots of the seedlings. In addition, it should be loosely packed so that the fine roots can penetrate it easily, and to avoid waterlogging that would lead to rotting of the embryo. You can either use special seed compost or mix ordinary soil with peat and sand in the ratio of 1:1:1. In order to kill all the germs present in this soil mix, place it in the oven for 30 minutes at a temperature of 210–250° F.

Time for sowing: The best time for sowing varies from species to species. You will find more precise information about sowing times in the respective plant descriptions. But there are a few general guide-lines that can be followed as a rule of thumb:

- You can sow seeds in a heated greenhouse, conservatory or on an indoor window-sill from February onwards. From mid-April to the end of May you can sow in an unheated greenhouse or conservatory, or directly in the chosen site, depending on the individual plant's need for warmth.
- Biennials that are sown in summer must be protected during the winter with a layer of brushwood and placed for instance in an empty window box on the balcony.

Sowing: Pressed peat or multi-pot flats are particularly suitable for sowing large seeds because they can be placed one per pot. Small seeds are best sown in seed trays , while very small seeds should be mixed with sand to prevent them from sticking to each other. The tray should be filled with seed compost – but not too deep – after which the compost should be smoothed to obtain an even surface. The seeds are sown loosely and then watered very gently with lukewarm water. The soil should never be allowed to dry out.

Dark germinators must be covered with a layer of compost while light germinators should only be pressed very lightly into the soil. It is important to follow the instructions on the seed packet.

If the tray has no cover or lid, you can use transparent plastic foil or a sheet of glass to cover the seedlings. It is essential to cover them in order to keep the air humidity high; this will encourage the seeds to germinate.

The best germination temperature is between 64–8° F for most plants. Exotic specimens have a higher germination temperature while species indigenous top temperate regions will germinate at a lower temperature. When the seedlings have germinated the cover can be removed.

Pricking out and subsequent care: When the seedlings have developed leaves and have become crowded in the seed tray as a result, they must be separated. If they have been sown in the final container they should be thinned out, keeping only the most vigorous specimens. If grown in a seed tray they should be pricked out into separate pots. Use seed compost or a 1:1:1 compost, peat and sand mixture to which a little fertilizer is added. Place the plants in a light place but not in direct sun. Pinch out the tips to encourage the seedlings to branch out and become bushy. This means pinching or snipping off the middle stem as soon as the seedling has developed three leaf stems, or in the case of standards when they have reached the desired height. Tender plants should be hardened off before they are taken outdoors, being gradually accustomed to cooler temperatures.

Vegetative propagation

Vegetative propagation, unlike growing from seed, makes it possible to produce a clone of your favourite plant in a very short time. This type of propagation is recommended in the case of plants that take a long time to develop from seed to the stage of a fully-grown plant, or in the case of sterile plants that do not produce seeds. This includes herbaceous perennials, grasses and bulbs as well as trees and shrubs.

There are several methods of vegetative propagation. You will find which method is suitable for which plant in the individual plant descriptions.

Timing: Most plants are best propagated by cutting in spring or early summer so that the young plants can benefit from the increasing daylight. Woody plants can also be propagated from cuttings taken in summer or autumn. The most important prerequisite for successful propagation from cuttings is that the mother-plant should be a healthy, vigorous-growing specimen, since all its characteristics will be passed on. The containers and compost used to propagate cuttings are the same as for raising plants from seed.

Methods: Cuttings can be taken from the tips of shoots (tip cuttings), pieces of stem (softwood or greenwood cuttings) and hardwood cuttings. Some plants can even be propagated from leaf cuttings (from whole leaves or pieces of leaves).

Softwood cuttings should be taken from the soft tip of a one-year old stem during the growing period. In the case of woody foliage plants and conifers these are called greenwood or semi-ripe cuttings. Cuttings from conifers are best taken in spring when growth has slowed down a little.

When taking cuttings it is important to cut just below a leaf node. The cuttings should be between 2–4 in long and have no more than four pairs of leaves, otherwise it will grow very slowly. It is best to remove the lower leaves.

Plant at a depth of about just under 1 in in the compost mix, press the compost around it to secure the cutting, water generously, cover with sheet of transparent plastic film and place in a light warm place. A warm soil temperature will promote rooting.

Reduce the leaf surfaces of cuttings with large leaves by half. This will reduce evaporation and promote rooting.

Cover the cuttings with a transparent lid or a sheet of transparent plastic cling film. However, it is important to ventilate the cuttings now and again. As soon as new leaves begin to develop, the cover can be removed completely. After the cutting has rooted, it should be repotted in a new container with fresh compost. Subsequently, treat the plants in the same way as seedlings, in other words put in a light place, pinch out the growing tip of a stem and harden off.

Hardwood cuttings: In this case cuttings are taken from young shoots of deciduous and evergreen plants after the growing period, mostly in late autumn. They should be 4–12 in long, not too thick, and have at least one eye. All the leaves must be removed. In order to remember which is the top and which is the bottom, cut the bottom diagonally. If you take the cuttings in winter, put them in sand and over-winter them in a frost-free place. In spring, they can be put directly into the compost so that that only one quarter of the length sticks out above the compost.

Grafting: This method is ideal when you want to combine the positive properties of a wild form, which usually serves as a stock, with those of the plant to be propagated, known as the scion. Grafting is a

Tips and tricks

- With cuttings and hardwood cuttings that are more difficult to root, it is advisable to use a rooting powder, available in garden centres, which will promote rooting.

- Usually, trimmings left after pruning in spring or early summer – for instance box or geraniums – can also be used as cuttings.

- Many cuttings will also root in water. Add charcoal to the water to prevent the submerged part from rotting.

- Hygiene is essential at all stages of propagation. In order to prevent infections, use clean containers and disinfected sharp knives.

skill that needs a little practice, so it is best to first try whip and tongue grafting of two equally vigorous plants. In this case the stock and scion are cut diagonally and placed on top of each other. The scion should be at least 4 in long and have one bud. The grafting is secured with a rubber band. Roses are propagated by T-budding. This means that a bud of the plant to be propagated (scion) is inserted in a T-shaped cut in the wild form (stock), an operation that should be carried out in summer. The graft is then secured and in spring the top part of the wild part (stock) is cut so that the bud of the scion can develop further.

Division: This is an easy way to propagate multi-stemmed plants such as herbaceous perennials and bamboos. The best

time is spring when the plants are repotted. If possible, the roots should be slightly loosened before dividing the plant with your hand, a knife or two spades back-to-back, depending on size. The separate pieces are then simply repotted in fresh compost. Make sure that each part has enough roots and leaf buds.

Bulbils: When the foliage is dying down, usually in early summer, the bulbils can be detached from the mother bulb and then planted in autumn after intermediate storage in a dry place. They will also grow in pots.

Separation of offsets: This is a very easy way to propagate plants. Offsets are completely formed mini-plants with roots that can be separated from the parent-plant and just simply planted again. A well-known example is the agave.

Suitable soil and compost

Plants that grow in a limited space and whose soil does not produce its own nutrients need very high quality compost in order to be healthy and vigorous. Its composition should be such that the main nutrients and trace elements are present in the correct quantity and in a balanced ratio. Good soil should be loose and structurally stable, well ventilated and not compressed. On the one hand, the water must drain away easily and on the other hand, enough of it should be retained to meet the plant's needs. The soil used for perennial container plants should be able to store nutrients for a long time because the plants will often remain in the same container for several years.

Organic components

White peat: This is a still fairly little-decomposed peat from the upper layer of a peat bog with a large number of pores that ensures the stable structure of the compost mixture. It improves the compost's aeration and it has the ability to store water and nutrients. A disadvantage is that if it dries out it is very hard to get it moist again.

Black peat: This is older, very decomposed peat with fewer pores than white peat. It improves the supply of nutrients but has a tendency to silt up. Excessive amounts of black peat in the compost may lead to waterlogging.

Compost: In this sense, compost is not the growing medium as a whole but a mixture of decomposed organic waste. It improves the ability of the soil to absorb water and nutrients, makes for better aeration and provides humus. The degree of decomposition and source of the organic detritus used play a decisive part in the quality of the compost (no sludge sewage because of the heavy metals it contains)

Bark humus: This composted waste product from the timber industry is increasingly replacing peat. It usually consists of crushed bark from conifers. The degree of aeration and water absorption depends on the level of decomposition.

Mineral components:

Clay: A mixture of various clay minerals that have a great water and nutrient absorption power. Aeration decreases as the amount of clay in the soil mixture increases.

Loam: A mixture of clay, poor clay and sand that improves water absorption and reduces air permeability.

Sand: The presence of sand in the soil mixture ensures good drainage and breaks up heavy soil. Because it is so heavy, it increases the stability of the plants. Sand is chemically neutral.

Aggregates

Expanded clay, expanded slate, pumice gravel: These are used to improve the aeration and water drainage of the soil mixture.
   Volcanic rock such as perlite and vermiculite and synthetic plastic foam such as expanded polystyrene have similar properties.

Products

You use either standard ready-made soil mixtures or mix them yourself. There are several kinds of soil mixes such as:

Standard soil mixes: These are produced industrially and consist chiefly of white peat, clay and humus, containing varying

---

Making compost on the balcony?
It is undoubtedly a desirable idea to make compost out of humus-rich plant detritus and kitchen waste. This can be done easily enough in a small garden but it is not really practical on a balcony. Apart from the space required, many soil creatures are necessary, from micro-organisms to earthworms, to decompose organic waste. To ensure that these creatures are able to penetrate the compost, it must rest on natural soil and not on a solid base such as concrete. There is also the matter of the smell given off by the decomposing organic material. So in these circumstances it is best to buy organic compost from garden centers, or possibly from official compost heaps in your area.
   Closed thermo-compost makers are ideal for small gardens. Once the enclosed container is filled the compost is not touched until it is ready, which may take as little as three weeks.

amounts of nutrients and aggregates depending on their use. Their advantage is the standard composition and quality while a pH of 5.6 to 6.5 is ideal for the majority of balcony and container plants. There are several kinds of standard soil mixes, ranging from seed soil, low in nutrients, to soil mixtures with slow-release fertilizer for long-term cultivation of perennials and shrubs.

Peat culture medium: The main component is de-limed white or sphagnum moss peat. It is true that white peat has a very loose structure but it has the disadvantage that it dries out very quickly and does not absorb water easily. In addition, it provides little stability, which is a serious disadvantage for large container plants. It is best used as an addition to heavy, loamy soil mixtures so as to loosen them up.

Potting soil: There is a very wide range of potting soils and they also vary considerably in quality. Inexpensive potting soil contains a high proportion of black peat which – if too high – is not ideal for plants. On the plus side, black peat is able to store nutrients but it is heavy, relatively badly aerated and has a tendency to becoming waterlogged. For these reasons is better to use high-quality potting composts, even if they costs a little more.

Special soil mixes: These are specially formulated to meet the requirements of particular plants such as palms, rhododendrons and so on.

Expanded clay, expanded slate: Soil-less mixes consisting of expanded clay have the advantage that they do not decompose unlike organic composts, and aeration always remains constant. Even with complete water-saturation, the roots still have sufficient oxygen. The need to water is greatly reduced because of the medium's great ability to store it. The disadvantage is that it does not store nutrients and plants must therefore be given regular applications of fertilizer.

Home-mixed composts: If you have a garden whose soil is loamy with a good humus content, as well as a compost heap, you can use it to make your own potting soil. A good recipe is: Take garden soil, well-rotted compost, sand and white peat in a 3:3:2:2 ratio. Mix well together and add some fertilizer according to requirements. The disadvantage is that the soil and compost may contain weed seeds, and also the quality will not be as consistent as commercial products.

Half-and-half:
You can also mix unfertilized or lightly fertilized garden soil with bought compost. A good mixture consists of soil, loamy soil and sand in the ratio of 1:1:0.2, to which you add organic fertilizer or slow-release fertilizer.

In order to halt the destruction of irreplaceable peat bogs, white or sphagnum moss peat is increasingly being replaced by the use of other components such as bark humus.

You can contribute to the protection of the environment by buying bark culture mediums instead of soil mixtures containing peat.

The right way to plant

Whether you have propagated the plants yourself or just bought them, there are a few important points to remember before you get to work.

- The best time for establishing most summer flowering plants is spring. However, container-grown plants can be planted all year round except during periods of frost.

- Plants kept indoors should be acclimatized gently to conditions outside by placing them in a sheltered position outdoors for a few days.

- The root ball must never be allowed to dry out. Before planting a new plant in its container, water it generously. If very dry, leave it to soak in a bucket or bowl of water.

- Newly planted specimens, especially flowering plants, will be a bit tender, so they should be protected from possible late frosts. Simply cover them in the evening with bubble wrap, straw matting or newspaper.

- Plants bought in plastic pots should be removed from the pots before planting, but pots made from peat or recycled waste paper need not be removed. Nonetheless the plants will root more easily if these are first lightly crushed or torn open.

- Repot plants at the same depth as before.

- Leave a space of about 1 in at the top so that the soil does not get washed over the edge when the plant is watered.

- All containers should have drainage holes. Re-used containers should be thoroughly washed with soft soap and water or a water and vinegar solution.

- Place shards of clay or expanded clay at the bottom of the container to improve the drainage.

- Young plants should be planted in small pots so that the roots quickly fill the pot.

- Then water the container generously so that the plants have sufficient moisture and any holes in the soil are washed together.

Looking for a stand-in for vacation

You all know the problem – who will look after your beloved plants, your pride and joy during vacation? If you are lucky you will have helpful neighbours who will be very happy to help. But there are also watering systems that can make your life much easier. Garden centers sell containers and hanging baskets for balconies fitted with water-tanks. This can give you up to 2 weeks free of watering, depending on the weather. More complicated automatic watering systems are also available.

To reduce evaporation you should put the plants in a shady position and cut off all the flowers. Larger specimens should be placed in a tray that is filled with water just before you leave.

Smaller containers can be watered using a wick. Push one end of the wick into the soil and the other end in a bowl or bucket filled with water. Make sure that the wick cannot slip out. It is best to use wicks made from artificial material so that as little water as possible evaporates. You can also place several pots in a bowl filled with clay granules, saturated with water.

Watering your plants

All container-grown plants must be watered regularly because unlike a garden there is no earth continually rained upon from which they can get further supplies of water. Remember this when choosing your plants and planning your balcony or terrace. Is there a water supply in the vicinity or will you have to carry watering-cans to and fro? How much you will have to water the plants depends on a number of factors:

How much water the plants need: Plants with large, soft leaves such as cottonweed (*Abutilon theophrasti*) or African hemp need a lot of water because of the surface area of their large leaves. Plants with fleshy, leathery or small leaves evaporate less water or can store it better so that they will more readily tolerate periods of drought. This includes agaves, purslane, laurel, citrus plants, myrtles and rosemary.

Containers: Small containers need to be watered more often than large containers, and plastic containers retain moisture longer than clay or terracotta.

Soil mix: Sandy soils dry out more quickly than loamy ones.

Weather and position: In sunny weather, dry air conditions or windy weather, plants will need much more water than in humid or sultry weather conditions, or if they are placed in a sheltered location.

The right way to water

- Check the water situation every day even in rainy weather. This is because much of the rainwater runs off the dense mass of leaves and never reaches the container.
- It is best to water in the morning or evening when it is not too hot. This gives the water sufficient time to reach the roots without evaporating before it gets to them.
- Never water the plants in the hot midday sun. Water directly onto the soil; do not pour water on the plant which will cause unsightly spots on the leaves, as well as encouraging mould and fungal infections to develop.
- Frequent, superficial watering is not as effective as a good soak, so it is better to water less frequently but more penetratingly. However, "thirsty" plants like angel's trumpets may need watering twice a day in very hot weather.
- In the case of succulent plants, such as agaves, wait until the soil is completely dry before watering.

- Waterlogging must be avoided at all cost because most plants will not tolerate it.
- If a container or pot has completely dried out, it is best to give it a good soak. Leave the plant and container to soak in a basin or tank until there are no longer any bubbles coming to the surface.
- You may be lucky enough to have a water-butt to collect rainwater. This is less cold and less alkaline than most tap water. It is important to use soft water such as rainwater for all lime-hating plants such as heathers, rhododendrons and hydrangeas. If you have no water-butt you can buy water-softening agents in specialist shops.

Many of the plants which are suitable for growing in containers will tolerate short periods of drought. They usually recover very quickly after generous watering. However, this should not be allowed to happen too often.

Balanced feeding

As important as water are the nutrients that are quickly used up by the plant. You can use a quick-acting organic fertilizer or a slow-release fertilizer that releases the nutrients over a long period. If necessary, you can also give the plant weekly applications of a quick-acting mineral compound fertilizer. If the plants look weak and stunted or if the leaves turn yellow and fall off, it usually means the plant is in desperate need of fertilizer.

Warning: Too much fertilizer can also be bad. For instance, an excess of nitrogen leads to weak, soft plant tissue that is extremely vulnerable to attacks from pests. It also encourages plants to produce leaves at the expense of flowers.

The right fertilizer

Mineral fertilizer

Mineral compound fertilizers: These compound fertilizers contain all the main nutrients and trace elements. These are applied in the form of chemical salts, which can be absorbed quickly by the plants. They are available as liquid fertilizer, powder or sticks. The latter provide the plants with food for several weeks. These mineral complete fertilizers are particularly suited for quick feeding during the main growth period, especially for plants that need a lot of food such as angel's trumpets, geraniums and petunias. Always follow the instructions on the package to avoid applying too much fertilizer and burning the plant.

Slow-release fertilizer: With these the nutrient salts are present in a neutral binder, usually in the form of small pellets that are gradually dissolved when watering the plants. The binder causes the nutrients to be released over a long period, which may be 3-4, 6 or 9 months depending on its effectiveness. If you have added slow-release fertilizer when planting you can usually wait a few weeks before applying more fertilizer. Another advantage of this type of fertilizer is that over-fertilizing is avoided because of the gradual release of nutrients.

Special fertilizer: If the plants lacks a particular nutrient, this need can be met by the application of a special single nutrient - or trace element fertilizer. These come in the form of single or compound fertilizer, for instance special iron fertilizer.

In the case of lime-hating plants like rhododendrons, hydrangeas or myrtles only special fertilizers that will not raise the acidity level of the soil should be used.

The particular needs of certain plants are met by specially formulated preparations, such as cactus fertilizer.

Symptoms of deficiency

Lack of... ... Main nutrients	Typical symptoms
Nitrogen (N)	Nitrogen is an important component of chlorophyll; older leaves become lighter and growth slows down.
Phosphorus (P)	Fewer flowers, reduced growth, the underside of the leaves and the stems turn reddish, the uppersides dark green; first affects the older leaves.
Calcium (Ca)	The tips of the shoots, the flowers and fruits become deformed and discoloured; the veins in the leaves turn brown and the stems may break; causes spots on apples and flower-bud rot in tomatoes.
Potassium (K)	This promotes the absorption of water and encourages growth of supporting tissue; deficiency causes wilting plants, leaf chlorosis, death of the affected areas, reduced frost resistance.
Sulphur (S)	Similar symptoms to nitrogen deficiency.
Magnesium (Mg)	Chlorosis between the veins of the leaves, especially in older leaves, which then die and drop off.
... Trace elements	
Iron (Fe)	Chlorosis of the leaves but the veins remain green.
Copper (Cu), Boron (B), Molybdenum (Mo)	Deformed, discoloured ends of shoots, flowers and fruits.
Manganese (Mn)	Spotted chlorosis on mature and young leaves.

Explanation:
Chlorosis: the leaves become lighter in color and turn yellow because the formation of chlorophyll is hampered.
Necrosis: the leaves turn brown and die off.

Organic fertilizer

These consist of animal or vegetable matter that must first be transformed in the soil into a form that can be assimilated. The advantage of this type of fertilizer is that because they decompose gradually they remain effective for a long time. In soil rich in humus they encourage the growth of micro-organisms, which in turn make it possible for the nutrients to be absorbed by the plants. However, it is important to mention at this point that the micro-organisms present in containers are already numerous enough.

The danger of over-fertilizing is small since the nutrients must first be converted. On the other hand, an acute lack of food cannot be corrected immediately by the application of an organic fertilizer. There are special organic fertilizers formulated for special requirements of plants such as citrus plants or cacti.
Organic fertilizers of vegetable origin: compost, crushed soy, crushed castor-oil plant and crushed rape.
Organic fertilizers of animal origin: guano, horn shavings or bone meal. Because of the BSE crisis, this has come under suspicion, but it is rich in phosphorus that is very beneficial to flowering plants.

Organic-mineral fertilizer

Pure organic fertilizers do not always contain all important nutrients and trace elements. This disadvantage is easily remedied by using an organic-mineral fertilizer. Besides making nutrient salts immediately available, they also contain slow-release organic compounds.

Plant tonic

These are substances that do not introduce food into the soil in themselves but rather improve the availability of nutrients in the soil through their positive physical and chemical properties. These substances include rock powder, valerian extract and algae.

Algae extracts contain many important trace elements, vitamins, enzymes, amino-acids, proteins and phyto-hormones that stimulate plant growth and are suitable for all types of plants. They can be applied when watering or sprayed as a leaf fertilizer.

Plant manure can be made for instance from stinging nettles, dandelions, field horsetail, garlic and comfrey. The result is both a plant tonic and a pest repellent.

Basic recipe for plant manure:
Put 2 lbs fresh, coarsely chopped herbal material in 2.5 gallons water (2 lb per gallon). Then put the container in a warm, sunny place. To ensure that animals do not fall into it, you should cover the container with a trellis. Stir the liquid manure daily and leave it to ferment for a week or two so that the active agents are released. When the liquid has turned dark and no longer foams, it is ready. Before using the manure, strain it and dilute with water (ratio 1:10). It can applied when watering or sprayed. This is best done in the evening in order to avoid burning the leaves.

Unfortunately, the process of fermentation produces unpleasant smells. This can be brought under control by adding rock powder or powdered stinging nettles, available in shops, every day to the fermenting manure.

Important rules for fertilizers

- It is better to apply weak concentrations of fertilizer frequently rather than high concentrations less frequently. High concentrations of fertilizer can damage the tender roots of plants. This is particularly true in the case of lime-sensitive plants. You should not introduce more nutrients into the soil than are being taken out. Always follow the instructions regarding dosage shown on the package.
- Only feed repotted plants after 4 to 6 weeks so that they have enough time to develop a root system.
- When applying slow-release fertilizer, only feed again after 10 weeks, or a period depending on the length of effectiveness of the particular slow-release fertilizer used.
- Do not feed container-grown woody plants or woody plants that have been planted out until the shoots have had time to mature fully before the winter.
- No not apply fertilizer if the soil is dry.
- Organic fertilizers promote the formation of humus and prevent over-fertilizing.

Time for repotting

- Fully-grown plants are usually repotted every 2–3 years; vigorous growing plants that need a lot of food should be repotted every year.

- Repotting is absolutely necessary when the container is completely filled with roots, which can then be seen growing out of the drainage holes, or when the soil looks hard and crusty. Do not wait until the plants shows signs of food deficiency.

- When repotting, loosen up the root ball and shorten excessively long roots. Remove all brown, rotten roots to encourage the formation of new roots.

- If necessary, all the roots can be cut back. But this must be done with great care, making sure that the root system and the rest of the plant remain in proportion.

- The best time to do this is spring as soon as growth resumes – for instance, when you are putting the plants outdoors again. At the same time the new compost will stimulate a powerful growth spurt.

- Never repot during the flowering season because this would encourage the plants to produce more shoots rather than flowers.

- The diameter of the new pot should never be larger than 1 in more than the previous pot in the case of small plants and 2–4 in in the case of larger ones. Do not forget to put a layer of drainage material at the bottom of the pot.

- Plant at the same depth as in the previous pot, otherwise the stem or trunk could rot.

- After repotting, keep the plants drier than usual for about two weeks so that they resume growth more quickly. Do not place newly potted plants in full sun.

Successful over-wintering

With the exception of annual summer flowers, herbs and vegetables, all container-grown plants must be protected from frost. But this protection varies depending on the degree of tenderness of the plant:

- Frost-resistant ornamental shrubs, fruit trees and herbaceous perennials can remain outdoors.

- The first priority is to protect the roots, which are sensitive to frost. The container can be wrapped in coconut matting, rush matting or bubble wrap and the top soil covered with dry leaves or straw. Covering the leaves or straw protecting surface with a mat will prevent the material from being blown away. Another possibility is to wrap the container in foil and place it in a larger container. You can further improve the insulation by filling the gap with leaves.

- Never put the container directly on the ground but on wooden laths, tiles or "feet" with a gap of at least 0.5 in. This both insulates the container and allows the water to drain away. In this way you will avoid waterlogging and frost damage to the roots and container.

- In winter move the plants to a sheltered position, such as against a house wall.

- Frost-sensitive parts of the plant such as the grafting point of standard roses should be protected with jute bags or brushwood. Evergreen plants like bamboos only need to be protected during periods of severe frost. The cover should be removed during the day.

- Evergreen herbaceous perennials such as Christmas roses or cyclamens should be protected with a layer of brushwood or dry leaves during lengthy periods of frost. Small containers should be grouped together.

- Similarly, it is recommended that the flowers of autumn-flowering herbaceous perennials should be protected from night frosts by covering them with fleece or similar material.

- Climbing plants trained against a support can be protected from severe frost with rush matting, which can then be easily removed on frost-free days.

- Evergreen plants should be watered in winter but only on frost-free days.

- Frost-sensitive, exotic container plants must over-winter indoors.

- They must be brought indoors before the first frost. Light, cool rooms, stairwells and conservatories are ideal for the purpose. Some plants will even survive in dark basements. However, it is important that the rooms should be aired regularly on frost-free days. Usually the temperature should be between 41 and 50° F but always check the particular requirements of your plants regarding light and temperature.

- Evergreen and winter-flowering plants will always need a light place to over-winter, but deciduous plants or plants that have been severely cut back can over-winter in a dark place.

- As a rule of thumb: the brighter and warmer the over-wintering room is, the more often the plant must be watered. But only water when the soil is dry.

- If you do not have much room and you would like to cut back large plants so as to accommodate them, make sure that the species will tolerate severe pruning. These species include angel's trumpets and fuchsias.

- Check regularly for pests and diseases and remove all affected parts.

- As the light increases, about the beginning of March, most plants begin to show signs of growth and produce new shoots. This is the time to prune them into shape or to the desired size – depending on the species – and if necessary repot and gradually accustom them to stronger light.

Pruning and cutting back

- Useful "transport aids" when bringing the plants in and taking them out are stands with rollers and trolleys. You could also simply install runners under wooden containers.

- If you do not have enough space at home, ask your gardener if he has an over-wintering service.

Make it a habit to remove dead blooms and cut back wilted shoots. In this way, the plant will direct its energy towards producing more flowers rather than seeds, unless you want the seeds for later use. This is recommended, for instance, for petunias, slipperworts (calceolaria), lobelias and alyssums after the main flowering. They will flower again later after a short pause. Herbaceous perennials such as phlox, gaillardia, American sneezewort and hardy herbaceous sunflowers also benefit from deadheading.

Most species flower more prolifically if they are cut back regularly. Regular pruning will keep older container plants in shape and promotes flowering. Pruning should take place in spring when dried and excessively long, thin shoots should

be removed. If you cut back lateral branches, the pruning will hardly be noticeable. If the plant is looking a little bare or seems to lack vigour and flowers less than expected, it needs rejuvenating pruning. This involves cutting back all the shoots; the older ones can even be cut down to ground level, or close to the trunk. Weaker shoots should also be removed, leaving only the most vigorous ones.

Lady's mantle (alchemilla), yarrow, catmint and sage will flower a second time after radical pruning. Campanulas and Indian nettles will produce fresh new foliage if completely cut back after flowering.

Plants that produce flowering shoots during the whole growing season can be cut back drastically during the rest period.

Spring-flowering produces flower buds on the previous year's wood. In this case, radical pruning is not advised, and only weaker shoots should be removed immediately after flowering.

Summer-flowering shrubs can be cut in February on a frost-free day. These

There are two kinds of purning:
Structural pruning: This is carried out on young plants to encourage good branching. It is important to emphasize the characteristic habit of the plant.
Maintenance pruning: This is carried out on older plants to maintain the shape and size, and to encourage the production of flowers.

plants include for instance forsythia, weigela, hogweed, guelder rose and deutzia. Spring-flowering plants such as ranunculus should only be cut after flowering.

When growing plants as standards, remove all the side-shoots of the young plant until it has reached the desired height. Then cut off the growing tip to promote the formation of lateral shoots. These must be continuously cut back until the crown has acquired its final shape. Shoots produced along the trunk must be removed.

Ideas for arranging plants

The range and variety of plants, containers and accessories is endless so that you can really give free rein to your imagination when designing your balcony or terrace. The designs we have illustrated here should give you some ideas when doing so. But while allowing your creativity to take over, you must remember the needs of the plants regarding position and cultivation so that you can enjoy your "garden room" to the full.

Combine plants of different sizes and shapes to create variety. Place tall-growing plants at the back of the container, bushy ones on the sides and hanging ones at the front.

Groups of pots and containers can be re-arranged depending on the season. Regularly flowering plants should be placed at the front. Any heavy containers that are hard to move should be planted with evergreens because they will be decorative in any season.

The arrival of spring

Spring flowers add a cheer to any balcony or terrace: primroses, hyacinths, lilies-of-the-valley and ornamental alliums. Remember that scented plants should be planted at face height.

Still life with tulips, crocuses, grape hyacinths and double dwarf campanulas. You can make delightful flower arrangements by putting a few simple pots together. Loose collars round the tulips prevent the stems from blowing over in the wind.

A blaze of summer color

In summer your balcony or terrace will be ablaze with color. This brightly coloured hanging basket contains trailing petunias, tuberous petunias, busy lizzies, forget-me-not, marigold and will also do well in partial shade. It is important to put together plants of similar vigour so no plant is overrun by another.

Abutilon and bog star compete for brilliance, the underplanting with white flowers sets them off to perfection and emphasizes the bright yellow of the abutilon and bog star. Tip: before filling the wicker basket with soil, line with a thin sheet of plastic and make a few holes to allow the water to run away.

An autumn atmosphere

Set against a wonderful autumn backdrop, this seat invites you to while away the time on sunny days. Autumn chrysanthemums, heather, asters and sedge complement each other beautifully.

A combination that is both beautiful and practical. These succulents include echeveria, crassula, kalanchoë and stonecrop, all needing very little water.

A double helping of nostalgia. These terra-cotta containers are filled with campanulas, hydrangeas and a small oleander next to a wicker basket containing Indian pinks and baby's breath.

Rose hips and other similar autumn fruits add a welcome touch of warm color at this time of year. The picture is completed with heather, cyclamen and ornamental cabbage.

Not just a visual delight – this prolific crop shows that growing vegetables in a window box is definitely worthwhile. Anyone would be delighted to receive such a magnificent gift hamper!

A mini herb garden with rosemary, marjoram, lemon balm, parsley and chervil for compulsive nibblers and gourmets. The delicious fragrances exuded by these herbs is more intense if they are placed in a sunny, dry position.

Container plants for a single season

Summer would only be half as beautiful without annual summer flowers, bulbs and tuberous plants. They look just as magnificent in pots, tubs, window boxes and hanging baskets as they do in flowerbeds. Not only do they add colour and structure but they also attract nature in the form of bees, bumblebees and butterflies to high-level windows and balconies.

Most annual species are sensitive to frost and can only be planted out after the danger of frost has passed. Annual summer flowering plants only need one season from sowing to flowering and the ripening of the seeds. Biennials produce only leaves in the first year and flower the following spring. Most biennials prefer a sunny position but there are also some that will grow in a shady corner. Both annuals and biennials produce better results in good quality soil. Some plants need a lot of watering while others need very little, but they all hate being waterlogged. Because container-grown plants have no food reserves in the soil, it is advisable to apply fertilizer in the form of slow-release fertilizer or organic fertilizer when planting out. Depending on the need for food of the particular plants, it is recommended to add fertilizer again after a few weeks either with fast-acting liquid fertilizer or fertilizer sticks. But do read the instruction regarding the amount required.

Annuals, biennials and bulbs are wonderful flowering and foliage plants for a single season but you should not lose heart when they die after the first night frost. In order to enjoy your favourite plants another year, gather the seeds, take cuttings or remove bulbils or bulblets for propagation. Pelargoniums and fuchsias can over-winter in a frost-free space.

Acalypha hispida

ⓘ

Location: 🌢 ☼ ⚠
Care: 🌡
Propagation:
Characteristics: ✖ ∞ ✿
*Pests: red spider mite, mealy
    bug, scale insect, white fly*
Flowering: summer – autumn

Red-hot cat's tail

Acalypha hispida

Also known as chenille plant, red-hot cat's tail, a member of the *Euphorbiaceae* family, is an erect, soft-stemmed shrub. In summer it produces numerous tiny, crimson flowers, borne on long pendent spikes. The large, soft catkin-like spikes are usually deep red but grey-white in the "Aba" variety. The large oval leaves are also extremely decorative. *Acalypha hispida* is an ideal container plant for balconies and terraces, reaching a height of about 35 in and a spread of 16 in. Ideally, it needs a constant temperature of 61° F throughout the year. It grows best in well-drained soil, in a sunny to partially shady position, sheltered from the wind. In summer it should be watered freely and fed every week. In winter, water sparingly. Light pruning in late winter promotes bushy growth. It is propagated from cuttings taken in early summer.

Pinwheel

Aeonium

ⓘ

Location: ◌ ☼-☀ ⚠
Care: 🌡
Propagation: ･°ﾟ   ❀✿
Charateristics: △ ∞ ✿ 🌼 ❄
Pests: aphids, mealy bug
Flowering: spring – summer

This genus which belongs to the family of the *Aeonium* includes about 40 species of rosette-forming succulents. This frost-tender plant is sensitive to cold and tolerates a minimum temperature of 41° F. It make an excellent container plants for balconies and terraces. *Aeonium* is a particularly popular species that forms dense, bushy round shrub about 24 in high. The short stems bear rosettes of thick, blue-green, spoon-shaped leaves with beautiful red edges. The terminal clusters of creamy-yellow flowers tinged with pink are borne in spring and early summer. The plant prefers light, well-drained soil, ideally cactus compost, and a sunny to partially shady position, with moderate watering. It should be fed once a month with an organic fertilizer or cactus fertilizer. Dead flower heads should be removed. It is propagated from seed in spring or from stem- or leaf cuttings.

*F*lossflower

Ageratum houstonianum

Ageratum in Greek means "not ageing". The name refers to the long flowering of this popular summer flowering plants which is particularly suitable as a container plant for balconies and terraces, where it looks very good planted with fuchsias and busy lizzies. In temperate climates, flossflowers, which have a dense, strongly branched habit, are usually grown as an annual. The oval to heart-shaped leaves are often covered with fine white hairs. In summer, the plant is covered with numerous clusters of tiny flower heads. Besides varieties with flowers in various shades of blue, there are other varieties with pink and white flowers. Flossflower prefers well-drained fertile soil in a very sunny, sheltered position. In high summer it needs plenty of water and should be fed every two weeks. Regular deadheading will prolong the flowering season. The plant contains cunarin, which can cause allergies.

Ageratum

ⓘ

Location: 💧 ☀ ⚠
Propagation: ⣀
Characteristics: ✖ ☉ ❀
Diseases: root rot
Flowering: summer – autumn

*L*ove-lies-bleeding

Amaranthus caudatus

This annual plant, a member of the *Amaranthus* family, does best in a sunny, sheltered position and looks well planted on its own in hanging baskets and containers. It reaches an impressive height of 60 in and looks good surrounded by containers with smaller annuals. The dark-red flowers are borne in long, drooping tassels from summer until early autumn. The axillary or terminal spikes, which are yellow-green in the variety "Viridis," last a long time. The plant's beauty is further enhanced by the vigorous, upright stems and large leaves. *Amaranthus* grows best in moderately fertile well-drained soil in a sunny position. In summer it must be watered freely to prolong flowering. It can be grown from seed in spring. Young plants should be pruned to encourage denser growth. Unfortunately it is prone to attacks from aphids, snails and caterpillars.

ⓘ

Location: 💧 ☀ ⚠
Propagation: ⣀
Characteristics: ☉ ❀
Pests: Aphids, caterpillars, slugs and snails
Flowering: summer – autumn

Antirrhinum majus

Location: ◌ ☼ ⧖
Propagation: ⸫
Characteristics: ✖ ☉ ❀
*Diseases: snapdragon rust,
   mildew*
Pests: aphids
Flowering: summer – autumn

Snapdragon

Antirrhinum majus

The ancient Greeks called this member of the *Scrophulariaceae Antirrhinum* family, which means "nose-like"; in French, on the other hand, it means "wolf's mouth". The comparison of the flower to the mouth of an animal is based on the 2-lipped structure of the flower and particularly on the prominent bulge of the underlip. These frost-sensitive plants are usually grown as annuals. The dwarf varieties, up to 8 in, are ideal for growing in containers on balconies, especially because snapdragons come in almost every colour of the spectrum. Flowering can be prolonged by deadheading regularly. The plants are easy to grow from seed and grow best in fertile, moist soil in a sunny, sheltered position, but they hate being waterlogged. They can be moved indoors to over-winter but they will then be prone to fungal infection. The plant can sometimes cause allergic reactions.

Asteriscus

Asteriscus maritimus

Location: ◌ ☼ ⧖
Propagation: ⸫
Characteristics: ☉ ❀
*Pests: aphids, white fly, leaf
   miner, thrips*
Flowering: spring – autumn

Asteriscus has recently become particularly popular among gardeners. This is due partly to its compact habit and decorative tufted growth but above all to its early, prolific flowering. The attractive, deep yellow flowers are produced uninterruptedly from April until November, unaffected by temperate weather conditions. *Asteriscus* is a dwarf species, grown as an annual, which reaches about 20 in in height and is therefore ideally suited as a container plant for balconies and terraces. It looks very attractive both on its own or combined with other plants. It grows best in well-drained soil and benefits from regularly feeding. It tolerates temperatures as low as 41° F. It should be deadheaded and watered regularly.

Summer cypress

Bassia scoparia

From a distance summer cypress, a member of the *Bassia* family, looks like a small conifer. Besides its attractive bright green feathery leaves, it also has a decorative oval to round habit. This annual, which grows up to 39 in high, does not mind pruning but it does need sufficient space to achieve its full effect. It provides a wonderful background for bright summer-flowering plants. The foliage of the "Childsii" variety remains lime-green even after the first frost while the leaves of the "Trichophylla" variety turn an attractive autumn red. The summer cypress thrives in fertile, well-drained soil and should be watered moderately even during the growing season. It grows best in a very sunny position protected from the wind. It will also benefit from 2-weekly applications of fertilizer. It is sown indoors directly in the pot, covering the seeds only lightly with a thin layer of soil.

Location: ◊ ☼ ⚠
Propagation: ⸫
Characteristics: ⊙ ☙
Flowering: summer

Begonia elatior hybrids

Begonia elatior group

Begonia elatior hybrids were developed at the end of the 19th century. This led to the creation in 1961 of "Rieger's Schwabenland," a variety that distinguished itself by compact growth, vigour and its easy propagation from leaf cuttings. It is now a very popular greenhouse plant that produces an abundance of white, pink or red flowers. It will also add a magnificent touch of colour to any balcony or terrace if placed in a sheltered position. This type is much more attractive than the tuberous begonias. The rose-like blooms contrast beautifully with the asymmetric, pale to olive-green leaves. Hanging or trailing forms such as the "Charisma" hybrids with double scarlet, pink or salmon-coloured flowers are ideal for hanging baskets.

Location: ◉ ☼ ⚠
Care: ⬡
Propagation: ⸫
Characteristics: ⊙/∞ ☙
Diseases: grey mould, mildew,
 stem and rhizome rot
Pests: caterpillars, mealy bugs,
 aphids, mites, thrips,
 weevils
Flowering: summer, in warm
 conditions autumn – winter

Semperflorens begonia

Location: ◗ ☼ ⚠
Propagation: ₀°°
Characteristics: ⊟ ✖ ☉ ❀
Diseases: grey mould, mildew,
  stem and root rot
Pests: caterpillars, mealy bugs,
  aphids, mites, thrips, weevils
Flowering: summer – autumn

Bedding begonias

Begonia: Semperflorens group

The ancestor of the "perpetual flowering" bedding begonia is native to Brazil. The leaves have a frosted, lacquer-like surface that make them very decorative additions to balconies and terraces. There are tall-growing and low-growing varieties with single and double blooms that flower prolifically throughout summer until late autumn. The "Cocktail" series includes bushy mini-plants with bronze-coloured foliage while the "Thousand Wonders" includes compact sun-resistant plants in various shades. Bedding begonias combine beautifully with verbena and dwarf marguerites. They grow best in partial shade in fertile, reasonably moist soil and will benefit from feeding every two weeks. Pinching out the tips will encourage a bushy growth. It is best to buy new plants because propagation is quite difficult.

Location: ◗ ☼ ⚠
Care: ❄
Propagation: ₀°°   ✂❀
Characteristics: ∞ ❀
Diseases: grey mould, mildew,
  stem and root rot
Pests: caterpillars, mealy bugs,
  aphids, mites, thrips, weevils
Flowering: summer

Tuberous begonias

Begonia: Tuberous group

Tuberous begonias are native to the South American mountainous regions. The mostly upright, bushy herbaceous perennials are very popular because of their decorative foliage and magnificent blooms. There are upright varieties for flowerbeds, containers and pots as well as large-flowered trailing begonias for hanging baskets. They come in almost every colour except blue and green and the attractive flowers can be single or double, sometimes with wavy-edged or ruffled petals. The plants rest in winter when the tubers should be lifted before the first frost, dried and stored at a temperature of 41–45° F. In early spring they can be planted with the eye facing upward in humus-rich, moist soil in a pot. They should only be taken outdoors when all danger of frost has passed, on the east side of the balcony or terrace, in a position where they are sheltered from the wind. The plants can be raised from seed or propagated from cuttings but the easiest way is by division of the tubers.

In summer these produce long fragile stems with a few mid-green leaves. The stems should be supported in the case of upright varieties. Throughout the summer, the plants produce clusters of two small, female flowers and a striking, double male flower. During the flowering season, tuberous begonias must be watered only sparingly with weekly applications of fertilizer. Flowering can be prolonged by removing the faded female blooms. The upright-growing varieties form the main group. The compact "Multiflora" begonias are grown for their numerous, small flowers while the hybrids of the "pendula" group are very suitable for hanging baskets.

Tuberous begonia hybrids

Bellis perennis

ℹ

Location: 💧 ☼–☀
Care: ❋
Propagation: ₀°° ✿
Characteristics: ∞ ❀
Flowering: spring

Common daisy

Bellis perennis

Common Daisy is a rosette-forming herbaceous perennial. The genus, which includes 15 species, is native to Europe, North Africa and Turkey. Common daisy is usually grown as a biennial, which means that the leaf rosette forms in the first year and flowers the following spring. Each rosette produces small flowers uninterruptedly from late winter until early summer. Flowers may be white, pink or crimson, fully double or pompon shaped. It is important to deadhead regularly in order to avoid self-seeding. The plants are raised from seed in summer or propagated by division after flowering. In winter the young plants are covered to protect them from the cold and moved to a frost-free place. These undemanding plants grow well in sun or partial shade in fertile soil and benefit from regularly watering.

Tickseed

Bidens ferulifolia

ℹ

Location: 💧 ☼
Propagation: ₀°° ✿
Characteristics: ⊔ ☉ ❀
Flowering: summer

The *Bidens* genus includes about 200 species grows in most hot to temperate regions of the world. Tickseed, which is native to Mexico and Arizona, has a bushy habit and grows about 20 in high. It has small, pinnate leaves with 1 to 3 leaflets and gold-yellow flowers that are produced from early summer until autumn. It is propagated from seed in spring, from cuttings in spring and autumn or division in early spring at the beginning of the growing season. Tickseed has a very spreading habit and should always be planted on its own in containers, pots or hanging baskets. This very undemanding, prolifically flowering plant does not need much food and will grow in any soil but needs a position in full sun. It is very sensitive to frost and is therefore grown as an annual. "Golden Goddess" and "Arizona" are very attractive and popular varieties.

Swan River daisy

Brachyscome iberidifolia

The genus to which this species belongs is native to New Zealand. It includes 60 to 70 annual plants and evergreen, mostly short-lived herbaceous perennials. The leaves are very different depending on the species but they are usually soft and deeply cut. The Swan River daisy produces numerous, small, daisy-like, fragrant brightly coloured flowers with an orange or brownish centre. The ray florets are usually purple, blue or white. Swan River daisies need a very sunny, sheltered position and fertile, well-drained soil. This bushy annual with its profusion of flowers is ideal for adding colour to any balcony or terrace. It can be raised from seed in spring. Unfortunately, snails also love the tender leaves.

Location: 💧 ☼ ⚠
Propagation: ₀°° 🐝🌿
Characteristics: ⚠ ⊙ ✿
Pests: slugs and snails
Flowering: summer

Brachyscome iberidifolia

Greater quaking grass

Briza maxima

ⓘ

Location: 💧 ☼ ⚠
Propagation: ⚬°°
Characteristics: ⊙ ✿
Flowering: spring – summer

Greater quaking grass has some 20 species that are found in the temperate regions of Europe and Asia. It owes its name to the fact that the spikelets quake at the slightest breath of wind. The greater quaking grass that is native to the Mediterranean can be raised from seed in spring indoors and planted out from April onwards. Cultivated as annual it grows best in full sun in fertile soil in dense tufts that grow up 24 in high. The flowers that appear from late spring until late summer are borne in beautiful small spikelets, which are themselves grouped into loose heart-shaped to round panicles. After flowering the panicles can be dried and used in their natural colour or artificially coloured as winter decoration or part of dried flower arrangements.

Bush violet

Browellia

ⓘ

Location: ⬦ ☼ ⚠
Propagation: ⚬°°
Characteristics: ⊙ ✿
Flowering: summer

Browellia is native to South America and Caribbean and is usually grown as an annual. It grows to a 32 in high bushy shrub with slightly sticky, matt green leaves. The violet-blue, blue or white flowers are produced singly or in clusters in the leaf-axils throughout the summer. Bush violets need plenty of light but do not like direct sun. They should only be watered moderately during the growing season. A weak dose of fertilizer every 2 to 4 weeks will encourage prolific flowering and promote bushy growth. Deadheading and removing dead leaves will prolong the flowering season. It can be grown from seed in spring and propagated from cuttings in summer. The young plants must be trimmed several times to encourage bushy growth.

Slipper flower

Calceolaria integrifolia

Slipper flower is native to the mountainous regions of Chile. It owes its name to the 2-lipped, slipper-like flowers whose smaller, lower lip is usually puffed out while the larger lower lip looks like an extended pouch. This evergreen herbaceous perennial is very sensitive to frost and therefore always grown as an annual. This semi-shrub, which can reach a height of 24 in, bears terminal clusters of yellow to bronze-coloured flowers from spring until autumn. However, it grows best in a cool, damp place, which must be bright and partially shaded. It is important that the very sensitive flowers are protected from the wind and that faded blooms and dead leaves are removed regularly. During the growing season, the plants must be watered generously and fed every 4 weeks with a compound fertilizer. It can be grown from seed in spring or propagated from cuttings in summer.

Location: 💧 ☼ – ☀ ⚠
Propagation: ⚬°°
Characteristics: ☉ ❀
Pests: slugs and snails
Flowering: spring – autumn

Calceolaria integrifolia

Calendula officinalis

ℹ️

Location: 💧 ☀ – ☀
Propagation: ⟋
Characteristics: ☉ ❀
Diseases: mildew
Pests: aphids
Flowering: summer – autumn

Callistephus chinesis

ℹ️

Location: 💧 ☀
Propagation: ⟋
Characteristics: ☉ ❀
Diseases: aster wilt
Pests: aphids, caterpillars
Flowering: summer

Pot marigold

Calendula officinalis

Calendula is native to southern Europe and is made up of 20 species. In the Middle Ages it was used to treat diseases such as smallpox, depression and constipation. Pot marigold is still used as medicinal herb today and is the only plant that is used both for both medicinal and culinary purposes. The petals are often used as a substitute for saffron in soups, rice and salads. It ranges in height from 8 in 12 to 28 in depending on the species. But all have a bushy growth with lanceolate, aromatic pale green leaves and daisy-like flowers that flower from summer until late autumn. It is propagated from seed in spring. *Calendula* grows in sun or partial shade in well-drained soil. The flowering season can be prolonged by removing the dead blooms and leaves or trimming back after the first flowering.

China aster

Callistephus chinensis

China Aster is native to China and Japan and has been cultivated in Europe for over 200 years. Is a very versatile plant in its uses because of its large number of species. There are low, bushy compact specimens and tall species that make ideal cut flowers. They also come in a very wide range of shapes and colors ranging from reddish, to violet-blue, white or yellow flowers, including some two-tone forms. They are usually sown in spring in consecutive batches in order to prolong flowering. This annual plant grows best in a warm, sunny position in well-drained, fertile soil and should be watered moderately. It does not tolerate waterlogging, which causes the dreaded aster wilt. Asters which are wilting for no apparent reason should be removed immediately. Asters should be deadheaded regularly and tall varieties should be supported.

Wire mesh plant

Calocephalus brownii

Calocephalus is native to Australia, where it grows as a small, evergreen shrub with needle-like, silver-grey, downy leaves. This densely branched shrub grows 40 cm (16 in) high. It only produces its inconspicuous, button-shaped flowers if the summer is very long and warm. It is usually sold as an autumn plant. It can be propagated from softwood cuttings between March and autumn and rooted under glass with high air humidity. The seedlings can be planted out when there is no longer any danger of frost. The plant tolerates periods of severe drought and needs very little food or water. It thrives in full sun and is easy to trim to shape. Usually grown as an annual, it can over-winter in an airy place. It provides a pleasant, neutral background for colourful summer flowering plants.

Location: ◌ ☼
Care: ❄
Propagation:
Characteristics: △ ∞ ⚘
Flowering: summer

Calocephalus brownii

ⓘ

Location: 💧 ☀ ⚠
Care: ❄
Propagation: ․° ✂❀
Characteristics: ∞ ❀
Pests: slugs and snails, weevils
Flowering: summer

Campanula

ⓘ

Location: 💧 ☀ – ☀ ⚠
Care: ⚠
Propagation: ․° ✂❀
Characteristics: ∞ ❀
Flowering: spring – summer

*I*talian bellflower

Campanula isophylla

Campanula includes some 300 species. Only a few are as ideally suited as Italian bellflower to growing in a container or hanging basket. This herbaceous perennial grows up to 8 in high and has a trailing habit. In summer it produces a mass of pale blue or white, star-shaped flowers. It can be propagated from seed or softwood cuttings in spring or division in autumn or spring. These tender plants appreciate an airy, bright, partially shaded position. They should only be watered moderately during the growing season and fed every 4 weeks with a liquid compound fertilizer. The shoots should be cut back in autumn when the plant is moved indoors to a bright place at 43–50° F and be kept moderately moist.

*C*anterbury bells

Campanula medium

This very handsome ornamental plant was already popular in the Middle Ages and is native to northern and central Italy. It is a slow-growing, erect biennial that develops leaf rosettes in the first year and flowers in the second year. The striking, bell-shaped flowers that grow along the stem appear in late spring and are produced throughout the summer. The colors range from blue, white to pink, depending on the variety. It can propagated from seed in spring or from cuttings or division. This frost-resistant species needs a sunny to partially shaded position, the colors holding better in partial shade. The soil should be fertile and moderately moist but never waterlogged. It also appreciates monthly applications of fertilizer. The stems can grow up to 35 in high and should be supported. The plant should be cut back after the first flowering to prevent self-seeding while promoting a second flowering.

Ornamental pepper

Capsicum annuum

Capsicum annuum

This genus of evergreen shrubs includes species that differ greatly from each other, such as the ornamental pepper, hot chilli (Cayenne pepper), sweet peppers and paprika used as a condiment. The number of species is enormous. On the whole, the smaller the fruit the hotter the taste. This highly frost-sensitive annual can be grown from seed indoors in late winter and later planted out, or bought as young plants and planted out after the last frosts in May. These deep-rooting plants need a very deep container that should be placed in a very sunny position. They need plenty of water during the growing season (the period when the unripe green fruits turn orange or red) and an application of liquid fertilizer every two weeks. The flowers should be sprayed every day to encourage the fruits to develop.

ⓘ

Location: ◗ ☼ ⚠
Propagation: ₀°°
Characteristics: ⊙ ❀
Diseases: viruses, wilt, mildew
Pests: aphids
Flowering: summer

Madagascar periwinkle

Catharantus roseus

This genus is native to Madagascar. It includes eight species that are grown as annuals although they are perennials. Madagascar periwinkle needs a very sunny location, monthly applications of fertilizer and only moderate watering even during the growing season. In winter it should be watered very sparingly, being very intolerant of waterlogging. These evergreen plants produce purple, pink or white flowers in spring and throughout summer. They grow bushier if pruned slightly. They can be grown from seed in spring and propagated from cuttings in summer. You should be very careful handling the plants when small children are present because all parts contain poisonous alkaloids.

ⓘ

Location: ◯ ☼ – ☀
Care: ❄ – ⌖
Propagation: ₀°°
Characteristics: ⚠ ✖ ⊙ /∞ ❀
Flowering: spring – summer

Cockscomb

Celosia spicata varieties

ⓘ

Location: 💧 ☀ ⚠

Propagation: ⠿

Characteristics: ☉ ✿

Diseases: stem rot, leaf spot

Pests: aphids

Flowering: summer

The *Celosia* genus includes 50 to 60 species. These herbaceous perennials are native to Asia, Africa and America but are normally cultivated as annuals. The common name of the plant was inspired by the shape of the inflorescence. Cockscomb grows 24 in high and bears pink, red, yellow or orange flowers depending on the species. They are very popular as cut flowers and are often used in dry flower arrangements. Because they flower more prolifically and colourfully in the sun in relatively moist air, they are best placed in a sunny but sheltered position. The soil must be kept evenly moist and watered only moderately or sprayed lightly. Plants benefit from weekly applications of a compound fertilizer. They need plenty of water in periods of very hot, dry weather. They are grown indoors from seed in spring.

Celosia

Cornflower

Centaurea cyanus

The blue-flowering cornflower owes its common name to the fact it is a "weed" that is often found in corn fields. In summer it produces small blue flowers that attract many bees and butterflies. Besides the well-known blue of the wild form, breeders have also developed varieties with white, pink or red flowers. Flowering can be prolonged by regular deadheading. This modest little annual needs well-drained soil and a sunny location. In regions where the climate is relatively mild, it can be sown in early autumn to produce flowers in early spring. Otherwise, sow in early spring indoors and plant out later when the seedlings are large enough.

Centaurea cyanus

Location: ◊ ☼
Propagation: ₒ°₀
Characteristics: ⊙ ❀
Diseases: mildew
Flowering: summer

Spider plant

Chlorophytum comosum

The genus includes 250 species and is native to South and West Africa. Spider plant is a bushy-shaped perennial with very narrow, grass-like leaves that can grow up to 12 in long. Depending on the variety, "Variegatum" or "Vittatum," the green leaves are marked with white or cream. In summer, the plant produces delicate white flowers that are borne in clusters. Spider plants are easily propagated from plantlets, removed from the mother-plant and rooted in jar of water or planted directly in the soil. Their undemanding nature and attractive appearance make them a very popular plant for balconies, terraces, as well as indoors. Although they tolerate irregular watering, they need plenty of water during the growing season and only moderate watering in winter.

Location: ◖ ☼ — ☼
Care: 🌡 — ❄
Propagation: ₒ°₀ ✂ ❧
Characteristics: ∞
Flowering: summer

Clarkia

Clarkia amoena

ℹ

Location: ♦ ☼ – ☼
Propagation: ₀°°
Characteristics: △ ☉ ✿
Diseases: stem and root rot
Flowering: summer

The *Clarkia* genus was named after Captain William Clarke who travelled across America in 1806 with his expedition and discovered it there. This annual has a bushy habit and striking spikes of funnel-shaped flowers in shades of pink. Although the flowering season in summer is relatively short, it flowers prolifically. Over-fertilizing only encourages the formation of leaves. The soil should be only moderately fertile, evenly moist and well-drained. Clarkia prefers a sunny to partially shaded location but dislikes excessive heat and moisture, which can hinder its development. These handsome plants also make excellent cut flowers. They are sown in early spring to flower at the beginning of autumn.

Cleome spinosa

Spider flower

Cleome spinosa

ℹ

Location: ♦ ☼ △
Propagation: ₀°°
Characteristics: ☉ ✿
Pests: aphids
Flowering: summer

The *Cleome* genus includes 150 species that are all native to the tropics and subtropics. The spider flower, grown as an annual, is particularly attractive with its large terminal flower heads with its prominent stamens. It is these very long stamens that have given the plant its common name. *Cleome* has serrated, hairy leaves, reminiscent of hemp. The intensely fragrant flowers may be pink, violet or white and appear in summer. The seeds are sown indoors in March in lightly fertilized soil and planted out in pots, bowls or tubs from May onwards. During the growing season, it must be watered generously and fed with liquid fertilizer every four weeks. Spider flower grows best in full sun. The flowering season can be extended by regular deadheading.

Parrot's bill

Clianthus puniceus

The genus consists of two species native Australia and New Zealand. This plant produces long red blooms, reminiscent of a parrot's bill. It is an evergreen climber that can reach 59 in high and if trained against a wall it can even reach a height of 16 ft. Parrot's bill is an upright creeping shrub that grows up to 24 in high. During the growing season it needs plenty of water and monthly applications of a liquid fertilizer. The soil must be well-drained. It grows best in a very sunny location sheltered from strong wind. It should be cut back immediately after flowering. It can be grown from seed in spring and propagated from cuttings in summer.

Location: 💧 ☼ ⚠
Care: ❄
Propagation: ⦿
Characteristics: ∞ ✽
Flowering: spring – summer

Ground blue convolvulus

Convolvulus sabatius

This frost-sensitive herbaceous perennial is native to Italy, Spain and North Africa. It is a dense, creeping or trailing plant that spreads rapidly, which makes it an ideal plant for hanging baskets or covering walls. The undemanding "Blue Mauritius" grows best in a very sunny, sheltered location in well-drained soil. It needs plenty of water during the growing season but in winter it only needs to be kept moist. The pale to deep blue flowers are produced throughout the summer until early autumn and open only during the day. The plant should be cut back vigorously after flowering in order to encourage the following year's growth. It can be propagated from seed, cuttings or by division.

Location: 💧 ☼ ⚠
Care: ⚠ – ❄
Propagation: ⦿
Characteristics: ∞ ✽
Pests: aphids
Flowering: summer – autumn

Cosmos bipinnatus

ⓘ

Location: 💧 ☀ ⚠
Propagation: ₀°°
Characteristics: ☉ ❀
Diseases: grey mould
Pests: aphids
Flowering: summer

Cosmos

Cosmos bipinnatus

Cosmos is native to Mexico and Brazil. This annual plant has an upright habit, elegant fernlike foliage and attractive flowers in white, pink and red shades, reminiscent of anemones. Because the production of flowers depends on decreasing daylight, the main flowering season is in late summer. Cosmos thrives in moderately fertile, moist soil in a very sunny location, sheltered from the wind, although it also tolerates partial shade. They are ideal plants for pots, tubs and hanging baskets but they need plenty of water during periods of drought. Flowering is encouraged by regular deadheading. Flowers should be cut shortly after opening. Cosmos are grown from seed, sown directly outdoors after the last frosts. The flowering season can be advanced by sowing and growing the seedlings indoors.

Crassula coccinea

ⓘ

Location: ⭕ ☀
Care: ❄ – 🌡
Propagation: ₀°°
Characteristics: ⚠ ∞ ❀ ❁
Pests: aphids, mealy bug,
   weevils
Flowering: summer

Crassula

Crassula coccinea

The *Crassula* genus includes over 150 annual and perennial, evergreen, succulent species, most of which are native to South Africa. *Crassula* comes from the mountainous region of the Cape and is frost-tender, so it should be kept indoors until danger of frost has passed and brought back inside in autumn. This succulent semi-shrub growing up to 24 in high produces several branches from the base and alternate pairs of leaves, sometimes tinged with red. The magnificent bright red and very occasionally white flowers are produced throughout the summer into the autumn. Crassulas grow best in a warm, sunny, dry place in well-drained, moderately moist soil with bi-weekly applications of cactus fertilizer. They are propagated from stem cuttings in spring and summer. The plant is prone to attacks from weevils.

Crocus

Crocus

Spring and autumn-flowering crocuses are ideal for adding colour to balconies and terraces before and after the summer. The genus is made up of about 80 species. The funnel-shaped flowers that are sometimes also two-tone come in a wide range of colors such as yellow, blue, lilac, light and dark purple and white. The bright orange stamens are very conspicuous. The leaves are grass-like and have a silvery white stripe in the middle. They develop at the same time as the flower or just afterwards. The corms of the spring-flowering varieties should be planted in autumn and those of the autumn-flowering varieties in spring, 2–4 in deep in well-drained soil. The soil must be kept dry in summer and moist in winter. The seeds can be harvested just before the seed pods burst open and planted in pots. Crocuses are usually propagated from offsets from the corms.

Crocus

ⓘ

Location: 💧 ☼
Care: 🗚
Propagation: ⊙°
Characteristics: ∞ ❀
Flowering: spring, autumn

Ornamental squash

Cucurbita pepo

The 9,000-year-long history of squash can be traced back to Central America. The annual species develop shoots up to 8 ft long. There are several varieties of ornamental squash whose fruit may be long and curved or round and of varying size. The smaller, compact-growing varieties are particularly suited for growing on balconies and terraces. They are sown indoors in spring, then planted out in fertile soil in larger containers when there is no longer any danger of frost. They thrive in sunny, partially shaded locations protected from the wind. The plants develop beautiful yellow or orange flowers. They need plenty of water and monthly applications of fertilizer. The green or yellow fruits ripen very quickly and can be harvested after a short time. In winter the plants should be moved to a frost-free, well-ventilated, cool place.

Cucurbita pepo

ⓘ

Location: 💧 ☼ – ☼ 🗚
Propagation: ⊙°
Characteristics: ⊙ ❀
Diseases: mildew, wilt
Flowering: summer

Turmeric

Curcurma

ⓘ

Location: ◗ ☀ ⚠
Care: ❄
Propagation: ⚬° ✿
Characteristics: ∞ ✿
Flowering: summer

Curcurma includes 40 herbaceous perennial rhizomatous species that are all native to the tropical regions of Asia and Australia. The broad leaves arranged in clusters dry up in autumn. This is also when the rhizomes of some species are harvested. They are used as condiment, food colouring and fabric dye. Turmeric is very popular in Indian cuisine, where the fresh or dried roots are used for flavouring curries and chutneys. They are grown from seed indoors in spring. In summer, they are placed outdoors in a partially shady location. During the growing season they need plenty of water and monthly applications of fertilizer. Being frost-sensitive, they must be brought indoors before the first frost and kept almost dry.

Cyclamen

Cyclamen

ⓘ

Location: ○ ☀
Care: ❄ – ❄
Propagation: ⚬°
Characteristics: ✖ ∞ ✿
Flowering: spring, autumn

Cyclamens can be found throughout Europe and Asia. It include 20 tuberous species that flower either in the spring or autumn. Cyclamens are very popular container plants for balconies and terraces because of their long flowering season of between two and three months, and the fragrance of their elegant flowers, which may be white, pink or red. The leaves are patterned and survive until spring in the case of the autumn-flowering varieties. They can be grown from seed between late winter and early spring. The seeds should be planted in trays and only covered with a thin layer of soil. The seed trays must be kept in complete darkness until germination. Cyclamen thrive in partial shade in well-drained, calcareous soil and benefit from moderate feeding. It is best to water the plants moderately along the inside edge of the container to prevent the tubers from rotting. All parts of the plant cause nausea if consumed.

Cyclamen

*P*apyrus

Cyperus papyrus

The *Cyperus* genus includes some 600 annual and evergreen perennial species that grow in the tropical and sub-tropical regions of the world. Papyrus plants are mainly grown for their handsome umbels of brown spikelets. In ancient Egypt the pressed and dried shoots were used to make papyrus, a paper-like material. Papyrus is an evergreen, clump-forming plant with leafless pulp-filled stems that form large umbels of spikelets. It is propagated from seed, sown in spring in moist, fertile soil, or by division. It can also be propagated by cutting the flower heads and placing them head down in a jar of water so that they can root. It thrives in full sun. The tray under the pot should always be full of water. If there is insufficient light the plant will produce only a few new leaves and, if too dry, the tips of the leaves will turn brown.

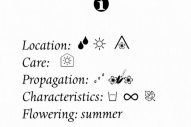

Location: 💧 ☼ ⚠
Care: ❄
Propagation: ⋰° ⚘
Characteristics: ⊟ ∞ ❀
Flowering: summer

Opposite page: Dahlia "Bantling"

Dahlia

Dahlia hybrids

ⓘ

Location: 💧 ☀ ⚠

Care: ❄

Propagation: ⚬° 🐛

Characteristics: ☉ / ∞ ❀

Diseases: mildew, mosaic virus, bulb rot (while over-wintering)

Pests: aphids, red spider mite, leaf bugs, slugs and snails, caterpillars

Flowering: summer – autumn

The *Dahlia* genus is native to the mountainous regions of Mexico and Central America. It includes some 30 species and there are over 20,000 hybrid varieties. After roses, dahlias are among the most popular ornamental plants. Spurred on by the great diversity in the colour and shape of flower heads, an impressive range of hybrid varieties has been developed. This vast assortment has then been classified into ten groups according to the shape of the flower head: single, decorative, pompon, ball, cactus, semi-cactus, anemone, collerette and water-lily flowered dahlias. The tenth group, miscellaneous, includes the more exotic forms such as the orchid dahlias or antler dahlias. They are very popular both as cut flowers and as container plants and border plants, not least because they flower throughout the summer well into the autumn until the first frost. They grow best in a sunny, sheltered location in well-drained soil, rich in humus. During the growing season they need plenty of water and food. The number of shoots should be reduced to five in large-flowered varieties and to ten in small-flowered varieties. It is also important to deadhead regularly. This will extend the flowering season. Dahlias usually attract large numbers of butterflies and bees. They can be propagated from seed or by division of the tubers. In autumn the tubers must be lifted and stored indoors at a temperature of 39–46° F and planted out again in spring.

Decorative dahlia

ⓘ

Location: 💧 ☀ ⚠
Care: ❊
Propagation: ⋅°° ⚘
Characteristics: ☉/∞ ❀
Diseases: mildew, mosaic
virus, bulb rot (while over-
wintering)
Pests: aphids, red spider mite,
leaf bugs, slugs and snails,
caterpillars
Flowering: summer – autumn

ⓘ

Location: 💧 ☀ ⚠
Care: ❊
Propagation: ⋅°° ⚘
Characteristics: ☉ ❀
Diseases: mildew, mosaic virus,
bulb rot (while over-
wintering)
Pests: aphids, red spider mite,
leaf bugs, slugs and snails,
caterpillars
Flowering: summer

Decorative dahlia

Dahlia "Berliner Kleene"

The group of decorative dahlias have magnificent blooms that are produced until late in the autumn. The flowers are double without clearly marked discs and the edges of the smooth petals are turned slightly inward. The numerous varieties of decorative dahlias are grouped according to the size of the flower head. Many varieties can grow up to 6 ft 6 in high and are therefore not very suitable for balconies. But there are also more compact varieties such as "Berliner Kleene" that only grows 16 in high. It produces salmon-pink flowers and is one of the most popular varieties. Other low-growing varieties are "Claudette" (purple), "Bluesette" (purple) and "Parkfeuer" (red). For more information on cultivation and care, see "Dahlia hybrids" above.

Collerette dahlias

Dahlia "Herz As"

One of the distinctive features of collerette dahlias is the single row of broad petals surrounding an inner "collar" of shorter petals with curled margins, which in turn encircle a central disc. The florets of the "collar" are in fact deformed stamens attached to the outer petals. Compared to the flower heads of other dahlia groups, which may be as much as 10 in across, those of collerette dahlias are relatively small, being only 4–6 in across. Collerette dahlias are not only popular with gardeners but also with bees and bumblebees. "Herz As" only grows 20 in high, making it an ideal container plant for balconies and terraces. It is a particularly decorative variety with pink flowers with a light centre. For more information on cultivation and care, see "Dahlia hybrids" above.

Cactus dahlia

Dahlia "Extase"

Until the late 19th century cactus dahlias were almost unknown but since their introduction in Europe they have become increasingly popular. The edges of the petals are rolled back and the tips of petals are pointed. The name cactus dahlia is a reference to the cactus-like appearance of the flowers. The "Extase" variety grows only 16 in high and has magnificent pink-yellow blooms; it is one of the most popular low-growing varieties. Equally attractive and "balcony-friendly" are the following varieties "München" (16 in, yellow), "Aspen" (semi-cactus flowered, 16 in, white), "Autumn Fairy" (16 in, orange), "Cheerio" (20 in, wine-coloured with white tips) and "Park Princess" (24 in, pale pink). For more information on cultivation and care, see "Dahlia hybrids" above.

Location: ◗ ☼ ⋀
Care: ❊
Propagation: ˒˳˳ ✻✿
Characteristics: ∞ ❀
Pests: mildew, mosaic virus, tuber rot
Pests: aphids, red spider mite, leaf bugs, slugs and snails, caterpillars
Flowering: summer – autumn

Single dahlia

Single flowered dahlia

Dahlia "Schloss Reinbeck'

Single dahlias are very unassuming, plain flowers that in spite of intense breeding have retained much of their Mexican ancestry. The centre of the single flowers, a cluster of tiny tubular flowers, is open and surrounded by a single row of broad petals. Some varieties have a second row of petals surrounding the central disc and these are known as duplex or peony dahlias. The dwarf varieties Mignon and Top-Mix are usually grown from seed and are ideal for small balconies. "Schloss Reinbeck" is a delightful variety that has orange blooms with a red centre and only grows 16 in high. Also very popular are "Irene van der Zwet" (24 in, yellow), "Nelly Geerling" (20 in, scarlet-red) and "Roxy" (16 in, purple). For more information on cultivation and care, see "Dahlia hybrids" above.

Location: ◗ ☼ ⋀
Care: ❊
Propagation: ˒˳˳ ✻✿
Characteristics: ⊙ – ∞ ❀
Pests: mildew, mosaic virus, tuber rot (while over-wintering)
Pests: aphids, red spider mite, leaf bugs, slugs and snails, caterpillars
Flowering: summer – autumn

*A*utumn chrysanthemum

Dendranthema indicum hybrids

This genus family is native to Europe and Asia and includes 20 species of herbaceous perennials with upright habit. They are among the oldest ornamental plants and have been grown since time immemorial for the magnificent, warm colors that they add to gardens and balconies in autumn. The flowers come in a wide range of colors such as white, yellow, brown, red or pink and have a distinctive tangy fragrance. Chrysanthemums are propagated in early spring from seed or cuttings. Autumn chrysanthemums grow best in well-drained soil and will benefit from monthly applications of a liquid compound fertilizer. Even during the growing season plants should only be watered when the top soil is dry. When grown outdoors, chrysanthemums should be placed in a sunny, sheltered location. For larger blooms, pinch out the lateral shoots. In winter, they should be moved to a bright, cool but frost-free place. All the parts of the plants can cause stomach upsets if consumed, while touching the leaves can cause skin allergies.

Dendranthema

ⓘ

Location: ○ ☼ — ☀ ⚠
Care: ❄
Propagation: .°°
Characteristics: ✖ ∞ ✿
Flowering: summer – autumn

*C*love pink

Dianthus caryophyllus

The *Dianthus* genus includes some 300 species. Dianthus caryophyllus, a perennial species that is native to the Mediterranean, has been used in the development of many hybrids. It has grey or pale green, linear to lance-shaped leaves and fragrant flowers that are sometimes multi-coloured. There is a very large number of varieties. They are ideal plants for flowerbeds, bowls and tubs while the alpine hybrids are particularly suited for growing in containers on balconies. During the growing season they should be watered moderately and fed every two weeks. Repeat flowering will be encouraged by cutting the plant back immediately after flowering. Pinching out the lateral shoots will help produce larger blooms. It is best grown from seed at the end of the winter with the tray placed on a window-sill. The seedlings should only be planted outdoors when there is no longer any danger of frost. A few varieties such as the biennial carnations are hardy.

ⓘ

Location: ○ ☼
Care: ⚠ *depending on species*
Propagation: .°°
Characteristics: ∞ ✿
Diseases: rust, fusarium-wilt
Pests: aphids, slugs and snails
Flowering: summer

Indian pink

Dianthus chinensis

This herbaceous perennial, usually grown as an annual or biennial, is native to China and Korea. It grows up to 16 in high and is ideal for balconies and terraces. Cultivars in the "Baby Doll" series only grow to a height of 8 in and produce large, single blooms that come in shades of red, pink or white. They are usually raised from seed in spring. If sown outdoors in autumn, they will need some protection against the cold and frost. They have a bushy habit with grey-green, lance-shaped leaves and produce a profusion of flowers in late spring and throughout the summer. The flowers come in various shades such as pink, red, pale purple or white and often have a purple centre. Indian pinks grow best in full sun. During the growing season the plants should be watered moderately and fed every two weeks. If cut back after the first flowering, the plants will produce new shoots and a magnificent second flowering.

Location: ◊ ☼
Care: ⚕
Propagation: ⸪°
Characteristics: ⊙/∞ ❀
Diseases: rust fungus, fusarium wilt
Pests: aphids, slugs and snails
Flowering: spring – summer

Dianthus chinensis

*D*iascia

Diascia

Location: ◊ ☼ – ☀
Care: ⚠
Propagation: ⸳°°
Characteristics: ☉ ✿
Flowering: summer – autumn

The *Diascia* genus is native to the mountainous regions of southern Africa and includes about 50 species. Their sprawling growth makes them ideal plants for hanging baskets on balconies and terraces. They are also very popular because of their long flowering season, which starts in early summer and continues until early autumn. The plants produce a profusion of pale pink, salmon-coloured or red flowers, depending on the variety. Diascias grow best in a sunny or partially shaded location, which should be well-ventilated to prevent the plant from rotting inside. Diascias are relatively easy to grow and will flower uninterruptedly throughout the summer with monthly applications of fertilizer and regular deadheading. They need plenty of water in dry weather and should be cut back after periods of drought. They will flower earlier if sown in spring indoors. They can also be propagated from cuttings taken in summer.

Diascia

Livingstone daisy

Dorotheanthus bellidiformis

This genus includes 10 species of low-growing, succulent annuals that are native to South Africa. It is the water stored in the plant's tissue that enables it to survive in the sandy mountains of its homeland. This mat-forming, summer flowering plant is ideal for growing along terrace walls. Daisy-like flowers are produced in white, crimson, pink-red, orange-yellow or brown-yellow shades throughout the summer until early autumn. Livingstone daisies are grown from seed indoors in early spring, the seedlings being planted outdoors after the last frosts. The soil should be sandy, well-drained and poor. Livingstone daisies should be watered sparingly because they store water. Excessive moisture causes rot. Because Livingstone daisies only open in the sun, it is important that they should be placed in a very sunny location.

Location: ○ ☼
Propagation: ₀°°
Characteristics: △ ⊙ ✿
Diseases: stem and basal rot
Pests: aphids
Flowering: summer – autumn

Echeveria

Echeveria

Echeveria

This genus of succulents includes over 150 perennial species. It is native to the semi-deserts of Texas, Mexico and Central-America. Echeverias are very popular because of their attractive, colourful foliage and magnificent red flowers, which are borne in terminal clusters on long stems. In temperate climates, echeverias (which are frost-tender) are cultivated as house plants that can be placed on the terrace or balcony during the summer months. They should be watered only moderately during the growing season and fed every month with a weak solution of a liquid compound fertilizer. In winter they should be kept almost dry. Generally speaking, echeverias need a lot of light and should be placed in a sunny, warm location. Even temperatures below 59° F can damage the plant. It can be grown from seed or propagated from leaf cuttings but the easiest way is to separate offsets and pot them individually in spring and summer.

Location: ○ ☼
Care: ⬆
Propagation: ₀°° ✄✿
Characteristics: △ ∞ ✿
Pests: aphids, mealy bug,
  weevils
Flowering: summer – autumn,
  according to species

Snow-on-the-mountain

Euphorbia marginata

Location: 💧 ☀
Propagation: ⸰⸰°
Characteristics: ✖ ☉ ✿
Diseases: grey mould
Pests: mealy bug
Flowering: summer – autumn

The *Euphorbia* genus originated in the tropics and sub-tropics but it also grows in the temperate zones. It comprises about 2,000 species that include shrubs, herbaceous perennials, annuals and succulents. Snow-on-the-mountain is a bushy, branched annual from North America. Like almost all euphorbia species, the milky juice contained in the plant is caustic and causes skin irritation. If it comes into contact with the eyes, it can cause temporary blindness. It is therefore advisable to wear gloves when handling euphorbias. *Euphorbia* grows very fast and has bright green, oval leaves with white margins. It produces small white flowers, surrounded by broad, white bracts. Euphorbias grow best in a sunny location in moist, well-drained soil. During the growing season, it needs additional feeding. It is grown from seed in spring. It can be prone to attacks by mealy bugs.

Eustoma

Eustoma

Eustoma grandiflorum

Location: 💧 ☀ ⚠
Care: 🗖–🗖
Propagation: ⸰⸰°
Characteristics: ☉/∞ ✿
Diseases: damping off (seedlings)
Flowering: summer

This genus is native to the United States. It is cultivated as an annual or biennial, as a single-stemmed plant when grown as a cut flower and multi-stemmed when grown as pot plant. It has slightly fleshy, oval, grey-green leaves and produces poppy-like flowers throughout the summer. Originally these flowers were blue but Japanese growers have developed the colour spectrum to include violet, pink and white. Eustomas grow slowly and make very good house plants and container plants for balconies and terraces as well as excellent cut flowers. They grow best in a sunny location, sheltered from the wind, in well-drained soil. During the growing season, they need plenty of water and feeding every two to three weeks, but during the winter they should be watered very sparingly. It is grown from seed sown at a temperature of about 68° F, in late winter for annuals and in late summer for biennials.

Persian violet

Exacum affine

The *Exacum* genus is native to the part of the world between Yemen and India. Persian violet is a bushy, evergreen, herbaceous perennial that is mostly cultivated as an annual. The glossy leaves are oval to elliptical. In summer it bears a profusion of fragrant, lavender-blue, pink or white flowers. Persian violet is also cultivated as a house plant and can be put out on the balcony or terrace when there is no longer any danger of frost. During the growing season it needs plenty of water and should be fed with a liquid compound fertilizer every two to three weeks. It grows best in full sun in a well-drained soil. It is propagated from seed or cuttings in early spring. The seeds should only be covered with foil or glass.

Exacum affine

ℹ

Location: 💧 ☀
Care: 📑
Propagation: ⚬°
Characteristics: ⊙ / ∞ ❀
Flowering: summer

Blue marguerite

Felicia amelloides

This bushy semi-shrub is native to South Africa and it is an ideal container plant for balconies and terraces. Blue Marguerite is usually cultivated as an annual because of its frost-sensitivity. The leaves are dark green and aromatic and the star-shaped flower heads are pale to dark blue with a yellow center. The profusion of flowers and long flowering season that starts in spring and continues until late summer make Blue Marguerite a very popular plant. The bushy growth can be further encouraged by pinching out the ends of shoots. Annuals are raised from seed in spring and propagated from cuttings in late summer. Plants should only be watered moderately during the growing season and the soil should be well-drained. Weekly applications of fertilizer are recommended during the growing season. The plants love full sun.

ℹ

Location: ○ ☀
Care: 📑
Propagation: ⚬°
Characteristics: ⊙ / ∞ ❀
Pests: aphids, red spider mites
Flowering: spring – autumn

Fuchsias — splashes of color in the shade

There are no better plants for shady corners than fuchsias. The genus includes about a hundred species and was first mentioned in the 16th century by the German botanist Leonhard von Fuchs, after whom the genus was named. Fuchsias are native to South America and Mexico, where they grow as perennial half-shrub, shrubs or even as small trees. They are particularly popular because of their magnificent flowers that may be single or double and grouped in axillary bunches or panicles. The four sepals are usually a different color from the four petals. They have eight long, striking filaments and a pistil that projects far beyond the corolla.

When cultivated as bedding plants and container plants, fuchsias are usually grown as annuals. However, they are easy to over-winter, even in a dark cellar. In such a situation the temperature must not exceed 50° F. If kept in a temperate conservatory, they will continue flowering for a while longer. F. magellanica is considered "hardy" in regions with mild climate. For containers, upright-growing species are better than hanging or trailing ones because of their growing habit. Upright species can also be trained as standards.

Fuchsias can be propagated from softwood cuttings, which can be taken between autumn and spring and rooted at 68° F. Regular pruning is recommended, especially in spring, to ensure bushy growth. The flowers are produced at the ends of the growing shoots and appear between six and ten weeks after pruning, depending on the species.

The varieties illustrated here are representative of a very large number of possibilities.

Opposite page (clockwise): Fuchsia "Beacon",
Fuchsia "Koralle",
Fuchsia "Mr. Hockin", Fuchsia "Dollar Princess"

Fuchsia

Fuchsia "Shadow Dancer"

ⓘ

Location: 💧 ☼ – ☼ ⚠
Care: ❋ *dark /* ⚱ *hell*
Propagation:
Characteristics: ∞ ❀
Diseases: rust, grey mould,
mildew
Pests: white fly, red spider mite,
aphids
Flowering: summer – autumn

The fuchsia types in the "Shadow Dancer" series are a recent addition to the range and have several advantages. They have very bushy growth and yet remain compact. They are trailing or upright depending on the species. In addition, they flower very early in spring and continue producing blooms well into the autumn. Unlike many other fuchsias there is no pause in the flowering season. The profusion of small, colourful flowers are a breathtaking sight with the flowers standing out beautifully against the foliage. These magnificent, colourful fuchsias are equally suitable as container plants for balconies and in hanging baskets, in borders and flowerbeds. In 2000 this series was awarded the Proven Winners prize, which is awarded by all the seedling firms of the world for the best innovation. For further information on care and cultivation, see the "Fuchsia" text above.

Fuchsia

Fuchsia "Dark Eyes"

ⓘ

Location: 💧 ☼ – ☼ ⚠
Care: ❋ *dark /* ⚱ *light*
Propagation: ₀°°
Characteristics: ∞ ❀
Diseases: rust, grey mould,
mildew
Pests: white fly, red spider mite,
aphids
Flowering: summer

The upright, densely branched shrub "Dark Eyes" can reach a height of 24 in and a spread of 30 in. Its long flowering season and prolific flowering make it a very popular garden plant. The flowers are double, medium-sized, measuring 1.5–2.5 in across, with deep red sepals and dark violet-blue petals. The magnificent blooms and dark colour of the petals give the plant a sophisticated charm and are faintly reminiscent of the heavily-made-up eyes of the glamorous Hollywood stars of the 1920s. Fuchsias grow best in a sunny to partially shaded location where they are sheltered from wind and excessive heat. They need plenty of water and monthly applications of fertilizer during the growing season. The regular removal of seed-heads will encourage more prolific flowering. The plants are trimmed to shape in spring. For further information on care and cultivation, see the "Fuchsia" text above.

Fuchsia

Fuchsia "Koralle"

ℹ️

Location: 💧 ☀️ – ☀️ ⚠️
Care: ❄️ *dark* / 💡 *light*
Propagation: ﹐°
Characteristics: ∞ ✿
Diseases: rust, grey mould,
mildew
Pests: white fly, red spider mite,
aphids
Flowering: summer

The "Koralle" variety is an erect, shrub-like hybrid whose flowers have very long tubes and short sepals, as do all hybrids in that group. It has velvety, olive-green leaves and robust stems. "Koralle" can reach a height of 35 in and a spread of 24 in in a short time, making it an ideal container plant for balconies and terraces. The variety owes its name to the intense coral red of its blooms. It bears terminal clusters of long-tubed, orange-red flowers in which sepals and petals are the same colour, unlike the typical fuchsia flowers which are usually a different colour. But like them, they thrive in a shady to partially shaded position where they are sheltered from wind and excessive heat. They need plenty of water and weekly applications of fertilizer during the growing season. They flower well into the autumn but when the temperature falls below 41° F they must be moved indoors. For further information on care and cultivation, see the "Fuchsia" text above.

Trailing fuchsia

Fuchsia "La Campanella"

ℹ️

Location: 💧 ☀️ – ☀️ ⚠️
Care: ❄️ *dark* / 💡 *light*
Propagation: ﹐°
Characteristics: ∞ ✿
Diseases: rust, grey mould,
mildew
Pests: white fly, red spider mite,
aphids
Flowering: summer

The name "La Campanella" not only sounds beautiful (it means "little bell") but it also refers to one of the most attractive trailing fuchsias, the ancestor of many varieties and cultivars. It owes its success to its magnificent double with white sepals and blue-violet petals and also to its sturdy resistance to pests and diseases. This trailing shrub reaches a height of 12 in, then trails downward. As a result, it is ideal as a container plant for balconies and it looks particularly stunning in a hanging basket. Because the wild form of this fuchsia is native to the misty mountain regions of Mexico and Chile, it will tolerate a certain lack of light. It is important to water and feed generously during the growing season. Although usually grown as an annual it will over-winter happily in a frost-free place, which may be bright or dark. For further information on care and cultivation, see the "Fuchsia" text above.

Trailing fuchsia

Fuchsia "Marinka"

F. "Marinka" is a particularly floriferous shrub in which both the flowers and the leaves are attractive. The crimson veins on the underside of the leaves contrast beautifully with the dark green leaves. The flowers are tinged with different shades of intense reds. The sepals are flushed with lighter shades of red while the petals are marked with darker shades of red. The plant reaches a height of 12 in and a spread 24 in. Like all trailing fuchsias, it looks very good in window boxes and absolutely magnificent in hanging baskets, where it can trail on all sides. Sometimes a single plant in a hanging basket can bear over 100 flowers. The sight is quite breathtaking when several young specimens are planted together in one hanging basket. For further information on care and cultivation, see the "Fuchsia" text above.

ⓘ

Location: 💧 ☼ − ☼ ⚠
Care: ❄ *dark /* 🔦 *light*
Propagation: ⸫
Characteristics: ∞ ❀
*Diseases: rust, grey mould,
   mildew*
*Pests: white fly, red spider mite,
   aphids*
Flowering: summer

Fuchsia

Fuchsia "Mrs Marshall"

"Mrs Marshall" is one of the few older varieties that are still commonly available today. In summer the bushy shrub is covered with a mass of delicate blooms with velvety, cherry-red petals and creamy-white sepals. It can also be trained as a standard. This is best done with young, well-rooted plants. To ensure that the plant increases in height, all the lateral branches and flowers are removed. When the plant has reached the desired height, the growing point must be pinched out. It is advisable to stake the plant during this phase. At this point side shoots are allowed to develop at the top of the stem. These will later form the crown of the standard. Other side shoots that may develop further down must be removed close to the stem. The shoots of the crown should be pinched regularly to encourage branching. It can take several years before a good round crown is formed, and the plant needs generous applications of fertilizer during the growing period. For further information on care and cultivation, see the "Fuchsia" text above.

ⓘ

Location: 💧 ☼ − ☼ ⚠
Care: ❄ *dark /* 🔦 *light*
Propagation: ⸫
Characteristics: ∞ ❀
*Diseases: rust, grey mould,
   mildew*
*Pests: white fly, red spider mite,
   aphids*
Flowering: summer

Trailing fuchsia

Fuchsia "Swingtime"

ⓘ

Location: 💧 ☼ – ☀ ⌂
Care: ❋ *dark* / 🔆 *light*
Propagation: ⸛
Characteristics: ∞ ❀
Diseases: rust, grey mould,
  mildew
Pests: white fly, red spider mite,
  aphids
Flowering: summer

The trailing variety "Swingtime" was developed in the United States in 1950. This vigorous growing shrub, which reaches of spread of 20 in, has large, double flowers with shiny, deep red sepals and white petals marked with fine red veins. The finely serrated, dark green, red-veined leaves are very reminiscent of those of Fuchsia "Marinka". Its spreading, trailing habit makes it an ideal plant for window boxes, pots and hanging baskets where it looks quite striking. Compared to other fuchsia varieties, "Swingtime" has the advantage that it is weather-resistant and will also grow in a sunny, warm location. It needs plenty of water and should be fed every week during the growing season. It is important to place the hanging baskets where they are protected from the wind. Containers with water tanks are recommended. For further information on care and cultivation, see the "Fuchsia" text above.

Trailing fuchsias

Treasure flower

Gazania

The *Gazania* genus includes about 16 species of low-growing annuals and herbaceous perennials. It is native to tropical and southern Africa. The colourful flowers that are very reminiscent to Gerberas come mainly in yellow, orange and red with a dark ring around the center. The grey-leaved varieties are also very handsome. Plants are sown under glass in spring or propagated from cuttings or by division in autumn. The young plants should only be planted outside after the last frosts. They grow up to 12 in high and do best in full sun because the flowers only open in the sun. They need only moderate watering but the soil should be well-drained because they hate to be waterlogged. Gazanias benefit from the application of a liquid compound fertilizer. Regular deadheading will encourage the production of more flower buds.

Location: ○ ☼
Propagation: ₀°° ✄
Characteristics: △ ☉ ❀
Diseases: stem and root rot
Pests: aphids, mites, thrips
Flowering: summer

Gazania

Gerbera

ⓘ

Location: 💧 ☼ – ☼
Care: 🏠
Propagation: ∙°° ✦
Characteristics: ∞ ✽
Diseases: leaf spot, root rot
Pests: aphids, white fly
Flowering: spring – summer

Gerbera

Gerbera jamesonii

This genus includes about 40 species of herbaceous perennials that are native to Africa, Madagascar and Asia. *Gerbera* produce white, pink, yellow, orange or red, single or double flowers almost throughout the year, depending on the variety and growing conditions. It is mainly known as a cut flower or house plant but it is also excellent as a container plant on balconies and terraces. However, it is important to make sure that the container is large and deep enough because the roots grow very deep. Because it is not frost-resistant it must be moved indoors again before the first frost. During the growing season it must be kept moist at all times and fed every week. It should be re-potted in spring and the soil must be fertile and well-drained. Gerberas need light and should therefore be placed in bright location. It is usually propagated from seed in autumn or spring.

Helianthus

ⓘ

Location: 💧 ☼ ⚠
Propagation: ∙°°
Characteristics: ✖ ☉ ✽
Diseases: mildew
Pests: aphids
Flowering: summer

Sunflower

Helianthus annuus

The Helianthus genus is native to America. The genus also includes Jerusalem artichoke, cultivated for its edible tubers. The fast-growing annual sunflower is one of the most important oilseed plants. It can grow up to 3 m high. Tall varieties make excellent cut flowers while shorter varieties such as "Big Smile" (16 in), "Sunspot" (23 in) and "Teddy Bear" (35 in) are better suited for use on balconies and in window boxes. The large flower heads that appear in summer have a brown center and yellow or reddish-brown petals, depending on the variety. Sunflowers grow best in well-drained soil in a sunny location where they are sheltered from the wind. It is important to water freely and feed regularly to obtain beautiful flowers. Plants are raised from seed in spring. Anyone who is prone to allergies should be careful when touching the leaves because they can cause skin irritation.

Straw Flower

Helichrysum bracteatum

The garden straw flower is native to Australia. It takes its name from the dry, papery bracts of the flowers which are often used in dried flower arrangements. This annual variety produces large flowers in shades of red, yellow, brown, violet or cream depending on the variety. The compact varieties such as "Bikini", raised from seed in spring, are excellent for window boxes. New varieties, propagated from cuttings, such as "Diamond Head," "Golden Beauty" and "Goldbusch" are ideal for hanging baskets because of their trailing habit. The straw flower needs well-drained, fertile soil which should be kept only moderately moist. In a sunny location sheltered from the rain it will produce a mass of flowers. It is important to remove the dead blooms regularly. Flowers intended for drying should be picked before they are in full bloom.

Location: ◊ ☼
Propagation: ⸱°°
Characteristics: △ ⊙ ✿
Diseases: mildew
Flowering: summer

Silver bush everlasting flower

Helichrysum petiolare

This species is native to South Africa, where it grows as a shrubby, evergreen foliage plant. Its main features are the densely branched, felted stems and the grey-woolly leaves, variegated with white or creamy-yellow. Varieties include "Rondello" (variegated creamy-yellow leaves) or "Silver" (leaves with a silvery sheen). In contrast, the white flower heads are quite inconspicuous. Silver bush everlasting flowers, usually grown as an annual, combine beautifully with colourful summer flowering plants in containers and hanging baskets. They grow best in sunny and slightly shaded positions. In spite of the thick foliage, they tolerate dry conditions quite well. This means they should be watered moderately but fed every week. Large specimens can be trimmed into shape. Silver bush everlasting flowers are easily propagated from seed and cuttings.

Helichrysum petiolare

Location: ◊ ☼ – ☀
Care: ❄
Propagation: ⸱°° 🍃
Characteristics: △ ⊙/∞
Diseases: mildew
Flowering: summer – autumn

Straw Flower

Helichrysum subulifolium

ⓘ

Location: ◊ ☼
Propagation: ₀°°
Characteristics: △ ⊙ ❀
Diseases: mildew
Pests: aphids
Flowering: summer – autumn

The annual straw flower, which is native to western Australia, forms a plant 20 in high with terminal yellow flower heads measuring 1.25 in across, borne on unbranched stems. Straw flowers are sold in summer as cut and dry flowers and look very decorative both fresh or dried because the colors remain just as brilliant when dried. Low varieties such as "Gold Braid" (14 in) make excellent container plants for balconies. Helichrysums need a very sunny location where they are also protected from rain. The soil must be well-drained and fed moderately. Straw flowers will flower for a long time if they are deadheaded regularly. They are sown indoors in early spring and planted out when all danger of frost has passed.

Heliotrope or Cherry pie

Heliotropium arborescens

ⓘ

Location: ♦ ☼ ⚠
Care: ❊
Propagation: ₀°°
Characteristics: △ ✖ ⊙/∞ ❀
Flowering: summer

Heliotropium is native to the Peruvian Andes and is usually grown as an annual. The deep-blue to reddish-violet flower heads exude a delicate vanilla fragrance that attracts large numbers of bees and butterflies. It is sown indoors from January onwards and the seedlings are planted outside after the last frosts. The plants should be tip-pruned several times to encourage bushy growth. Heliotropes are propagated from cuttings in spring or summer. They thrive in a sunny location, sheltered from rain and wind, and benefit from applications of a liquid fertilizer once or twice a month. They are very sensitive to excessive wet and dry conditions and should therefore be watered with great care. If the root ball dries out the leaves will become limp and the plant is unlikely to recover. During the winter it should be moved to a light, frost-free place with a temperature of 41–50° F. The plants contain poisonous alkaloids.

Heliotropium arborescens

*F*oxtail barley

Hordeum jubatum

The 20 species of annual and perennial grasses making up the *Hordeum* genus can be found in all temperate regions. Foxtail barley is an annual or biennial ornamental grass that grows in tufted clumps. The light green leaves that grow upright or curved can reach a length of 6 in. Broad, dense panicles of silky, blue-green spikelets, tinged with red or purple and later beige, are produced throughout the summer. The feathery multi-fruits maintain their silky appearance even when they are cut before they are fully ripe and used in dry flowers arrangements. Plants are raised from seed in spring, or in autumn, which means the young plants must spend the winter indoors in a frost-free place. Foxtail barley thrives in a sunny location in well-drained, moderately fertile soil. It does not tolerate being waterlogged.

Location: ○ ☼
Care: ❄
Propagation: ⸳₀°
Characteristics: ⊙ / ∞ ❀
Flowering: summer

Opposite page: Hyacinthus

Hyacinthoides hispania

Location: ☀ ○
Propagation: ⠀bulbils
   Characteristics: ❄ ✖
Flowering: spring

ℹ

Location: ◗ ☀—☀
Care: ❄
Propagation: ⠀bulbils
Characteristics: ✖ ∞ ❀
Flowering: spring

Spanish bluebell

Hyacinthoides hispania

This bulbous perennial species that grows wild in the woods in Spain, Portugal and North Africa is ideal for planting under standards or in containers as vigorous spring flowering plants. Large clumps of erect, narrow, dark green leaves emerge from the 2.5 in bulbs. The blue, bell-shaped flowers are borne in spring in erect, conical clusters. The cultivars "Excelsior,": "La Grandesse" and "Rosabella" produce flowers in shades of violet-blue, white and violet-pink. Contact with Spanish Bluebells can cause skin irritation and severe nausea if consumed. They are propagated from seed immediately after the seeds have ripened or from bulbils in summer. If not dead-headed after flowering before the seeds mature, it will self-seed itself. Spanish Bluebells grow in any soil but do best in fertile, moist, well-drained soil.

Hyacinth

Hyacinthus orientalis

Strongly scented hyacinths flower in spring and are native to Asia Minor and Central Asia. Available in many colors and shades, they are a wonderful addition to balconies and terraces and combine beautifully with other spring-flowering plants such as bergenias, candytuft and pansies. Hyacinths can be propagated by planting the bulblets that are separated from the mother-bulb in summer. The bulbs are planted in autumn at a depth of 4 in and well watered. The flowers are magnificent in the first year but become increasingly weak as the years go by. This is why they are usually grown as annuals. It is also possible to lift the bulbs after they have flowered, store them in a dry place and plant again in autumn. Hyacinths need a very sunny location in soil that should always be moist. All parts of the plant are poisonous if consumed and contact with the skin may cause irritation.

Hymenostemma

Location: 💧 ☀
Propagation: ⸫
Characteristics: ⊙ ❀
Diseases: *leaf spot*
Pests: *aphids, leaf miners*
Flowering: *summer – autumn*

Dwarf marguerite

Hymenostemma paludosum

This annual plant is native to southern Europe and the temperate regions of Asia. It has a bushy, compact habit and produces flowers with whitish ray florets and yellow centers that contrast beautifully with the fresh green background of the foliage. It is a very undemanding plant and ideal for very small balconies because it only grows 12 in high. It grows best in a sunny, airy location in well-drained, moderately fertile soil which should be kept moist at all times. It should be deadheaded regularly and pruning after the first flowering will encourage a prolific second flowering. Plants can be propagated from seed under glass in early spring, while later they can also be sown directly on site.

Location: 💧 ☀ ⚠
Propagation: ⸫
Characteristics: ❀
Diseases: *mildew*
Flowering: *summer*

Polka dot plant

Hypoestes phyllostachya

The *Hypoestes* genus is native to South Africa and Madagascar. The leaves of the polka dot plant are speckled with pinkish-violet, a feature that gives the plant its common name. The tiny, pink flowers that appear in summer are rather inconspicuous in comparison. This undemanding but frost-sensitive plant is mostly known as a house plant but is also an excellent container plant that will be very decorative on any balcony during summer. It is sown indoors in spring and planted outdoors when all danger of frost has passed. It should be pruned regularly to encourage bushy growth. These softwood cuttings can then be used for propagation, for which a temperature of 68° F is needed. It is important that the soil is well-drained and kept moist at all times. *Hypoestes* appreciate occasional spraying and feeding every two to three weeks. They grow best in a partially shaded position where they are also protected from the wind.

Hypoestes phyllostachya

*C*andytuft

Iberis umbellata

This species is native to southern Europe, where it grows as a densely branched 20 in high annual or biennial. It has narrow, lanceolate dark green leaves and dense clusters of small white, pink, red or violet flowers that appear in late spring and summer. The plant grows best in full sun but it will also grow well in partial shade in a warm place. It is an ideal plant for borders and as an edging plant but also looks very good combined with other summer flowering plants in window boxes and containers on balconies. In addition, it lasts a long time as cut flowers. Candytuft is sown in spring or autumn. If sown directly outdoors the site should be covered to protect it from the cold. It thrives in well-drained soil, rich in humus, that should be kept moist at all times. Cutting back after flowering will encourage a compact shape and second flowering.

Iberis

Location: ◊ ☼ /⟋⟍
Care: /⟋⟍ in half-shade
Propagation: ₒ∘°
Characteristics: ∞ ❀ ❄
Pests: slugs and snails,
    caterpillars
Flowering: spring, autumn

Busy lizzie

Impatiens walleriana

ⓘ

Location: 💧 ☼ – ☀ ⚠
Propagation: ⦙
Characteristics: ⊙ ❀
Diseases: damping off, grey
mould
Pests: red spider mite, white fly,
aphids, weevils
Flowering: spring – autumn

Busy lizzie is native to the mountainous regions of East Africa. The flowers come in white, orange, pink, red and violet, and they may also be two-toned or double. Busy lizzies are usually grown as annuals because of their frost-tenderness, but apart from that they are very robust and undemanding. They will grow in partial or complete shade where they are protected from the wind and not too hot. Even rainy summers will not affect the plant's prolific flowering. It is important that the soil should be kept moist at all times and fed with a weak solution of fertilizer during the growing season. Leaves and stems wilt very quickly if the soil is allowed to dry out but new shoots are produced just as quickly as soon as the plant is watered. It is sown in spring at a temperature of 68° F. The plant must be staked if the shoots become too long.

Impatiens walleriana

Busy lizzie

Impatiens New Guinea group

As might be expected, the ancestors of the Impatiens New Guinea group originated in New Guinea. This group flowers uninterruptedly as do the other species in the genus. The flowers come in a wide range of colors such as red, orange, pink, purple or white and the leaves are green or bronze-coloured. Apart from the dwarf varieties, the New Guinea group are larger than their relatives and grow 12 in high. They grow best in partial shade but also do well in the sun if watered well. These robust plants with large blooms are ideal for growing in window boxes or in containers with other plants. During summer, they should be watered generously and fed with weak solutions of fertilizer. The soil must be kept moist at all times but not allowed to become waterlogged because this would lead to rotting of the plant. It is propagated from seeds or cuttings in spring and summer. Cuttings root very easily in a glass of water.

Iris

Iris

The 300 species that make up the *Iris* genus produce tuberous rhizomes or bulbs and are mostly found in the northern hemisphere. The exotic flowers have three outer petals or "falls" that droop and three inner petals or "standards." All the varieties of the dwarf iris make excellent container plants and look very good in window boxes. They come in various shades of blue and violet, frequently with a yellow spot and ridge in the center of each "fall" or outer petal. They need well-drained soil, rich in humus, which should kept evenly moist during the growing season and only fed twice during this period. After flowering they should be watered more sparingly. Dwarf irises grow both in sun and partial shade. The offsets are planted in pots in autumn and covered during the winter if left outdoors or moved indoors to a frost-free place. All the parts of the plant are poisonous.

Impatiens New Guinea

🛈

Location: 💧 ☼ – ☀ ⚠
Propagation: ⊙°
Characteristics: ⊙ ✿
Diseases: damping off
*Pests: red spider mite, white fly,
    aphids, weevils*
Flowering: summer

Iris

🛈

Location: 💧 ☼ – ☀
Care: ⚠ ❄
Propagation: ⊙° ✿
Characteristics: ✖ ∞ ✿
*Diseases: rhizome rot, leaf spot,
    grey mould*
Pests: slugs and snails, aphids
Flowering: spring – summer

Shrimp plant

Justicia brandegeana

ⓘ

Location: 💧 ☀ ⚠
Care: 🏠
Propagation:
Characteristics: ∞ ❀
Pests: red spider mite, white fly
Flowering: summer – autumn

The flowers of this species are very similar to those of the common hop. The long-lasting, brown-red bracts that surround the white flowers are particularly attractive against the fresh green foliage. They are borne in terminal, pendulous clusters and flower throughout the year except during the winter months. The actual flowers are quite inconspicuous and drop very quickly. This frost-sensitive plant is well-known as a house plant but it also looks very decorative on balconies where it can be placed after all danger of frost has passed. It grows best in partial shade where it is sheltered from the wind in well-drained soil that should be kept moist at all times during summer. It is important to feed the plant every week during the growing season. In winter, it should be watered sparingly and moved to a place with a temperature of 50–59° F. After repotting in spring, it is cut back and the cuttings that root easily can be used for propagation. Young plants should be pruned several times in order to encourage a bushy, branched growth. It is best to plant several of them in the same container.

Justicia

Lagurus ovatus

Hare's-tail grass

Lagurus ovatus

The *Lagurus* genus has one species that grows in the wild in the Mediterranean. This can be grown either as an annual or biennial. Hare's-tail grass owes its name to the fluffy soft panicles of spikes, reminiscent of a hare's tail. At first the panicles are tinged with pale green or lilac, turning later a creamy yellow-brown. Depending on the time of sowing, which could be late summer or spring, the grass flowers between May and August. It grows to a height of 20 in and will form dense tufts if it has enough room. It looks very good in a large container and is also very decorative planted along a terrace wall. Because it dries very well it is often used in dried flower arrangements. It thrives in full sun in moderately fertile, well-drained, reasonably moist soil.

ⓘ

Location: ◊ ☼
Care: ⚞ — ❄
Propagation: ⋱
Characteristics: ☉/∞ ❀
Flowering: spring – summer

*I*ce plant

Lampranthus

This genus of attractive succulentsis native to South Africa It produces an abundance of daisy-like flowers in a variety of colors including white, yellow, pink and dark red throughout the summer. The fleshy leaves are arranged in pairs along the stems and are able to store water. *Lampranthus* is an ideal container plant for balconies and terraces but it must be moved indoors well before the first frost because it is very sensitive to cold. A conservatory would be ideal but the main thing is that it should be cool and dry. In summer, it needs a sunny, well-ventilated location and is only watered to prevent it from drying out. The soil should be sandy and poor but in summer it should be fed every two to three weeks. It is propagated in spring from seed or cuttings.

Location: ○ ☼
Care: 🌡
Propagation: ₀°
Characteristics: ∞ ❀
Pests: mealy bug, aphids
Flowering: summer – autumn

Lantana

*S*hrub verbena

Lantana camara hybrids

The genus includes evergreen herbaceous perennials and shrubs that are predominantly native to South America. It is not frost-resistant in temperate zones. Young plants grow 12 in high but perennials can reach a height of 39 in. They produce tiny flowers grouped in round heads, which change colour during the flowering season, opening yellow and turning red later. There are creamy-coloured, yellow, yellow-red but also pink, red or white forms. Shrub verbena is a very versatile plant that can be used as a container plant or trained as a standard. Plants need a sunny location where they are also protected from the rain. In summer, they need plenty of water and weekly applications of fertilizer. In autumn it must be moved indoors to a bright room with a temperature of 41–50° F. It can be cut back in spring when cuttings can also be taken. All the parts of the plant are poisonous.

Location: ◖ ☼
Care: ❋
Propagation:
Characteristics: ⚠ ✖ ∞ ❀
Diseases: mildew
Pests: white fly, red spider mite
Flowering: summer – autumn

Rock isotome

Laurentia axillaris

This summer flowering plant is native to Australia where it grows as a herbaceous perennial. In temperate zones it is cultivated as an annual because of its sensitivity to frost. The star-shaped flowers are sky blue, pink or white depending on the variety and they are produced throughout the summer until the autumn. *Laurentia* forms a bushy, compact shrub that grows 10 in high. With its long-tubed, star-shaped flowers, it is an attractive addition to any balcony or terrace, either as "underplanting" in a tub or in a hanging basket. It grows best in the sun but will also grow well in partial shade. It needs a sandy soil, rich in humus but does not tolerate being waterlogged. In summer, it must be watered regularly and fed every week. It is grown from seed in spring or autumn but if sown at the latter date, they will flower later in the season.

ⓘ

Location: ◊ ☼ — ☀
Propagation: ⦁°°
Characteristics: △ ⊙ ✿
Pests: aphids
Flowering: spring

Sea lavender

Limonium sinuatum

This large genus includes about 300 species and can be found in all the temperate zones of the world. Also known as statice, Sea Lavender is native to the Mediterranean and is upright, bushy herbaceous perennial that is usually cultivated as an annual in temperate zones. It produces a profusion of small flowers in a wide range of colors throughout the summer until early autumn, attracting many butterflies. Sea Lavender is better known as a cut flower and is frequently used in dried flower arrangements. But it also makes an excellent container plant that looks very attractive on balconies and terraces. It needs a sunny, dry location and sandy, well-drained soil. It should be watered and fed very sparingly even in summer. It is sown indoors in spring and seedlings should only be planted out after all danger of frost has passed.

Limonium sinuatum

Location: ◊ ☼
Propagation: ⦁°°
Characteristics: ⊙ ✿
Diseases: mildew
Flowering: summer

Toadflax or Baby snapdragon

Linaria maroccana

Location: ◊ ☼ – ☀
Propagation: ∘°
Characteristics: ☉ ✽
Diseases: mildew
Pests: aphids
Flowering: spring – summer

The 100 species of this genus are all native to the Mediterranean and West Europe As its name indicates *Linaria maroccana* is native to Morocco. It is a fast, upright-growing annual with stems covered with sticky hairs and alternate, lanceolate, pale green leaves. It bears clusters of pink, red, lilac, violet, apricot, yellow, creamy-coloured and white snapdragon-like flowers throughout the summer. This very adaptable plant prefers fertile, well-drained soil and a sunny to partially shaded location. It needs very little water. Pruning after the first flush of flowering will encourage a second flowering. Toadflax is grown from seed in spring after which it will self-seed very easily.

Trailing lobelia

Lobelia erinus "Richardii"

Location: ◖ ☼ – ☀ ⚠
Propagation:
Characteristics: ☉ ✽
Diseases: grey mould
Flowering: summer – autumn

The wild form of trailing lobelia is native to South Africa. The popular annual cultivar "Richardii" has a very long flowering season and is an ideal plant for hanging baskets, window boxes and tubs. The narrow, oval leaves are concealed by a mass of pale blue flowers with a white centre. There are other trailing cultivars such as "Azuro" and "Saphir," which have deep blue flowers, and the "Pendula" series whose flowers are all one colour. They all prefer sandy soil, rich in humus and a sunny to partially shaded location. It is important that they are watered regularly and fed every two weeks with a compound fertilizer. Unlike the upright species, trailing lobelias are propagated from cuttings taken between November and March. They must not be planted too close together so that the trailing shoots that will develop later have sufficient space to grow.

Lobelia erinus "Richardii"

Upright lobelia

Lobelia fulgens

This rhizomatous herbaceous perennial is native to North America. It is classified among the tall-growing lobelias that can grow up to 24–47 in high depending on the species. The irregular flowers consist of three lower and two small upper petals and they are borne in summer grouped in one-sided spikes. Most are scarlet-red but there are also pink- and violet-flowering varieties. They make very attractive container plants for balconies and terraces but they are only half-hardy. This is why it is best to move them indoors for winter, where they should be placed in bright, cool place. Otherwise, they can be grown from seed in late winter. They grow best in a sunny location and must be watered regularly and fed every week during the growing season.

ⓘ

Location: 💧 ☼ – ☀ ⌂
Care: ⌂ ❄
Propagation: ⚬°
Characteristics: ∞ ❀
Diseases: leaf spot
Pests: slugs and snails
Flowering: summer – autumn

Sweet alyssum

Lobularia maritima

Location: ○ ☀ — ☀
Propagation: ⸬
Characteristics: ⊙ ✿
Diseases: mildew, white rust
Pests: slugs and snails, flea
  beetles
Flowering: summer – autumn

This clump-forming, slightly trailing annual is native to the Mediterranean. It produces a mass of tiny flowers that may be white, pink or violet depending on the species, and its honey-like scent attracts bees. It flowers throughout the summer until the autumn and is often used as an edging plant on terrace walls, in pots and in window boxes. This undemanding plant grows best in full sun or partial shade. It should only be watered when the top soil is dry. Although it should only be fed sparingly, it must be fed very generously after the first flowering in order to encourage a prolific second flowering, which is also stimulated by regular deadheading. It can be grown from seed indoors in early spring and the young plants are planted out after all danger of frost has passed.

Parrot's beak

Lotus

Location: ◐ ☀ — ☀
Care: 🏠
Propagation:
Characteristics: ∞ ✿ ❀
Pests: mealy bug, aphids, red
  spider mite
Flowering: summer – autumn

The *Lotus* genus is a very architectural plant. Its unusual, needle-like leaves and clusters of exotic scarlet flowers make it a wonderful container plant for balconies and hanging baskets. Parrot's Beak, native to the Canary Islands, flower, in spring with bright orange to scarlet blooms that contrast beautifully against the background of silvery-green, needle-like leaves. It is a perennial but not frost-resistant. In summer it prefers a sunny to partially shaded, airy location. The soil should be light and rich in humus. It is important to water regularly but without letting the plants become waterlogged. They should be fed every week during the growing season. In winter they should be moved indoors to a bright, well-ventilated room with a temperature of about 54° F and watered only sparingly. Plants are propagated from softwood cuttings in spring or late summer.

Lupinus

Dwarf lupine

Lupinus nanus

The genus has about 200 species including herbaceous annuals, herbaceous perennials, shrubs and semi-shrubs that are often used as cattle feed by farmers. But these fast-growing plants with their imposing, colourful flower spikes carried on tall stems are also very popular ornamental garden plants. The dwarf lupine, native to California, only grows 2 in high and is therefore ideal as a container plant for balconies. In summer it bears spikes of flowers 8 in long that may be blue, white, pink or lavender depending on the variety. Dwarf lupines grow best in a sunny location in well-drained, moderately fertile, sandy soil. They should be watered regularly and fed sparingly. Regular deadheading is important to prevent self-seeding. It is usually sown in spring. If consumed the seeds will cause severe nausea.

ⓘ

Location: ◖ ☼
Propagation: ｡°°
Characteristics: ✖ ☉ ✿
Pests: slugs and snails
Flowering: summer

Loosestrife

Lysimachia congestiflora

Location: ♦ ☼ – ☼
Propagation:
Characteristics: ☉ ✿
Pests: slugs and snails
Flowering: spring – autumn

The *Lysimachia* genus is native to China. The genus was named after King Lysimachos, who ruled in ancient Greece and who is said to have calmed a raging bullock with such a plant. In temperate zones it is grown as an annual. It produces small, golden-yellow flowers with an orange eye against a background of dark green or yellow and green variegated leaves. Because of its trailing habit, loosestrife is particularly suited for growing in hanging baskets but it also looks very good in window boxes. It grows best in well-drained soil in partial shade. Although it needs plenty of water, it hates being waterlogged. In addition, it should be fed every week with a compound fertilizer. Dead blooms should removed. It is propagated from softwood cuttings in late summer.

Brompton stock

Matthiola incana

Location: ○ ☼ ⚠
Propagation: ⠼
Characteristics: ☉ ✿
Diseases: wilt, stem rot,
   damping off (seedlings)
Pests: leaf miners, flea beetles,
   caterpillars
Flowering: summer – autumn

In the past, stocks were found in almost every cottage garden. Besides the tall cut flower varieties, there are also a series of more compact, smaller, fragrant types that look very decorative on balconies and terraces. The red, violet, white or pink to mauve flowers are fragrant throughout the day but this fragrance becomes even more intense in the evening and in cloudy weather. They grow best in well-drained soil in a sunny, warm location where they are protected from the wind. Stocks are propagated from seed in spring. This frost-sensitive plant can also be placed on the window-sill before being planted out when all danger of frost has passed. It is usually grown as an annual.

Melampodium

Melampodium paludosum

Melampodium is native to southern Europe. It is a fast grower that flowers prolifically and is very robust and adaptable. This annual owes its popularity to its sparkling appearance, reminiscent of a bright, starry night. Throughout the summer it produces a mass of small, daisy-like flowers with pale yellow, whitish yellow or bright yellow ray florets and an orange center that stand out attractively against the dark green background of the foliage. In spite of this vigorous growth, *Melampodium* only grows 8 in high and is therefore ideally suited as a container plant on balconies and terraces. It prefers a sunny location and well-drained soil that must be kept moist at all times. It only needs moderate amounts of fertilizer. It is propagated from seed in early spring.

Location: �♦ ☼
Propagation: ₀°°
Characteristics: ⊙ ✿
Pests: *white fly, red spider mite, aphids*
Flowering: *spring – autumn*

Mesembryanthemum

Mesembryanthemum crystallinum

This genus of succulents is native to Cape Province in South Africa. *Mesembryanthemum* is an annual succulent mat-forming ground covering plant that grows 4 in high. Their distinctive feature are the small, swollen glands on the top of the leaves that sparkle in the sun and give the plant a crystalline appearance. In summer this undemanding succulent produces 1 in white, red, pink and occasionally yellow flowers depending on the variety. It is extremely easy to grow; all it needs is a position in the sun and sandy soil. It should only be watered and fed in moderation. It is grown from seed in spring and must be moved indoors before the first frost and only put out when there is no longer any danger of frost.

Mesembryanthemum

Location: ◊ ☼
Propagation: ₀°°
Characteristics: ⊙ ✿
Diseases: *fungus disease (from excessive damp)*
Flowering: *summer*

Monkey flower

Mimulus

ⓘ

Location: 💧 ☀ — ☀ ⚠
Propagation: ⚬° ⚘
Characteristics: ⊙ ∞ ✿
Diseases: mildew rot
Pests: slugs and snails
Flowering: summer – autumn

Monkey flower is native to America. A master of disguise, it comes in many forms and colors and the flowers are often marked with dark blotches or speckled. Today it is becoming increasingly popular as a container plant for balconies and terraces. The large-flowered hybrids are the most suitable for the purpose. They have funnel-shaped flowers, speckled with red up to 2 in long. They prefer a sunny to partially shaded, airy, cool location in moist to wet, fertile soil. They must be fed every week during the summer months. If cut back after the first flowering, they will bloom again a second time. Although they are perennials, the hybrids are mostly cultivated as annuals. They can be grown from seed but specimens propagated from cuttings usually produce larger, more colourful flowers.

Molucella laevis

Shellflower

Molucella laevis

Location: 💧 ☀
Propagation: ⚬°
Characteristics: ⊙ ✿
Flowering: summer

The *Molucella* genus includes four annual species that are native from the eastern Mediterranean to north-west India. Shellflower is a summer flowering annual that originates in the Caucasus. It is ideal for mixed planting on terraces and also produces beautiful cut flowers that can be used fresh or in dry flower arrangements. It grows up to 39 in high and has round, light green leaves. The apple-green, shell-shaped calixes round the rather inconspicuous white to pale pink flowers are grouped in whorls and borne on long spikes. The calixes acquire an almost paper-like appearance when the seeds ripen. This frost-sensitive plant thrives in a sunny, warm location in moist, well-drained and moderately fertile soil. It flowers from June until September and can be grown from seed in late spring. The seeds should soaked before sowing.

Grape hyacinth

Muscari

This vigorous genus consists of 30 species. The fleshy, mid-green to grey-green leaves appear soon after planting in autumn. The white or blue, bell-shaped flowers that are borne in dense spikes on leafless stems develop the following spring. *Muscari* is one of the most popular bulb plants for spring. It is an ideal container plant for terraces and balconies. Grape hyacinths thrive in a sunny or partially shaded position in fertile, well-drained soil. The bulbs are lifted in summer and the bulbils separated from the mother-bulb. After a period of rest in summer, the bulbs are planted in autumn about 4 in deep. Feed once after the leaves have developed.

Location: ◊ ☀ – ☀ ⁄⅍
Care: ⁄⁂
Propagation: ☙✔❀
Characteristics: ✖ ∞ ❁
Diseases: virus diseases
Flowering: spring

Myosotis sylvatica

Forget-me-not

Myosotis sylvatica

The Greek word *Myosotis* means "mouse-ear" and the genus has been given this name because of the pointed leaves of its roughly 50 annual and perennial species. These undemanding spring-flowering plants will thrive almost anywhere as long as the conditions are warm and not too dry. They grow best in a sunny and partially shaded location in well-drained fertile soil. The short lifespan of forget-me-nots is easily compensated by their prolific self-seeding. Feeding before the flowering season will encourage more abundant flowering. The small flowers are borne in dense flower heads. Many varieties have been developed from the small forget-me-not, that are usually grown as annuals or perennials. The lavender-blue, pink or white flowers are produced from spring until early summer. It can be grown from seed in early spring if sown indoors or directly outdoors in summer. The young plants of varieties grown as biennials should be covered during winter.

Location: ❧ ☀ – ☀
Care: ⁄⁂
Propagation: ∴°
Characteristics: ⊟ ☉ / ∞ ❁
Diseases: mildew
Pests: slugs and snails
Flowering: spring – early
    summer

Daffodil

Narcissus

ℹ

Location: ◐ ☼—☼
Propagation: ✿✐✿
Characteristics: ✖ ∞ ✿ ❅ —⟁
Diseases: Fungus and virus
diseases
Pests: narcissus fly, bulb eel
worms, slugs and snails
Flowering: spring – early
summer

The *Narcissus* genus includes many species and varieties that are among the most popular early spring-flowering bulbs. Large-cupped daffodils produce the most handsome cut flowers while the very decorative wild forms look more attractive in rock gardens and borders, and as container plants on balconies and terraces. Daffodils are very popular not only for attractive, fragrant flowers but also for their elegant foliage. The cyclamineus daffodil, "Tête-à-tête", is quite famous as a container plant. The bulbs are planted in autumn 4–6 in deep in fertile, well-drained soil and placed in a sunny or partially shaded location. They should be watered generously during the growing season but then allowed to dry out once the leaves begin to wilt. Deadheading will prolong the flowering season. The application of a potash fertilizer, poor in nitrogen, will encourage the production of flowers. They are propagated from offsets removed from the main bulb or by division of the clumps. The sap of the plant can cause allergies.

Narcissus

Nemesia

Nemesia

The *Nemesia* genus consists of colourful annuals grown for the border and as container plants for balconies and terraces. The most cultivated are hybrid varieties. The large trumpet-shaped flowers are produced throughout the summer until the autumn in a wide range of colors from white to yellow, red and blue and borne in dense clusters. The bushy, branched plants grow 16 in high. Nemesias thrive in a sunny, sheltered location and cool temperatures. The soil should be fertile, kept evenly moist and well-drained. They need plenty of water in periods of drought but waterlogging will quickly lead to stem rot at the base. They benefit from weekly applications of fertilizer. They must be deadheaded regularly, and cutting after flowering will encourage a second flowering. Nemesias are grown from seed in spring and young plants should be pruned to encourage a bushy, branched growth.

Location: 💧 ☼ ⚠
Propagation: ⸰°
Characteristics: ⊙ ❀
Diseases: stem rot
Flowering: summer – autumn

Nemesia

Tobacco plant

Nicotiana x sanderae

ⓘ

Location: 💧 ☼–☼ ⚠

Propagation: ⸰°

Characteristics: ✖ ☉ ✿

Diseases: grey mould, virus diseases

Pests: slugs and snails, caterpillars, aphids, white fly

Flowering: summer – autumn

The *Nicotiana* genus is a member of the nightshade family. All parts of all the plants are poisonous (leaves, flowers and stems). The tobacco plant was first introduced into Europe from South America at the beginning of the 16th century. *Nicotiana x Sanderae* with its many colourful varieties is the most popular ornamental nicotiana and is usually grown as an annual. The older species open their fragrant tubular flowers on warm, still, summer's evenings while the flowers of new varieties open all day. Nicotianas thrive in rich, well-drained soil in full sun or partial shade, in a sheltered location. They need plenty of water and during the growing season they also benefit from weekly applications of fertilizer. They grow up to 16 in high and as a result provide an excellent framework for plant arrangements. They are not easy to raise from seed and it is therefore best to buy new seedlings that can be planted out when all danger of frost has passed. Taller varieties should be staked and regular deadheading prolongs the flowering season.

Nicotiana

Cupflower

Nierembergia hippomanica

Cupflower is native to South America. This small, bushy herbaceous, cushion perennial is usually grown as an annual and reaches a height of 8 in. It is ideal for planting in empty corners in the garden but also along terrace walls and in tubs and hanging baskets on balconies. It flowers throughout summer until autumn with violet-blue or white flowers with yellow throats depending on the variety. The slender, upright stems that carry dark green, lanceolate, hairy leaves are strongly branched and should be cut back after flowering. The frost-sensitive cupflower grows best in moist but well-drained soil in a sunny to partially shaded location. It appreciates regular watering and occasional applications of fertilizer. It is grown from seed in spring or propagated from tip cuttings in summer.

Location: 💧 ☼ — ☀ ⚠
Propagation: ⊙°
Characteristics: ✖ ⊙ ❀
Diseases: tobacco mosaic virus
Pests: slugs and snails
Flowering: summer – autumn

Love in a mist

Nigella

Nigella is particularly popular with gardeners because of its attractive flowers and decorative seed-heads, often used in fresh and dry flower arrangements. Love-in-a-mist produces spurred, many-petalled flowers in shades of blue, white or pink, followed by balloon-like brown seed-heads. The variety "Transformer" already starts flowering in late spring. It has bluish-green leaves and terminal yellow flower heads, followed by particularly attractive flower heads, very similar to upturned umbrellas, that are often used in dry flower arrangements because of their very decorative appearance. *Love-in-a-mist* has intensely blue flowers. It grows best in a very sunny location in fertile soil, rich in humus. It is grown from seed in late spring. Regular deadheading will prolong the flowering season but naturally prevents the formation of seed-heads.

Nigella

Location: ◊ ☼ ⚠
Propagation: ⊙°
Characteristics: ⊙ ❀ ❄
Flowering: spring – summer

Chilean bellflower

Nolana paradoxa

The *Nolana* genus is native to Chile, Peru and the Galapagos Islands. The Chilean bellflower only reaches a height of 8 in with a spread of 20 in. It flowers prolifically throughout the summer, producing funnel-shaped, blue-violet, axillary blooms with yellow-white throat borne in singly or in clusters. The flowers only open in full sun. Because of its creeping, twining, climbing growth it makes excellent ground cover and also looks very attractive in hanging baskets and tubs on balconies. It is best grown as an annual in a sunny location, sheltered from the wind, in well-drained soil, rich in humus. In summer it should watered regularly and fed every 14 days. Deadheading will prolong the flowering season. Bushy growth will encouraged by pruning young plants.

ⓘ

Location: ◊ ☼ ⚠
Propagation: ⸰ᵒ
Characteristics: ⊙ ❀
Pests: aphids
Flowering: summer

Osteospermum

ⓘ

Location: ◊ ☼ ⚠
Care: ❄
Propagation:
Characteristics: ∞ ❀
Diseases: mildew, verticillium wilt
Pests: aphids, thrips, leaf miner, white fly
Flowering: spring – autumn

Osteospermum

Osteospermum ecklonis

Osteospermum, is native to South Africa. From late spring until autumn it produces a profusion of large daisy-like flowers that may be white, pink, violet or yellow depending on the variety. Interesting new varieties have been developed such as those with spoon-shaped petals. The compact plant 28 in high has glossy, dark green leaves that look particularly attractive as container plants on balconies and terraces. In winter it must be moved to a frost-free place. *Osteospermum* grows best in a sunny location, sheltered from the wind, in moderately fertile, well-drained soil. It must be watered moderately but regularly and fed every seven days with a weak solution of fertilizer. This ensures that the plant continues flowering even in periods of very hot weather. It is propagated from tip cuttings in spring; growing from seed should be left to the expert. It is important to deadhead regularly.

Common poppy

Papaver rhoeas

The *Papaver* genus includes about 70 annual, biennial and perennial species. Some are considered weeds. The common poppy is native to Europe and Asia Minor. This fast-growing, small-branched annual with the charm of a wild flower produces delicate-looking, saucer-shaped scarlet-red flowers with a black centre. The opium poppy, cultivated for the production of opium and related drugs, produces white, pink, red or violet flowers that are often double. Grown as annuals and biennials, poppies thrive in a fertile, well-drained soil in a sunny location. They need plenty of water during the growing season. They are propagated from seed in spring or autumn. Regular deadheading is important to prevent self-seeding. Poppies will cause nausea if consumed.

ⓘ

Location: ◆ ☀
Propagation: ₀°°
Characteristics: ✖ ⊙ / ∞ ❀ ❄
  (wild form)
Diseases: wilt
Pests: aphids
Flowering: summer

Papaver rhoeas

Pelargoniums – nostalgic and modern

Geranium is the popular name for the plants of the genus Pelargonium *because they were originally included in the genus* Geranium. Pelargos *in Greek means "stork" and refers to the resemblance of the schizocarp to the beak of a stork. They are native to Cape Province in South Africa and were introduced in Europe at the beginning of the 17th century. There are over 200 species and a large number of varieties, including many large-flowered varieties developed by breeders. The varieties illustrated here are but a selection of the wide range available.*

Geranium oil is widely used in the perfume and cosmetic industry, often replacing more expensive rose oil.

Scented-leaved pelargoniums have experienced a real revival in recent years. Some of the varieties include Pelargonium radens, P. x graveolens, P. capitatum *and* P. odoratissimum. *With their small flowers grouped in umbels they have preserved their original appearance better than garden varieties.*

Geraniums are best known as bedding- and window box plants. They will happily over-winter in a bright room with a temperature of 50 to 59° F and are ideal for cultivating as perennial container plants. In winter they should be kept relatively dry but in summer they need plenty of water. They are easily propagated from softwood cuttings, taken in summer or spring. Zonal pelargoniums can be propagated from seed but this takes longer. Older specimens can be cut back in spring – in fact this is recommended in the case of ivy-leaved pelargoniums to ensure a bushy growth.

Scented-leaved pelargonium

Pelargonium "Fragrans Group"

ⓘ

Location: ◊ ☼ ⚠
Care: 🏠
Propagation: ˳°°
Characteristics: ⊙ / ∞ ❀ ▨
Diseases: grey mould,
  black spot, rust fungus
Pests: weevils, aphids,
  caterpillars, white fly
Flowering: summer – autumn

Scented-leaved pelargoniums are native to South Africa. The leaves of these vigorous, densely branched plants often contain ethereal oils that smell of peppermint, eucalyptus, lemon, apple, rose and many other fragrances. The scent becomes even more intense if the leaves are rubbed lightly. *Pelargonium* grows to a height and spread of 12 in. The small, heart-shaped, grey-green leaves exude a pine- and apple-scented fragrance. "Mabel Grey," the most fragrant of the geraniums, has evergreen, rough-textured, lemon-scented leaves and mauve flowers marked with red. The small, round leaves of the "Aroma" variety have a very sweetish scent while the leaves of "Attar of Roses" are rose-scented. *Pelargonium* "variegatum" has midgreen, lemon-scented leaves with a creamy margins. This aroma is even stronger in the lemon-scented geraniums, whose leaves are also slightly apple-scented.

Zonal pelargonium "Frank Headly"

Ivy-leaved geranium

Pelargonium peltatum

Location: ◊ ☼ ⚠
Care: 🌡
Propagation:
Characteristics: ☉ / ∞ ❀
*Diseases: grey mould, black
    spot, rust fungus*
*Pests: weevils, aphids,
    caterpillars, white fly*
Flowering: summer – autumn

Ivy-leaved geraniums, also known as trailing geraniums, are among the most popular plants for window boxes, hanging baskets and containers. The effect of their long, trailing shoots and profusion of flowers that last until the autumn is unrivalled. They are also weather-resistant, and some varieties, such as those of the "Cascade" series, with single flowers, drop their flowerheads when over. The red and white "Mexikanerin" and violet "Amethyst Starlight" both have semi-double flowers with petals displaying dark-purple and white, feather-shaped markings. The single, large-flowered "Blizzard" varieties are a recent development. Trailing geraniums need a sheltered place so that their long shoots do not break off. They are usually propagated from cuttings.

Pelargonium

Pelargonium x hortorum "Vancouver Centennial"

Upright geranium

Pelargonium x hortorum

This large hybrid group was developed from a South African wild form. They are compact plants that grow up to 24 in high whose single or double flowers come in numerous shades and are grouped in long-stemmed umbels. The leaves are usually marked with a dark "zone" that in foliage-geraniums such as "Vancouver Centennial" is bronze-coloured and in "Mrs Pollock" even multi-coloured. The semi-double zonal pelargonium "Grand Prix" produces bright red flowers and "Schöne Helena" has salmon-coloured flowers. "Brasil" and "Tango Pink" have pink-lilac flowers. The vigorous-growing "Salmon Flash" with light salmon-coloured, star-shaped flowers is a recent innovation. It combines beautifully with other varieties. Regal pelargoniums have particularly large flowers. Upright geraniums need more sun and warmth than their trailing relatives and are prone to weather damage. It is important that they are deadheaded regularly.

Location: ◊ ☼
Care: 🏠
Propagation: ⚬°°
Characteristics: △ ⊙ / ∞ ✿ ▧
Diseases: grey mould,
black spot, rust fungus
Pests: weevils, aphids,
caterpillars, white fly
Flowering: summer – autumn

African fountain grass

Pennisetum setaceum

ⓘ

Location: 💧 ☼ ⚠
Care: ⚠
Propagation: ∘° 🐝✿
Characteristics: ☉ ✿
Flowering: summer – autumn

This deciduous, tuft-forming, perennial grass is native to the African tropics. The plants look very attractive in containers or planted along the edge of a terrace. The dense tufts reach a height of 39 in and a spread of 20 in. They have rough-textured stems and long, narrow leaves. In summer they bears panicles of copper-coloured, bearded spikelets. The panicles are ideal for drying and are therefore often used in dried flower arrangements. African fountain grass needs feeding every two weeks and dead leaves should be removed regularly. This undemanding grass grows best in a sunny position in light, well-drained soil, which should be kept very moist in summer. It can propagated from seed in spring or by division in early summer. If the plants are left outdoors during winter, they should be cut back and covered with thick layer of dry mulching material.

Pennisetum setaceum

Egyptian star

Pentas lanceolata

This bushy, rounded shrub, also known as Star cluster, is native to Arabia and tropical Africa. It has light green, lanceolate leaves, covered with soft hairs and umbel-shaped clusters of small star-shaped flowers that are pale pink, red, violet or white depending on the variety. They are produced throughout the summer. This frost-sensitive plant is not only ideal for cut flowers, but it also makes an excellent house plant that can be placed in window boxes and pots on balconies and terraces in summer. Dwarf varieties are particularly good for this purpose. Taller varieties can be pruned to keep them to the required size. *Pentas* thrive in moist but well-drained soil in a sunny to partially shaded position. Regular watering, weekly feeding and occasional pruning will encourage flowering. The plant is propagated from seed in summer and stem cuttings in summer. During winter, it must be moved to a light, frost-free place.

ⓘ

Location: 💧 ☀ — ☀ ⚠
Care: 🗍
Propagation: ₒ°°
Characteristics: ∞ ✿
Pests: aphids, red spider mite
Flowering: spring – summer

Cineraria

Pericallis x hybrida

Cinerarias have serrated, coarse-textured leaves arranged in rosettes. The showy, colourful flowers grouped in dense heads are produced from spring until autumn in shades of pink, red, violet and white. There are also two-tone varieties. The herbaceous perennial is usually grown as an annual and, because it only grows 12 in high, it makes an ideal container plant for balconies and terraces. The frost-sensitive cineraria is very tolerant of heat, sea-air and poor soil but will not tolerate excessive humidity in the air or being waterlogged. It grows best in well-drained soil in a bright to partially shaded location. During the growing season it needs regular watering and weekly feeding. It can be propagated from seed but this is best left to the expert.

ⓘ

Location: 💧 ☀ ⚠
Propagation: ₒ°°
Characteristics: ⊙ ✿
Diseases: aphids, red spider mite, thrips, white fly, leaf miner
Flowering: spring – autumn

Opposite page: Petunia "Surfinia"

Trailing petunia

Petunia "Surfinia"

ℹ️

Location: 💧 ☀ ⚠
Propagation: ⚬°°
Characteristics: ✖ ⊙ ❀
Diseases: *mosaic virus, wilt*
Pests: *aphids, white fly*
Flowering: *spring – autumn*

"Surfinia" petunias are types propagated from cuttings that have been developed by Japanese breeders. The name is now applied to all trailing petunias, although there are many trailing types developed by other breeders. These robust, vigorous-growing and unusually weather-resistant trailing petunias produce many more flowers than traditional petunias, but only if they are watered and fed regularly. Because of the large mass of leaves and flowers, the plants need very large amounts of food and water. The stems can grow up to 5 ft long. However, it is very important that they are sheltered from the wind. They also make excellent ground cover. These types, available only as young seedlings, do not need pruning and thinning. Although usually grown as annuals, you could also try over-wintering the plants at a temperature of 50° F and propagating from cuttings.

Garden petunia

Petunia x atkinsiana

ℹ️

Location: 💧 ☀ ⚠
Propagation:
Characteristics: ✖ ⊙ ❀
Diseases: *mosaic virus, wilt*
Pests: *aphids, white fly*
Flowering: *spring – autumn*

The annual, frost-sensitive garden petunias are members of the poisonous nightshade family. There are erect and trailing types whose single or double flowers come in almost every colour. Like the large-flowered Grandiflora group, the floriferous Multiflora group with medium-sized flowers also make excellent container plants for balconies and terraces. The disadvantage of the Grandiflora petunias is that they are not weather-resistant and are therefore prone to botrytis. They need well-drained, fertile soil and a sunny position where they will be sheltered from the wind. During the growing season they need plenty of water and weekly applications of fertilizer. Regular deadheading will encourage a more prolific flowering. They are raised from seed in spring and planted after the last frosts have passed. Pruning the young plants encourages bushy growth.

Phlox

Location: ♦ – ◌ to ☼ – ☀
Care: ⚐
Propagation: ₀°°
Characteristics: ∞ ✿
Diseases: mildew, leaf spot
Pests: leaf gall, nematodes
Flowering: spring – summer

Annual phlox

Phlox drummondii

The fast-growing, annual summer-flowering phlox that produces an abundance of flowers in purple, white, pink, red and lavender blue from late spring until autumn is an ideal plant to add colour to balconies and terraces. The small, flat flowers are grouped in dense terminal clusters that contrast beautifully with the pale green, lance-shaped leaves. The varieties in the "Sternenzauber" series have serrated petals that give the flowers a star-shaped appearance. Phloxes grow best in a sunny to partially shaded location in well-drained, fertile soil, rich in humus. In summer, they must be watered regularly and freely. They flower badly in wet summers, but regular deadheading encourages flowering. Annual varieties are raised from seed in spring. Phloxes are prone to attacks by red spider mites and mealy bugs and are vulnerable to mildew and leaf spot.

Plectranthus

Location: ♦ ☼ ⚐
Propagation:
Characteristics: ☉ ✿
Flowering: summer – autumn

Swedish ivy

Plectranthus forsteri

In the past Swedish ivy could usually be found in and around farms because its penetrating, unmistakable odour kept vermin away. The herbaceous perennial grown as an annual is native to south-east India. Its aromatic, colourful leaves and white tubular flowers that appear in summer make it a very popular plant. It has a spreading habit with stems reaching up to 39 in in length. It is an ideal container plant for balconies and also looks very good in hanging baskets. This frost-sensitive plant grows best in partial shade in well-drained, moist soil. It needs plenty of water and monthly applications of fertilizer during the growing season. It can be cut back at any time. It is easily and quickly propagated from cuttings taken in spring.

Miniature bamboo

Pogonatherum paniceum

This elegant, 16 in high house-bamboo is not related to the true bamboo. It is beautiful plant that is native to South-East Asia and has elegant, slender stems and attractive narrow leaves. Cats are very fond of this grass. It is an undemanding pot-plant but not frost-resistant and is therefore better known as a perennial house plant. In summer it can be placed outdoors on a terrace or balcony. It needs a warm, bright location but dislikes direct sun. The root ball should never be allowed to dry out because the withered stems are very difficult to remove. Water and food should be reduced to one-third during winter. Miniature bamboo is propagated by division in spring.

ⓘ

Location: ♦ ☼ ⊿
Care: ❄
Propagation: ✄ ✿
Characteristics: ∞

Sun plant

Portulaca grandiflora

In its native habitat in Argentina and Brazil, sun plants grow on very sunny, dry, sandy slopes. The small, succulent, fleshy leaves are able to store water so that they need very little water and food even in cultivation. In warm, dry summers they produce an abundance of large, rose-like, single or double flowers in many colors, including orange, pink, red, yellow and white. Because of their spreading, trailing habit, these frost-sensitive annuals are ideal as container plants and in hanging baskets for balconies and terraces. They are also excellent ground cover and provide attractive edging in borders. They need very little water and are very undemanding. Moreover, they will survive in many places where other plants will not. They can be propagated from seed in spring and from cuttings in summer.

Portulaca grandiflora

ⓘ

Location: ◊ ☼
Propagation: ˖ᵒ
Characteristics: △ ⊙ ✿
Diseases: stem rot
Pests: aphids
Flowering: summer

Fairy primrose

Primula malacoides

ⓘ

Location: ♦ ☀ ⚠
Care: 🎍
Characteristics: ✖ ∞ ✿
Diseases: viruses, root rot, grey
  mould
Pests: aphids, red spider mite,
  weevils, slugs and snails
Flowering: Winter – spring

Like pansies and bulbs, this attractive spring-flowering plant is a popular herald of spring in gardens and balconies. A frost-sensitive herbaceous perennial native to China, it is better known as a house plant but it is also looks very nice on balconies and terraces in summer. It grows up to 12 in high and has pale green leaves with slightly fringed margins. The delicate whorls of flowers are borne on slender stems, covered with soft hairs from late winter onward, depending on the weather. The flowers come in a wide range of colors including light purple, pinkish red and white. *Primula* has particularly attractive, dense umbels. All primroses need not too dry, well-drained soil, rich in humus and partial shade. The soil should never be allowed to dry out or become waterlogged. During the growing season, plants must fed every two weeks and wilted parts removed. Primroses are grown from seed but this should be left to experts. Contact with the skin can lead to irritation.

Ranunculus

ⓘ

Location: ○ ☀ – ☀ ⚠
Care: ❄
Propagation: ∴ 🌱 tubers
Characteristics: ✖ ∞ ✿
Diseases: mildew
Pests: slugs and snails, aphids
Flowering: spring–early
  summer

Persian buttercup

Ranunculus

Ranunculus was introduced from Asia Minor into Europe in 1596 is one of the most attractive heralds of summer. It is a bulbous perennial but is not frost hardy. The round, double flowers that come in white, pink, red, yellow and orange depending on the species appear in late spring. The tall varieties make magnificent cut flowers while the low, more compact varieties are more suited for containers, pots and window boxes. The plants need a sunny to partially shaded location and well-drained soil. They benefit from regular watering and 2-weekly applications of fertilizer. After flowering when the leaves have died, the bulbs are lifted and stored in well-ventilated, dry place with a temperature of 45–50° F. They are planted out again in autumn or spring. It can also be raised from seed indoors in autumn or late winter. Skin contact can cause irritation.

Black-eyed susan

Rudbeckia hirta

The annual Black-eyed Susan is native to North America. It bears colourful flower heads with pretty, purple-brown conical centers on branched or unbranched erect stems. The petals surrounding the center are bright yellow to reddish brown, occasionally also two-tone. The flowers can be single or double. Tall varieties make excellent cut flowers while low varieties are ideal for filling gaps in window boxes and containers. The annual, frost-tender Black-eyed Susan grows best in a sunny location in well-drained soil, rich in humus. Although undemanding and easy to grow it needs plenty of water and food during the growing season. Dead blooms must be removed regularly. It is sown indoors in spring and only planted out when there is no longer any danger of frost.

Rudbeckia hirta

Location: 💧 ☼ ⚠
Propagation: ⠐⠌
Characteristics: ☉ ❀
Pests: slugs and snails
Flowering: summer

Painted tongue

Salpiglossis sinuata

Painted tongue is an annual native to the southern Andes. Its extremely attractive flowers are very similar to those of the petunia, to which it is in fact related. It has an upright habit with slender, branched stems and can soon reach 24 in in height. The funnel-shaped, strikingly veined flowers appear in the upper axils of the bright green, lanceolate leaves and are produced throughout summer until the beginning of autumn. They come in a wide range of colors such as red, orange, yellow, blue and reddish violet. The plant is quite demanding but the effort is worth it. It is vital that it is placed in a sunny, warm location where it is protected from the wind to ensure that it flowers prolifically. The plant may not flower at all in a cold, wet summer. This frost-tender plant grows best in fertile, well-drained soil that should be kept moderately moist at all times. It must be fed weekly during the growing season and deadheaded regularly. Tall varieties should be staked. It is grown from seed in early spring.

Location: 💧 ☼ ⚠
Propagation: ⠐⠌
Characteristics: ☉ ❀
Diseases: grey mould, root rot
Pests: aphids
Flowering: summer – autumn

Salvia

Salvia coccinea

ⓘ

Location: 💧 ☼ ⚠

Propagation: ₀°°

Characteristics: ☉ ❀

Pests: slugs and snails, red spider mite, aphids

Flowering: summer – autumn

This annual is native to North America and Mexico. It has a bushy, loosely branched habit with fern-like foliage and grows 24 in high. It bears bright red flowers, grouped in slender spikes, until the first frosts in autumn. The leaves are oval and crenate. "Lady in Red" with bright red flowers and salmon-coloured "Coral Nymph" are very popular varieties. Salvias love warm, sunny locations. They need plenty of water and food to ensure prolific flowering. The soil must be fertile and well-drained to prevent waterlogging. This variety of salvia looks very good planted in a group, but it is also ideal for filling gaps in window boxes. As far as colour is concerned, these salvias combine beautifully with heliotropes and marguerites. It is sown indoors in late winter and planted out after all danger of frost has passed.

Mealy sage

Salvia farinacea

ⓘ

Location: 💧 ☼ ⚠

Propagation: ₀°°

Characteristics: ☉ ❀

Pests: slugs and snails, red spider mite, aphids

Flowering: summer – autumn

Salvia farinacea is native to Texas and Mexico. It owes its name to the "floury" or "mealy" fluff covering the stems and spikes. The small 2-lipped flowers are grouped in dense spikes on long, slender stems and are a little reminiscent of lavender flowers. They are frost-hardy down to 23° F and besides the blue-flowering varieties there are also white varieties. With a height of 12–28 in, salvias make excellent cut flowers and dried flowers, and they look equally attractive in containers and borders. They look particularly good with roses. Like all salvias, they like a sunny location and plenty of water and food to ensure prolific flowering. The soil must be well-drained to make sure it does not become waterlogged. Regular deadheading will prolong flowering. They are grown from seed in spring indoors.

Scarlet sage

Salvia splendens

This exotic sage originated in Brazil where it grows as a herbaceous perennial. It is grown as annual in temperate zones because of its frost-tenderness. The low-growing varieties that only reach 10–12 in in height are ideal for terraces and balconies. These include for instance the dark-violet "Laser Purple," the bright red "Feuerzauber" and salmon-coloured "Melba." "Carabiniere" has distinctive dark foliage and red flowers. The tubular lipped flowers are grouped in dense clusters and are produced until the autumn. The bright red varieties look very good with yellow-flowering plants such as slipperwort. They need a sunny position where they are protected from wind and rain. The soil must be fertile, rich in humus and moist at all times during summer. Every week it should be fed with a weak solution of fertilizer. Regular deadheading will encourage a second flowering. Seeds are sown at a temperature of about 68° F from March onwards.

Location: 💧 ☼ ⚠
Propagation: ⠿
Characteristics: ☉ ✽
Pests: slugs and snails, red spider mite, aphids
Flowering: summer – autumn

Salvia viridis

Salvia

Salvia viridis

The most distinctive feature of this species of sage are the striking bracts, grouped in dense whorls, rather than the inconspicuous paler flowers. These can be violet-blue, pink, red or white depending on the variety. This species is native to the Mediterranean where it grows as a biennial or herbaceous perennial. In temperate zones it is usually grown as an annual. It grows 16–28 in high and is often cultivated as a source of cut flowers but it also looks very decorative in borders, pots and window boxes. The flowers are very popular with butterflies. Because of their natural charm, they combine beautifully with wild flowers and foliage plants. Like all other salvias they grow best in a sunny, warm location in fertile, well-drained soil. They do not tolerate being waterlogged. They are sown indoors in spring and from May onward. They can also be sown directly outdoors but in this case, it will flower later.

Location: 💧 ☼ ⚠
Propagation: ⠿
Characteristics: ☉ ✽
Pests: slugs and snails, red spider mite, aphids
Flowering: summer – autumn

Creeping zinnia

Sanvitalia procumbens

ⓘ

Location: ◊ ☼ ⚠
Propagation: ₀°°
Characteristics: ⊙ ✿
Flowering: summer – autumn

The annual creeping zinnia is native to Mexico and Guatemala. Because of the deep yellow, daisy-like flowers with almost black center and its dwarf habit (8 in) this species is sometimes called "miniature sunflower." "Aztekengold" with gold-yellow flowers and dark foliage is a very popular variety. "Mandarin Orange" has deep orange flowers. Creeping zinnia is strongly branched, prostrate annual that flowers uninterruptedly from early summer till autumn when the first frosts arrive. It is an undemanding plant that is ideal for hanging baskets, pots, window boxes and in containers where it can be planted in front of taller plants. It is sown in spring directly in the pots, which will be placed outdoors when all danger of frost has passed. It grows best in a sunny, sheltered location in sandy, well-drained soil. It must be regularly deadheaded, fed every two weeks and watered moderately. It tolerates dry conditions better than being waterlogged.

Sanvitalia

*F*an flower

Scaevola saligna

The 96 species of this Australian genus are not hardy but some are grown as house plants and balcony plants. This is true in particular of the blue fan flower, which was only introduced to Europe in 1988. It is a trailing plant that is often grown in hanging baskets and window boxes. It is extremely weather-resistant and even tolerates short periods of drought. To ensure prolific flowering fan flowers need a sunny to partially shaded location, well-drained soil, soft water and weekly applications of a weak solution of fertilizer from spring until late summer. Because of its frost-tenderness, it can only be placed outdoors at the end of May. It is propagated from softwood cuttings in late summer under mist, which is why it is best left to the experts. The violet-blue "Blue Wonder" variety is a classic. It looks very good with trailing geraniums.

Location: ◊ ☼ – ☀
Propagation:
Characteristics: ⊙ ✿
Pests: leaf miner, white fly
Flowering: spring – autumn

*P*oor man's orchid

Schizanthus x wisetonensis

This annual, poisonous plant, is native to Chile. The petals are deeply cut or lobed, hence its botanical name. The yellow-black center is reminiscent of orchids and this explains one of its common names, poor man's orchid. It is also known as butterfly flower. The plant produces terminal, bell-shaped, 2-lipped flowers in shades of white, blue, pink, red or red-brown throughout the summer until the autumn. Low varieties (8 in high) are ideal for window boxes and containers to which they will add colour and an exotic touch. They need well-drained soil and a sunny location where they will be sheltered from the wind, for instance an inner courtyard. In summer, the plant needs plenty of water but only moderate amounts of fertilizer. Otherwise the stems become too soft. It is preferable to buy young plants than to try and raise them from seed. Young plants should be pruned regularly to encourage branching. Cutting back after the first flowering will encourage a second flowering.

Location: ♦ ☼ ⟁
Propagation: ∴
Characteristics: ✖ ⊙ ✿
Flowering: summer – autumn

Scilla

Scilla siberica

This species is native to Eastern Europe, Asia and Africa like all others in the genus. It has strap-shaped, basal leaves and delightful, star-shaped, blue flowers that are borne on 6 in tall leafless stems in early spring. The blue-flowering variety "Spring Beauty" only reaches 6 in in height and it is ideal for containers and window boxes. The variety "Alba" has white flowers. The leaves wilt very quickly when the plant has finished flowering. The frost-hardy bulbs are planted in early autumn in bowls, baskets or window boxes in well-drained soil, which should be covered with some brushwood during winter. Scillas should be watered sparingly during the growing season and not at all during the rest period. During the growing season, scillas benefit from moderate amounts of fertilizer every two weeks. Propagation from off-sets is only possible outdoors in open ground; for growing in containers, they are best grown from seed. Both bulbs and seeds are poisonous.

ℹ

Location: ○ ☼ − ☼ △
Care: △ ❆
Propagation: ∴ ✿ bulbils
Characteristics: ✖ ❀
Diseases: viruses
Flowering: spring

Senecio cineraria

ℹ

Location: ○ ☼ △
Propagation:
Characteristics: ✖ ☉ ∞ ❧
Diseases: rust fungus, mildew
Pests: aphids
Flowering: summer – autumn

Cineraria

Senecio cineraria

The plant owes its name common name, cineraria (from the Latin meaning "ashes") to the grey leaves, covered with white woolly hairs. It is native to the Mediterranean. Most varieties of this popular foliage plant grow about 8 in high and provide an "architectural" framework to late summer flowering plants. The leaves are deeply lobed or broadly serrated depending on the variety. The mustard-yellow flower heads that appear in summer are only produced by perennial species that survive outdoors in regions with mild winters. Cineraria is used to warmth and dry conditions; it needs very little water but it requires a very sunny location. During the growing season it needs feeding once a month. The soil should be too moist because this would lead the leaves to turn green, the white hairs being only a protection against heat and drought. The plant contains poisonous alkaloids.

Gloxinia

Sinningia speciosa

Gloxinia, a very popular container- and house plant, is the best-known species of the Latin American genus *Siningia,* includes 80 bulbous herbaceous perennials. It owes its great popularity to the strikingly beautiful flowers, which come in a wide range of colors. They are large, bell-shaped with delicately marked, velvety petals with curly margins. They grow above a rosette of pale green, equally velvety leaves which are hairy on top and tinged with red underneath. They are planted in spring in fresh, well-drained soil. Gloxinias grow best in a bright location but not in direct sun. When placed on a balcony or terrace, they should be well protected against the rain. They should be watered regularly with lukewarm water and fed every week until the end of the flowering season. During winter the tubers should be stored dry in a frost-free place. Propagation from seed is best left to professionals.

Sinningia

ⓘ

Location: 💧 ☀️
Care: 🌡️
Propagation: .°°
Characteristics: △ ∞ ✿
Pests: leafhoppers, thrips
Flowering: summer

Aubergine or Eggplant

Solanum melongena

Like the potato and tomato, the eggplant or ornamental aubergine is a member of a family that grows throughout the world. Its fruits edible can be braised, fried or roasted. But be careful: all the other parts of the plant are poisonous! The annual eggplant can be found from tropical Africa to India. Not ony does it have only decorative fruits but also pretty reddish violet flowers that are produced in summer until autumn at the same time as the fruits, which are white at first before ripening to a warm golden yellow. The seeds are planted in spring in sandy, well-drained soil in a large container. The young plants are placed outdoors in a sunny location when all danger of frost has passed. The plant needs plenty of water and weekly applications of fertilizer to produce a good crop. It is important to stake the plants firmly.

Solanum melongena

ⓘ

Location: 💧 ☀️ ⚠️
Propagation: .°°
Characteristics: ✖ ☉ ✿
Pests: aphids
Flowering: summer – autumn

Solenostemon

ⓘ

Location: ♦ ☼ – ☼ ⚠
Care: ❄
Propagation: ₀°
Characteristics: ☉ / ∞ ✿
Pests: white fly
Flowering: summer

Coleus

Solenostemon scutellarioides

Coleus is native to tropical Africa and Asia, where it grows as a bushy, herbaceous perennial, not grown for its inconspicuous flowers that appear in summer but for its colourful, speckled, serrated foliage. Being frost-sensitive it is mostly cultivated as an annual but it can also over-winter in the house at a temperature of 50° F. In autumn, it should be cut back and re-potted in spring in fresh, well-drained soil, rich in humus. The exotic colors of the decorative leaves, covered in fine hairs, are shown to their best advantage in a partially shaded, sheltered location. It needs plenty of water and weekly feeding during the growing season. If the flowers are pinched out, the leaves will grow larger. Because the foliage loses some of its colour in the second year, it is best to propagate every year from softwood cuttings.

Sparrmannia africana

ⓘ

Location: ♦ ☼ ⚠
Care: ❄
Propagation:
Characteristics: ∞ ✿ ✿
Pests: red spider mite, white fly
Flowering: winter – spring

African hemp

Sparrmannia africana

African hemp has been grown as a house plant for 200 years and belongs to the same family as the lime tree. It is native to South Africa and Madagascar, where it grows to a tree 13 ft high. The white flowers with reddish-violet or yellow stamens are borne in attractive clusters that appear in spring. African hemp needs plenty of water during the growing season but does not tolerate being waterlogged. In summer it should be fed every 2 weeks. It grows best in a bright, sheltered location where it is sheltered from the wind but not in full sun or too hot because this would lead to leaf drop. In winter it should be placed in a warm, cool place (no higher than 50° F and watered very sparingly. It should be repotted every 2 years in fertile, well-drained soil. The plant can be cut back after flowering and the resulting cuttings will root very easily.

Sutera

Sutera diffusus

Sutera has a creeping or hanging habit that makes it particularly suitable as a container plant for balconies and terraces. These frost-sensitive plants have small leaves that are arranged in clusters or opposite. The flowers appear from late spring until autumn and are white, pink, reddish-violet or blue depending on the variety. Because *Sutera* produces only few, small flowers in the shade, it is best to place it in full sun in fertile, well-drained soil. It should be watered regularly and fed every two weeks. It can be grown from seed or propagated from cuttings. It can be trimmed lightly 6 to 8 weeks before flowering.

Location: ◖ ☼ ⚠
Care: ⬆
Propagation: ⸰ᵒ
Characteristics: ☉ ❀
Diseases: grey mould, root rot
Pests: thrips, aphids, white fly
Flowering: spring – autumn

African marigold

Tagetes erecta

The annual African marigold that is native to Mexico and Guatemala is one of the most popular summer flowering plants. Today there are many varieties of this species, which include single, chrysanthemum-like flowers and double, carnation-like blooms with a rather pungent aroma. They appear in late spring and are produced throughout the summer until autumn in various shades of orange. The bright colors of the flowers contrast beautifully with the dark green, feathery foliage. Depending on the species, they grow from 8 to 39 in high, the low-growing varieties being more suited for growing in containers and window boxes. The vigorous-growing but frost-sensitive *African marigold* also makes a good edging plant. They thrive in full sun but will also grow in partial shade. In summer the soil should be kept moist at all times and the plant fed every week. It is important to deadhead regularly. Seed are sown indoors in late winter. Both leaves and sap can cause allergies.

Tagetes erecta

Location: ◖ ☼ – ☼
Propagation: ⸰ᵒ
Characteristics: ⚠ ✖ ☉ ❀
Diseases: grey mould
Pests: aphids, red spider mite,
    slugs and snails, caterpillars
Flowering: summer – autumn

Tagetes patula

ⓘ

Location: 💧 ☼ – ☼
Propagation: ⣀
Characteristics: ✖ ☉ ✿
Diseases: grey mould
Pests: aphids, red spider mite,
slugs and snails, caterpillars
Flowering: summer – autumn

French marigold

Tagetes patula

The varieties of the *Tagetes patula* species are very suitable for growing in containers and window boxes because of their small size. Their blooms are smaller than those of the larger sibling but much more prolific and less sensitive to rain. The bushy plant grows between 8 and 24 in, depending on the variety, producing single or double flowers in red, yellow, orange or various shades of brown. They are also often two-tone. *Tagetes patula*, which is also native to South America, is an even more dainty wild form, covered in a mass of small, single flowers that come in shades of yellow, orange or brown and attract large numbers of butterflies and bees. It only grows 8 in high and has fine, feathery foliage. It grows both in sun and partial shade in fertile, light potting compost. It is propagated from seed in spring.

Torenia fournieri

ⓘ

Location: 💧 ☼ ⚠
Propagation: ⣀
Characteristics: ☉ ✿
Pests: aphids, white fly
Flowering: summer – autumn

Wishbone flower

Torenia fournieri

In recent years the wishbone flower that produces blooms in shades of blue, pink or violet has become a very popular house plant or summer flowering garden plant. The *Torenia* genus includes over 300 species and is native to South Vietnam. While the "Clown" F1-hybrids have an upright, bushy growth and are propagated from seed every year, the "Summer Wave" varieties, propagated from cuttings, have a trailing habit that makes them ideally suited for growing in window boxes and hanging baskets. The blue, lipped flowers are produced in profusion throughout the summer until the beginning of autumn. They grow best in well-drained soil, rich in humus, in shade or partial shade where they are protected from the wind. In summer they need plenty of water and should be fed every week. They hate being waterlogged.

Common nasturtium

Tropaeolum majus

This annual species of the *Tropaeolum* genus is native to Peru and includes upright, scrambling and climbing varieties. The latter are ideal for covering pergolas and walls in a very short time. The funnel-shaped, spurred, bright red, yellow or orange flowers are borne in the leaf-axils of shoots that can reach up to 6 ft 6 in in length. The plant is also medicinal: besides being a tonic it has diuretic, expectorant, bactericidal and fungicidal properties. Because of their sharp taste, leaves and flowers are sometimes used in cooking such as in salads, while the seeds are sometimes used as a substitute for capers. Nasturtiums need plenty of sun and water. They should be fed only every two months with a low-nitrogen fertilizer. They are raised from seed in late spring, even in situ in milder regions.

Location: 💧 ☼
Propagation: ◦°
Characteristics: ⊙ ❀
Pests: aphids, caterpillars, flea beetles, white fly
Flowering: summer – autumn

Tropaeolum majus

Tulipa

ⓘ

Location: ○ ☀ ⚠
Care: ⚠ – ❄
Propagation: 🌱bulbils
Characteristics: ✖ ∞ ❀
Diseases: bulb rot, fungus
Pests: slugs, snails, nematodes
Flowering: spring

Tulip

Tulipa

The tulips grown today are native to central and western Asia. The genus includes about 100 species but the number of varieties is in the thousands. The shorter, botanical tulips look particularly good in window boxes and bowls. The bulbs are planted in October at the latest in light, sandy soil but not as deep as they would be in the garden – 1.25 in is enough. The pots containing the bulbs are then placed in a dark, frost-free place until the leaves begin to emerge. The pots should only be watered sparingly and waterlogging must be avoided at all costs because this would lead the bulbs to rot. They only need feeding once before flowering. When moving the pots outdoors, place them in a sunny, sheltered position and deadhead regularly. The flowers must be protected from frost. Offsets are rarely produced in pots. All parts of the plant cause nausea if consumed, and they may lead to allergenic reactions.

Verbena

ⓘ

Location: ❥ ☀
Propagation: ⚬⚬
Characteristics: ⊙ ❀
Diseases: mildew
Pests: thrips, aphids
Flowering: summer – autumn

Garden verbena

Verbena

The wild forms of the roughly 200 herbaceous perennials and shrubs of the *Verbena* genus are native to South America. These mostly fragrant summer flowering plants usually have serrated, wrinkled leaves and brightly-coloured flowers with a white eye. The hybrid varieties 16 in high that are grown as annuals are particularly recommended for window boxes and containers. The flowers are produced throughout summer until autumn and are borne in dense umbels. The weather-resistant plants are sown in spring in sandy soil, rich in humus. Verbenas thrive in a sunny or partially shaded, sheltered location. During the growing season, they need regular watering and weekly applications of a weak solution of fertilizer. The root ball should never be allowed to dry out. It is important to remove faded blooms as quickly as possible. Garden verbena is propagated from cuttings and is excellent for growing in hanging baskets. A herbaceous perennial with violet-red flowers that is grown as an annual it reaches a height of 24 in.

Pansy

Viola x wittrockiana

Who does not know these small, brightly coloured plants that go on flowering for so long? Like most other *violas*, the varieties in this species have large single flowers consisting of five overlapping petals. They come in almost every color; some are one color while others are multi-coloured, not forgetting the very popular varieties with a dark blotch in the middle. Also much loved is the dainty little horned violet. They look very good combined with narcissi, forget-me-nots, tulips and daisies. Because pansies become rather unsightly when they grow in the shade, it is best to place them in the sunniest location possible. Pansies need regular watering but hate being waterlogged. Dead blooms should immediately be removed. Autumn-flowering pansies are sown in summer. Plants sown indoors in winter will flower two or three months later. If biennial pansies are left out during winter, it is advisable to cover them with brushwood.

Arum lily

Zantedeschia aethiopica

This tuberous perennial 39 ft high is native to South Africa. Its creamy-white, funnel-shaped spathes (a petal-like leaf) envelop spikes of tiny flowers borne on long stems that rise above the deep green, arrow-shaped, basal leaves. But there are also varieties with different coloured spathes such as yellow or red. The small, creamy-white flowers are grouped in dense, finger-like spikes (spadix), which is one the distinctive features of all members of the genus. Arum lilies grow best in a sunny, warm location in well-drained soil, rich in humus. Being marginal water plants they do not tolerate drought. During the growing season they need plenty of water and should be fed every week. The should only be watered sparingly during the rest period after the leaves have died. They are propagated from seed or by division. Being frost-sensitive, they must be moved indoors during winter.

Viola x wittrockiana

🛈

Location: 💧 ☼ — ☼
Care: ⚘
Propagation: ⦙
Characteristics: △ ⊙ / ∞ ❀
Diseases: grey mould, mildew
Pests: aphids
Flowering: spring and autumn

Zantedeschia aethiopica

🛈

Location: 💧 ☼ ⚘
Propagation: ⦙ ✶
Characteristics: ✘ ∞ ❀ ❄
Pests: aphids
Flowering: spring – autumn

Perennial container plants

Annual and biennial spring and summer-flowering plants are always associated with container plants. However, most of them flower only once and they should only be planted after mid-May because of their sensitivity to frost.

In recent years plants suitable for containers, have started to include an ever-larger range of frost-hardy woody plants and herbaceous perennials that are native to cooler climates, which until now were only seen in gardens. These plants considerably prolong the season on the balcony or terrace. A few species such as hellebores already start flowering in late winter while others such as aubrietias flower in early spring. Evergreen ferns such as Dryopteris affinis or grasses such as Carex morrowii embellish the balcony or terrace with their attractive foliage. By carefully selecting of plants you can enjoy greenery and flowers on your balcony or terrace all year round.

While woody plants survive the winter, with or without leaves depending on whether they are evergreen or not, the parts of herbaceous perennials that are above ground usually die off. It is their underground parts such as roots or rhizomes that survive over the winter, from which new shoots sprout in spring. One important aspect to be taken into consideration when growing plants in containers is their reduced frost-hardiness. The roots are more exposed than they would be in the ground and rather restricted by lack of space. This is why it is recommended to protect container-grown plants during prolonged periods of frost, even though they would otherwise be hardy in a normal flowerbed. This can be achieved by covering the plants with brushwood while protecting the container with bubble wrap or insulating material. Remember also that shallow-rooted plants are better suited for growing in containers than deep-rooted ones.

Achillea millefolium

ⓘ

Location: ◊ ☼
Propagation: ✂🌱
Characteristics: ⚠ ∞ 🧫 ❄
Diseases: powdery mildew
Pests: aphids
Flowering: summer – autumn

*A*chillea

Achillea millefolium

This is one of the 85 species of the *Achillea* genus that is a member of the large *Compositae* family. It is a herbaceous perennial that is native to Europe and the moderate regions of Asia with narrow, feathery, dark green, aromatic leaves. It produces white, cream or pink-to-red flower heads. *Achillea* is frost-hardy, robust and spreads easily in the garden. It grows best in a sunny, dry location in well-drained soil, rich in nutrients. Only growing to a height of 12–20 in, it is ideally suited for rock gardens, flowerbeds and wild gardens but is also suitable for growing in containers, for instance on roof terraces. In addition, it is an excellent cut flower and is also very popular in dry flower arrangement. It can be propagated by division in late winter or from cuttings in winter. It is recommended to remove the dead blooms after flowering or at the latest in winter. This will promote a vigorous growth in spring, when it is also advisable to feed the plant.

*S*lender sweet flag

Acorus gramineus

ⓘ

Location: 💧 ☼ – ☼
Care: ⚠ ❄
Propagation: ✂🌱
Characteristics: ⎍ ∞ 🌿
Flowering: summer

The *Acorus* genus, a member of the *Araceae* family, only has two species of grass-like, evergreen perennials. Because the flower spikes that appear in spring are rather inconspicuous, *Acorus* is usually planted for its dense, dark green foliage, which is particularly fragrant when dried. Depending on the species, the leaves may be variegated with a yellow or white stripe. *A. gramineus* is a Japanese miniature plant that only grows 6–12 in high. As a marginal aquatic plant it is ideal for planting in wet or very moist soil, for instance near a water tank. Varieties such as "Pusillus" are recommended for planting in aquariums, planted in a basket at a depth of 4 in, where they will grow happily at a temperature up to a maximum of 72° F. These plants are easy to look after and should be cut back in late winter. If left outdoors during winter they should be well protected against frost. It is safer to bring them indoors where they can over-winter in frost-free conditions.

Maidenhair fern

Adiantum raddianum

This *Adiantum* genus, a member of the *Adiantaceae* family, forms vigorous, arching fronds that grow in dense clumps. In summer this warmth-loving house plant can also be placed outdoors on the balcony or terrace in partial or complete shade. The maidenhair fern grows best in well-drained soil, rich in humus, which should kept moist at all times. During the growing season it should be fed twice a month with a weak solution of liquid fertilizer. In late summer, old fronds should be cut back to encourage a dense new growth. Re-potting should be done with great care because the roots are very delicate. When moving the plant from a moist to a dry location, it is best to make the change gradually. It can be propagated in spring by division of the rhizome or raised from spores. Maidenhair ferns are sensitive to frost and do not tolerate temperatures below 45° F.

Adiantum raddianum

ⓘ

Location: 💧 ☀ – ☀ ⚠
Care: ▦
Propagation: ·°° ❀
Characteristics: ∞ ⚘
Pests: scale insects

Mexican giant hyssop

Agastache mexicana

The genus includes 20 perennial species and belongs to the family of the *Labiatae*. *A. mexicana*, Mexican giant hyssop, is a bushy, short-lived perennial with grey-green, fragrant, oval pointed leaves, native to Mexico. It grows up to 35 in high and produces red, pink or white flower spikes 12 in long from mid to late summer. It thrives in full sun in well-drained, fertile soil. If using fresh potting compost, the plant needs no further applications of fertilizer. They are ideally suited for planting in mixed borders, containers and window-boxes but they can only tolerate a minimum of 32° F, so it is advisable to bring young plants indoors before the first frost. Giant hyssop can be raised from seed in early spring at a temperature of 55–64° F. It can easily be propagated from semi-ripe cuttings in early summer. The plants are prone to mildew in dry summers.

ⓘ

Location: 💧 ☀
Care: ⚠
Propagation: ·°°
Characteristics: ∞ ✿
Diseases: powdery mildew
Flowering: summer

Ajania

Ajania pacifica

Location: ○ ☼
Care: ⚠
Propagation: ✂ ✿
Characteristics: ∞ ❁
Flowering: autumn

This genus with 30 species belongs to the *Compositae* family and is native to the exposed, rocky regions of central and eastern Asia. *Ajania pacifica* is a low, well-branched herbaceous perennial with sinuate, mid-green leaves with a silvery edge, covered with woolly hairs underneath. Ajania flowers in autumn with enchanting umbels of yellow flower heads. The plants grow best in a sunny position in well-drained, fertile soil. It is an excellent plant for rock gardens and herbaceous borders. It also looks very good in containers with other autumn flowering plants such as *Acorus* or *Carex* species. However, it does need a little protection in winter in colder regions. The seeds can be sown in spring directly in pots, which should be kept frost-free. They can also be propagated from cuttings.

Ajania pacifica

*B*ugle

Ajuga reptans

This herbaceous perennial, a member of the *Labiatae* family, grows in the wild in the cooler regions of Europe, Africa, Asia and Australia. *Ajuga reptans* is a creeping, evergreen, rhizomatous perennial that spreads very quickly by means of runners. The attractive, basal leaf rosettes produce spikes of dark blue tubular flowers in spring and early summer. The color of the leaves ranges from brownish-red to bright purple-red and even variegated. Common bugle is also used for medicinal purposes as a mild analgesic and astringent herb with laxative properties. A frost-hardy groundcover, it thrives in moist , humus-rich soil in partial shade or full shade. It should be protected from direct sun while a layer of mulch such as bark will help keep the soil moist. *Ajuga reptans* combines beautifully with *Arabis*, *Lysimachia* and *Saxifraga*.

Ajuga reptans "Catlius Giant"

ⓘ

Location: 💧 ☀ — ☀
Propagation: 🌿
Characteristics: ∞ ❀ ▩ ❄
Diseases: powdery mildew
Flowering: spring – summer

*L*ady's mantle

Alchemilla mollis

The *Alchemilla* genus that belongs to the *Rosaceae* family includes some 300 species of frost-hardy herbaceous perennials, native to Europe and Asia. *A. mollis* is particularly popular because of its beautiful, yellow-green flowers, which are borne in summer, and the grey-green, round, palmate or lobed hairy leaves. *A. mollis* is also known under the name *A. vulgaris*. It is an ideal ground cover and excellent edging plant but it is also suitable for growing in a container. In addition, it is also a very good source of cut flowers. The serrated leaves divided into shallow lobes are very beautiful when covered in rain drops or dew. *Alchemilla* grows best in partial shade in a well-drained soil. It is trouble free and demands very little care. The seeds should removed as soon as they ripe because the plant spreads very quickly by self-seeding. In winter it should be cut back to the ground. Propagation is by division in spring.

ⓘ

Location: ○ ☀ – ☀
Propagation: ∘∘° 🌿
Characteristics: ∞ ❀ ▩ ❄
Pests: slugs and snails
Flowering: summer

Alyssum

Alyssum

ℹ

Location: ◊ ☼
Propagation: ₒ∘°
Characteristics: ∞ ❁ ❄
*Diseases: downy mildew,
    white rust*
Pests: aphids, flea beetles
Flowering: spring – summer

The *Alyssum* genus belongs to the *Cruciferae* family and is native to Europe, north Africa and Asia. The plant produces dense clusters of white, creamy, yellow or pink flowers that appear in spring and early summer. As a cushion-forming plant it is ideal for rockeries, flowerbeds and even cracks in walls, growing best in a sunny position. It will also thrive on sunny, dry balconies and terraces either in window boxes or as under-planting in larger containers. One of the best-known alyssums is *A. saxatile*, which flowers in various shades of yellow. *Alyssum murale* is a larger variety with grey-green leaves and yellow flowers. *A. spinosum* has grey-green, silvery leaves and white flowers that later fades to purple. Alyssum is frost-hardy and thrives in dry, well-drained soil. It benefits from an application of fertilizer after the flowering period. This is also the time to take cuttings. Alternatively it can be grown from seed in spring.

Windflower

Anemone blanda

ℹ

Location: ♦ ☼ – ☼
Care: ⚠ ❋
Propagation: ₒ∘° ✂❀
Characteristics: ∞ ❁
*Diseases: leaf spot, powdery
    mildew*
*Pests: caterpillars, slugs and
    snails*
Flowering: spring

The genus, a member of the *Ranunculaceae* family, comes from the temperate regions in Asia. Anemones are delicate, tuberous herbaceous perennials that form dense clusters of deeply divided leaves and spread very fast. *Anemone blanda* is hardy but should be protected against severe frost. It flowers in spring with open, saucer-shaped, starry blooms that come in shades of white, pink or blue. Anemones grow best in well-drained, humus-rich soil in sun or partial shade and will not tolerate waterlogging. Feed with a compound fertilizer during summer. Anemones self-seed very easily but they can also be grown from seeds or division during the rest period. Anemones should be kept dry during their rest period after flowering. "Atrocoerulea" with deep blue flowers and "Radar" with red flowers and white center are particularly popular varieties.

Columbine

Aquilegia

The *Aquilegia* genus that belongs to the *Ranunculaceae* family includes many species that grow in meadows, light woodland and mountainous regions in the northern hemisphere. A. *caerulea* is an upright, short-lived herbaceous perennial, native to the Rocky Mountains in North America, with deeply lobed leaves. Aquilegias produce large, spurred flowers in shades of red, yellow or brown depending on the species, borne from early to mid-summer on slender leafy stems. It grows best in rich but light soil in sun or partial shade and is very undemanding. They also make beautiful cut flowers. A. *flabellata* comes from east Asia and has palmate, grey-green leaves. The nodding, purple-blue flowers with white to creamy-white tipped petals appear in early summer. There is also a dwarf variety of this species that only grows 6 in high and is ideal for growing in containers. It can be grown from seed or divided in spring.

Location: ◗◗ ☼ — ☼
Propagation: ∘ᵒ ✂
Characteristics: ∞ ❀ ❄
Diseases: powdery mildew
Pests: aphids, sawflies, leaf miners, caterpillars
Flowering: spring – summer

Aquilegia vulgaris

Wall rock cress

Arabis caucasica

Arabis caucasica is one of about 120 mostly evergreen herbaceous perennials belonging to the *Cruciferae* family. It is native to the rocky regions of Europe, Asia and north Africa. As a result they are all very undemanding and easy plants to grow. They are ideal for growing in rockeries, as edging of terraces or in gaps in walls where they spread quickly by means of small rhizomes, formong dense clusters of leaves. Rock cress also does very well in containers. This mat-forming evergreen plant develops loose rosettes of grey-green, serrated leaves. In late spring, it bears dense spikes of fragrant, white flowers. It grows best in a sunny location in well-drained soil and tolerates hot, dry conditions extremely well. Because it is a very vigorous grower it needs plenty of space when combined with other plants. It can be cut back vigorously in winter. It is propagated by division in spring.

ⓘ

Location: ◊ ☼
Propagation: .°° ✀✐✎
Characteristics: ∞ ✿ ❄
Diseases: downy mildew, white rust
Pests: mites, aphids
Flowering: spring

Rock cress

Arabis procurrens

Arabis procurrens, a species of the *Arabis* genus that itself belongs to the *Cruciferae* family, occurs in the wild in the rocky regions of Europe, Asia and North-Africa. It is a mat-forming, evergreen herbaceous perennial with dense, flat rosettes of narrow, glossy green leaves with creamy-coloured edges and sometimes also variegated with pink. It produces loose spikes of white flowers in late spring. It should be cut back after flowering to ensure a compact, bushy growth. It thrives in rich, well-drained soil in a sunny location. It benefits from an application of a slow-release or organic fertiliser in spring. It is propagated from seed in autumn or softwood cuttings in summer. However, the quickest way to propagate rock cress is by division. Because it is such a vigorous grower it should be given sufficient space when combined with other plants.

ⓘ

Location: ◊ ☼
Propagation: .°° ✀✐✎
Characteristics: ∞ ✿
Diseases: downy mildew, white rust
Pests: gall midges, aphids
Flowering: spring

Thrift

Armeria maritima

Armeria is a genus with 80 bushy, cushion-forming, evergreen herbaceous perennials that belong to the *Plumbaginaceae* family. Common thrift grows in the coastal regions of Europe and is often planted in rockeries, flowerbeds, pots and large containers. This grass-like herbaceous perennial with narrow, dark green leaves bears white, pink or purple flower heads on long stems from late spring until summer. It grows best in well-drained, light sandy soil in a sunny location and needs plenty of water in dry summers. Make sure they are not waterlogged in winter. Apart from this, it is a very undemanding plant. The flowering period can be prolonged by deadheading very regularly. It is important to remember that it spreads very readily.

Armeria maritima "Düsseldorfer Stolz"

Location: 💧 ☼
Propagation: 🐝
Characteristics: ∞ ❀ ❄
Pests: spider mites, aphids
Flowering: spring – summer

Wormwood

Artemisia

The *Artemisia* genus, a member of the *Compositae* family, includes 300 species of evergreen and deciduous herbaceous perennials, native to the northern hemisphere. Wormwood is cultivated mainly for its aromatic, silvery grey leaves, which also have a deter insects. The clusters of tiny flowers are quite inconspicuous. In fact, one species, *A. dracunculus* or tarragon, is a popular culinary herb. *A. absinthium* is ideal for flowerbeds and rockeries while *A. schmidtiana*, which only reaches 10 in in height, is excellent for growing in containers. It grows best in a sunny location in light, fertile soil. *A. lactifora* prefers a slightly moister soil. Alpine species such as *A. glacialis* look beautiful in gaps in the wall. Most species will slowly die if waterlogged. It can be divided after flowering and should be pruned vigorously in spring.

Artemisia "Oriental Limelight"

Location: 💧 – ◌ *acc. to variety* ☼
Propagation: ⸪ 🐝
Characteristics: ∞ ❀ ❄
Diseases: powdery mildew
Pests: aphids
Flowering: summer

Aruncus dioicus

ℹ

Location: 💧 ☀ — ☀
Propagation: ⚬° ✂
Characteristics: ∞ ❀ ❄
Pests: blackfly, sawflies
Flowering: summer

ℹ

Location: ○ ☀—☀
Propagation: ⚬° ✂
Characteristics: △ ∞ ❀ ❄
Diseases: rust fungus (from wet)

Goat's beard

Aruncus dioicus

The *Aruncus* genus is native to the damp forests and mountains of the northern hemisphere and is a member of the *Rosaceae* family. It only includes three species of rhizomatous herbaceous perennials whose long flower plumes are reminiscent of giant astilbes. Goat's beard is an ideal cut flower, the female plumes being creamy-white while the male ones are white. They are produced from early to mid-summer. This herbaceous perennial is dioecious (having the male and female reproductive organs in separate flowers on separate plants). The large leaves consist of oval leaflets, arranged in opposite pairs. Goat's beard thrives in moist, rich soil in partial to full shade. A layer of mulch at the base of the plant will help retain moisture. It is an extremely undemanding plant but it needs to be cut down to ground level in winter. With its imposing height of 6 ft it is an ideal container plant for balconies and terraces with little sun.

Maidenhair spleenwort

Asplenium trichomanes

This vast genus belongs to the *Aspleniaceae* family and includes over 700 deciduous and evergreen species that can found throughout the world except the Antarctic. They have short erect or creeping rhizomes and develop dense crowns of fronds. The smaller species are ideal for rock gardens, Alpine troughs and cracks in walls, while the larger species are grown in combination with woody plants and in shady borders. Maidenhair spleenwort is one of the most vigorous species of the genus. This highly decorative plant is often seen in the cracks of old town walls and fortifications. Its pinnate, linear fronds with dark stem are very attractive. It is evergreen, frost-hardy and only grows 4 in high, so it is ideal for even the smallest container. Being epiphytic, it grows best in dry, sandy soil in partial shade. The same is true of *A. rutamuraria*.

Alpine aster

Aster alpinus

Aster alpinus is a spreading hardy herbaceous perennial that grows throughout Europe and Asia. It is a member of the *Compositae* family and grows about 8 in high. The daisy-like flowers that are borne singly on mostly branched stems appear in early summer. Depending on the species, the flowers come in a variety of colours but always with yellow disc florets. The "Dark Beauty" variety has dark violet flowers, "Wargrave Park" has pale pink flowers tinged with purple, while "Albus" and "White Beauty" have white flowers. Alpine asters grow best in limy, sandy, well-drained soil. They grow both in sun and partial shade. They should be covered with a layer of mulch after being cut back in autumn. They are propagated by division in spring and can be rejuvenated after they have finished flowering. They attract butterflies and bees and harmonise very well with *Achillea* or *Gypsophyla*.

Aster alpinus

ⓘ

Location: ◌ ☼ – ☼
Care: /❅
Propagation: ❦❧
Characteristics: ∞ ❀
Diseases: fusarium wilt, leaf
*   spot, grey mould*
Pests: aphids, slugs and snails,
*   nematodes*
Flowering: spring – summer

Aster dumosus

Aster dumosus

This species is native to Europe and North America and there are many varieties of this herbaceous perennial 10–12 in high. The daisy-like flowers are borne in loose clusters on erect, mostly branched stems. *Aster dumosus* forms round, cushion-shaped rosettes with white, pink, carmine, violet and blue flowers depending on the variety; for instacne, the variety "Silberblaukissen" has silvery blue flowers. The intense colours of *A. dumosus* are particularly beautiful in the sun. They grow best in rich soil. They should be cut back to ground level after flowering and protected with a layer of brushwood during winter. New plants are best planted out in spring when an application of a slow-release fertilizer is recommended. The plants can be divided in spring and after flowering, greenwood cuttings can be taken in winter. By planting Grass of Parnassus with asters you will keep threadworms at bay.

ⓘ

Location: ◌ ☼
Care: /❅
Propagation: ❦❧
Characteristics: ∞ ❀
Diseases: powdery mildew
Pests: aphids, slugs and snails,
*   nematodes*
Flowering: autumn

Aster novi-belgii

ⓘ

Location: ◌ ☼ — ☀
Care: 🗚
Propagation: 🐌🪰
Characteristics: ∞ ❁
*Diseases: fusarium wilt, leaf
    spot, grey mould, powdery
    mildew*
*Pests: aphids, slugs and snails,
    tarsonemid mites, nematodes*
Flowering: autumn

Aster novi-belgii

Aster novi-belgii

The *Aster* genus includes over 250 species of deciduous and evergreen herbaceous perennials that are all suitable for growing in containers on balconies and terraces. Aster novi-belgii is native to the east coast of North America where they grow in the wild from Newfoundland down to Georgia. The flowers are borne in loose sprays from late summer to mid-autumn and have violet ray florets with yellow disc florets in the center. The leaves are narrow and smooth. It is from this wild form that the various cultivars flowring a wide range of colours have been developed. The colours range from bright pink to violet and blue. They grow best in moist, fertile soil in a sunny location. The soil should never be allowed to dry out. Tall varieties also look very good on balconies and terraces and they are an excellent source of cut flowers. However, it is important that they should be staked together so that they do not fall apart. Mulching is recommended after cutting back in the autumn.

Astilbe

Astilbe

ⓘ

Location: 💧 ☼ — ☀
Care: 🗚
Propagation: ⸬ 🐌🪰
Characteristics: ∞ ❁
*Diseases: powdery mildew,
    leaf spot*
Flowering: summer

Saxifragaceae grow in the wild in damp places in south-east Asia and North America. Their long plume-like spikes of tiny flowers that come in shades of red, pink, violet and white, depending on the variety, are very striking. They turn an attractive brown color when they fade and also look very decorative in winter. They also make very good cut flowers. The hybrids of *A. x arendsii* have particularly long spikes. "Bressingham Beauty" is extremely handsome. It grows 35 in high and has mid-green leaves tinged with bronze and spires of bright pink flowers in mid-summer. However, lower varieties such as the bright red "Fanal" are better suited for growing in containers. This is also true of the compact varieties of *A. chinensis* that are 8-16 in high. Astilbes grow best in moist soil in shade and high humidity. They also benefit from an application of compound fertilizer at the end of the winter. They should be cut back vigorously in winter and protected with a layer of mulch.

Astilbe "Europa"

*A*ubrietia

Aubrieta hybrids

The genus *Aubrieta* is a member of the *Cruciferae* family, an evergreen, cushion-forming perennial that grows in the wild from the Mediterranean to the Balkans as far as Asia Minor. In spring it produce dense clusters of flowers that may be in shades of blue or red, depending on the species and variety. Much loved by butterflies, aubretias are ideally suited to rock gardens, dry walls and in sunny places such as in containers on balconies and terraces where they will provide magnificent splashes of color. There are many varieties of *A. deltoides* that are preferable to the species because of the wide range of color. "Argenteovariegata" has mid-green leaves with silvery variegation and pink flowers while "Blaumeise" has blue flowers. Aubretias grow best in sandy, limy soil in full sun. They can be raised from seed or propagated by division in spring. In summer and autumn they can also propagated from semi-ripe cuttings. Plants should be repotted as soon as you notice that they are flowering less prolifically.

Location: ◊ ☼
Propagation: ˳°˳ ✿✄
Characteristics: ∞ ✿ ❄
Diseases: white rust
Pests: aphids, nematodes
Flowering: spring

Bergenia

Bergenia hybrids

ⓘ

Location: 💧 ☀ — ☀
Propagation: ⸰⁰ ✿
Characteristics: ∞ ❀ ❉
Diseases: leaf spot, brown rot
Pests: slugs and snails,
*   caterpillars, weevils*
Flowering: spring

The *Bergenia* genus is a member of the *Saxifragaceae* family and native to the Altai mountains in Mongolia and Siberia. Plants form powerful rhizomes and dense rosettes of large, leathery, glossy leaves which may be rounded or spatula-shaped. Garden varieties frequently turn a beautiful reddish shade in winter and in spring produce large, loose clusters of funnel to bell-shaped flowers, often borne on red or purple stems. The pink-flowering "Morgenröte" grows to 16 in high and is ideally suited for growing in pots and containers. "Silberlicht" is quite different from other aubretia varieties and has white flowers tinged with pink. Bergenias grow best in moist but well-drained soil in sunny or partially shaded locations. It is interesting that the winter colours are more intense specimens that have been fed less. The flowering season can be prolonged by regular deadheading. They are grown from seed or propagated by division in spring.

Bergenia

Quaking grass

Briza media

Briza media

The annual and perennial grasses in this genus that belongs to the *Poaceae* family are native to the temperate regions of Europe and south-west Asia. *Briza media* is a bushy ornamental grass with narrow, mid-green leaves, slightly hairy along the edges. In summer it produces about 30 nodding brownish-purple spikelets grouped in loose panicles that quake and rattle in the breeze, hence the name. They make excellent dried flowers, which are sometimes also coloured. After flowering the flowers tend to dry out on the plant. Quaking grass grows best in moderately fertile, sandy soil that is kept slightly moist at all times. It is an extremely undemanding plant that must be cut back at the end of the winter. It can be divided in spring.

Location: ○ ☼ – ☼
Propagation: ✄
Characteristics: ∞ ❄
Flowering: spring – summer

Lesser calamint

Calamintha nepeta ssp. Glandulosa

This very aromatic, hardy herbaceous perennial belongs to the family of the *Labiatae* and grows in the temperate regions of the northern hemisphere. It spreads by means of creeping rhizomes. The leaves of some of the species are used for medicinal purposes and as herb tea. The lesser calamint is an aromatic, bushy plant with an erect habit and oval, often serrated, dark green leaves. In summer it bears loose spikes of blue flowers that are white in the "White Cloud" variety. The species owes it name to its similarity to catmint (*Nepeta*). *C. grandiflora* has violet-pink flowers. This undemanding herbaceous perennial is ideally suited to the rock garden and flower beds as well as window boxes. It is also good as underplanting in containers on balconies and terraces. It tolerates sun but prefers shade. The soil should be rich in humus and be kept moist at all times. It can be raised from seed or propagated by division in spring.

Location: ◗ ☼ – ☼
Propagation: ∴ ✄
Characteristics: ∞ ❄
Diseases: powdery mildew
Flowering: summer

*S*cotch heather

Calluna vulgaris

ⓘ

Location: ◌ ☼ – ☀
Propagation:
Characteristics: ∞ ❀ ❄
Diseases: grey mould, root rot
Flowering: summer – winter

This evergreen bushy shrub that belongs to the *Ericaceae* family grows on the moorlands and heathlands of northern and western Europe as well as in Asia Minor. In late summer it produces single or double bell-shaped flowers, grouped in dense clusters, in shades of red, violet, pink or white. Scotch heather always attracts a large number of butterflies. Recently developed varieties whose flowers do not open keep them well into the winter. The narrow, dark green leaves often turn purple in winter. Scotch heather has a bushy, upright habit and grows 8–31 in high. It grows well both in sun and partial shade but needs acid soil, low in nutrients such as rhododendron compost for instance. Scotch heather must be deadheaded every year – but not in autumn or winter – to promote flower production. This is also the right time to take cuttings for propagation. An application of organic or mineral fertiliser is also recommended.

Calluna vulgaris

Bellflower

Campanula carpatica

This species of the *Campanula* genus, a member of the *Campanulaceae* family, is native to the Carpathian mountains as the name suggests. It is a bushy plant up to 12 in high that forms dense clumps of green, heart-shaped leaves. In early summer it produces a mass of white or blue, bell-shaped flowers which are borne singly on long, leafless stems. It includes some known varieties such as "Blue Clips" with sky blue flowers and "White Clips" (pure white). The species grows about 10 in high and is not invasive. It is therefore ideally suited for containers, window-boxes and hanging-baskets. It grows best in a sunny location in humus-rich, fairly limey soil. If planted in a hanging basket, it should be sheltered from the wind. It can be divided in late winter while cuttings can be taken after flowering. It recovers quickly from frost damage. Slugs and snails can be a problem, depending on the location.

Location: ○ ☼ — ☼ ⚠
Propagation: ·°° ⚒
Characteristics: ∞ ✿ ❄
Diseases: powdery mildew
Pests: slugs and snails
Flowering: spring – summer

Campanula glomerata "Joan Elliott"

Clustered campanula

Campanula glomerata

This species grows in the wild throughout Europe and Asia as far as the Caucasus and Iran. The rhizomatous perennial has an upright habit and produces blue-violet or white flowers, depending on the species, borne on square, leafy stems. The flowers are grouped in tight clusters in the leaf axils. Being rhizomatous, it can become very invasive but is easily divided after flowering. It can be raised from seed in spring. It should be cut after the first flowering to encourage a second flowering. Cuttings can be taken at the same time. It is a very undemanding plant but it hates being waterlogged. It grows best in partial shade in fertile soil that should be kept only moderately moist. Because it is rather invasive it is best planted on its own in a large container. The white "Schneekrone" and violet "Joan Elliot" varieties are particularly beautiful.

Location: ○ ☼
Propagation: ·°° ⚒
Characteristics: △ ∞ ✿ ❄
Diseases: powdery mildew
Pests: slugs and snails
Flowering: summer

Campanula persicifolia

ℹ

Location: ◊ ☼ — ☀
Propagation: ₀°°   ✿✿
Characteristics: ∞ ❀ ❆
Diseases: powdery mildew, rust
Pests: slugs and snails
Flowering: summer

Narrow-leaved bellflower

Campanula persicifolia

This species is another member of the large Campanula genus that belongs to the *Campanulaceae* family, native to southern and eastern Europe and the temperate zones of Asia. It grows 32 in high and forms dense rosettes with very narrow leaves 3 in long. The large blue or white cup-shaped flowers that appear in early to mid-summer, grouped in loose spikes, are borne on long, leafless stems. *C. persicifolia* spreads through rhizomes and therefore best grown in separate container as this will prevent it from spreading excessively. It needs plenty of sun and grows best in loamy, humus-rich soil. It combines very well with astilbes and day lilies and they are very long-lasting. "Grandiflora Alba" with white flowers and "Grandiflora Caerulea" with brilliant blue flowers are among the most beautiful varieties. It can be sown directly in the pots in spring or divided after flowering.

Wall harebell

Campanula portenschlagiana

ℹ

Location: ◊ ☀
Propagation: ₀°°   ✿✿
Characteristics: ∞ ❀ ❆
Diseases: powdery mildew
Pests: slugs and snails
Flowering: summer

This campanula species, native to the mountainous regions of Croatia, is an ever-green mat-forming, compact perennial which only grows 4-6 in high. It spreads fast by means of runners. It is also known under the name of *Campanula muralis*. The erect, loosely branched clusters of funnel-shaped, blue violet flowers are borne on leafy stems in mid to late summer above a carpet of irregularly serrated, mid-green leaves. It flowers again in autumn. These typical rock garden plants are ideally suited for growing on old walls and plant troughs. It is extremely undemanding and grows best in sandy, loamy soil, which should not be allowed to dry out. It can be raised from seed in autumn or divided after flowering. Cuttings taken in early summer will root very easily. Watch out for snails and slugs and powdery mildew in damp weather.

Trailing bellflower

Campanula poscharskyana

The trailing bellflower is native to Croatia like the wall harebell. It is better known than its relation but, like it, it has milky sap in its stems and leaves and spreads by means of runners. The lavender-blue, star-shaped flowers grouped in loosely branches heads are borne in late spring on long leafy stems. The mid-green leaves are heart-shaped. It develops up to 28 in long, trailing shoots that make it ideally suited for hanging baskets. It is important to plant self-contained space to restrict its spreading since it could easily overpower neighbouring plants. It looks particularly attractive when trailing down a wall. "Laurence" and "Stella" are highly recommended varieties. Bellflowers grow best in moderately fertile, well-drained soil in sun or partial shade where it is protected from the wind. It is propagated like the other campanula species.

Location: ◊ ☼ — ☀ ⚠
Propagation: ⁖ ⚒
Characteristics: ∞ ❀ ❄
Diseases: powdery mildew
Pests: slugs and snails
Flowering: summer

*Campanula poscharskyana
and Campanula carpartica*

Steeple bellflower

Campanula pyramidalis

Location: ◊ ☼–☼ ⚠
Propagation: ⸳°° ⚜⚘
Characteristics: ∞ ❀ ❄
Diseases: powdery mildew
Pests: slugs and snails
Flowering: summer

Steeple bellflower is native to northern Italy and the north-west of the Balkans. This short-lived, erect herbaceous perennial grows up to 47 in high is usually cultivated as a biennial. It forms loose rosettes of serrated, mid-green leaves and tall, narrow spires of blue or white star-shaped flowers borne on tall stems, covered with sessile leaves, that appear in summer. Because of its size steeple bellflower is best planted on its own in a container. It also looks very attractive trained against a trellis while creating a beautiful visual screen at the same time. It should be cut back after the first flowering to encourage repeat flowering and prevent it from self seeding. It will grow in full sun but the stunning colours of the flowers come into their own in partial shade.

Carex

Leatherleaf sedge

Carex buchananii

Location: ♦ ☼
Care: ⚠
Propagation: ⚜⚘
Characteristics: ∞ ❧
Pests: aphids
Flowering: summer

Carex is a vast genus of perennial, deciduous or evergreen ornamental grasses. It is a member of the *Cyperaceae* family. Most of the species thrive in moist soil and are ideal for growing in bog gardens and near ponds. They are mostly cultivated for their magnificent, colorful foliage while some are also grown for their striking pendent flower spikes. The leatherleaf sedge is a bushy, herbaceous perennial from New Zealand which grows 16 in high. The long, copper-coloured leaves with arching tips are very decorative. In summer it produces brown, insignificant spikelets. Frost-hardy to 23° F, it looks very attractive in winter when covered in hoar-frost and is therefore only cut back at the end of the winter. It can be divided in late spring. It looks very good on its own but can also be combined with other plants. It grows best in sandy, moderately fertile soil in a sunny location.

Goldband carex

Carex morrowii

The evergreen goldband carex is native to Japan, where it grows in moist soils and humid marshland. Its narrow, pointed, mid-green leaves form a loose clump. In spring it bears rather inconspicuous, yellowish flowers. "Variegata," which has dark green, white rimmed leaves, and "Variegata Aurea," which has yellow stripes and only grows 10 in high, are among the most attractive varieties. It introduces variety in containers and combines well with autumn plants. *C. hachijoensis* "Evergold" whose yellow leaves have green edges is very popular for that reason. Goldband carex grows best in moderately fertile, very moist but well-drained soil. It prefers shade but the variegated forms tolerate more sun. It is frost-hardy down to 23° F.

Location: 🌢 ☼ – ☀
Care: /※\
Propagation: ✿🐛
Characteristics: ∞ 🦋
Pests: aphids
Flowering: summer

Red valerian

Centranthus ruber

This genus that belongs to the *Valerianaceae* family is native to the Mediterranean. Red valerian is particularly popular as an ornamental plant because of its long-lived flowers that are produced in large numbers. This herbaceous perennial forms clumps 16–39 in high. The blue-green leaves are slightly fleshy. It bears dense clusters of small, star-shaped, fragrant flowers, produced from early summer until autumn. They range from dark red to pale pink depending on the variety. The "Albus" variety has white flowers. Red valerians are very undemanding plants and only need plenty of sun and well-drained alkaline soil. They will tolerate long periods of drought and need hardly any fertilizer. Red valerians attract bees and butterflies. Regular deadheading is recommended to prevent them from self seeding. They can be divided at the beginning of spring.

Centrathus ruber and Geranium

Location: ◊ ☼
Propagation: ⟡° ✿🐛 🦋
Characteristics: ∞ 🦋 ❊
Flowering: summer – autumn

Snow-in-summer

Cerastium tomentosum

ℹ

Location: ○ ☼ — ☀
Propagation: ∘°° ✀✄
Characteristics: ∞ ❀ ❅
Diseases: powdery mildew
Flowering: spring

The *Cerastium* genus, a member of the *Caryophyllaceae* family, can be found in almost all temperate regions of the northern hemisphere as far as the Arctic. *C. tomentosum* is native to the mountains of southern and eastern Europe and is a vigorous, spreading, mat-forming ground-cover plant with narrow, silvery green leaves. In late spring and summer it bears a profusion of loose clusters of white, star-shaped flowers. This is why it looks particularly attractive against a dark background. Planted along the edge of a terrace, the dense foliage will prevent weeds from growing. It also looks very pleasant in troughs and as underplanting in containers. It combines beautifully with avens, flax and tall bellflowers. Snow-in-summer is easy to grow and is easily propagated by division after flowering. It grows best in sandy, well-drained soil in a sunny location but also grows quite well in partial shade.

Delphinium

Delphinium grandiflorum

ℹ

Location: ♦ ☼ ⚠
Care: ⚠
Propagation: ∘°°
Characteristics: ✘ ⊙ / ∞ ❀
Diseases: leaf spot, powdery
    mildew
Pests: slugs and snails, lead
    miners
Flowering: summer

Members of the *Ranunculaceae* family, delphiniums are are very popular garden plants because of their large, majestic spikes of intensely blue flowers. *Delphinium grandiflorum* (syn. *D. chinense*) is a short-lived herbaceous perennial that is usually grown as an annual in regions with harsh winters. The hood-shaped, single flowers which come in shades of blue, violet, pink or white flowers are produced in summer. Compact varieties that only reach a height of 10 in such as "Delfy Bau" and "Blauer Zwerg" are particular suited for growing on balconies and terraces. They grow best in a sunny location in light, sandy soil. Delphiniums should never be allowed to be waterlogged. Deadheading after the first flowering will encourage a second flowering in autumn. If consumed the leaves can cause stomach upsets while contact with the skin can cause irritation.

Delphinium grandiflorum

Common pink

Dianthus plumarius

Dianthus plumarius

Common pinks are native to south-eastern Europe and members of the *Caryophyllacea* family. *D. plumarius*, a perennial forming hummocks or mats, grows 8–12 in high. It includes many varieties that look very good not only in borders and rock gardens but also in window boxes and containers on balconies and terraces. It has blue-green, grass-like leaves and intensely fragrant flowers that come in white, pink or red, depending on the variety. They form a dense, fragrant carpet of flowers. Common pinks thrive in standard potting compost which should be light and well-drained. They prefer a sunny to partially shaded location. They can be grown from seed in early spring or by division between autumn and the beginning of spring. There are also varieties with magnificent double flowers such as "Altrosa" that is pink, "Diamant" that is white and "Heidi" that is red.

ⓘ

Location: ○ ☼ – ☀ ⚠
Propagation: ∘°° ✄❀
Characteristics: ∞ ❀ ❄
Diseases: rust, fusarium wilt
Pests: slugs and snails, aphids
Flowering: spring – summer

Dicentra spectabilis

ⓘ

Location: ◗ ☀
Propagation: ✄✿
Characteristics: ∞ ✿ ❄
Pests: slugs and snails
Flowering: spring – summer

Bleeding heart

Dicentra spectabilis

Dicentra spectabilis is a widely distributed, hardy herbaceous perennial that produces red and white, heart-shaped flowers borne on arching stems in late spring and summer. It is a member of the *Papaveraceae* family and is native to the eastern part of North America. Bleeding heart grows about 32 in high and makes an excellent container plant while the dwarf variety *D. eximia* only grows 8 in high and is ideal for smaller containers. But be careful, the plants spread very quickly because of the creeping rhizomes. Bleeding hearts grow best in partial shade in humus-rich soil which must be kept moist at all times, but it hates being waterlogged. The fern-like leaves die down after flowering but soon grow again the following year. The application of a compound fertilizer at the end of the winter encourages growth. This is also the time when the plants can be divided. Cuttings can be taken in early summer.

Male fern

Dryopteris

ⓘ

Location: ◗ ☀ – ☀
Care: ⚠
Propagation: ✄✿
Characteristics: ∞ ✿
Pests: slugs and snails

The male fern, a member of the *Dryopteridaceae* family that includes about 200 species of deciduous and evergreen ferns, is native to the forest areas of the northern hemisphere. Many of the frost-resistant varieties have very decorative, pinnate fronds and are ideal for growing in pots and containers. They prefer a location in shade or partial shade where they are sheltered from the wind. Dead fronds should always be removed. *D. affinis* has green, leathery fronds that last well into the winter. Equally imposing is the male fern 39 in tall; there are also more compact varieties. The broad buckler or shield fern *D. dilitata* is smaller with fronds 12 in long and is therefore suitable for growing in containers on balconies. They all thrive in fertile, humus-rich, moist soil. They are propagated by division in spring. In cold winters a light protection is recommended.

Dryopteris

Coneflower

Echinacea purpurea

This genus, a member of the *Compositae* family, is well known for its medicinal properties and includes nine species that are all native to the United States. The thick roots are edible and those of *Echinacea angustifolia* and *E. purpurea* are dried and used to improve the body's natural defence against colds. The coneflower or *Rudbeckia purpurea* is an attractive flowering herbaceous perennial with narrow, dark green leaves and large flower heads with a reddish-brown cone-shaped center surrounded by purple-red, pink-red or white ray florets, depending on the variety. The large, terminal flower heads are borne singly on 35 in tall stems and are excellent cut flowers. Regular deadheading is important to prolong flowering. They thrive in fertile soil, preferably in a sunny location. It is propagated from seed in spring or division.

Echinacea purpurea

Location: ◐ ☼ ⚠
Propagation: ⸴° ✂🖊
Characteristics: ∞ ❀ ❄
Pests: mealy bugs
Flowering: summer

Heather

Erica

Location: 💧 ☀
Propagation:
Characteristics: ∞ ❀ ❄ ⚠
Diseases: root rot and stem rot
Flowering: summer – spring,
   according to variety

The *Erica* genus that belongs to the *Ericaceae* family includes about 800 species of small-leaved, floriferous, evergreen shrubs. Most of these are native to South Africa but a few varieties can also be found in the rest of Africa and in Europe. The varieties native to Europe have small, bell-shaped flowers in shades of white, pink and red. The many attractive varieties of the hardy alpine heath *Erica carnea* produce white, pink or red flowers throughout the winter until early spring. The bell heather *E. cinerea* flowers throughout the summer until the autumn. It may need a little protection in winter.

Erica

Mexican fleabane

Erigeron karvinskianus

The genus, a member of the *Compositae* family, exists in all the temperate regions of the earth but especially in North America. *Erigeron karvinskianus* is a spreading, clump-forming, half-hardy perennial that is native in Mexico and other parts of Central America. In regions with a mild climate it produces numerous, small white flowers, tinged with pink or purple all year. In temperate regions it must be pruned more frequently because it has a tendency to spread and overpower neighbouring plants. "Profusion" is very floriferous variety that produces flowers with pink or white ray florets. Its trailing habit makes it an ideal plant for growing in hanging baskets and containers. Fleabane grows well in sun or partial shade in well-drained, sandy soil. It is grown from seed indoors in early spring, the plants flowering about three months after sowing.

Location: ☀ ☼–☼ ⚠
Care: ⚠
Propagation: ⚬°°
Characteristics: ∞ ✿
Flowering: spring – autumn

Fescue

Festuca

This genus belongs to the *Poaceae* family and includes some 300–400 species of clump-forming, perennial grasses with linear, evergreen leaves and tiny, flat panicles of spikelets, produced throughout summer. A few species have become quite popular as ornamental grasses because they tolerate periods of drought and severe frost without suffering any damage. Neither are they choosy about position. *Festuca glauca*, blue fescue, an evergreen grass 8 in tall with upright to arching, blue-green leaves and similarly blue-green panicles is particularly decorative. "Blaufuchs" has bright blue leaves, "Blauglut" silver-blue leaves and purple flowers and "Silbersee" white blades; all three are very beautiful. Grasses grow best in a sunny location in sandy, well-drained soil. Large specimens can be divided in spring.

Festuca

Location: ○ ☼
Propagation: ⚘✿
Characteristics: ∞ ▨ ❄
Flowering: summer

Fragaria

ⓘ

Location: ◗ ☼ ⚠
Propagation: 🌱 *runners*
Characteristics: ∞ ❄
Diseases: grey mould
Flowering: summer

Wild strawberry

Fragaria hybrids

The genus, a member of the *Rosaceae* family, can be found in all the temperate regions of the northern hemisphere. The creeping, clump-forming herbaceous perennials are often grown as decorative ground cover as well as for their delicate fruits. Their three-lobed leaves are glossy and the white or pink flowers have five petals. The modern varieties can bear fruits up to six months of the year, and in warm climates almost all year round. These hardy plants prefer well-drained, fertile soil that should be kept moist at all times. Fungal infections can occur in excessively wet conditions. The top soil should be covered with straw so that the fruits do not rot. Wild strawberries thrive in full sun where they are sheltered from the wind, especially those growing in hanging baskets. The application of an organic fertilizer in spring will stimulate growth and the production of flowers.

ⓘ

Location: ◌ ☼
Care: ⚠
Propagation: ⠐
Characteristics: ∞ ❀
Diseases: downy mildew
Pests: slugs and snails
Flowering: summer – autumn

Blanket flower

Gaillardia pulchella

The 30 species in the *Gaillardia* genus, which belongs to the *Compositae* family, are mostly native to Central and North America. They can be found throughout the northern hemisphere where they flower throughout summer until the first frosts in autumn. The flowers are reminiscent of sunflowers but are much more colorful. The flower heads with yellow-tipped red ray florets are quite striking. The more compact varieties such as the 10 in high "Kobold" are ideal for balconies and terraces. *Gaillardia pulchella* is a short-lived, sun-loving herbaceous perennial that in winter should be covered with brushwood to protect it against frost. It is frequently cultivated as an annual. The flowering season can be prolonged until late summer by regular deadheading. It can be propagated from seed or cuttings in spring.

Gentian

Gentiana

The *Gentiana* genus, a member of the *Gentianaceae* family, is common in all the temperate regions, mostly in mountain and forest areas. The large, trumpet- or bell-shaped flowers are usually bright blue but they also come in white and red. They are produced from spring until autumn, depending on the species and variety. The lime-hating, stem-less species like *Gentiana clusii* that flowers in spring or *G. sino-ornata* which flowers in autumn are particularly attractive. They need an acid, moist soil and prefer partial shade. As a result they are ideal for combining with ferns such as *Dryopteris*. The summer flowering gentian *G. septemfida* var. *lagodechiana*, on the other hand, bears flowers on stems 2 in high and will also grow in the sun in calcareous soil. The smaller, robust varieties are ideal for growing in containers. However, they should be covered in winter to protect them from the cold. They are grown from seed in autumn but they can also be propagated by division.

ⓘ

Location: ♦☀—☀ *acc. to variety* /❅\
Care: /❅\
Propagation: ₀°° ✂❀
Characteristics: ∞ ❀
Diseases: gentian rust, stem rot
Pests: slugs and snails
Flowering: spring, summer or
  autumn

Geranium

Cranesbill

Geranium

Cranesbill belongs to the *Geraniaceae* family and can be found in all temperate regions of the world. The long-stemmed, often fragrant leaves are rounded, lobed and deeply cut. The beautiful flowers, often grouped in loose clusters, come in shades of pink, blue, violet and white. The compact species and varieties such as *Geranium cinereum*, which only grows 6 in high, are particularly suitable for growing on balconies and terraces. A very pretty variety is "Ballerina," which has pale purple flowers with dark violet veins and centre. *G. dalmaticum* and *G. sanguineum* are very low-growing with a compact habit. As a result, they are ideal for underplanting. They are very undemanding and will grow in sun and partial shade in fertile, well-drained soil. Dead flowers and leaves must be removed regularly to promote growth and prolong the flowering season. It is propagated by division or from seed in spring.

ⓘ

Location: ◊☀—☀
Propagation: ₀°° ✂❀
Characteristics: ∞ ❀ ▦ ❄
Diseases: downy and powdery
  mildew
Pests: slugs and snails, sawfly
  larvae, weevils
Flowering: spring – summer

ⓘ

Location: 💧 ☀–☀
Propagation: ·°° 🪴/🌱
Characteristics: ∞ ❀ ❄
Pests: sawflies
Flowering: spring – summer

Avens

Geum avens

The genus *Geum*, a member of the *Rosaceae* family, grows in mountainous regions, along riverbanks and and in forests of the arctic and temperate regions of the world. Besides the scarlet-flowering species *G. chiloense* and orange-flowering *G. coccineum*, there are also numerous hybrids. They produce anemone-like, single or double flowers in orange and red shades that appear in spring. The pinnate leaves are equally attractive, making these flowering herbaceous perennials 10–20 in tall perfect for balconies and terraces. They look very good with other herbaceous perennials, for instance the tall-growing primrose varieties. They are all hardy and grow best in fertile, well-drained soil in sun or partial shade. In winter they can be cut back to the ground. They are propagated from seed or by division in spring.

Ground ivy

Glechoma

ⓘ

Location: 💧 ☀
Propagation: *runners*
Characteristics: ☉/∞ 🍃 ❄
Pests: slugs and snails
Flowering: spring – summer

The genus *Glechoma* belongs to the *Labiatae* family includes twelve species of creeping, mat-forming, hardy perennials that grow almost everywhere in Europe. Their stems root at the nodes and quickly form a carpet of coarsely toothed, round to oval, hairy leaves. In summer, plants produce small, fragrant, blue-violet tubular flowers which emerge from the leaf axils. These fast growing plants are excellent for growing in hanging baskets or as underplanting in containers. They grow best in fertile, moist but well-drained soil in partial shade. They should never be allowed to dry out because the brown leaves are rather unsightly. When touched the leaves emanate a very distinctive smell. In the "Variegata" variety they are marbled with white. The runners are easily separated and root quickly. These herbaceous perennials are usually grown as annuals.

Glechoma hederacea

Baby's breath

Gypsophila

The *Gypsophyla* genus is a member of the *Caryophyllaceae* family and has over 100 species that can be found throughout Europe, Asia and North Africa. It is often used by florists in flower arrangements for its elegant white or pink flowers. *G. paniculata* is usually grown as an annual herbaceous perennial that in spring produces beautiful sprays of tiny white flowers. These may be used fresh or dry in flower arrangements. The plant should be planted in a large container in well-drained soil, enriched with fertilizer. Cut back after flowering to encourage a second flowering. *G. repens* only grows 12 in high and bears sprays of pink flowers. It is ideal for window boxes on balconies and terraces and for underplanting. It grows best in a sunny position and prefers dry conditions. It is grown from seed in spring or propagated from cuttings in early summer.

Gypsophila

Location: ◗ – ◌ *acc. to variety* ☼
Propagation: ₀°₀°
Characteristics: ⊙/ ∞ ❀ ❅
Pests: stem rot
Flowering: spring – summer

Hakonechloa macra

ℹ

Location: 💧 ☼—☼
Propagation: ✂️🌼
Characteristics: ∞ 🌼 ❄️
Flowering: summer

Golden Japanese forest grass

Hakonechloa macra

This small, perennial ornamental grass belongs to the *Graminae* family. It has only one species, which is native to Japan. It is a slow-growing, herbaceous grass that only reaches 12 in in height. In colder regions the deep green leaves of the species turn a beautiful bronze color in autumn. There are also decorative, variegated forms such as "Aureola" that looks very particularly striking in light shade. It can be planted on its own or in groups and is quite an eye-catcher on a balcony or terrace. This hardy grass is very slow growing and ideal for permanent planting in pots and containers. It grows best in humus-rich, fertile soil, which must be kept fairly moist at all times. But it should be not allowed to become waterlogged. The grass will grow in sun or partial shade. It is easily propagated by division in spring.

Shrubby veronica

Hebe

ℹ

Location: ○ ☼
Propagation:
Characteristics: ∞ 🌼 🌼
*Diseases: leaf spot, root rot,
    downy mildew*
Pests: aphids
*Flowering: spring, autumn
    according to species*

These shrubby, evergreen plants are members of the *Scrophulariaceae* family and native to New Zealand and Chile. The range of *Hebe Andersonii* hybrids with variegated leaves has greatly increased in recent times. For instance, *Hebe buchananii* and *H. pinguifolia* are evergreen, hardy species that produce delicate, white flowers in spring. *H. ochracea* has striking, scale-like, olive green leaves, tinged with ochre. *H. cupressoides* "Boughton Dome," also with scale-like leaves, forms a grey-green dome. These species grow very slowly and are ideal for permanent planting on balconies and terraces. Early planting raises the plant's frost-hardiness. It tolerates dry conditions better than being waterlogged and benefits from regular feeding. It grows best in full sun and the broad-leaved varieties should be cut back after flowering. They are propagated from cuttings between spring and autumn.

Hellebore

Helleborus

This genus belongs to the *Ranunculaceae* family and is native to Europe and west Asia. It includes 15 species of herbaceous perennials that flower in winter and spring. The best-known of these species is the Christmas rose *Helleborus niger*. It already starts flowering in December producing white, saucer-shaped flowers and is therefore often available as a pot plant at Christmas. If grown outdoors, it should be protected slightly from the cold. The mid-green, deeply lobed leaves are evergreen. Hellebore hybrids grow about 16 in high and produce flowers in shades of purple, yellow and white, flushed with pink, which appear in spring. They are vigorous growers and fully hardy. They all need humus-rich, moist soil and prefer shade or partial shade. They look very good combined with ferns and heather. All species, especially the seeds, are poisonous, and the sap can cause skin irritation.

Helleborus

ⓘ

Location: ◑ ☀ — ☀
Propagation: ₀°
Characteristics: ✘ ∞ ❀ ❄
Diseases: leaf spot, black rot
Pests: aphids, slugs and snails
Flowering: winter – spring

Alumroot

Heuchera micrantha

The *Heuchera* genus, a member of the *Saxifragraceae* family, is native to the rocky regions of North America and is particularly common in the Rocky Mountains. *H. micrantha* is a bushy, evergreen herbaceous perennial with heart-shaped, grey-marbled leaves which in the "Palace Purple" variety are a coppery-purple. Loose sprays of small, tubular, reddish white flowers are produced in early summer. Breeders have developed many varieties of this popular foliage plant. "Bressingham Bronze" has magnificent glossy dark purple-red leaves while "Snowstorm" has greenish-white leaves and sprays of bright red flowers. Plants can be grown in window boxes or containers – depending on their size – in sun or partial shade. At the end of winter they can be cut back to the ground. Plants grown from seed often fail to come true to type. For this reason it is better to propagate by division.

ⓘ

Location: ◑ ☀ — ☀
Propagation: ₀° ❦✿
Characteristics: ∞ ❀ ❦ ❄
Pests: aphids, weevils
Flowering: spring – summer

Plantain lily

Hosta

ℹ

Location: 💧 ☀️
Propagation: ⦾° 🐝
Characteristics: ∞ 🍂 ❄️
Diseases: virus diseases
Pests: slugs and snails, aphids,
weevils
Flowering: summer

The genus *Hosta* is native to Japan and China and includes hardy, herbaceous perennials that are grown mainly for their decorative foliage. Formerly included in the *Liliaceae* family, they now belong to the *Hostaceae* family which was created specially for them. The often strongly textured, broad, lanceolate leaves appear in shades of blue-green, yellow-green, variegated or with differently coloured margins, depending on the species and variety. Violet or white trumpet-shaped flowers, borne in racemes, are produced in summer. Leaves and blooms are often used in flower arrangements. Hostas are ideal for planting in pots and containers on partially shaded balconies and terraces where, for instance, a blue-green variety would like particularly beautiful. They need fertile, well-drained soil which should be kept evenly moist at all times. They need regular feeding during the growing season. Unfortunately they are particularly attractive to slugs and snails. They are easily propagated by division or from seed in spring.

Right and opposite page: Hosta

Bluet

Houstonia caerulea

Location: 💧 ☀
Propagation: 🌱 ✂
Characteristics: ∞ ❀ ❄
Flowering: spring

The genus, a member of the *Rubiaceae* family, includes 50 herbaceous perennials, annuals and biennials that are all native to North America. The bluet is a short-lived herbaceous perennial that is best grown as a biennial. This means that it is sown indoors in winter and planted out in spring when the young plants had developed sufficient roots. They grow 6 in high and look very good in rockeries and in containers on terraces and balconies. Their star-shaped, blue or white flowers with yellow eye appear in spring. They need acid, humus-rich soil that should be kept moist at all time, and partial shade. They must always be watered with lime-free water otherwise they may not survive long. For this reason they combine well with heathers and other lime-hating plants. They are grown from seed or propagated by division.

Houttuynia

Houttuynia

Location: 💧 ☀
Care: ⚠
Propagation: ✂
Characteristics: ⊔ ∞ 🍂
Pests: slugs and snails
Flowering: spring – summer

The genus *Houttuynia* belongs to the *Saururaceae* family, and its only species which is native to east Asia. It is an excellent ground cover with spreading rhizomes. The oval to heart-shaped, bluish or grey-green leaves with red edges are a real eye-catcher. When crushed the leaves exude an orangey scent. The tiny, greenish-yellow flowers, which are grouped in dense spikes surrounded by white bracts at the base, appear in spring. The "Chamaeleon" variety with bright green-yellow-red variegated leaves is very decorative. An additional advantage is that it is less invasive than the species and is therefore ideally suited for growing in containers. Plants grow best in moist, humus-rich soil and will even grow in shallow water. The colorful foliage looks particularly good in dappled shade. They should be cut back vigorously at the end of autumn and covered with brushwood. They are propagated by division in spring.

Candytuft

Iberis saxatilis

This genus belongs to the *Cruciferae* family and consists of about 50 species of herbaceous annuals and perennials as well as evergreen sub-shrubs, which are mostly native to southern Europe, north Africa and west Asia. *Iberis saxatilis*, which is common in southern and central Europe, produces large, very decorative clusters of white flowers that appear in spring. It grows 4 in high and branches very easily. It is indispensable in the rockery and is ideal for quickly filling gaps in large containers. If it is cut back after flowering it will flower again in autumn. Candytuft needs a very sunny location. If it is in partial shade, it must protected from frost in winter. It grows best in well-drained, fertile soil, which should be on the dry side rather than wet. Cuttings can be taken in early summer. *I. Sempervirens* also produces clusters of white flowers.

Iberis

Location: ○ ☼ ⚠
Care: ⚠ *in half-shade*
Propagation: ⚬°
Characteristics: ∞ ✿ ❄
Pests: *slugs and snails,*
        caterpillars
Flowering: *spring, autumn*

Hen and chickens houseleek

Jovibarba globifera

The *Jovibarba* genus consists of evergreen, succulent perennials. It is closely related to the *Sempervivum* genus and, like them, is a member of the *Crassulaceae* family. They form rounded rosettes, sometimes tinged with red, depending on the species. *Jovibarba globifera* is also known as *J. sobolifera*. The species produces evergreen rosettes with pale green, fringed leaves that become reddish at the tip with age. In summer it bears clusters of bell-shaped, greenish-yellow flowers. "Bronce ingot," a variety of *J. heuffelii*, has bronze-coloured leaves. The rosettes die off after flowering but leave numerous offsets, which produce new plants. These undemanding plants are hardy and need sandy, well-drained soil such as for instance cactus compost. They need a sunny, dry location.

Jovibarba globifera

Location: ○ ☼ ⚠
Propagation: ✿ *baby rosettes*
Characteristics: ∞ ✿ ❄
Flowering: *summer*

Kirengeshoma

Kirengeshoma palmata

ⓘ

Location: ◦ ☼
Propagation: ◦ ✿
Characteristics: ∞ ❀ ❊ ❆
Pests: slugs and snails
Flowering: summer

The only species in the genus, this elegant plant belongs to the *Hydrangeaceae* family and is native to the forests of Japan and Korea. It is an upright, bushy herbaceous perennial growing 24 in high and has arching, black stems with large, bright green palmate leaves and narrow, cream-coloured, funnel-shaped flowers that appear in summer. It is completely hardy and needs moist, fertile, humus-rich but lime-free soil in light shade. It combines well with hostas and other lime-hating plants. It can be grown from seed sown after it has ripened or in spring. However, this is not always successful. Propagation by division in spring is much more reliable. Watch out for snails, which are very fond of the leaves and young shoots.

Red-hot poker

Kniphofia

ⓘ

Location: ◦ ☼ ⚠
Care: ⚠
Propagation: ✿
Characteristics: ∞ ❀
Pests: thrips
Flowering: summer – autumn

The genus, a member of the *Asphodelaceae* family, has about 70 species of herbaceous perennials, some of them evergreen, which are all native to southern and eastern Africa. Red-hot pokers form bushy clumps with arching, strap-shaped, bright to mid-green or blue-green leaves. The leaves of the deciduous species are usually grass-like while those of the evergreen species are long and strap-shaped. The numerous pendent, tubular flowers, which may be red, orange, yellow or white depending on the species, are grouped in large, upright, candle-like spikes. Many flowers are red when they first come out but soon fade to yellow, resulting in a two-tone spike. Red-hot pokers are very attractive to bees. The plant requires a sunny, sheltered location where it can over-winter safely. It is also advisable to protect it with some leaves or brushwood. It should only be watered sparingly during winter. Plants can be divided in early spring.

Kniphofia

Yellow archangel

Lamium galeobdolon

Most species of the evergreen *Lamium* genus, a member of the *Labiatae* family, can be found in Europe, north Africa and Asia. This dead nettle is a rhizomatous herbaceous perennial that spreads rapidly by means of runners, thus forming a dense carpet of leaves up to 12 in high. In summer it produces whorls of tubular yellow flowers, flecked with brown, measuring nearly 1 in across. "Florentinum" has silver-marked leaves that turn reddish in autumn. Less aggressively invasive are "Hermann's Pride" with silvery-green leaves and "Silver Angel" with a creeping habit. Spreading can be controlled by pruning at the beginning of spring. The plant can also be divided. If planted near other plants make sure that the latter do not get suffocated by the spreading deadnettle. These excellent foliage plants grows best in moist soil in partial shade.

Location: 💧 ☀ – ☀
Propagation: ⚘🌿❀
Characteristics: ∞ 🍃 ❄
Pests: slugs and snails
Flowering: summer

Striped dead nettle

Lamium maculatum

Location: 🌢 ☀ – ☀
Propagation:
Characteristics: ∞ 🥀 ❄
Pests: slugs and snails
Flowering: summer

The wild form of the perennial *Lamium maculatum* or spotted deadnettle has spread from Europe and western Asia to North America. This semi-evergreen, mat-forming perennial must cut be back during the growing to restrict its vigorous spreading. The toothed, mid-green leaves usually have a white stripe running down the center and are quite eye-catching. The clusters of white, pale pink or dark red flowers are borne in mid-spring. This excellent ground cover plant is ideal for growing on terrace walls or in window boxes, containers and hanging baskets. "White Nancy" has white-variegated, mid-green leaves and white flowers while "Argenteum" has silvery leaves with green margins, and both are particularly suited for this purpose. "Chequers" has pink-lilac flowers. They all grow best in very moist, humus-rich soil in a shady location.

Lewisia cotyledon

Bitterwort

Lewisia cotyledon

Location: ◊ ☀
Care: ⚘
Propagation: ˳˳˚
Characteristics: △ ∞ ❀
Diseases: stem rot
Pests: slugs and snails, aphids
Flowering: spring – summer

The genus *Lewisia* is a member of the *Portulaceae* family of about 20 species of deciduous or evergreen herbaceous perennials that are all native to the Rocky Mountains. *L. cotyledon* is an evergreen herbaceous perennial with fleshy, dark green leaves, arranged in basal rosettes. The dense clusters of white, yellow, pink or purple-red flowers, depending on the variety, are borne from late spring to late summer. *L. cotyledon* grows 12 in high but there are also very attractive, more compact varieties. These undemanding, vigorous-growing plants only need moderately moist, fertile, well-drained soil and a lightly shaded, dry location. They do not tolerate being waterlogged, which would lead to stem rot. A layer of mulch around the plant will help prevent this. However it is advisable to protect the plants in winter. It is propagated from seed in spring or leaf cuttings in summer.

Blazing star

Liatris spicata

Liatris spicata is native to central and eastern North America. It is not immediately apparent that *L. spicata* is a member of the *Compositae* family because its flowers are so different. Also known as button snakeroot, this low-growing herbaceous perennial forms basal tufts of grass-like leaves, the leaves on the stems becoming increasingly narrow towards the top. The red-violet, white or pink flowers, borne in tall spikes, open from the top downwards and attract many butterflies and bees. It is a robust plant that will grow in any fertile soil. It benefits from an application of fertilizer in spring. Although it prefers dry conditions, it will also adapt to moist growing conditions. It is an undemanding perennial that is ideal for growing along terrace walls and in containers on balconies. It should be cut back vigorously in winter and can be propagated from seed in spring.

Location: ◊ ☼
Propagation: .∘° ✍
Characteristics: ∞ ❀ ❄
Pests: slugs and snails
Flowering: summer

Sea lavender or Statice

Limonium tetragonum

Sea lavender, also known as statice, belongs to the *Plumbaginacea* family. There are about 150 species that can be found in coastal zones and wasteland throughout the world. *Limonium tetragonum*, native to China, Korea and Japan, is an upright herbaceous perennial with a basal rosette of narrow leaves 6 in long. The tiny spikes of pink flowers with hairy, white calixes appear in autumn. Grwoing to 8 in high, sea lavender is a very popular cut flower but it is only half-hardy. It is best grown as a container plant on balconies and terraces. It grows best in well-drained soil in a sunny location. Because it is only semi-hardy, it should only placed outdoors after all danger of frost has passed. Sea lavender should only be watered moderately and fed with a weak solution of fertilizer. Although a herbaceous perennial, it is usually grown as an annual or biennial and grown from seed in spring.

Location: ◊ ☼
Care: ❄
Propagation: .∘°
Characteristics: ∞ ❀
Diseases: powdery mildew
Flowering: autumn

Purple toadflax

Linaria purpurea

This frost-hardy, herbaceous perennial grows up to 39 in high and is a member of the *Scrophulariaceae* family. Its mid-green leaves up to 2.5 in long are arranged in a whorl at the base and alternately higher up the stem. The racemes of pink-violet flowers are produced from mid to late summer. There are many varieties of the species that come in a wide range of colours. For instance, the tall-growing variety "Canon Went" has pale pink flowers while "Springside White" has white flowers. In order to flower prolifically *Linaria* needs fertile, well-drained soil and a position in full sun. It needs very little water. It is propagated from seed or cuttings in early spring and it also self-seeds very easily. The plant is prone to mildew and attacks by aphids but is otherwise resistant.

ⓘ

Location: ◊ ☼
Propagation: ₀°
Characteristics: ∞ ✿ ❄
Diseases: powdery mildew
Pests: aphids
Flowering: summer

Linum

Flax

Linum

Linum includes about 200 species, mostly from the temperate regions of the northern hemisphere. Flax is a plant with a long flowering season that produces blooms in a wide range of colours such as yellow, white, blue, red or pink, depending on the variety. It is a very decorative plant that looks well in containers and window boxes on balconies and terraces, in borders and as edging. Most species and varieties such as bright yellow golden flax *L. flavum* "Compactum" are frost-resistant but perennial species such as *L. narbonense* need to be protected against the cold with a layer of brushwood or moved indoors to a frost-free place. Flax grows best in fertile, well-drained soil in a sunny location sheltered from the wind. After flowering the plants should be cut back vigorously. It is propagated from seed in spring or autumn. Perennial species can be propagated from cuttings in early summer.

ⓘ

Location: ◊ ☼ ⚠
Care: ❄ – ❄ *according to variety*
Propagation: ₀°
Characteristics: ☉/∞ ✿
Pests: slugs and snails, aphids
Flowering: summer

Lobelia

Lobelia x speciosa

The genus *Lobelia* includes 300 species of annuals, herbaceous perennials and shrubs that grow in the temperate regions of the world, especially in America and Africa. They are members of the *Campanulaceae* family and are much loved for their magnificent flowers and foliage. Less well known than trailing lobelias are the numerous attractive varieties of tall-growing hybrids *Lobelia x speciosa*, which produce pink, reddish-violet or bright red blooms, borne on spikes that flower from the top downwards. These short-lived herbaceous perennials must be protected in winter or moved to a frost-free, cool, light place. Because they flower considerably less prolifically after two years, it is best to grow them as annuals. They prefer a sunny to partially shaded position and fertile soil that must be kept moist at all times. Varieties are grown from seed in spring.

Location: ◆ ☼ — ☀
Care: ⬘ ❄
Propagation: ⸫
Characteristics: ☉/ ∞ ✿
Diseases: *leaf spot*
Pests: *slugs and snails*
Flowering: *summer*

Lobelia x speciosa

Lupinus

ⓘ

Location: 🌢 ☼
Propagation: ˳°°
Characteristics: ✖ ∞ ❀ ❄
Flowering: summer

*L*arge-leaved lupin

Lupinus polyphyllus

The *Lupinus* genus has 200 species of annual and herbaceous perennials and shrubs that are native to southern Europe, north Africa and north America. Lupins or lupines are undemanding plants of the *Leguminosae* family, bearing magnificent, brightly coloured spikes of flowers. The four-leaved lupine is also used as forage plant and as green manure to improve the quality of the soil. The many hybrids, including Russell lupins, that are now available on the market produce spectacular blooms in shades of blue, red, pink, yellow or white, on spikes up to 20 in long. They are ideal container plants for balconies and terraces where they are a real feast for the eyes. But care must be taken because the plant is poisonous. Lupins grow best in fertile soil which should be kept moist at all times. If cut back immediately after flowering in summer, they may flower again in autumn. Propagation is by seed or cuttings.

Lychnis coronaria

ⓘ

Location: ◌ ☼
Propagation: ˳°° ⚘🖊❀
Characteristics: ∞ ❀ ❄
Diseases: slugs and snails
Flowering: summer

*R*ose campion

Lychnis coronaria

Also known as crown pink, *Lychnis* is a short-lived herbaceous perennial native to south-east Asia, central Asia and the Himalayas. This undemanding, very floriferous member of the *Caryophyllaceae* family has silver-grey felted leaves and hairy silvery stems that contrast beautifully with the brightly coloured flowers that appear in summer in shades of dark pink, purple and scarlet red. *Lychnis* grows best in moderately fertile, well-drained soil in a sunny location. Watering and feeding are hardly necessary, and indeed the silvery color of the leaves develops even better in dry than moist soil. It is recommended to deadhead *lychnis* regularly in order to prolong the flowering season and prevent unwanted self-seeding. It is easiest to propagate by division in spring.

Dotted loosestrife

Lysimachia punctata

Lysimachia is native to central and southern Europe and Turkey and is somewhat surprisingly a member of the *Primulaceae* family. This extremely hardy, tuft-forming herbaceous perennial can reach 39 in in height with broad, bright green leaves with wavy margins. The numerous bright gold-yellow flowers are grouped in whorls on high terminal spikes. Dotted loosestrife is also used in flower arrangements. It looks very attractive in borders and elegant containers on balconies and terraces. It also grows well in shade. It needs fertile, moist, well-drained soil to grow well. If watered generously it will also do well in sun. Spring is the best time to divide the plants.

Lysimachia punctata

ⓘ

Location: 💧 ☀
Propagation: ✂🌱
Characteristics: ∞ ❀ ❄
Pests: slugs and snails
Flowering: summer

Musk mallow

Malva moschata

The genus has 30 species of herbaceous annuals, biennials and perennials that are native to Europe, north Africa and Asia. A member of the *Malvaceae* family, *Malva moschata* has a bushy habit and grows up to 32 in high with woody stems at the base. The plant takes its name from the delicate musk fragrance that emanates from the leaves. The magnificent pale pink flowers appear in spring and are produced until the beginning of autumn. The white-flowering variety "Alba" is also very attractive. Musk mallow is extremely easy to grow. All it needs is well-drained, fertile soil and a sunny to partially shaded location. Mallows have a natural charm that will enhance any corner of the garden, balcony or terrace. They should be cut back after the first flowering to prevent them from self-seeding. They can be propagated from seed in spring or cuttings in early autumn.

ⓘ

Location: 💧 ☀ — ☀
Propagation: °°°
Characteristics: ∞ ❀ ❄
Diseases: rust fungus, leaf spot
Flowering: summer

Meconopsis

ℹ

Location: 💧 ☼ – ☼ ⚠
Care: ❋ – ❄
Propagation: ∘°° 🦗 🌼
Characteristics: ☉/∞ ❀
Diseases: powdery mildew
Flowering: spring – summer

Meconopsis

Meconopsis

Meconopsis is a member of the *Papaveraceae* family and includes annual, biennial and short-lived herbaceous perennials, native to the Himalayas. The bright colours and delicate beauty of the saucer-shaped, silky flowers are a real feast for the eyes. Whether planted along terrace walls or in containers and window boxes, the flowers will always add a wonderful touch of color to the surroundings. *Meconopsis x sheldonii* is up to 39 in tall and has sky blue flowers while *M. cambrica* , up to 20 in has yellow to orange flowers. These hardy plants thrive in fertile, well-drained soil which must be kept moist at all times. However, they hate being waterlogged as much as dry conditions and heat. That is why they should be placed in a cool, partially shaded location. They are propagated from seed or by division in spring.

ℹ

Location: 💧 ☼ – ☼
Propagation: 🦗 🌼
Characteristics: ∞ 🦋 ❋
Diseases: powdery mildew, rust
  fungus
Flowering: summer

Apple mint

Mentha suavolens

The *Mentha* genus, a member of the *Labiatae* family, numbers 25 species of aromatic, perennial herbs that are native to Europe, Africa and Asia. Apple mint grows around the Mediterranean and is very popular because of its aroma and taste, although some people do not like using it because of its hairy leaves. This fast-growing herbaceous perennial that grows up to 39 in high has arching stems with rounded, grey-green leaves, splashed with white in the "Variegata" variety. The tubular, white or pink flowers that appear in spring attract many bees. Mint looks very good combined with other plants in hanging baskets and window boxes. It prefers sandy, humus-rich soil and need plenty of water and careful feeding. It will grow in sun or partial shade. It can be propagated from cuttings or seed in spring or autumn.

Monkey flower

Mimulus

This genus *Mimulus* belongs to the *Scrophulariacae* family and includes about 180 species that are all very different from each other. The tubular- to funnel-shaped flowers come in a variety of shades, some being speckled or flecked. *M. cardinalis* is a herbaceous perennial that grows about 20 in high and it is particularly suited for growing in containers. It flowers with scarlet blooms that are produced throughout the summer until the first frosts in autumn. Because the delicate flowers are easily damaged by rain and wind, it is best to place them in a sheltered location. They grow best in a sunny, dry location as does *M. cupreus,* which that is not frost-resistant. The latter grows about 8 in high and comes in many shades of red and yellow. It needs fertile, moist soil and should be fed every week during the summer months. It needs to be protected against the cold during winter. It is propagated from seed, cuttings and by division in spring.

Purple moor grass

Molinia caerula

This genus of perennial grasses only has two species that grow on heath and moorland in Europe and Asia. Its gold brown autumn colours and elegant habit make it a very decorative container plant for balconies and terraces. Purple moor grass forms mounds of slender, upright leaves 20 in long. The violet-coloured flowers borne in slender panicles are produced from spring until autumn. In contrast to the species, which can reach a height of 5 ft, the white-striped "Variegata" variety only grows 24 in high. The "Moorhexe" variety that has dark purple panicles is also a very good choice. This hardy grass grows best in acidic soil that must be kept moist at all times in full sun or partial shade. It combines very well with heathers. It can be grown from seed or propagated by division. Plants raised from seed do not come true to type.

ⓘ

Location: 🌢 ☀ – ☀ ⚠
Propagation: ⸳°° ✿
Characteristics: ☉/∞ ✿
Diseases: mildew rot
Pests: slugs and snails
Flowering: summer – autumn

Molinia caerulea

ⓘ

Location: 🌢 ☀ – ☀
Propagation: ⸳°° ✿
Characteristics: ∞ ⬚ ❄
Flowering: spring – autumn

Bergamot

Monarda hybrids

Location: ○ ☼ – ☀
Propagation: °°°
Characteristics: ∞ ❀ ❄
Flowering: summer

The genus *Monarda* belongs to the *Labiatae* family and is native to America. Its aromatic, green and sometimes violet leaves are used among other things to flavour tea. The flowers may be white, red or violet, depending on the variety, and they are reminiscent of sage. They are produced from mid-summer till early autumn, attracting large numbers of bees and butterflies. "Adam" has bright red flowers, "Beauty of Cobham" has pink flowers with a purplish calyx and "Schneewittchen" has white flowers. *Monardas* grow 39 in tall and make beautiful container plant that look very imposing on balconies and terraces. They are undemanding, hardy plants that grow in sun and partial shade. They tolerate dry conditions better than excessive moistness. Nevertheless, the soil should never be allowed to dry out in summer and in winter it should not be too wet. In winter, they can be cut down to the ground if necessary and an application of fertilizer in spring will encourage growth. It is propagated by division or from cuttings.

Monarda "Squaw"

Catmint

Nepeta x faassenii

Nepeta, a member of the *Labiatae* family, grows everywhere in the northern hemisphere. It is a bushy, clump-forming perennial with lavender-blue flowers arranged in whorls on long, dainty spikes. The silver-green leaves of *N. x faassenii* exude a distinctive aroma when crushed, but unlike the other species in the genus and in spite of its common name, it does not attract cats. It grows to 20 in high and spreads considerably. This is why it is an ideal border plant and is particularly suited for growing in large containers. It grows best in full sun in fertile, well-drained soil. It thrives in hot, dry conditions. However, it should be cut back after the first flowering in order to maintain its compact growth and also to encourage a second flowering. It is propagated from seed, cuttings or by division.

Location: ◊ ☼
Propagation: ₀°°   ✄
Characteristics: ∞ ✿ ❊
Diseases: powdery mildew
Pests: slugs and snails
Flowering: summer – autumn

Evening primrose

Oenothera

The genus *Oenothora* is native to the temperate zones of North América and has over 100 species of annuals, biennials and perennials. Most species except for *Oenothera speciosa* (which has pink flowers) have bright yellow flowers that grow up to 12 in high and are produced throughout summer. The flowers usually open only in the evening when they also exude their distinctive fragrance. The well-known evening primrose oil is extracted from the tiny black seeds. They prefer sandy, well-drained soil in full sun and do not enjoy dry conditions. *O. tetragona* is particularly recommended for balconies and terraces. The variety "Fryverkeri" grows 16 in high, has purple brown leaves and bright yellow flowers. "Rosea" is also very decorative with white flowers flushed with pink and a yellow center. The modern hybrid species are less frost-hardy and are usually cultivated as annuals or biennials.

Location: ◊ ☼
Care: 🕯 *hybrids*
Propagation: ₀°°
Characteristics: ⊙/∞ ✿ ❊
Flowering: summer

Snake's beard

Ophiopogon

Location: 🌢 ☼ – ☼
Care: ⊛ *O. planiscapus*
❄ – 🏠 *O. jaburan*
Propagation: ∘°° ⚶
Characteristics: ∞ ❀ 🍃
Pests: *slugs and snails*
Flowering: *summer*

Native to east Asia, *Ophiopogon* is a member of the *Convallariaceae* family and is particularly appreciated for its tufts of handsome, evergreen grass-like leaves. *O. jaburan* is native to Japan and not frost-hardy; it is therefore best cultivated as a container plant in temperate zones. *O. planiscapus* is half-hardy and will tolerate a light frost. However, it is still advisable to protect it against frost. Depending on the variety, the linear, arching leaves are dark green, green with a white stripe down the centre or almost green-black as in "Nigrescens." In summer, spikes of white, bell-shaped flowers appear among the grass-like leaves. "Nigrescens" only grows 8 in high and is an ideal container plant for balconies and terraces. Plants grow best in shade or partial shade, in well-drained, fertile soil. In summer, they should be watered moderately and fed every month. They can be propagated from seed or by division in spring.

Oregano

Origanum laevigatum

Location: ◊ ☼
Propagation: ∘°° ⚶
Characteristics: ∞ ❀ ❄
Flowering: *summer – autumn*

Origanum is a genus of herbaceous perennials, native to the Mediterranean and south-west Asia. It is especially known as a culinary herb through two species in particular, *O. vulgare* (oregano) and *O. majorana* (marjoram). A member of the *Labiatae* family, oregano is grown not only for its aromatic fragrance but also for its dark green, often bluish or purplish leaves and decorative flowers. The frost-hardy perennial species *O. laevigatum* produces a profusion of purple flowers throughout the summer that project above the dark green leaves. The flowers always attract large numbers of bees and butterflies. The "Herrenhausen" variety grows 16 in high with green leaves tinged with dark purple and deep violet flowers. Oregano grows best in poor, sandy soil in a very sunny location. It should be watered very sparingly even in summer and does not require much feeding.

Origanum

Royal fern

Osmunda

The twelve or so species in this genus, which belongs to the *Osmundaceae* family, grow almost everywhere in the world except in Australia. The largest species, *Osmunda regalis* or royal fern, can reach a height of 39 in. The "Gracilis" variety only grows 24 in high and is an ideal container plant for terraces and balconies. In summer it forms dense clumps of bright green ferns that turn yellow or golden brown in autumn. The upright, reddish brown fertile fronds that emerge from the inner fronds ensure the fern's propagation. The royal fern grows best in moist, well-drained, fertile soil in a partially shaded location. It is propagated by spores in summer or division of existing plants in autumn.

Location: 💧 ☀ — ☀
Propagation: ⋅°° 🌿
Characteristics: ∞ 🪴 ❄
Flowering: summer

Sorrel

Oxalis

There are about 500 species of the *Oxalis* genus and they are very popular among plant-lovers because of their delicate compound leaves and colorful, flat or cup-shaped flowers, which close at night like the leaves. They are members of the *Oxalidaceae* family and are mostly native to southern Africa and South America. Besides the popular *O. tetraphylla*, the good luck plant that is often offered as a gift at New Year, there are also perennial species that make excellent container plants for balconies and terraces. One such species is *O. adenophylla* with glossy silvery leaves and pink flowers with a white throat. Oxalis plants thrive in a warm, sunny position in moderately fertile, acid soil that must be kept moist at all times and should only be fed moderately. *O. acetosella* prefers a shady location. They are propagated in spring from seed or by division of the rhizomes.

ⓘ

Location: ◗ ☼ – ☼ ⚠
Care: ❄ – ❋ *according to variety*
Propagation: ⚬° ✎
Characteristics: ∞ ❀
Diseases: rust fungus
Pests: slugs and snails
Flowering: spring – summer

Switch grass

Panicum virgatum

Many of the 400 species of the *Panicum* genus, a member of the *Poaceae* family, are particularly popular with florists for their elegant panicles of spikelets. Switch grass is an excellent visual screen and provides effective protection against the wind on balconies and terraces because it can grow up to 39 in high. Specimens are particularly decorative when planted on their own in a large container. The stems and leaves turn pale to reddish brown in autumn. The large, arching panicles of tiny spikelets appear in late summer and acquire a reddish to bronze sheen in autumn. Switch grass grows in sun or partial shade in moderately fertile, well-drained soil. Although it will tolerate dry conditions, it should be watered regularly and be kept wet rather than moist. Moderate feeding is recommended. After the winter, it can be cut back and propagated from seed or by division.

ⓘ

Location: ◗ ☼ – ☼
Propagation: ⚬° ✎
Characteristics: ∞ ❀ 🍂 ❄
Flowering: summer

*I*celand poppy

Papaver nudicaule

There are about 70 species in the *Papaver* genus, which belongs to the *Papaveraceae* family. These species grow in Europe, Asia, Africa, North America and even the Arctic. The most famous species of this genus are the corn poppy and the notorious opium poppy used in the production of opium. The Iceland poppy, which is native to Asia and parts of North America, is usually grown as an annual or biennial, forming a bushy plant about 12 in high. It is an ideal container plant for balconies and terraces, for instance combined with blue fescue and saxifrage. The deliciously fragrant, single, saucer-shaped flowers appear in spring above the pale green foliage and are produced in shades of white, yellow, orange and red. The Iceland poppy has poisonous sap. It grows best in a sunny location in light sandy soil, which must not be kept too wet. Regular watering and feeding will prolong the flowering period.

Location: ◊ ☼ ⚠
Propagation: ₀°°
Characteristics: ✖ ∞ ❀ ❄
Diseases: downy mildew
Flowering: spring – summer

Papaver nudicaule

Pennisetum alopecuroides

Location: ○ ☼ ⟁
Care: ⟁ – ❄
Propagation: ⚬° ❧
Characteristics: ∞ ❀
Flowering: summer – autumn

Chinese fountain grass

Pennisetum alopecuroides

This wonderful clump-forming, evergreen fountain grass, a member of the *Poaceae* family, is native to Asia and Australia. This extremely decorative species is mostly grown for its imposing, bottlebrush-like flower spikes that are much loved by florists. The 8 in long, pale green to purple flower spikes produced throughout summer until autumn are particularly impressive on a dewy morning. The pale green leaves up to 24 in long are flat and quite inconspicuous in comparison. Fountain grass grows best in a sunny location in well-drained, moderately fertile soil. It only needs moderate watering and feeding. The varieties are only half-hardy and should be brought indoors or protected against frost during winter if left outdoors. Dead leaves should only be cut back in spring. This is also the time when it can be sown or older plants can be divided.

Phlox

Phlox

Location: ◖ – ○ acc. to variety ☼ – ☼
Care: ⟁
Propagation: ⚬°
Characteristics: ∞ ❀
Diseases: powdery mildew,
   leaf spot
Pests: leaf galls, nematodes
Flowering: spring – summer

The genus *Phlox* belongs to the *Polemoniaceae* family and includes over 60 species of annuals and hardy perennials. These species, which are mostly native to North Africa, are very popular because of the colorful, fragrant flowers produced in profusion. They add a colorful note to balconies and terraces, the taller forms such as the *Phlox paniculata* hybrids looking particularly good in containers while the low-growing, cushion-forming species such as *P. douglasii* are more suitable for window boxes. The tall-growing varieties need a lot of water during the growing season while the low-growing types will tolerate drier conditions but they all need plenty of sun. Phloxes will flower for weeks if a few flowering stems are cut back after the first flowering and the plant has been fed generously in spring. Both species should be protected from frost with brushwood or peat. Varieties can be propagated from cuttings taken in summer.

Phlox

Balloon flower

Platycodon grandiflorus

The only species in its genus, this member of the *Campanulaceae* family is native to east Asia. The balloon flower has an upright habit and grows 12-24 in high depending on the species. It forms thick tuberous roots. The large, broadly bell-shaped flowers may be white, pink, blue or violet, appearing in summer above the lanceolate, bluish-green leaves. These undemanding plants grow best in loamy, moist but well-drained soil in a sunny to partially shaded position. Plants needs occasional feeding during the growing season. These herbaceous perennials are ideal for rockeries, pots and containers. They combine very well with switch grass and evening primroses. They can be cut back vigorously in winter and propagated from seed in spring. The stems contain a milky sap.

Platycodon

Location: 💧 ☼ – ☀
Propagation: ⋰°
Characteristics: ∞ 🏵 ❄
Pests: slugs and snails
Flowering: summer

Polystichum

ⓘ

Location: 💧 ☀ – ☀
Care: /⁂\
Propagation: ✂🌿
Characteristics ∞ 🦋

Soft shield fern

Polystichum

The *Polystichum* genus belongs to the *Dryopteridaceae* family and grows in the mountainous regions of Europe and Asia. These very popular ornamental foliage plants have much-divided, bipinnate leathery fronds and are ideal for rather shady balconies and terraces. *P. setiferum* has long, soft fronds that remain green even in winter. The crosiers and stems of the fronds are covered with large brown scales. They grow 20–40 in high, depending on the species, and will grow in window boxes or on their own in large containers. Soft shield ferns thrive in shade or partial shade and grow best in humus-rich soil that should be kept very moist at all times but not waterlogged. It is important that the roots are in well-aerated soil so that they not rot. This fern dislikes being disturbed but large specimens can be divided in spring. In colder regions they should be protected against frost.

ⓘ

Location: 💧 ☀ – ☀
Propagation: ·°° ✂🌿
Characteristics: ∞ 🦋 ❄
Diseases: root rot, grey mould
*Pests: aphids, weevils, slugs and
    snails*
Flowering: spring

Drumstick primrose

Primula denticulata

This very varied genus, a member of the *Primulaceae* family, is widely distributed throughout the temperate regions of the northern hemisphere. Almost half of them are native to the Himalayas. The drumstick primrose comes from the humid mountainous regions of Asia. Striking clusters of flowers in shades of pink to purple, white and red with a yellow eye, depending on the variety, are borne on strong stems in spring. The rosettes of broadly lance-shaped, mid-green leaves are only formed after the plant has flowered. The species grows best in shade to partial shade in fertile, humus-rich soil that must be kept moist at all times. Plants will tolerate a little sun if the soil is kept very moist. They combine beautifully with bleeding hearts, hyacinths, forget-me-nots, ferns and shade-loving grasses. They can be raised from seed in spring or divided after the flowering.

Japanese candelabra primrose

Primula japonica

Primula japonica

As the name suggests, this species is native to Japan where it grows in damp meadows and shady, lightly wooded marshland. It also grows in mountainous regions where it can still be found at altitudes of 13,000 ft. This is why it is prefers shade to partial shade when grown as a container plant on balconies and terraces. It needs fertile, lime-free humus-rich soil that must be moist but well-drained. *Primula japonica* also does well in bog gardens and near water. The species has strong stems growing up to 20 in high. Being a candelabra type, the flowers, which are crimson in the species and white in the "Alba" variety, are arranged in whorls along the stem. *P. bulleyana*, also a candelabra type, has whorls of fragrant orange-red or yellow flowers. They also look good in containers on balconies and terraces. The plants can be divided after flowering or propagated from seed.

Location: 🌢 ☼ — ☼
Propagation: ⋰° ✿
Characteristics: ∞ ✿ ❄
Diseases: root rot, grey mould
Pests: aphids, slugs and snails
Flowering: summer

Cowslip

Primula veris

Primula veris

The cowslip *Primulus veris* is native to Europe and western Asia where it grows in dry, sunny meadows. In contrast to the *P. japonica* species, it also grows on alkaline soil, which should be fertile and rich in humus. The fragrant yellow flowers with orange-flecked throat are produced in spring and borne on strong stems. As many as 30 flowers can be grouped in one umbel. Cowslips look particularly good in rock gardens and containers because of their "wildflower" appearance. *P. auricula*, which grows 4 in high, has many brightly coloured varieties and *P x pubescens* with pastel-coloured flowers also flower in spring and thrive in full sun. Propagation is similar to that of the other species.

Location: ◌ ☼ — ☼
Propagation: ⋰° ✿
Characteristics: ∞ ✿ ❄
Diseases: root rot, grey mould
Pests: aphids, weevils, slugs
and snails
Flowering: spring

Primula vulgaris

Primrose

Primula vulgaris

ⓘ

Location: ◦ ☼ – ☼
Propagation: ₀° ❀
Characteristics: ∞ ❀ ❆
Diseases: root rot, grey mould
*Pests: aphids, weevils, slugs and
    snails*
Flowering: spring

The wild form of this stemless *Primula* species is native to western and southern Europe. It forms rosettes of oval to lanceolate, wrinkled, mid-green leaves with serrated margins that are covered with fine hairs on the underside. While the species has pale yellow flowers with a dark center produced in early spring, the many varieties come in every possible shade. The fragrant flowers have five petals and are grouped in dense clusters. Like bulbs, primroses will add color to balconies and terraces in spring. However, the flowers are sensitive to frost. They grow in sunny to lightly shaded locations, in fertile, loose soil that should be kept very moist. Varieties are usually grown from seed. The flowering period can be prolonged by combining early- and late-flowering varieties. If you need space in the window boxes for summer flowering plants, you can plant out the primroses in the garden.

Chamois cress

Pritzelago alpina

ⓘ

Location: ◊ ☼ – ☼
Propagation: ₀° ❀
Characteristics: ∞ ❀ ❆
Flowering: spring – summer

This carpet-forming, herbaceous perennial is native to southern Europe and the Balkans. A member of the *Cruciferae* family, it is often still referred to by its former botanical name *Hutchinsia alpina*. In spring clusters of pure white flowers emerge from this carpet of leaves which grows up to 4 in high. This species is a very popular herbaceous plant for rock gardens because it soon covers any gaps with greenery. It is also ideal for filling spaces in window boxes and containers on terraces and balconies. You could also create your own little rock garden in a large container on your balcony or terrace. It looks very good with low-growing campanulas and whitlow grass (*Draba*). Plants grow best in dappled shade in lightly moist soil, which should also be able to dry out well. It is propagated from seed or by division.

Pasque flower

Pulsatilla vulgaris

The pasque flower belongs to the *Ranunculacaea* family and is native to the mountainous regions of Eurasia and North America. It is grown for its delicate, finely divided, fern-like leaves and elegant nodding flowers. The foliage only develops after the appearance of the single, tufted, bell-shaped flowers covered in silky hairs in spring or early summer. Pasque flower forms bushy clumps and has a vigorous, woody rootstock. It prefers rich, rather dry, well-drained soil and a location in full sun. It dislikes cold, wet weather. The wild form is a protected plant. It does not like being disturbed but large specimens can be divided in spring. It can also be propagated from seed and root cuttings.

Location: ◊ ☼ ⛰
Propagation: ⸲°° ✂
Characteristics: ✖ ∞ ❀ ❄
Flowering: spring

Pulsatilla vulgaris

Firethorn

Pyracantha

Location: ◊ ☼ — ☀
Propagation: ∘°°
Characteristics: ✖ ∞ ❁ ❄
Flowering: spring

Pyracantha, a member of the *Rosaceae* family, is native to the Mediterranean and the temperate regions of Asia. It is much loved by gardeners because of the profusion of bright red, yellow or orange berries that appear in autumn and winter. The very vigorous *P. coccinea* can reach a height of 6 ft 6 in but it can also be grown in a container and must be cut to the appropriate size. However, when cutting it back it is important to remember that it flowers on wood that is two years old. Clusters of little white flowers are produced in early summer, later followed by the bright berries that remain on the shrub well into the winter. *Pyracantha* does not need much food and does not mind dry conditions. It will grow in full sun or partial shade. It is grown from seed or propagated from cuttings. The fruit can cause nausea if consumed.

Pyracantha

Salvia

Salvia nemorosa

Th genus *Salvia* has 900 species of annual and perennial herbaceous plants, shrubs and sub-shrubs, making it the largest genus in the *Labiatae* family. *S. nemorosa* grows everywhere in the world except in tropical rain forests and in very cold regions. It has the typical salvia flowers, namely tubular and two-lipped with the lower lip flat and the upper lip in the shape of a hood. This bushy, perennial salvia grows 12–20 in high, depending on the species. In summer it produces slender, erect spikes of flowers in shades of pink, reddish-violet and blue. It thrives in full sun and prefers dry conditions to wet ones. The soil should be rich and the plant benefits from regular feeding. If cut back immediately after flowering it will flower a second time. In spring it can be propagated from cuttings or by division but it can also be grown from seed.

Salvia nemorosa

Location: ◊ ☼
Propagation: ∘° ⚑❀
Characteristics: ∞ ❀ ❄
Flowering: summer

Sage

Salvia officinalis

Salvia officinalis is a decorative sub-shrub that is native to the Mediterranean region and like many herbs it belongs to the *Lamiaceae* family. The young shoots and leaves of the strongly aromatic plant can be harvested throughout the summer and used for flavouring many dishes. For a restoring tea, the leaves should be harvested shortly before the plant flowers. The leaves can be preserved successfully by freezing or drying. The very vigorous muscatel sage smells even more strongly and is grown for cosmetic purposes and as an ornamental plant. Sage prefers a well-drained, dry soil and plenty of sun in a location protected from the wind. It should be kept fairly dry and fertilized only once a month. Propagation is possible through offsets, cuttings or division. In spring, strong cutting back is recommended. In classical antiquity, sage was known as a cure for inflammation and sores, hence its name *Salvia*, from the Latin word *salvere* meaning "to feel well."

Salvia officinalis "purpurascens"

Location: ◊ ☼ ⚠
Propagation: ∘° ⚑❀
Characteristics: ∞
Diseases: root rot
Pests: slugs and snails, aphids,
  spider mites, white fly
Flowering: summer (harvesting)

Lavender cotton

Santolina chamaecyparissus

Location: ○ ☼ ⚠
Care: ⚠
Propagation:
Characteristics: ∞ ✾ ❧
Flowering: summer

Santolina is native to the dry, rocky regions of the Mediterranean and belongs to the *Compositae* family. *S. chamaecyparissus* is a round, evergreen sub-shrub that grows 12 in high. The branches are covered with long, finely dissected, grey-white, woolly leaves that produce a pleasant fragrance. In summer, it produces bright yellow flowers. Particularly beautiful are "Lambrook Silver" with its silver-grey foliage and deep yellow flowers and the fairly compact "Lemon Queen" with grey-green foliage and cream flowers. Lavender cotton thrives in sheltered, dry, sunny places. It is hardy in milder regions but protection during winter is still recommended. It grows in ordinary potting soil and can be cut into shape at the end of the winter. It is propagated from cuttings taken in spring.

Santolina chamaecyparissus

Saxifrage

Saxifraga

The genus *Saxifraga* includes about 440 species, mostly evergreen, that are native to the temperate zones and Alpine and sub-arctic regions of the northern hemisphere. They are members of the *Saxifragaceae* family. There are many species and varieties available which are well suited for growing on terraces and balconies. *S. x apiculata* and *S. Arendsii* hybrids forms dense, evergreen mounds of small lanceolate leaves. *S. x apiculata* has yellow flowers that are produced in spring while the varieties flower in shades of red, pink, yellow and white. *S. umbrosa* forms rosettes of dark green leaves with small, white, star-shaped flowers, grouped in loose clusters, borne on upright, branched stems. All the species mentioned above grow best in partially shaded, dry sites and will therefore not tolerate being waterlogged. The soil must be rich in humus and be kept moderately moist. Propagation is by division in spring.

Location: 🌢 ☼
Propagation: ✿
Characteristics: ∞ ❀ ❄
Pests: aphids, spider mites, weevils
Flowering: spring

Scabiosa

Pincushion flower

Scabiosa caucasica

This genus *Scabiosa* that includes about 80 annual and perennial species grows in all temperate regions. It belongs to the *Dipsacaceae* family. It is very popular as a cut flower and for planting in borders. In summer it produces large flower heads with frilled petals that may be pink, red, reddish-violet and blue, depending on the variety. This bushy plant with mid-green leaves grows up to 31 in high. Its wild-flower appearance makes it ideally suited for growing in containers on balconies and terraces. It does not tolerate being waterlogged and is not absolutely hardy. This is why it needs a sheltered position and protection against frost during winter. It can be cut back to soil level at the end of the winter to promote new growth. It is propagated by division, by cuttings or grown from seed in spring.

Location: ◊ ☼ ⚠
Care: ⚹
Propagation: ⋅°° ✿
Characteristics: ∞ ❀
Flowering: summer

Easy-care succulents

Sedum spectabile

Are you one of those people who tend to forget watering now and again or never have time to do so? This is not the end of the world because we shall suggest a few plants here that can survive short or longer periods of drought without any problem.

Succulents such as sedums, sempervivums and saxifrages are all native to the dry desert and mountain regions of the earth and they are real survivors. They store water in their fleshy leaves and survive for quite a long time on these water reserves. This means that the task of watering and feeding can be reduced to minimum. In fact, excessive watering and feeding normally leads to weakening of the plant tissues, which in turn would make them vulnerable to pests and diseases. They will thrive in full sun or in shady, well-drained soil.

In summer, cacti or succulents such as Aenium *or* Echeveria *that normally live on a window-sill can be placed outdoors. Besides these true succulents there are other plants that do not need watering every day either. These include annual summer flowering plants such as rose moss (*Portulaca*), Livingstone daisy (*Dorotheanthus*),* Helichrysum petiolare, *parrot's beak (*Lotus berthelotii*), wax begonias (*Begonia semperflorens*), ivy-leaved pelargoniums, gazanias and spurge (*Euphorbia*). Among herbaceous perennials wormwood (*Artemisia*), santolinas, wall daisies (*Erigeron karvinskianus*), blanket flower (*Gaillardia*) and well-known sun-loving herbs such as oregano, thyme and sage also need very little watering.*

Wall-pepper

Sedum acre

ⓘ

Location: ◊ ☼
Propagation: ･° ✄❀
Characteristics: ✖ ∞ ❀ ❄
Diseases: root rot
Pests: slugs and snails
Flowering: summer

The *Sedum* genus includes about 400 species of usually succulent, evergreen or deciduous annuals and biennials, herbaceous perennials, sub-shrubs and shrubs. Most species are native to the mountainous regions of the northern hemisphere. Wall-pepper is a typical representative of the mat-forming, evergreen, frost-hardy species. The fleshy leaves form a mat 4 in high, covered in summer with yellow, star-shaped flowers. Wall-pepper is an ideal rockery plant and it grows best in sandy, well-drained soil in a sunny, dry location. It tolerates periods of drought better than excessive moisture. It self-seeds very easily but can also be propagated by division in spring. If consumed, wall-pepper can cause slight nausea.

Sedum acre

Stonecrop

Sedum telephium

Sedum telephium grows in the wild throughout Europe as far as Siberia. Like *S. acre*, it is a member of the *Crassulaceae* family. This rhizomatous plant has a bushy habit and grey-green leaves, arranged alternately on vigorous stems. The broad, flat, rust-reddish flower heads that appear in late summer are very popular with bees and butterflies. The plant is decorative throughout the year and should therefore only be cut in early spring. Small varieties are ideal for window boxes while larger ones look very good in an attractive pot or container. It is important that they should be placed in a sunny location. Because stonecrop can store water in its fleshy leaves and stems, it does not need to be watered very often. If not repotted, it will need some feeding to encourage new growth and the production of flowers.

Sedum "Matrona"

Location: ◌ ☼
Propagation: ₒₒ° ✂️🌸
Characteristics: ✖ ∞ 🌼 ❄️
Diseases: stem and root rot
Pests: slugs and snails
Flowering: summer – autumn

Houseleek

Sempervivum

The genus *Sempervivum* includes some 40 species of evergreen, perennial succulents. It is native to Europe and west Asia and belongs to the *Crassulaceae* family. Almost all species have small, star-shaped flowers that may be yellow, white or in shades of pink or red depending on the species and variety. The most important feature of these plants are their beautiful, symmetric, leaf rosettes that form dense, ground-covering mats. The cobweb houseleek *S. arachnoideum* took its name from the white, cobweb-like hairs that cover the green leaf rosettes. It flowers throughout the summer with terminal pink to red flowers. Like all succulents, houseleeks grow well in dry conditions and need very little food. They need sandy, well-drained soil and a sunny location. They often only flower after a few years. Houseleeks can be propagated by planting the ready-rooted offsets between spring and summer.

Sempervivum "Black Prince"

Location: ◌ ☼
Propagation: ✂️🌸
Characteristics: ∞ 🌼 ▨ ❄️
Diseases: rust fungus
Flowering: summer

Lamb's ears

Stachys byzantina

Location: ◊ ☼
Propagation: 🐝 🌿
Characteristics: ∞ 🍃 ❄
Diseases: powdery mildew
Pests: slugs and snails
Flowering: summer

This genus belongs to the *Labiatae* family and includes some 300 species of annual herbs, herbaceous perennials and evergreen shrubs. It is native to the more northern regions of the temperate zones of the world. It used to be cultivated in the herb garden because many species were thought to have medicinal purposes. Its flowers attract numerous bees and butterflies. Lamb's ears acquired its name from the appearance of its lanceolate leaves, covered with white woolly hairs. In summer it produces whorls of pink-red flowers. The leaves are prone to rotting in cold, wet weather. This is why it is recommended to position the plant in a sheltered, very sunny location. It should be fed during the growing period but watered only moderately. It can be cut down to the base in late winter and propagated by division in spring.

Right: Stachys byzantina
Opposite page: Terrace with Stachys byzantina, Salvia and Lavender

*S*tipa

Stipa

The wide-spread genus *Stipa*, a member of the *Poaceae* family, includes 300 species of clump-forming ornamental grass, many of them native to the Mediterranean region. It produces striking feathery plumes that are borne on long stems. The individual spikelets develop the long beards that are a special feature of this genus and move in the wind. The leaves are very long and narrow. Larger species such as *S. tenacissima*, up to 2 ft and *S. barabata*, up to 32 in are best grown on their own so that they do not overpower neighbouring plants. The more compact *S. pennata* only grows 16 in high and is therefore also suited for larger window-boxes. All species grow best in light, sandy, limey soil in full sun. However, they do not like long periods of rain. They should be cut back in spring. They can be propagated by division in early summer and grown from seed in autumn.

ⓘ

Location: ◊ ☼ ⚠
Care: ⚠
Propagation: ∘° ✁
Characteristics: ∞ ⚘
Flowering: summer

Tanacetum parthenium

*F*everfew

Tanacetum parthenium

The *Tanacetum* genus consists of rhizomatous perennials and belongs to the *Compositae* family. According to Greek mythology Ganymede became immortal after drinking a tea made from parsley fern, which is one of the *Tanacetum* species. *Tanacetum* plants have been used in the past to treat menstrual problems, hysteria, skin complaints, sprains, contusions and bruises and rheumatism. *T. parthenium* or feverfew is one of the traditional popular medicinal herbs, used to treat fever, shivering fits and also opium overdose. Nowadays, it is grown mainly for its beautiful, single or double, long-lasting flowers with white ray florets and yellow disc florets. These frost-hardy plants with yellow-green leaves are very short-lived and are therefore grown as annuals that are sown every year.

Location: ◊ ☼
Care: ⚠
Propagation: ∘°
Characteristics: ✖ ☉/∞ ⚘
Pests: aphids, leaf miners
Flowering: summer

Lemon thyme

Thymus x citriodorus

The genus includes about 350 species of aromatic evergreen herbaceous perennials, shrubs and sub-shrubs that turn woody at the base. They are native to the dry grasslands of Eurasia and belong to the *Labiatae* family. As compact, upright shrubs or prostrate mat-forming plants, most species are suitable for growing on balconies and terraces. They will grow well in window boxes and terracotta pots. Lemon thyme is a bushy, rounded shrub with narrow, yellow-green leaves. The variety "Silver King" has silvery-grey variegated leaves. It exudes an intense lemony fragrance and is often used to flavour dishes. In summer it produces lilac flowers that attract large numbers of bees. It needs sandy, not too fertile soil and a very sunny, warm location. It should be protected against frost during cold winters. It is easily propagated by division.

ⓘ

Location: ◊ ☼
Care: ⚠
Propagation: ✿✂
Characteristics: ∞ ✿ 🍃
Flowering: summer

Thymus

Globeflower

Trollius chinensis

Location: 💧 ☼ — ☀
Propagation: ✄
Characteristics: ∞ ❀ ❄
Diseases: powdery mildew
Flowering: summer

With their rounded, bright yellow blooms and liking for damp places, these clump-forming perennials are rather similar to buttercups, to which they are related. They belong to *Ranunculaceae* family and are native to Europe and the temperate regions of Asia. *Trollius chinensis* forms a dense bushy shrub that grows 39 in high. It flowers in spring with brilliant orange-yellow, bowl-shaped blooms on tall stems above the decorative, deeply divided leaves. It is a very undemanding plant but needs humus-rich soil that must be kept moist at all times. The variety "Gold Queen" will also tolerate dry conditions. It grows best in sun or partial shade and looks very good in combination with hostas and *primula elatior*. They can be cut back before or after the winter to encourage new growth. Propagation is by division in spring.

Trollius chinensis

Periwinkle

Vinca minor

The genus belongs to the *Apocynaceae* family and includes seven species of ever-green sub-shrubs and herbaceous perennials that grow in the forests of Europe, North Africa and Central Asia. They are grown both for their beautiful leathery, glossy dark or variegated leaves and their pale blue to violet flowers, which appear in late spring. *Vinca minor* can be grown not only as groundcover but also as trailing plants in hanging baskets and containers. The variety "Rubra" has reddish-violet flowers, "Gertrude Jekyll" has white flowers while "Variegata" has white-variegat-ed leaves. They are ideally suited for growing in partial and full shade in light, humus-rich soil. Because it is periwinkle is failry invasive, it should be cut back regularly. In cold regions it should be protected during winter. *V. minor* can be propagated by separating already rooted shoots from the mother plant and re-planting them else-where. All parts of the plant are poisonous.

❶

Location: 💧 ☀ — ☀
Care: ⚠
Propagation: ✂
Characteristics: ✖ ∞ ❀ ▨
Diseases: rust fungus
Flowering: spring – summer

Viola cornuta

Horned violet

Viola cornuta

The large *Viola* genus, a member of the *Violaceae* family, includes about 500 species of annuals, biennial and evergreen herbaceous perennials that grow in all the temperate regions of the northern hemisphere. The horned violet, also known as the horned pansy, is a spreading, evergreen herbaceous perennial with creeping root-stock. Between spring and late summer it produces a mass of lightly fragrant flow-ers that stand out beautifully against the oval, toothed leaves. These are smaller and more graceful than their larger sibling, the pansy. They come in wide variety of colors, ranging from yellow, blue and red to white. They grow best in a sunny to partially shaded location in ordinary potting soil and will also tolerate periods of drought. They are usually grown as annuals or biennials, being sown in spring or late summer.

❶

Location: ○ ☀ — ☀
Care: ⚠
Propagation: ⦾ ✂
Characteristics: ∞ ❀
Diseases: rust fungus, powdery
  mildew
Pests: aphids, spider mites,
  slugs and snails
Flowering: spring – summer

Architectural plants as focal points

Opposite page (clockwise from top left): Federborstengras, Hosta, Hakonechloa macra and Polystichum setiferum

Flowering plants are not the only ones that can embellish balconies and terraces. There are also striking foliage plants that provide a framework, background and contrast, as well as greenery all year round in the case of evergreens. If you look around you will notice plants with the most remarkable colors and forms that offer amazing possibilities for many locations, including shady corners.

What gives a plant its architectural quality is its habit. This may be spherical, columnar, erect or trailing. Whatever it is, if it is strongly defined it will create a focal point on the balcony or terrace. The concept of texture depends on a combination of the color and the smoothness or roughness of the leaves. The leaves may be one color only or variegated, and with a rough, smooth or shiny surface. Their shape too can vary enormously: large and round, serrated or finely feathered, to name but a few. The budding leaves of hostas and ferns are quite a sight in themselves.

You many need just one architectural plant as a focal point on a balcony or terrace but sometimes groups work better. Delicate ornamental grasses such as Pennisetum combines very well with other plants while creating an interesting contrast. Different textures often only work if they are repeated several times. Single plants are not as eye-catching as groups of plants – this is even more true if the plant is small. In this case it is best to use plants of similar appearance but in larger numbers to avoid an excessively busy effect. For instance, the dark leaves of bergenias placed next to the yellow-variegated leaves of Salvia "Icterina" will create an interesting contrast. Similar leaf shapes in different colors, as with some fuchsias for instance, may also be very attractive.

Container plants

Container plants are very versatile and will give a lot of pleasure. They can be endlessly re-arranged according to your whim or fancy. Mediterranean and sub-tropical plants will remind you of wonderful holidays while evergreens will provide greenery all year round. Many of our traditional pot plants are native to warmer climes. In their native habitat they grow in the wild as perennials but where the climate is cooler they must be over-wintered in a light, frost-free room between October and May. As a rule of thumb: the brighter the room where the plants over-winter, the more water they will need. But only water when the root ball is dry. Continue to watch out for pests even when the plants are over-wintering indoors. If space is at a premium, there are species that can be pruned before you bring them indoors. You can check in the "Plant Descriptions" section if, when and how the plants can be pruned. The plants can be returned to the terrace or balcony again after mid-May when there is no longer any danger of frost. Put the plants out on a cloudy day so that they have time to get accustomed to the light and do not get sun-scorched.

Frost-hardy container plants bring a double benefit: you enjoy your shrub or tree all year round and you save yourself the trouble of bringing the plants in and out again. However, even these need some protection during winter. The roots of container-grown plants are more exposed and therefore more vulnerable during prolonged periods of frost than those growing in flowerbeds. It is therefore advisable to insulate the container adequately against frost. Remember also that evergreen plants should still be watered during winter, although this should be carried out only on frost-free days.

Abutilon megapotamicum

Location: 💧 ☼–☀ ⚠
Care: 🌡
Propagation:
Characteristics: △ ∞ ❀
Diseases: grey mould (in winter)
Pests: aphids, white fly, spider mites
Flowering: summer

Chinese lantern

Abutilon megapotamicum

This member of the *Malvaceae* family originates from South America. It has a shrub-like habit and grows up to 5 ft tall. It flowers in summer with yellow petals and red calyx, while the variety "variegatum" has yellow-flecked leaves. There are also many *abutilon* hybrids with flowers in a wide variety of colors. They prefer a sunny, warm location but not the strong midday sun. In summer the plant must be watered generously. During the growing period it should given a complete fertilizer every week. It is best propagated during summer by tip cuttings. For over-wintering, *abutilons* should be kept in a sunny location where the temperature will not go below 41–50° F because otherwise they would lose their leaves. During this period the plants need very little water. Large plants can be cut back drastically before being brought indoors, although pruning is best done in early spring. Watch out for aphids and whitefly and check for grey mould while the plant over-winters.

Mimosa

Acacia

Acacias are members of the *Mimosaceae* family. They are native to Australia and have become naturalised in the Mediterranean. Grown in containers, they will reach a height of 6 ft 6 in. The fragrant yellow flowers appear in spring on *A. dealbata* (Silver Wattle) while the "four-seasons mimosa" *A. retinodes* flowers almost all year round. The finely pinnate pseudo-leaves that are in fact leaf stalks make them ideally suited to dry conditions. They flower only in warm, sunny places and need generous, continuous watering and a slightly acid soil. Although the root ball must never be allowed to dry out, it must not become waterlogged. During the growing period it must fertilized every week. It is propagated from seed in spring or summer, scratching the hard seed shell lightly before sowing. During winter it should be placed in a sunny location where the temperature will not go below 41° F; in a conservatory the temperature can be higher. Pruning or cutting back, whether light or vigorous, should take place after flowering. Mimosas are prone to spider mites.

Location: 💧 ☼ ⚠
Care: ❄ 🌡
Propagation: ∴
Characteristics: ∞ ❀
Pests: spider mites
Flowering: spring – winter

Ash-leaf maple

Acer negundo

This species native to North America is a member of the maple family (*Aceraceae*). The male flowers that appear in spring are grouped in large pendulous clusters and they are particularly striking. In the wild this deciduous tree can reach a height of 66 ft. However, less vigorous forms are better suited for growing in containers. For instance, the "Flamingo" variety with green and pink flecked leaves that are completely pink when they first come out has particularly decorative foliage. Ideally, they need a sunny to partially shaded location. Although maples prefer damp soil they do tolerate occasional drying of the root ball. During summer a maple should be given fertilizer every two weeks. Unwanted shoots can be cut back in late autumn and winter. It is propagated from soft cuttings in early summer or varieties may be propagated by grafting (splice grafting or oculation). Although maples are frost-resistant, the containers should be well protected. Besides mildew, maples also suffer from leaf spot and brown spot if the compost is too wet.

Japanese maple

Acer palmatum

This species is native to Japan, Korea and China. The trees are very decorative, usually with a round to umbel-shaped crown and reach a height of 10 ft when grown in containers. The purple flowers that appear in June are grouped in small clusters. In autumn the green leaves turn brilliant orange to red. For instance, the "Red Pygmy" variety has striking brown-red leaves that are finely, and deeply cut while "Dissectum" has bright green foliage that turns orange-yellow in autumn. Maples prefer partial shade and thrive in rich, well-drained soil with a low pH. They require regular watering and prefer organic fertilizers because excessive lime in the soil and fluctuating moisture levels can cause the leaves to turn brown from the edges and finally die completely. Unwanted shoots can be cut back in late autumn and winter. For propagation, over-wintering and plant protection, see *Acer negundo*. Young plants should be protected from cold winds.

Location: ◆ ☀–☀
Propagation:
Characteristics: ∞ 🌿 ❄ *with*
   container protection
Diseases: mildew, leaf roll
Pests: caterpillars, aphids,
   spider mites, gall mites
Flowering: spring

Acer palmatum

Location: ◆ ☀ ⚠
Propagation:
Characteristics: ∞ 🌿 ❄
Diseases: leaf roll
Pests: caterpillars, aphids,
   spider mites, gall mites
Flowering: spring

ⓘ

Location: ◊ ☼ − ☀
Propagation:
Characteristics: ∞ 🏵 ❄ *with*
   container protection
Diseases: leaf roll
Pests: aphids, spider mites, gall
   mites
Flowering: spring

Agapanthus

ⓘ

Location: ◖ ☼ − ☀
Care: ✻
Propagation: ◖◗✿
Characteristics: ∞ ✿
Diseases: rhizome rot
Pests: aphids, slugs and snails
Flowering: summer

Norway maple

Acer platanoides

This species grows in the wild in a woodland environment in Europe and Asia Minor. The bright yellow, fragrant flowers grouped in dense umbel-shaped clusters appear in spring and are very popular with bees. The shiny, green pointed leaves have striking autumn colors that vary from gold-yellow to red. The "Globosum" variety with its spherical crown is a particularly decorative plant for growing in a container. It will grow in a sunny to partially shady location and will thrive in moderately dry to moist soil, preferring acid soil to an excessively limey one. In summer it should be fertilized about every two weeks. This variety of maple is frost- and pollution-resistant and tolerates periods of drought without suffering serious damage. "Globosum" is usually grafted on a rootstock and grows in a harmonious shape without requiring any pruning. Besides aphids, this species sometimes suffers from leaf spot in the case of excessive moisture of the soil.

Agapanthus

Agapanthus africanus

Also known as the African lily, agapanthus is native to South Africa. It is a member of the lily family (*Liliaceae*) and when grown in containers it will reach a height of 5 ft. The evergreen *A. praecox* is also a very popular container plant. Broad, strap-shaped leaves grow from fleshy rhizomes. The impressive, eye-catching umbels, which may be white or blue depending on the variety, appear in summer. These should be removed after flowering. Agapanthus will grow both in sunny and partially shady location. In summer they need plenty of water and weekly applications of fertilizer but they hate being waterlogged. In winter, the plants should be allowed to over-winter in a light, cool location at a temperature of 41° F to ensure plenty of buds. If necessary a fairly light basement will also do. The rhizomes should kept almost dry to ensure they do not rot. Agapanthus is easily propagated by division of the rhizomes, an operation best performed in spring after the winter period of dormancy. The plants should only be repotted when the container looks as if it is completely full.

Agave

Agave americana

Agaves (*Agavaceae*) are native to Mexico but have also become naturalised in the Mediterranean. With their succulent leaves they are ideally suited to dry conditions but they require a lot of space because the leaves of their rosettes can reach a length of 3 ft. For safety it is advisable to cover the pointed, extremely sharp ends of the leaves, for instance with corks. Agaves only flower when 10 to 15 years old, after which the plant dies. They need a lot of sun and very little water. Always allow the soil to dry out before watering. Do not fertilize too much during the growing period, in fact give at most one or two applications of cactus fertilizer. In winter, agaves can be kept in a dark or light place at a temperature of 41° F with low humidity. Keep them almost dry during this period. They can be propagated from secondary rosettes, taken from the base and potted. Agaves are not prone to pests.

Location: ◊ ☼ ⚠
Care: ❄
Propagation: ✂ *offsets*
Characteristics: △ ∞
Pests: scale insects and woolly aphids (in young plants)

Agaves

Silk tree

Albizia julibrissin

Location: ♦ ☼ ⛰
Care: ✸
Propagation: ∘°°
Characteristics: △ ∞ ❁
Diseases: root rot
Pests: spider mites, white fly
Flowering: summer

This mimosa-like plant has a tree-like to shrubby habit and is native to the tropics and sub-tropics. The large feathery leaves consist of numerous small single leaflets that fold up at night time. For this reason it has been called the "sleep tree." The bright pink fragrant flowers that appear in summer look like brushes with their long filaments. *A. iophanta* has yellow inflorescences similar to those of the callistemons. *Albizia* prefers partial shade but needs warmth. In summer it requires a lot of water because lack of water causes leaf drop. However, it hates being waterlogged as this would lead to root rot. During the growth period it should be fertilized on a weekly basis. The skin of the seeds should be scratched a little before sowing. In winter, the plant should put in a bright place, at a temperature of 41–50° F, and be watered only sparingly. The umbel-shaped crown is pruned regularly to maintain its shape while older specimens can be rejuvenated by vigorous pruning. *Albizias* are occasionally troubled by spider mites.

Lemon verbena

Aloysia triphylla

Location: ♦ ☼ — ☼
Care: ✸
Propagation:
Characteristics: ∞ ❁ ✿
Pests: aphids, white fly
Flowering: summer

The *Aloysia* genus is a member of the vervain family (*Verbenaceaea*) and grows in the wild from California as far south as Chile. In the wild it reaches a height of almost 16 ft. It is particularly popular because of its delicious, lemon fragrance that intensifies when the leaves are crushed. The leaves are much used a medicinal herb tea and in the cosmetics industry. The small, bluish-white flowers that appear in mid-summer are grouped in long panicles. Lemon verbena grows best in a sunny to partially shaded location but not in the fierce midday sun. In summer it must be watered generously and fertilized regularly. In winter, it must be put in a cool, bright, well ventilated place at a temperature of 36–41° F. Lack of light will lead to leaf drop. Before taking out in the spring, plants can be pruned lightly or cut back vigorously. This is the ideal time to propagate from tip cuttings, which root very easily. Lemon verbena is prone to attack by whitefly and greenfly.

Kangaroo paw

Anigozanthus

The Australian kangaroo paw, a member of the *Haemodoraceae* family, flowers in early spring in its native country but in temperate zones the flowers appear in summer. They are yellow-green or red tubular-shaped flowers borne in terminal clusters or spikes at the end of stems the up to 16 in long. Besides *A. flavidus* and *A. manglesii*, there is also a series of hybrids. They all prefer a warm, sunny location and well-drained soil. They need regular watering in summer, ideally with lime-free water. They do not tolerate being waterlogged or a dry root ball. They only need weak solutions of fertilizer. Regular dead-heading is recommended while older plants will benefit from occasional thinning out. The plants can be propagated from seed at room temperature but also by division of the rhizome, which is quicker. In winter, these evergreen plants must be placed in a bright, well-ventilated room and a temperature of about 50–59° F. They are sometimes prone to root rot and leaf spot.

Anigozanthus flavidus

Location: ◊ ☼ ⚠
Care: 🌡
Propagation: ∘°° ✂🐝
Characteristics: △ ∞ ❀
Diseases: root rot, leaf spot
Pests: slugs and snails, caterpillars
Flowering: spring, summer

Cape mallow

Anisodontea capensis

The "fleshy lizzy," a member of the *Malvaceae* (mallow) family, is native to South Africa. It has a shrubby habit and can grow up to 5 ft in height. It is often cultivated as a standard. It flowers continuously from spring to autumn with delicate pinkish-red blooms. It thrives in a warm, sunny location but not in strong midday sun. It is important to remove the dead flowers regularly. In summer it requires large amounts of food and water. The soil must never be allowed to dry out but waterlogging must be avoided, otherwise the leaves will go yellow and drop. It also needs weekly applications of fertilizer. Watering should be reduced in winter. During winter the temperature should be 41–59° F depending on the intensity of the light. Before taking out again, the long shoots can be cut back to three or four pairs of leaves while larger specimens can be rejuvenated by vigorous pruning. Spring is the ideal time to take tip cuttings, which root easily. The plants can also be propagated from seed but the seedlings will not be true to type. Watch out for greenfly and blackfly.

Anisodontea capensis

Location: ◊ ☼ – ☼ ⚠
Care: ❄ 🌡
Propagation: ∘°°
Characteristics: ∞ ❀
Diseases: leaf drop
Pests: aphids, white fly
Flowering: spring – autumn

Paris daisy

Argyranthemum frutescens

Location: 🌢 ☼ ⚠
Care: ❄ 🛈
Propagation:
Characteristics: ∞ ❀
Diseases: blue mould
Pests: white fly, aphids, spider
  mites, leaf miner
Flowering: spring – autumn

This bushy semi-shrub is a member of the aster family (*Asteraceae*) and native to the Canary Islands. The daisy-like flowers are in fact inflorescences with yellow tubular center florets surrounded by white, pink or yellow ray florets, depending on the variety. Outdoors they flower continuously throughout the summer while in a conservatory they flower even longer. In order to ensure this prolific flowering, they require a lot of sun, water and food. During periods of hot weather, they must often be watered twice a day. In the growing period they must be given weekly application of a complete fertilizer. They need to be placed in a sheltered position where they are protected from the wind. Dead flowers should be removed regularly. Larger specimens are cut back in spring and if there is limited space for over-wintering, this can be done earlier, in the autumn. Depending on the brightness, the plants should over-winter in a well-ventilated room to prevent grey mould at a temperature of 41–59° F. The easiest way to propagate is from tip cuttings in spring. Watch out for greenfly and blackfly.

Argyranthemum frutescens

Blood flower

Asclepias curassavica

This evergreen semi-shrub, a member of the *Asclepiadaceae* family, is native to the tropical regions of America. All parts of the plant contain a milky sap. The orange to dark-red flowers that first appear in spring and last until the autumn are grouped in umbels and are very popular with butterflies. The long, erect fruit pods contain numerous seeds that can be sown from January onward at a temperature of about 68° F. The plant needs a warm, sunny location. During the growing period, it needs to be watered generously. It important to start fertilizing the plant in spring as soon as it shows signs of growth. It should over-winter in a light room at a temperature of 50–54° F and only watered occasionally. A lack of light will delay the flowering while excessive moisture will cause root and basal stem rot. Watch out for whitefly and greenfly. If well supported during the early stages, the plant will branch out better. It can also be trained as a standard. Otherwise, prune moderately in spring.

Asclepias curassavica

ⓘ

Location: 💧 ☼
Care: 🌡
Propagation: ₀°°
Characteristics: ⚠ ∞ ✿
Diseases: fungal rot
Pests: white fly, aphids
Flowering: spring – autumn

Aspidistra

Aspidistra elatior

It may be hard to believe but aspidistra has recently been classified in the *Convallariaceae* family, like lily-of-the-valley. This evergreen herbaceous perennial is native to China. It is known mainly as a house plant but in summer it can also be put outdoors. While the large, leathery leaves are impressive, the flowers that develop at the base in spring are very inconspicuous. Aspidistra requires very little care and attention. It also thrives in shade but does not tolerate strong sun. It can tolerate draughts and fluctuations in temperature. In summer, it should always be kept moist and be given weekly applications of fertilizer. In winter it should be placed in a bright location in a temperature of about 50° F and kept drier. If repotted in spring, the rhizomes can be divided and each repotted with two or three leaves attached. Watch out for spider mites and thrips.

ⓘ

Location: 💧 ☼ – ☼
Care: ❄
Propagation: ⚘✿
Characteristics: ∞ 🍃
Pests: spider mites, thrips, scale
insects, woolly aphids
Flowering: spring

Opposite page: Aucuba japonica

Aucuba

Aucuba japonica

ⓘ

Location: ◊ ☼ — ☀
Care: ❄
Propagation:
Characteristics: △ ✖ ∞ ❦
Diseases: leaf drop
Pests: scale insects, spider mites
Flowering: spring

The aucuba, an evergreen shrub and a member of the *Cornaceae* family, reaches a height of 16 ft in its native country of China. The very striking leaves may be yellow or green-flecked depending on the variety. Aucubas are dioecious, meaning that the male and female flowers grow on separate plants. If pollination takes place, red, slightly poisonous fruits develop. It is a very robust plant that prefers a shady location. However, forms with variegated foliage will turn green in permanent shade. Because of the leathery leaves the plant transpires less but it still needs regular watering in summer. It also needs good drainage and weekly doses of fertilizer. It can remain outdoors during winter if placed in a sheltered position. However, it is safer to put it in a light, frost-proof place at a temperature of about 41–50° F. If it is too warm and the air too dry the leaves will drop. Cuttings can be taken in spring or summer. Watch out for scale insects and spider mites.

Berberis

Berberis thunbergii

ⓘ

Location: ◊ ☼ — ☀
Propagation: ✄
Characteristics: ✖ ∞ ❁ ❄
  with container protection
Diseases: mildew
Pests: aphids
Flowering: spring

This evergreen *Berberis* species, a member of the *Berberidaceae* family, originates from China and Japan. Tall varieties of this frost-resistant, densely branched shrub are often used as hedges. The lower-growing varieties are ideal for cultivating in containers while dwarf forms are perfectly suited for growing underneath. Berberis has reddish brown, black-red or green leaves; the latter usually turning red in autumn. The yellow flowers appear in spring and later develop into coral-red berries that are poisonous. *B. thunbergii* thrives in sunny and partially shaded places and prefers slightly acid, well-drained soil. When grown in a container it must be watered regularly and fertilized about every two weeks. It does not mind being cut back at all although it is best to remove dead wood in spring. It can be pruned very vigorously to rejuvenate it. It is propagated from half-ripe cuttings that root very easily in summer or by division in the case of bushy species.

Bamboos — a touch of the exotic

Few plants create such an exotic atmosphere in gardens or balconies as bamboos. There are numerous genera and species that all belong to the Poaceae family. Bambusa, Thamnocalamus and Fergesia have short rhizomes and grow into dense bushes while Phyllostachys form runners. The plants all have the same structure: they have an underground rhizome, stems and leaves. The stems are mostly green but they can also be yellow, brown or black, and single-coloured, flecked or patterned. Depending on the species, they grow upright or arching. The young decorative stems stand out beautifully if the older stems are cut away regularly. The panicles of flowers are very similar to those of grasses. An interesting feature of bamboos is that they flower at very long intervals, sometimes only after 100 years. Because the formation of flowers uses up such a lot of the plant's energy, most of them die afterwards. The only thing you can do if this happens is to buy a new plant.

Most species prefer partial to full shade where they are also protected from the wind. Only Phyllostachys will thrive in the sun. All species need regular watering. Waterlogging leads to root rot but lack of water will cause the leaves to curl up. Bamboos benefit from weekly applications of fertilizer between spring and late summer.

The plants are best divided when new shoots appear, or you can cut and plant a piece of rhizome with at least one stem. Most species can be left outside during winter if the container is sufficiently protected. It is probably safer for bamboos to over-winter in a frost-free but very bright place.

Opposite page: Bougainvillea glabra

Bougainvillea

Bougainvillea glabra

This magnificent plant with its striking flowers was discovered by sailors who brought it back from South America and introduced it to the Mediterranean. A member of the *Nyctaginaceaea* family, this climbing plant easily reaches a height of 33 ft. When grown as a container plant it can be trained as a bushy shrub, a standard or against a trellis. The colorful bracts that envelop the small white flowers come in various colors. The plant must be watered regularly during the flowering period. If left dry, the leaves will drop, but waterlogging is equally damaging. It must be fertilized every week until the beginning of autumn. By cutting back the long shoots in summer, the development of numerous side-shoots with new buds is encouraged. During the winter it should be placed in a light room at a temperature of 50–59° F or in a dark place at a temperature of 41–50° F. It will then drop all its leaves and must be kept dry during this period. Soft tip cuttings and half-ripe cuttings can be taken all year round.

Angel's trumpet

Brugmansia

All the plants in the *Solanaceae* family are native to South America where they grow as shrubs or small trees. Their large, trumpet-shaped flowers that are particularly fragrant in the evening flower well into the autumn. They thrive in a sunny to partially shaded location and must be protected from the wind and the strong midday sun. On hot summer days they must watered morning and evening because the soil must never be allowed to dry out. Soft tip cuttings and half-ripecuttings can be taken almost all year round, ideally out of the flowering season. It can be pruned in spring and larger specimens may be reduced before being taken in for over-wintering. In winter it should be placed in a light room with a temperature of 50–59° F or in dark place at 41–50° F. It is best repotted every year in a larger container. All parts contain poisonous alkaloids that are still used as a drug by the Indians today. They are prone to attacks by lygus bugs.

ⓘ

Location: 💧 ☀ ⚠
Care: ❄ 🌡
Propagation:
Characteristics: ∞ ✿
Diseases: leaf drop
Pests: spider mites, white fly, aphids
Flowering: spring – autumn

Brugmansia

ⓘ

Location: 💧 ☀ ⚠
Care: ❄ 🌡
Propagation:
Characteristics: ⚠ ✖ ∞ ✿
Diseases: virus diseases
Pests: leaf bugs, weevils, suckers
Flowering: summer – autumn

Box

Buxus sempervirens

ℹ

Location: ◌ ☼ – ☀
Propagation:
Characteristics: ✖ ∞ ▓ ❄
  with container protection
Diseases: fungus rust
Pests: boxwood aphid, gall
  midges
Flowering: spring

Box is an evergreen plant and a member of the *Buxaceae* family that grows all round the Mediterranean even as trees. It is normally grown as a hedge, low edging plant or topiary. In addition, this dense, evergreen shrub is an excellent visual screen. The flowers that appear in spring are very inconspicuous. Box will grow both in the shade and in the sun but prefers well-drained, limey soil. Like all container plants it must be watered and fertilized regularly. Large specimens can be pruned into shapes which are then maintained by pruning every year in summer. Older plants are rejuvenated in spring. Soft wood cuttings or slightly woody cuttings can be taken between early summer and autumn. But be careful because they contain poisonous alkaloids. The container should be well insulated during the winter. If the air is too dry, the plant may be attacked by box suckers.

Buxus sempervirens

*B*ottlebrush

Callistemon citrinus

Callistemon citrinus (*Myrtaceae*), an evergreen shrub, is native to Australia. The shrub owes its common name to the striking flower spikes with long, red stamens that appear from spring until summer. The adjective *citrinus* is a reference to the lemony smell of the leaves when crushed. It grows best in a warm, sunny location, sheltered from the wind. In summer it must be watered regularly. If the root ball is allowed to dry out, the plant can die. However, waterlogging is equally damaging since it leads to the development of fungi in the soil. Water only with lime-free water and give the plant applications of an acidic rhodendron fertilizer every two weeks. Older specimens can be cut to the desired shape or pruned vigorously to rejuvenate them. The most successful method of propagation is cuttings taken in late summer or spring. They should over-winter in a cool, bright place at 41–50° F and the soil must not be allowed to dry out.

Location: 💧 ☼ ⚠
Care: ❄
Propagation:
Characteristics: △ ∞ ✿
Diseases: *putrefactive agents*
Pests: *spider mites, scale insects,*
   woolly aphids
Flowering: *spring – autumn*

Callistemon citrinus

Camellia japonica

ⓘ

Location: 💧 ☼ ⚠
Care: ❄
Propagation:
Characteristics: ∞ ❀ ❧
Diseases: stem and root rot,
   flower and bud rot
Pests: scale insects, thrips
Flowering: autumn – spring

Camellia

Camellia japonica

Camellia is a member of the *Theaceae* or tea family and it is native to Japan and Korea where it grows as an evergreen shrub or tree. The flowering period stretches from late autumn to spring. Besides the flowers, which may be single, semi-double or double and range in color from red, pink or white depending on the variety, camellias also have decorative, dark green shiny leaves. *C. japonica* prefers a bright to partially shaded, airy location but out of the strong midday sun. Water regularly with lime-free water and make sure the soil does not dry out or become waterlogged. Spray the plants now and again until the buds start developing. Camellias that are lime-sensitive need weekly applications of fertilizer, ideally an azalea fertilizer. Because the buds already begin to form in summer, they must be pruned immediately after flowering, cutting back to a bud or side branch. At the same you can also taken tip cuttings. In winter, they must placed in a bright, cool room 41-57° F ; over 59 degrees the buds will start to drop.

ⓘ

Location: 💧 ☼ ⚠
Care: ❄
Propagation: ✂❀
Characteristics: ⊔ ∞ ❀
Diseases: grey mould, rhizome
   rot
Pests: spider mites, aphids, slugs
   and snails
Flowering: summer – autumn

Canna

Canna indica

This plant is native to Central America. The long, decorative leaves and up to 5 ft tall flower stems develop from the creeping rhizomes of this marsh-plant. The flowers come in a large range of colors. They need a warm, sunny location, sheltered from the wind. In summer, they need large amounts of water and generous weekly applications of fertilizer. Dead blooms should be removed regularly. The rhizomes can easily be divided in late winter and spring, making sure that each piece has two or three eyes. Damaged parts can be protected from rotting by dusting with charcoal. In autumn, the dead leaves and dried stems are cut back to 4–8 in from the ground and the rhizomes are lifted and stored in a cool, dry place at 41–50° F. If it is too damp, the rhizomes will develop grey mould. Cannas are prone to attacks by spider mites, greenfly and snails.

Caryopteris

Caryopteris x clandonensis

Caryopetris is native to Japan and eastern China and a member of the *Verbenaceae* family. The bushy, deciduous shrub has deep green, fragrant leaves that are barely 0.5 in long. It has small, bright blue, tubular flowers grouped in dense clusters that appear between late summer and autumn. It is very popular with butterflies. Caryopteris need a sunny, warm location and well-drained soil, rich in humus. It thrives in hot, dry conditions, which is why it should be watered only moderately during the growing season. The container must be well protected before the first frosts to prevent the roots being damaged by frost. It is even safer to move the container to a frost-free place. The previous year's growth must be cut back in spring. The seeds collected in autumn are sown in spring. However, it is quicker to propagate plants from greenwood cuttings, taken between spring and summer.

Canna indica

Location: ◌ ☼ ⟁
Care: ✳
Propagation: ₒºº
Characteristics: ∞ ❄ *to -15 °C (5 ° F)*
Pests: leaf bugs
Flowering: early summer – autumn

Cassia

Cassia corymbosa (syn. Senna corymbosa)

Cassia corymbosa, previously classified in the *Leguminosae* family and now a member of the *Ceasalpiniaceae* family, is native to South America. This robust but tender plant can reach a height of 10 ft. Besides the attractive pinnate leaves, *C. corymbosa* has beautiful golden yellow flowers grouped in clusters that appear in spring and continue until autumn. It prefers a sunny, warm, airy location such as a roof terrace. In summer, it needs plenty of food and a lot of water. This means that the soil must never be allowed to dry out. It requires weekly applications of fertilizer and dead blooms should be removed regularly. Fresh seeds germinate very quickly and the best time for this is late winter or early spring. In winter, it should be placed in a sunny room at a temperature 50° F or in a cool, dark room. However, in the latter conditions, it will lose its leaves. Water sparingly in winter but do not allow the root ball to dry out. But excessive moisture can lead to fungal rot. Cut back the year's growth in spring.

Location: ◖ ☼
Care: ✳
Propagation: ₒºº
Characteristics: ∞ ❀ ❋
Diseases: rot
Pests: aphids, white fly
Flowering: spring – autumn

Candlebush

Cassia didymobotrya

ⓘ

Location: 💧 ☀
Care: 🌡
Propagation:
Characteristics: ∞ ❀ ❧
Diseases: rot fungus
Pests: aphids, white fly
Flowering: spring – autumn

Candlebush takes its name from its striking, erect clusters of flowers. While the open flowers are yellow, the buds at the top end of the clusters are still dark. They stand out beautifully against the background of the green, pinnate leaves that smell like peanut butter when touched. *Cassia didymobotrya* originates from tropical Africa where it grows to a small tree that can reach a height of 10 ft. All *cassias* can by grown as standards. They need a warm, sunny location and must be watered and fed generously during the growing season. The flowering season can be prolonged well into the winter if the dead blooms are removed regularly. This species does not produce seeds when cultivated and should therefore be propagated from cuttings. They must over-winter in a sunny room at a temperature that is no lower than 50° F. Do not allow to become waterlogged and look out for aphids. Cut back the year's growth in spring.

Cassia didymobotrya

Red cestrum

Cestrum elegans

A member of the *Solanaceae* family, red cestrum is native to Mexico and was first introduced into cultivation at the beginning of the 20th century. The reddish-purple flowers appear throughout the summer at the end of the slender purple-coloured branches, followed by round, dark-red berries. It makes a bushy shrub with a height of up to 10 ft. Although cestrums tolerate full sun, they are best planted in partial shade because of their great need of water during the summer. Feed weekly from spring to late summer and every two to three weeks during winter. Dead blooms should be removed regularly. Place in a light room at a temperature of 50–59° F or in a dark place at a temperature of 41–50° F. In this case the plant will lose its leaves. Dampness will lead to grey mould. Rejuvenate the plant by cutting back older shoots down to the base before over-wintering. It is easily propagated from tip cuttings or semi-ripe cuttings taken in spring. The plant is poisonous.

Cestrum elegans

Location: 💧 ☼ – ☀ ⚠
Care: ❄ 🏠
Propagation:
Characteristics: ✖ ∞ ❀
Diseases: *grey mould, herb rot*
Pests: *aphids, white fly*
Flowering: *summer – autumn*

Lawson cypress

Chamaecyparis lawsoniana

Lawson cypress, a member of the *Cupressaceae* family, is native to the Pacific coastal regions of North America. In the wild, Lawson cypresses can reach 65–165 ft in height but garden varieties remain considerably smaller. They are usually columnar and conical but rarely round. They are ideal as a visual screen because of their overlapping leaves, borne on flattened branches and arranged in sprays. The foliage ranges in color from green to blue, grey and golden. They prefer a sunny to partially shaded location. Apart from this, the conifer is very undemanding and it can also be cut back as required. But remember that they need watering regularly when grown in a container, as well as a regular application of conifer fertilizer. They can be left outdoors in winter if the container is suitably protected. It is propagated from cuttings from this year's growth taken in late summer and autumn. It can also be grown from seed collected from the fir-cones in autumn. The leaves can cause allergies.

Chamaecyparis lawsoniana "White Spot"

Location: 💧 ☼ – ☀
Propagation: ⸲°
Characteristics: ✖ ∞ ❀ ❄
Diseases: *die-back*
Pests: *conifer red spider mite, leaf miners, aphids, scale insects*

Chamaecyparis "Sungold"

Location: ♦ ☼ — ☼
Propagation: .°°
Characteristics: ∞ 🦋 ❄
Diseases: die-back
Pests: conifer red spider mites, leaf
   miners, aphids, scale insects

Chamaerops humilis

Location: ◊ ☼
Care: ❄ 🗔
Propagation: .°° 🐛
Characteristics: △ ∞ 🦋
Diseases: putrefactive agent
Pests: spider mites, mealy bugs

Sawara cypress

Chamaecyparis

Sawara cypress is native to Japan where it can reach a height of 165 ft. It is a slender conical tree but the garden varieties vary enormously in habit, height and colouring. For instance, there is the semi-spherical variety "Filifera Nana," and "Filifera Sungold" and "Plumosa Aurea" that have golden-yellow foliage. They will thrive in a sunny or partially shaded location and require very little care. They can also be pruned if necessary. Dwarf varieties grow very slowly, which make them ideally suited for growing in containers. But remember that plants grown in containers require plenty of water and regular applications of fertilizer. In winter they can remain outdoors but the roots should be well protected. They can be propagated from cuttings of the current year's wood taken between late summer and autumn. They can also be grown from seeds, collected from the cones in autumn. Varieties are usually grafted.

European fan palm

Chamaerops humilis

European fan palms are native to the Mediterranean. They may form one or more trunks and usually do not reach more 6 ft 6 in in height when grown in containers. If well looked after, they may flower after a few years but they will not develop fruit. They need a very sunny, airy location. This otherwise undemanding palm tolerates hot, dry conditions and even a little frost. They should only be watered moderately even in summer but not inside the leaves because this could lead to rot, as may excessive watering. Feed sparingly even during the growing season. In winter they should be put in a cool, dark place at a temperature of 32–41° F and accustomed very gradually to light in spring. If allowed to over-winter in the house, they should be watered occasionally. They are grown from seed. Suckers may be removed in spring. They are usually not troubled by pests but the prickly stalks can be quite dangerous.

Mexican orange blossom

Choisya ternata

This evergreen shrub, native to Mexico, bears a profusion of sweetly scented white flowers whose fragrance is reminiscent of oranges. The flowers are borne in clusters and first appear in late winter and continue until early summer. The leathery leaves are also highly aromatic. Mexican orange blossom will grow up to 5 ft high and does best in partial shade. In summer it requires a lot of water, which should be very low in lime. The plant needs weekly applications of fertilizer until the beginning of the autumn to ensure that the leaves will be very dark green. If kept drier after the first flowering in summer, they will flower a second time in autumn. Cuttings can be taken all year round although summer cuttings root most easily. In winter, it is best placed in a bright, not too light room 41° F to a maximum of 59° F. If the room is too dark, it will lose its leaves. Old branches that have grown too long can be cut back but otherwise pruning is not necessary. It is usually pest-free.

Rock rose

Cistus

Rock roses are evergreen shrubs native to the Mediterranean that can grow up to 5 ft high in the wild. The flowers are borne in cymes at the end of the branches and appear in early summer. *C. ladanifer* has white flowers and *C. x purpureus* pink flowers while those of *C. laurifolius* are also fragrant. They prefer a sunny, warm location. In summer they need plenty of water but do not tolerate being waterlogged. Plants should be given weekly applications of fertilizer until the end of the summer. Large specimens can be cut back after flowering but otherwise they do not need any pruning. Seedlings will develop into bushy shrubs in only a few years. *Cistus* can also be propagated from cuttings taken in summer. In regions where winters are mild they can remain outdoors in winter. Otherwise they should over-winter in frost-free conditions at a temperature of 41–50° F. Good ventilation is paramount to prevent grey mould. Greenfly and white fly may be a problem.

Location: 💧 ☀
Care: ❄ 🗼
Propagation:
Characteristics: △ ∞ ❁ 🍃
Pests: *spider mites, aphids, slugs and snails*
Flowering: *spring, autumn*

Cistus

Location: 💧 ☀ △
Care: ❄
Propagation: ∘°°
Characteristics: △ ∞ ❁
Diseases: *grey mould (in winter)*
Pests: *aphids, white fly*
Flowering: *summer*

Caring for citrus plants

The dream of re-creating a "little piece of the Mediterranean" back home can come true on your balcony or terrace. Citrus trees are native to Asia and Australia, where they grow as evergreen shrubs or trees. They delight almost all year round with their deliciously scented flowers and fruit that are frequently borne at the same time. The leaves, flowers and fruit of citrus plants all contain a strongly aromatic oil that is responsible for their intense fragrance.

In summer citrus plants need plenty of water, which however must be able to drain off freely because waterlogging will lead to root rot. The soil must be allowed to dry out before watering again. It is important to use soft water, for instance rainwater, which will not increase the acidity (pH level) of the soil. Special citrus fertilizer is also recommended.

The best over-wintering conditions are a light room and a temperature of about 50° F. Lime trees prefer warmer conditions, 58–64° F. Citrus plants flower less prolifically immediately after pruning. However, older or untidy specimens may be pruned by removing shoots that have finished flowering. You can either cut off the entire branch or up to a side shoot.

Citrus plants are usually propagated by grafting. Seedlings rarely come true to type and usually only flower after ten years at the earliest. Cuttings usually do not grow as bushy as grafted specimens but it is always worth trying them.

Remember when planting a citrus tree that they do not like being repotted. It is therefore advisable to choose a container that is slightly too large.

Opposite page: Citrus hybrid

Citrus limon

ⓘ

Location: ◌ ☼ ⚠
Care: 🔼
Propagation:
Characteristics: ⚠ ✖ ∞ ✿
Diseases: grey mould
Pests: aphids, woolly aphids,
scale insects, spider mites
Flowering: spring – winter

ⓘ

Location: ◌ ☼ ⚠
Care: 🔼
Propagation:
Characteristics: ⚠ ✖ ∞ ✿
Diseases: grey mould
Pests: aphids, woolly aphids,
scale insects, spider mites
Flowering: spring – winter

Lemon

Citrus limon

Citrus limon or lemons are originally native to India but are now cultivated on a large scale all round the Mediterranean. They belong to the same family as the sweet orange and are as much appreciated for their evergreen foliage as for their fruit. The leaves are aromatic and the flowers very fragrant but the ethereal oils they contain can cause skin irritation. Citrus plants need a warm, sunny place. Lemons need the same care as sweet oranges. They also need weekly applications of special citrus fertilizer. Yellowing leaves are the sign of being waterlogged causing root rot, or of lack of air, especially when it is much colder during the night than during the day. A tip: if the tree does not flower, keep it dry for about a week. This will prompt it to flower. Lemons are prone to scale insect and mealy bug infestation.

Sweet orange

Citrus sinensis

Like all subtropical citrus plants, sweet oranges belong to the *Rutaceae* family. They may flower all year round although their main flowering season is in spring. Both the white flowers and foliage are highly aromatic. These evergreen plants need a sunny, warm location. Only use lime-free water and only when the soil has dried out. Do not repot too frequently but instead work organic fertilizer into the top soil. Give weekly applications of special citrus fertilizer until the end of the summer and monthly applications of iron-based fertilizer. In winter the plant should be placed in a bright, airy room at a temperature of 50–59° F and watered only sparingly. Before taking the plant out, trim it to shape and remove all dead wood. It can be propagated in summer through grafting using the same methods as for roses. Propagation from cuttings is not as successful. Sweet orange is prone to scale insect and mealy bug infestation.

*J*apanese cleyera

Cleyera japonica

Location: 💧 ☀
Care: 🏠
Propagation:
Characteristics: ∞ ❀ 🍃
Pests: *woolly aphids, scale*
insects, spider mites
Flowering: *summer*

Cleyera, a member of the *Theaceae* or tea-plant family, is native to Japan and China. The evergreen, summer flowering shrub grows very slowly and when grown in a container will reach 5 ft in height. The "Tricolor" variety with its dark-green leaves almost 4 in long edged with yellow to creamy-white is a very decorative foliage plant. The fragrant yellowish-white flowers appear in summer. Cleyeras thrive in partial shade but do not like full sun. The soil must be kept moist at all times and it is best to use soft water. The shrub will benefit from weekly applications of fertilizer until the beginning of autumn. In winter they should be moved to a light position with a temperature of about 50° F. Low air humidity will encourage the plant to produce new growth in spring. It can be propagated from semi-ripe cuttings taken in spring. Young plants should be pruned regularly, after which pruning is no longer necessary. Watch out for woolly aphids and scale insects.

*C*abbage palm

Cordyline australis

Location: 💧 ☀ — ☀
Care: ❄
Propagation: ⦁°°
Characteristics: ∞ 🍃
Pests: *spider mites, scale insects*
Flowering: *summer*

These palm-like trees that form one or more trunks grow up to 40 ft tall in their native habitat of New Zealand. The large, lanceolate or sword-like leaves are grouped in a bunch at the end of the branches. The leaves may be green with yellow stripes, reddish or purple depending on the variety. The numerous white, sweet-scented flowers are borne in striking plumes that can be up to 39 in long. Large container plants can easily be kept to the desired height by pruning. The resulting heads of leaves and pieces of trunk can be used as cuttings for propagation. It can also be grown from seed but this takes longer. Cabbage palm prefers a sunny location but will also grow in partial shade. It is important that the soil is kept consistently moist. If the soil is dry for too long the leaf ends will turn brown and if waterlogged, the roots will rot. During the growing season plants should be given weekly applications of fertilizer. Ideally, they should over-winter in a light room at a temperature of 41–50° F but a light basement or cellar will also do.

Cordyline

Red-barked dogwood

Cornus alba

This deciduous dogwood, a member of the *Cornaceae* family, grows in the wild from Easter Europe as far as North Korea. In the wild, this erect plant has a very spreading habit. The yellowish to creamy-white flowers appear in spring, followed by whitish fruit. The varieties "Argenteomarginata" which has green leaves with white edges and "Spaethii" with green leaves and yellow edges are particularly attractive varieties. *C. alba* "Sibirica" has brilliant coral-pink stems. These undemanding, frost-resistant shrubs will grow in a sunny or partially shaded location. In summer the soil should be kept consistently moist and well-drained. They can be pruned at the end of the winter so that they do not grow too big. The color of the bark of new stems is particularly intense. Tip: cut back only part of the stems so that the plant still flowers. *Cornus* is propagated by soft wood cuttings taken in summer or hardwood cuttings in autumn.

Location: ○ ☼ — ☀
Propagation:
Characteristics: ∞ 🌱 ❄
Flowering: spring

Corokia

ⓘ

Location: ○ ☀ − ☀
Care: ❋
Propagation:
Characteristics: △ ∞ ❀
*Pests: scale insects, woolly
   aphids*
Flowering: spring

Wire netting bush

Corokia cotoneaster

Wire netting bush acquired its name from its intertwining, zig-zagging branches. It grows relatively slowly and will barely reach 6 ft 6 in when grown in a container. Formerly classed as a *saxifrage*, it is now part of the *Escalloniaceae* family. The fragrant, yellow, star-shaped flowers that are borne in spring stand out beautifully against the background of the round, dark green leaves. The flowers later develop into round, orange-red fruits. This vigorous shrub will grow in the shade although it prefers partial shade. It should be watered moderately and regularly but it must never become waterlogged. It must be fed every week from spring till autumn. It is easily propagated from greenwood cuttings taken in spring. In winter, the plants should be moved to a light place with a temperature of 41–50° F. Young plants should be pruned several times, while older specimens need only be thinned out.

Smoke bush

Cotinus coggyria

ⓘ

Location: ○ ☀
Propagation: ₒₒ°
Characteristics: △ ∞ ❀ ❉ ❋
*Diseases: mildew, verticillium
   wilt*
Flowering: spring

This deciduous shrub is a member of the *Anarcardiaceae* family and it is native to Southern Europe and Asia. It has a spreading habit and can grow up to 10 ft high. The green leaves of this species turn brilliant orange to deep red in autumn. The leaves of the variety "Royal Purple" are black-red all year round. The yellowish flowers that appear in spring are borne on 8 in long panicles, followed in late summer by striking, multiple fruits covered with downy hairs. These frost-resistant plants will tolerate not only hot, dry conditions but also strong sun. They look best in a place where they are sheltered from the rain. They thrive in moderately fertile, well-drained soil. Dead shoots should be removed. Semi-ripe cuttings taken in spring and dusted with rooting powder root very easily. Plants can also be raised from ripe seeds, which germinate quickly. Varieties with red leaves are prone to mildew.

Cotoneaster

Cotoneaster

Cotoneasters belong to the *Rosaceae* family and are native to China. Evergreen or deciduous, they range from prostrate mat-forming or cushion types to large, erect bushes and are therefore suitable as groundcover or standing on their own. *C. dammeri* "Coral Beauty" is usually grown as a standard. Cotoneasters are very popular for their red but poisonous berries. which remain on the tree for a long time. *C. franchetti* grows up to 6 ft 6 in high and has beautiful, white to pink flowers, followed by attractive oval berries in autumn. All tolerate dry conditions and will grow in both sun and partial shade. In summer they will benefit from regular watering and applications of fertilizer every four weeks. Most species and varieties are frost-resistant but *C. franchetti* is a little more sensitive. It is recommended to protect the roots in the winter months. Bushes can be trimmed to the desired shape in late winter and will even tolerate vigorous pruning. They are propagated from cuttings taken from spring to late summer. Varieties are usually grafted.

Cotoneaster

Location: ⬡ ☼—☀
Propagation:
Characteristics: ✖ ∞ ✲
Diseases: fire blight
Pests: aphids, woolly aphids,
    spider mites, tortrix
    caterpillars
Flowering: spring

Monterey cypress

Cupressus macrocarpa

A member of the *Cupressaceae* family, this cypress is native to California, hence its common name. It is fast growing and cone-shaped when young but develops a broad crown as it gets older. The golden yellow needle foliage becomes darker with age. "Goldcrest" is one of the most famous varieties. The Italian cypress *C. sempervivens* is a very popular container plant. Cypresses grow best in a bright, sunny location. They must be watered regularly and given weekly applications of fertilizer. If the tree is subjected to a period of prolonged drought, the foliage will turn brown. Cypresses do not mind being pruned but container-grown specimens usually do not need pruning to keep their shape. Although they will tolerate a light frost, it is recommended to keep them in a bright, well-ventilated, frost-free place 32° F. They can be grown from fresh seeds or propagated from cuttings taken in spring or autumn. Cypresses are prone to coryneum canker, which can cause the whole tree to die.

Location: ⬡ ☀
Care: ✽
Propagation: ⸱°°
Characteristics: ∞ ❦
Diseases: canker

Cycas revoluta

ⓘ

Location: ◊ ☼
Care: 🏠
Propagation: ⋰°
Characteristics: △ ✖ ∞ 🥀
*Pests: scale insects, woolly
    aphids, spider mites*

ⓘ

Location: ◊ ☼
Propagation:
Characteristics: ✖ ∞ ❀ ❄
Diseases: leaf spot, mildew
*Pests: spider mites, aphids, gall
    mites*
Flowering: spring

Sago palm

Cycas revoluta

Cycas revoluta is a member of the *Cycadaceae* family. Although it is usually associated with the Mediterranean, it is native to Japan and south-east Asia. The short, thick trunk can reach 10 ft in height. The large pinnate leaves consist of many small leathery leaflets and they form a crown of palm-like fronds. It needs space and prefers partial shade. The soil should always be slightly moist especially during the growing season. Nevertheless, it prefers dry conditions to excessive moisture. It also benefits from small, weekly applications of fertilizer. In winter, it should be kept in a bright room at a temperature of 50–59° F. It is particularly sensitive to light in spring when it is first taken outdoors. It is grown from seed in spring at a temperature of 86° F, but it rarely produces seeds when cultivated. It is prone to attacks by scale insects and spider mites. All parts of the plant are very poisonous.

Broom

Cytisus decumbens

A member of the *Fabaceae* family, this genus includes tender Mediterranean species but also many others that are native to Europe and the Balkans and are therefore hardy. Dwarf species like *C. decumbens* are ideal for growing in containers. They are densely branched and grow no higher than 20 in. The bright yellow flowers that appear in late spring and continue until early summer, standing out beautifully against the green foliage. *C. decumbens* thrives in a sunny, warm location. During the growing season, it needs plenty of water and food. The soil should be well-drained. It will tolerate dry conditions but not being waterlogged. In winter, the container should well protected against frost. *Cytisus* is propagated from semi-ripe cuttings taken in summer when pruning after the plant has finished flowering. All parts of the plant are poisonous.

Broom or Genista

Cytisus x racemosus

This broom is native to the Mediterranean and a member of the *Papilionaceous* family. *C. x racemosus* is a densely branched, evergreen shrub that can grow up to 6 ft 6 in high in a container. The clusters of bright yellow flowers appear early in spring and are deliciously fragrant. They are followed by the characteristic legumi-nous pods. *C. canarensis*, *C. maderensis* and *C. monspessulanus* are popular container-grown species. They need plenty of light and regular watering in summer. Excessively dry conditions will lead to leaf drop while being waterlogged will lead to root rot. In addition the plant needs weekly applications of fertilizer. In winter, it must be placed in a bright room at a temperature of 41–50° F. In order to encourage growth, pruning the plant vigorously after flowering is recommended. Plants are easily propagated from green cuttings taken from the soft tip of a stem in early summer. Watch out for aphids and spider mites.

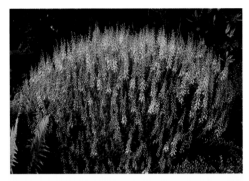

Cytisus x racemosus

Location: ◌ ☼
Care: ❄
Propagation:
Characteristics: ∞ ❀
Pests: aphids, spider mites, gall mites
Flowering: spring

Dracaena palm

Dracaena draco

The dracaena palm (*Dracaenaceae*), previously included in the agave-family, is native to the Canary Islands and Madagascar, where it grows as a densely-branched tree, 66 ft high. It has a decorative, sturdy trunk and an attractive head of long, grey-green, lanceolate leaves. The whitish flowers that appear in summer are borne in dense clusters. Container-grown plants grow more slowly and take a while before reaching an impressive height. These succulents thrive in a sunny, warm location. They do need regular watering in summer but they hate being waterlogged, excessive moisture leading to root rot. During the growing season the plant needs weekly applications of fertilizer. In winter they must be placed in a bright room where the temperature does not go below 50° F. A plant that has grown too large can be cut back. New plants can be grown from seed in spring in a heated frame at a temperature of 68–77° F.

Location: ◌ ☼ ⚠
Care: 🕯 ❄
Propagation: ⋅°°
Characteristics: ∞ ❧
Diseases: root rot
Pests: spider mites
Flowering: spring, summer

Echium

Echium

Echium is a member of the *Boraginaceae* family and is native to the Canary Islands. The shrub can grow up to 6 ft 6 in high and has striking, compact spires of small red flowers. It is grown as a biennial, which means that it forms a rosette of leaves the year it is sown and flowers the following year. The plant dies after fruiting. But it produces a lot of seeds from which new plants can be grown. It needs a sunny location but should be slightly protected from the midday sun. In summer it needs plenty of water but only from the bottom and not in the leaf rosette, or the plant will rot. Do not forget to apply generous weekly applications of fertilizer. It should over-winter in frost-free conditions with a temperature of up to 50° F. If the temperature is not cool enough, the plant will not flower the following year. Water sparingly in winter.

ℹ

Location: 💧 ☼
Care: ❄
Propagation: ⚬°°
Characteristics: △ ∞ ❀
Diseases: root rot, grey mould
Pests: slugs and snails, spider mites, white fly
Flowering: summer

Tree heath

Erica arborea

Tree heath, a member of the evergreen *Ericaceae* family, is native to southern Europe and east Africa where it can grow to fairly tall tree. The fragrant grey-white flowers, borne in dense terminal clusters, appear in spring. Because of its small, needle-like leaves, the plant does not transpire much, which means that it does not mind prolonged periods of drought. They prefer a sunny location but need plenty of lime-free water during the growing and flowering season; however they must not be waterlogged. Although tree heath is more tolerant of lime than other species, it should be planted in peaty soil. It will tolerate slight frost but it is best to over-winter it in a light, well-ventilated room at a temperature of 41–50° F. It needs regular watering even during the winter. It can be propagated from semi-ripe cuttings taken from non-flowering shoots in mid-spring. Older specimens can be cut back if necessary.

ℹ

Location: 💧 ☼
Care: ❄
Propagation:
Characteristics: ∞ ❀
Diseases: heather die-back, grey mould, mildew
Pests: scale insects
Flowering: spring

Cockspur coral tree

Erythrina crista-galli

This undemanding shrub is native to South America, where it grows as a shrub or small tree. The striking scarlet-red flowers that are borne in summer in long terminal spikes on the arching branches stand out beautifully against the background of the large, blue-green leaves. The plant thrives in a sunny, warm location, preferably south-facing. In summer, it needs plenty of water. Although it needs well-drained potting soil, the root ball must never be allowed to dry out. In addition, the plant requires weekly applications of fertilizer until late summer. Dead blooms and dead wood should be removed in autumn or winter. In winter the plant drops its leaves and can therefore over-winter in the dark at a temperature that should not exceed 50° F. Older specimens can be kept completely dry until spring during this rest period while younger plants should be watered occasinally. Semi-ripe cuttings grow more quickly than seedlings. The plant contains poisonous alkaloids.

Location: 💧 ☼ ⚠
Care: ❄
Propagation: ⚬°°
Characteristics: ✖ ∞ ❀
Pests: spider mites, woolly aphids
Flowering: summer

Erythrina crista-galli

Eucalyptus

Location: 🌢 ☼
Propagation: ∴
Characteristics: ∞ 🐾 ❄
Diseases: grey mould
Pests: aphids
Flowering: summer, winter

Eucalyptus or Gum

Eucalyptus

The evergreen gum tree species are native to Tasmania and Australia, where they can be found almost everywhere from the wet coastal regions to the dry desert areas. Their size ranges from small shrubs to gigantic trees. *E. gunnii* is an extremely popular species because it tolerates temperatures as low as 5° F. It is a fast-growing tree that can be cut back to keep the size down. The blue-green juvenile leaves are striking but the yellowish-white flowers that appear in winter are rather inconspicuous. Eucalyptus trees love a warm, sunny location. If grown in containers, they must be watered regularly and generously. If left to dry out, they will probably not recover. Use lime-free water and lime-free soil, and feed sparingly. In milder regions, eucalutpus plants can be left outdoors; otherwise they need a light, well-ventilated place with a temperature of 41–59° F. Seeds sown in spring germinate very quickly.

Pineapple flower

Eucomis bicolor

Location: ◊ ☼
Care: ❋
Propagation: ∴ ✂❀
Characteristics: △ ∞ ❀
Pests: slugs and snails, spider mites
Flowering: summer

Pineapple flowers belong to the *Hyacinthanceae* family and are native to South Africa. The 12 in long leaves are oblong with a wavy margin. The greenish-yellow flowers with purple edges are borne on tall spikes of about 24 in, crowned by a cluster of green, leaf-like bracts. The pineapple flower needs a sunny, warm location. As soon as the leaves begin to develop, increase the watering and apply small, weekly doses of fertilizer. Reduce the watering outside the growing-season. In winter, store the container or just the bulbs in a dark place at a temperature of 41–50° F. Propagate by dividing the clumps in spring. Growing from seed requires more patience. Snails and slugs may be a problem.

Spindle or Burning bush

Euonymus alatus

The burning bush or winged spindle, a deciduous tree and member of the *Celestraceae* family, is native to east Asia. It is a densely-branched, spreading shrub growing up to 10 ft high and wide. The greenish-yellow flowers that appear in spring are quite inconspicuous but the green leaves turn a fiery red in autumn. The spindle tree "Red Cascade" (*E. europaeus*) is very popular because of its autumn colors and red fruit. *Euonymus* grows is sun or partial shade. It is very undemanding but needs regular watering in summer like all container-grown plants as well as an application of fertilizer every 14 days. The soil should be slightly acid. Unwanted shoots can be removed and larger specimens can be trimmed to the required shape. Green cuttings taken in spring, dusted with rooting powder, will root very easily. Varieties of *E. fortunei* are grown as standards and are also propagated by grafting. The containers should be protected from frost.

Japanese spindle

Euonymus japonicus

This evergreen shrub belonging to the spindle family (*Celastraceae*) is native to Japan and Korea, where it can reach a height of 26 ft. The greenish flowers that appear in spring are followed by striking pink fruits containing orange seeds. The glossy leathery leaves are dark green and marked with white or yellow depending on the variety. Japanese spindles prefer partial or full shade although the variegated forms needs more light. In summer the plant should be watered moderately and in winter more sparingly. However, if the root ball dries out, the leaves will drop. Feed sparingly. Although *E. japonicus* will tolerate short periods of slight frost, it is best to keep it in a light, frost-free place where the temperature does not exceed 50° F. Larger specimens can be cut back as required. It can be propagated from semi-ripe cuttings, which can be taken throughout the year. Watch out for spider mites and scale insects in summer and mildew and root rot in winter.

ℹ

Location: ◊ ☀
Propagation:
Characteristics: ∞ 🍃 ❄
Diseases: mildew
Pests: aphids, spider mites,
   tortrix caterpillars
Flowering: spring

Euonymus japonicus "Elegantissima Aurea"

ℹ

Location: ◊ ☀– ☀
Care: ❋
Propagation:
Characteristics: ∞ 🍃
Diseases: mildew, root rot
Pests: spider mites, scale insects
Flowering: spring

Resin bush

Euryops

Location: 🌢 ☼ 🜨
Care: ❋ 🌡
Propagation:
Characteristics: ∞ ✿
Diseases: grey mould
Pests: sucking insects, leaf
  miners
Flowering: spring – summer

Euryops is a member of the aster family (*Asteraceae*) and native to South Africa, where it grows as a small evergreen shrub or semi-shrub. Unlike its relative, the Marguerite or Paris daisy (*Argyranthemum*), the yellow flower heads are produced from spring to late summer. To ensure a profusion of flowers it needs a warm, sunny location where it is protected from the wind. It needs plenty of water during the summer and on particularly hot days it may even need watering twice a day. During the flowering season, fertilizer should be applied once a week and dead blooms removed regularly. Large specimens can be cut back in spring and even in autumn if space is at a premium in the place where they are over-wintered. Move to a light, frost-free place with a temperature of 41–50° F, well-ventilated to avoid grey mould. Propagate from greenwood cuttings in spring. Watch out for aphids, white fly, spider mites and leaf miners.

Euryops

Exochorda

Exochorda x macrantha

The most famous variety of this deciduous shrub, a member of the *Rosaceae* family, is "The Bride." It is a spreading shrub with arching branches whose height and spread can exceed 6 ft 6 in. Its slow growth and prolific flowering even as a young plant make it a very popular container plant. The striking white flowers that are borne in spring in long clusters pale green leaves contrast beautifully against the background of pale green leaves. Exochorda thrives both in the sun and partial shade, preferring acid to neutral, well-drained soil. Water and feed regularly during the growing season. After flowering, cut back shoots that have finished flowering to a strong new shoot or bud. It can be propagated from softwood cuttings taken in spring and raised from seed in autumn. It is usually trouble free. Protect the container from frost in regions where winters are harsh.

ⓘ

Location: 🌢 ☼ — ☼
Propagation: ₀°°
Characteristics: ∞ ❀ ❄
Flowering: spring

Castor oil plant

Fatsia japonica

Fatsia (*Araliaceae*), an evergreen shrub, is native to Japan and Korea, where it grows up to 16 ft high. There are also slower growing varieties such as "Variegata," which are ideal as container plants. It has particularly attractive glossy, leathery, palmate leaves that can be up to 16 in long. The small, white flowers are borne in autumn in clusters, followed in older plants by round, black fruits. *Fatsias* do well in a shady position where they are sheltered from the wind. They need plenty of water but it is best to water them twice a day in summer rather than a larger amount once a day because too much water can lead to root rot. Although they will tolerate slight frost, in colder climates it is best to move them to a frost-free place where the temperature should be between 41–50° F. Large specimens can be cut back drastically if necessary. *Fatsias* can be raised from seed in late winter to mid-spring and varieties are propagated from cuttings taken in mid to late summer.

ⓘ

Location: 🌢 ☼ — ☼ ⟁
Care: ❆
Propagation: ₀°°
Characteristics: ∞ ❧
Diseases: root rot
Pests: spider mites, woolly
  aphids
Flowering: autumn

Ficus carica

ℹ

Location: 💧 ☀ ⚠
Care: ❄
Propagation:
Characteristics: ∞ 🐚 ❄
Diseases: verticillium wilt, grey
    mould
Pests: spider mites, aphids
Flowering: spring

*C*ommon fig

Ficus carica

The Mediterranean fig is a member of the *Moraceae* family. It is a very decorative plant with beautiful foliage consisting of large, deeply lobed leaves. In addition, it produces fruit and is very easy to look after. The flowers that appear in spring are rather inconspicuous. Originally, pollination was ensured by gall-wasps but nowadays most varieties are self-pollinating. A fig tree needs a sunny, warm location where it is sheltered from the wind. In summer it requires plenty of food and water but does not tolerate being waterlogged. In regions with a mild climate it can remain outdoors in winter if protected from cold winds. Indoors this deciduous plant can be over-wintered in a dark, cool place between 32–50° F. Young plants should be trimmed regularly but older specimens should only be cut back if necessary. *Ficus* is propagated from hardwood cuttings in late winter or from ripe greenwood cuttings in summer.

ℹ

Location: 💧 ☀– ☀ ⚠
Care: ❄
Propagation:
Characteristics: ⚠ ∞ ❀
Diseases: rust fungus, grey
    mould
Pests: white fly, spider mites,
    aphids
Flowering: summer

*F*uchsia

Fuchsia hybrids

Ladies' eardrops (*Onagraceae*) are native to South America where they grow as perennial semi-shrubs, shrubs or even small trees. The flowers of the garden varieties, which may be single or double, are borne in axillary clusters or panicles. Frequently, the four sepals are a different color from the four petals. Fuchsia triphylla hybrids differ from other hybrids in that the flowers are in clusters while *F. magellanica* with its crimson sepals and petals resembles the wild form and is considered hardy in regions with a mild climate. Fuchsias are ideal for brightening up shady places. It is important to water regularly because the root ball must never be allowed to dry out or become waterlogged. Apply fertilizer frequently but in small doses. Dead blooms and fruit should be removed regularly. In winter plants must be moved to a bright or dark place where the temperature will not exceed 50° F. Fuchsias are pruned in spring when softwood cuttings can be taken at the same time.

Gardenia or China flower

Gardenia augusta

The evergreen gardenia or opera flower (*Rubiaceae*), also known as *G. jasminoides*, is native to China and Japan, where it grows to a 5 ft shrub. It has decorative, glossy, dark green leaves and beautiful large, deliciously scented white flowers, often double, that appear in summer. These house plants need warmth but they can be moved outdoors in summer, where they should be placed in a bright location but not in direct sun. Gardenias need a lime-free proprietary soil, rich in peat. Water only with lime-free water, moderately in summer and in winter only just enough to prevent the root ball from drying out. Feed weekly with a special acid fertilizer. In winter, gardenias need a lot of light, a temperature of 50–59° F and high humidity. Cold conditions and waterlogging will cause root rot. Cuttings can be taken in summer or spring. Young plants should be pruned regularly, older plants only when necessary.

Gardenia jasminoides

ⓘ

Location: ◊ ☀ ⚠
Care: ⬍
Propagation:
Characteristics: △ ∞ ✾
Diseases: root rot
Pests: spider mites, scale insects
　　and woolly aphids
Flowering: summer

Broom

Genista maderensis

Broom is a member of the papilionaceous family (*Fabaceae*) family and *G. maderensis* has recently been classified in it. Often still referred to as *Cytisus maderensis*, the species is native to Madeira, where it grows to an evergreen shrub 23 ft high. It is covered with gold-yellow, fragrant flowers that are borne in terminal clusters from late spring to early summer. Brooms like plenty of light but not direct midday sun. In summer, they must be watered generously but especially very regularly. Excessively dry conditions will lead to leaf drop while waterlogging will cause root rot. In addition, brooms need weekly applications of fertilizer. In winter, they should be moved to a bright place where the temperature is between 41–50° F. To encourage growth brooms should be cut back vigorously after flowering. Softwood cuttings taken in summer root very easily. Watch out for aphids and spider mites.

ⓘ

Location: ◖ ☀
Care: ❄
Propagation:
Characteristics: ∞ ✾
Pests: aphids, spider mites
Flowering: spring

Dyer's greenweed

Genista tinctoria

ⓘ

Location: ◊ ☀
Propagation:
Characteristics: ✖ ∞ ❀ ❄
Pests: aphids
Flowering: summer

The deciduous Dyer's Greenweed is native to central Europe and western Asia. This small slow-growing prostrate to erect shrub is a member of the *Fabaceae* family and rarely grows higher than 32 in. It has glossy green leaves and bright yellow flowers that appear in early summer, followed by the typical brown pods. The dwarf form "Plena" has double flowers. *G. tinctoria* grows best in a sunny location and does not mind hot, dry conditions. It is therefore ideal for exposed places such as roof terraces. The soil must be well-drained and not too rich. The plant can be cut back by one-third after flowering in order to keep it in the right shape. At the same time softwood or greenwood cuttings can be taken, which will root very easily. The container must be well protected during winter. Note that all the parts of the plant are poisonous.

Ginkgo biloba

Ginkgo

Ginkgo biloba

ⓘ

Location: ◊ ☀ — ☀
Propagation: ₀°°
Characteristics: ∞ ❧ ❄ *with*
*   container protection*
Flowering: spring

Ginkgo biloba belongs to the *Ginkgoceae* family and is the only species of its genus. This deciduous tree is native to China, where it grows in the wild to a height of 100 ft. When young, the ginkgo is cone-shaped, slowly spreading as it gets older. The leaves are fan-shaped with parallel veins; they are pale green in spring, turning a beautiful golden yellow in autumn. The ginkgo is a robust tree that will grow in sun and partial shade. It is frost-resistant and tolerates urban pollution and wind. Unwanted shoots and branches can be cut back in late winter or spring. To ensure the production of seeds male and female trees are necessary. The female flowers develop into plum-like fruits. These can be harvested in mid-autumn when the flesh is removed and the seeds stored in a refrigerator for sowing in spring. Ginkgo can also be raised from softwood cuttings taken between spring and early summer.

Silky oak

Grevillea

Like all members of the *Proteaceae* family, silky oak is native to the southern hemisphere, where it grows as a shrub or tree. Because silky oaks usually do not flower in cultivation, species such as *G. banksii* and *G. robusta* are mostly grown as decorative foliage plants. However, older specimens of varieties such as *G. rosmarinifolia* have beautiful orange-red flowers. While *G. robusta* prefers partial shade, *G. rosmarinifolia* is happier in full sun. However, they are easily damaged by rain. The soil must never dry out completely or be waterlogged. It is important to use soft water when watering so that the plant does not suffer from iron deficiency. It should be given small, weekly applications of fertilizer. In winter it should be moved to a bright, well-ventilated place where the temperature is between 41–59° F. *G. robusta* can also over-winter in a dark place but in that case it will lose its leaves. Older plants can be cut back lightly or vigorously as required. It can be grown from seed almost all year round. It can also be propagated from summer cuttings but these root very slowly.

Kahli ginger

Hedychium gardnerianum

Most species of this genus of the *Zyngiberaceae* family are native to China and Indonesia. These rhizomatous perennials are used as a culinary condiment, as a component in dyes and fragrances as well as for medicinal purposes. Only *H. gardnerianum* is available as a container plant. It grows up to 6 ft 6 in high and the lanceolate leaves can be as long as 16 in. The golden-yellow, fragrant flowers are borne in late summer in terminal spikes. The stamens that protrude far out of the flowers are quite striking. This plant needa a warm, sunny location where it is protected from the rain and wind in order to flower. During the growing and flowering season it needs regular watering. It will tolerate short periods of drought but not being waterlogged. While growing it needs to be fed weekly. It does best in humus-rich soil enriched with compost. In winter it should be moved to a bright, dry place with a temperature of 50–59° F. It is propagated by division of the rhizomes.

Location: 💧 ☼ – ☼ *some vars.* ⚠
Care: ❄ 🗓
Propagation: ⚬°°
Characteristics: △ ∞ ❀ *some vars.* 🍃
Flowering: summer

Hedychium gardnerianum

Location: 💧 ☼ ⚠
Care: 🗓
Propagation: ⚘⚘
Characteristics: △ ∞ ❀
Pests: aphids, spider mites
Flowering: summer

Day lily

Hemerocallis hybrids

ⓘ

Location: 💧 ☼ – ☼ ⚠
Care: ⚠ ❋
Propagation: ✂❋
Characteristics: △ ∞ ❀
Diseases: rust fungus, stem and leaf rot
Pests: gall midges, slugs and snails, sucking insects
Flowering: summer

These evergreen or semi-evergreen plants are native to Japan, China and Korea. In contrast to the wild species, *Hemerocallis hybrids* are less spreading and are becoming increasingly popular as container plants. The strap-shaped, dark green leaves grow in dense clumps from the fleshy rhizomes. The large colorful flowers appear in summer. Day lilies grow well in the sun or partial shade. They need plenty of water in order to produce buds and a compound fertilizer every two to three weeks. They should be planted in fertile soil, rich in humus. They hate being waterlogged and are best left undisturbed. Larger specimens can be divided every two or three years, either after flowering or early spring. In winter, the container should be protected against frost. During periods of alternating frost and thaw, the plant is prone to stem and leaf rot.

Hibiscus

Hibiscus rosa-sinensis

ⓘ

Location: 💧 ☼ ⚠
Care: 🕯 ❋
Propagation:
Characteristics: △ ∞ ❀
Diseases: root rot
Pests: aphids, woolly aphids, spider mites, white fly
Flowering: spring – autumn

Hibiscuses are members of the *Malvaceae* family, native to tropical Asia. Even when grown in containers they can reach a height of 10 ft. The large single flowers come in many colors and are borne singly until autumn, standing out beautifully against the glossy dark green leaves. The plants thrive in a sunny, sheltered location and dislike being disturbed. In summer they need plenty of water – preferably soft water – and an application of a compound fertilizer at least once a week. If the soil dries out the flower buds will drop. In winter, these rather tender plants should be moved before the first frosts to a bright place where the temperature is between 50–59° F. If they are kept in a conservatory where the temperature fluctuates around 68° F, they will continue flowering for a little longer. It can be propagated from semi-ripe cuttings taken in spring and summer. Young plants should be pinched out regularly and older specimens can be thinned in spring or cut into the required shape. They are prone to aphids.

Hibiscus rosa-sinensis

Common hibiscus

Hibiscus syriacus

This deciduous hibiscus, a member of the *Malvaceae* family, is native to China and Japan. It is also very common in the Mediterranean. Even when grown in a container, this bushy, erect shrub can reach a height of 6 ft 6 in. The striking single, axillary flowers that come in a wide variety of colors appear in summer. Besides pink ("Woodbridge") and white ("Red Heart," white with a red center), there are also red and purple varieties. They will flower prolifically if placed in a sunny, sheltered position and watered and fed regularly. The soil should be well-drained and rich in nutrients. It is advisable to repot the plants every spring. When repotting, remove all the lateral shoots and cut back the main shoots by one third. In winter the plants should be moved to a sheltered location and the container protected against frost. Shoots damaged by frost can easily be removed. Softwood or heel cuttings taken in spring or summer root very easily.

Location: 💧 ☀ ⚠

Propagation:

Characteristics: ∞ ❄

Diseases: mildew

Pests: aphids, woolly aphids, spider mites, white fly

Flowering: summer

Kentia palm

Howea

This genus of palms belongs to the *Areaceae* family and is native to the islands of the South Pacific. The two species both have large pinnate leaves and are very popular container and house plants. In the wild they grow from a single stem but when cultivated they are trained to develop several stems. Besides *H. belmoreana*, *H. forsteriana* is the best known species. Unlike its relative, its stem is more robust and the large fronds do not arch. Both dislike full sun, preferring a partially shaded position. But above all they need warmth, young plants needing as much as 68° F all year round. They must be watered regularly, preferably with soft water to prevent the formation of brown leaf spot. In addition, they should be given weekly applications of fertilizer. In winter they should be moved to a bright place and a temperature of 50–59°F. *Howeas* can be grown from seed in spring but germination can take several months.

Hydrangea

Hydrangea macrophylla

These deciduous shrubs of the *Hydrangeaceae* family are native to east Asia where they grow up to 5 ft high. The flowers are borne in rounded, flat or conical heads depending on the variety. They all prefer partial shade without direct sun. Water exclusively with lime-free water. Hydrangeas need acid soil such as azalea or rhododendron compost to release the metal elements necessary to develop their famous blue color. Besides applications of fertilizer every 14 days, the blue varieties also need a monthly application of aluminium sulphate or they may revert to pink. Because the buds are very sensitive to frost, hydrangeas should be moved to a bright or dark place where the temperature is between 32–41° F. In winter the plants should be watered only sparingly. From February onward, the plants need more light again. Dead blooms should be cut back to next new shoot and older specimens can be pruned hard after flowering. They is propagated from semi-ripe cuttings in summer. The leaves can cause skin allergies.

Hydrangea macrophylla

Holly

Ilex

Holly, a member of the *Aquifoliaceae* family, grows in the tropics as well as in temperate regions. These mostly evergreen shrubs or small trees have very decorative leaves that can be uniformly green or variegated with white or yellow, with smooth or spiny margins. The small, white, delicately scented flowers are followed by red or black poisonous berries. The compact, slow-growing varieties *I. Crenata* and *I. x meservae* are ideally suited for growing in containers. They tolerate dry conditions and frost. Nevertheless, do not forget to water them. They thrive in sunny and partially shaded locations and in lime-free, well-drained soil, rich in humus. If necessary, the plants can be cut back in summer to maintain the desired shape. They can be propagated from semi-ripe cuttings in late summer and from ripe wood in autumn and winter. The root balls must be protected against frost.

Ilex

Location: ◊ ☀
Propagation:
Characteristics: ✖ ∞ ▩ ❄
Diseases: root rot
*Pests: leaf miners, aphids,
   scale insects*
Flowering: spring

Jasminum mesnyi

Location: 💧 ☀—☼
Care: ❋ ☒
Propagation:
Characteristics: ∞ ❀
Pests: aphids, woolly aphids
Flowering: summer

*J*asmine

Jasminum

The numerous jasmine species are members of the *Oleaceae* family and they can be found almost everywhere in the world. These deciduous and evergreen climbers all have intensely fragrant flowers that are white in the common white jasmine (*J. officinale*) and yellow in *J. mesnyi* and *J. odoratum*. *J. sambac* has a double, gardenia-like flowers. Jasmine prefers a warm, sunny location. In summer it must be watered generously and given applications of fertilizer once a week. Except for *J. sambac*, which even in winter needs a minimum temperature of 59° F, the other species should be overwintered in a well-ventilated cooler position of 41–50° F. They will even tolerate short periods of frost. In the case of larger shrubs, either cut back the flowering shoots after flowering or cut back vigorously to the desired shape. Plants can be propagated from softwood or semi ripe cuttings taken in spring or summer.

*C*reeping juniper

Juniperus horizontalis

Location: ◊ ☀—☼
Propagation:
Characteristics: ✖ ∞ ▩ ❄
Diseases: die-back
Pests: spider mites, leaf miners, aphids, scale insects

These evergreen plants with their characteristic mat-forming habit are native to North America. Many varieties such as "Bar Harbor" have bluish green foliage that turns reddish-purple in autumn. Some of them make a spread of some 6 ft 6 in but only grow 20 in high. The "Winter Blue" variety is less spreading than others. Slow-growing varieties of *J. sinensis,* such as "Old Gold" are also suitable for growing in containers. They also look good in combination with heathers, planted together in large containers. These frost-resi}stant shrubs prefer a sunny location and will even tolerate periods of drought. They will even grow in poor soil, which should be acid rather than limey. Feed occasionally with a special conifer fertilizer. Juniper can be propagated from semi-ripe cuttings taken in late summer. The leaves can cause skin allergies.

Blue star juniper

Juniperus squamata

This evergreen shrub grows in the wild in the mountainous regions of Afghanistan and China. They are either prostrate and sprawling or erect and bushy. Sometimes they even grow as small trees. The grey-green to silvery blue-green foliage is very decorative. Compact, slow-growing varieties such as the mound-forming "Blue Star" with silvery foliage or the mat-forming "Blue Carpet" with blue-green foliage are ideal for growing in containers. These undemanding, frost-resistant shrubs prefer a sunny location and will even tolerate prolonged periods of drought. They are therefore ideal plants for roof terraces. They need sandy soil, rich in humus, and will even tolerate a chalky soil. Feed every 4 weeks with a conifer fertilizer. They can be propagated from semi-ripe cuttings taken in late summer. Fungal infections can lead to die-back. Yellow and dead branches must be removed immediately and burnt.

Location: ◊ ☼ — ☀
Propagation:
Characteristics: ✖ ∞ 🐞 ❄
Diseases: die-back
Pests: spider mites, leaf miners, aphids, scale insects

Sheep laurel

Kalmia angustifolia

These plants, members of the Ericaceous family (*Ericaceae*), are native to the damp forests and marshlands of North America. The small evergreen shrubs grow 39 in high and spread almost as much. Their Latin name (*angustifolia*) refers to their narrow, lanceolate, leathery, blue-green leaves. The rosy-red, bell-shaped flowers are borne in summer in dense clusters. The "Rubra" variety has bluish pink flowers. They prefer partial shade but will also grow in the sun if the soil is sufficiently moist. The soil should have a medium level of acidity and must always be kept moist. In spring the soil should be mulched or a slow-release fertilizer should be applied. Dead branches should be removed regularly and if necessary the shrub can be cut back drastically. It is propagated from softwood cuttings in summer and ripe wood cuttings in winter. It can also be grown from seed in spring. If swallowed, all parts of the plants will cause nausea.

Location: 🌢 ☼ — ☀
Propagation: ⦁°°
Characteristics: ✖ ∞ 🌸 ❄
Flowering: summer

Opposite page: Lantana

Crepe myrtle

Lagerstroemia indica

ℹ

Location: � ☼ /⚠\
Care: 🔆 ❄
Propagation: ∘°°
Characteristics: ∞ ✿
Diseases: mildew
Pests: white fly, spider mites
Flowering: summer

This deciduous plant is a member of the *Lythraceae* family and is native to China and Korea, where it grows as a shrub or tree up to 33 ft high. The single flowers have wavy petals like crepe paper and are borne in long clusters until autumn. The colors are pink, white or purple depending on the variety. The plant needs plenty of sun and warmth to ensure flowering and in cooler regions it flowers late or not at all. Because the young shoots break easily, crepe myrtle should be planted in a sheltered position where it is protected from the wind. It is important to water regularly to prevent the buds from dropping . During the growing season, it should be given weekly applications of fertilizer. In regions where winters are mild, older trees can stay outdoors during the winter. However, it is best to move the plants to light place indoors with a temperature of about 59° F. In spring, flowering shoots of the previous year can be cut back. It can be propagated from softwood cuttings taken in spring while pruning. Watch out for mildew, which can cause the buds and flowers to drop.

Shrub verbena

Lantana Camara hybrids

ℹ

Location: ◗◦ ☼
Care: ❄
Propagation:
Characteristics: ✖ ∞ ✿
Diseases: grey mould
Pests: white fly, spider mites, aphids
Flowering: summer – autumn

These evergreen shrubs, members of the *Verbenaceae* family, are native to tropical America. Grown as shrubs or small standards they can reach a height of 39 in. The frounded heads of flowers are produced in summer. Flowers of different colors often appear on the same shrub. They thrive in the sun but should first be placed in light shade when being put outdoors again in spring. The soil should never be allowed to dry because this can cause the wrinkled leaves to go brown and die. Fertilizer should be given weekly until September. The best time for propagation by cuttings is between spring and summer. In winter it should be moved to a light, well-ventilated place with a temperature of 41–50° F. Long, straggly shoots can be pruned in spring or the entire plant can be vigorously cut back if required. If the plant is cut back just before overwintering, it can be moved to a cool, dark place with a temperature of about 41° F. All parts of the plant are poisonous.

Laurus nobilis

ⓘ

Location: ◌ ☼ – ☀ ⚠
Propagation:
Characteristics: ∞ 🏵 🌡
Diseases: mildew
Pests: scale insects, woolly aphids
Flowering: spring

Bay laurel

Laurus nobilis

This evergreen shrub or tree (*Lauraceae*) is native to the Mediterranean, where it can grow to quite a tall tree. It is a very popular container plant because of its deliciously fragrant glossy, dark green leathery leaves. Bay trees seldom flower or produce fruit when cultivated because a male and female plant are needed to achieve pollination. Both leaves and berries are used as a condiment, fragrance and herbal medicine. It is ideal as an all-year round visual screen, growing happily in sun or partial shade. In summer it must be watered regularly although it will tolerate short periods of drought. It must not be waterlogged. If the soil is fertile and rich in humus it will only need weekly applications of a compound fertilizer during the summer. Cuttings can be taken all year round. It should over-winter in a bright, cool place with a temperature of around 34–41° F.

Lavandula

ⓘ

Location: ◌ ☼
Care: ⚠ 🌡
Propagation: ˳∘˳
Characteristics: ∞ 🏵
Diseases: grey mould
Pests: aphids
Flowering: summer

Lavender

Lavandula

Lavender, a member of the *Lamiaceae* family, is native to the Mediterranean, where it grows as a herbaceous perennial, evergreem semi-shrub or shrub. It has linear leaves, covered with fine white hairs, that exude a typical lavender scent and purple-blue, pink or white flowers depending on the variety. Old English lavender (*L. angustifolia*) is a popular container plant that is frost-resistant even in a temperate climate. This variety also produces lavender oil. The flowers of *L. stoechas* and *L. dentata* are borne in purple-red spikes. They all require a warm, sunny location in order to develop their full aroma. Although they tolerate periods of drought, they need well-drained soil that should be kept moist at all times. They do not need much food until the end of the summer, when usually a small application of fertilizer suffices. In winter, it is safer to move them to light, frost-proof place where the temperature will not exceed 50° F. Older specimens should be thinned out every year. Lavender can be propagated from softwood cuttings or raised from seed in spring.

Tree mallow

Lavatera arborea

Tree mallows (*L. arborea*) and shrub mallows (*L. olbia*) are native to the Mediterranean and Australia. In the wild these deciduous shrubs of the *Malvaceae* family grow to a height of 6–10 ft. The tree mallow has large, purple-red flowers marked with dark veins that appear in summer, while the shrub mallow has smaller, pink to purple flowers. They prefer a sunny, warm, sheltered location where they are protected from the wind to prevent them from drying out too much. In summer they need plenty of water. Lack of water would cause the flower buds to drop. Mallows also need plenty of food, which is why they should be given weekly applications of fertilizer until the end of the summer. Pruning is not necessary. Very large specimens can be thinned out lightly in spring or cut back vigorously if so required. It is propagated from cuttings in spring or autumn. In winter, the plants should be moved to a bright, well-ventilated space with a temperature of between 41–50° F. Aphids can be troublesome during spring and summer.

Location: ◆ ☼ ⚠
Care: ❋
Propagation:
Characteristics: ∞ ✿
Diseases: *stem rot, rust fungus*
Pests: *aphids, spider mites,
    white fly*
Flowering: *summer*

Lavatera

Garden tree mallow

Lavatera thuringiaca

ⓘ

Location: ◗◖ ☼ ⚠
Propagation: ∘°°
Characteristics: ∞ ✿ ❄
Diseases: stem rot, rust fungus
Pests: aphids, spider mites,
white fly
Flowering: summer

This tree mallow, also a member of the *Malvaceae* family, is native to central and southern Europe. It is also considered a valuable medicinal plant. It is a bushy shrub that can reach a height and spread of 6 ft 6 in. The striking, large, funnel-shaped flowers that may be pink or white depending on the variety appear in summer. The green leaves are made up of five lobes. The garden tree mallow needs very little care. It thrives in full sun in well-drained, only moderately fertile soil. In summer it requires plenty of water but not too much since being waterlogged can cause the shoots to rot. Rust can also be a problem. It is best planted in a sheltered location such as against a wall of the house where it is protected from cold winds. It can be grown from seed or propagated from cuttings in spring. The plant can be cut back to the base in early spring to rejuvenate it. The root ball should be well protected against frost.

Tea tree

Leptospermum scoparium

ⓘ

Location: ◗◖ ☼ ⚠
Care: ❄
Propagation:
Characteristics: ∞ ✿
Pests: spider mites, aphids
Flowering: winter, spring

The tea tree (*Myrtaceae*) is native to Australia, where it grows as an evergreen shrub or small tree. The small needle-like leaves are very aromatic and are used by the Aborigines to make tea. The tea tree usually flowers in spring but in a conservatory it already starts flowering in late winter. There is a large number of varieties: as well as the white-flowering varieties, there are also pink and red-flowering varieties with single or double flowers. It needs a warm, sunny location in rather acid soil and regular watering. The soil must never be allowed to dry out or become waterlogged. Use only soft water to water the plant. Apply a rhododendron fertilizer every 14 days. Large specimens can be cut back after flowering. In winter the plant should be moved to a light, well-ventilated room with a temperature of 50° F to ensure the prolific formation of buds. Water sparingly during the winter. It is propagated from cuttings and young plants should be pruned several times.

Leptospermum scoparium

Privet

Ligustrum

Most *Ligustrum* species (members of the *Oleaceae* family) are native to east Asia and eastern India. The only species native to Europe is the common privet (*Ligustrum vulgare*). *L. lucidum* is an evergreen privet that is a popular container plant because of its large shiny leaves. The leaves may be dark green or yellow depending on the variety. The small white, fragrant flowers are borne in late summer in large conical clusters. *L. indicum* flowers in late spring. The flowers are followed by black berries that are mildly poisonous. Privet will grow both in sunny and partially shaded location. In summer plants need plenty of water and nutrients. *L. lucidum* is grown as a tree while the other varieties are often clipped into a particular shape or hedge. This is why they are regularly pruned during the growing season. That is also the best time to take cuttings, which will root very easily. In winter, move the plant to a bright place with a temperature of 41–50° F. If placed in a dark room, privet will lose its leaves.

Location: ◗ ☼ – ☼
Care: ❄
Propagation:
Characteristics: ✖ ∞ ❀ ✾
Diseases: leaf spot, wilt
Pests: aphids, scale insects,
  woolly aphids
Flowering: spring, summer

Lily

Lilium hybrids

ℹ

Location: 💧 ☀ – ☀ ⚠

Care: ⚠ ❄

Propagation: ⚬°° ✎✿

Characteristics: ∞ ❀

Diseases: grey mould

*Pests: lily beetles, slugs and
   snails, aphids*

Flowering: spring, summer

Lilium is part of the *Liliaceae* family and the genus includes almost 100 species that are distributed across all the temperate regions of the world. Smaller varieties such as the oriental hybrids and botanical species are ideal as container plants. The flowering period stretches from spring to summer, depending on the variety. The large, funnel-shaped flowers come in every color imaginable except blue. Lilies thrive in a bright location but not in direct sun. They need fertile, well-drained soil and will benefit from the application of a slow-release fertilizer in spring. They need plenty of water in summer. Plant the bulbs in autumn or spring at a depth of about 4 in and store at a temperature of 41–50° F, keeping the soil moderately moist. As soon as the leaves begin to develop, move the pots to a lighter, warmer place. Lilies can be grown from seed or propagated from scales or bulbils in late summer. Containers should be moved to a frost-free place or protected against frost.

Lilium hybrids

Blue potato bush

Lycianthes rantonnetti

This member of the nightshade family (*Solanaceae*)is still known to many gardeners under its previous name *Solanum rantonettti*. It is native to South America, where it grows as a shrub or standard with arching branches. The striking violet-blue flowers with yellow center are followed in autumn by reddish, poisonous fruits. The potato vine (*Solanum jasminoides*), a climber, has white to bluish flowers borne in clusters. Both thrive in the sun and *S. jasminoides* will also do well in partial shade, provided it is also protected from the wind. The plant needs regular watering and applications of fertilizer, otherwise the leaves turn yellow and drop off. In winter the plant should be moved to a bright, well-ventilated place with a temperature of about 50° F or to a dark place with a temperature of 41° F. In this case the plant would lose its leaves. Climbers or larger specimens can be cut back before taking indoors for over-wintering but the best time for pruning is spring. Cuttings can be taken between spring and the beginning of autumn.

Lycianthes rantonnettii

ⓘ

Location: ◆ ☼ – ☼ ⚠
Propagation:
Characteristics: ✖ ∞ ✿
Diseases: grey mould, tomato
  spotted wilt virus
Pests: aphids, white fly
Flowering: spring – autumn

Southern magnolia

Magnolia grandiflora

This evergreen tree of the magnolia family (*Magnoliaceae*) is native to North America, where it grows up to 80 ft high or more. The large, glossy, dark green leaves are reddish-brown underneath. They contrast beautifully with the cup-shaped, creamy-white flowers 6 in wide, which are also intensely fragrant. Magnolias love sun but they should be gradually accustomed to the light when being taken out again in spring. During the growing period, they need plenty of water but only soft water. In addition, the plant should be given weekly applications of fertilizer until the end of the summer. Magnolias can be pruned into shape and more mature specimens can be pruned hard if necessary. In winter a temperature of 41° F will be enough but there must be sufficient light. *M. grandiflora* can be grown from seed and propagated from cuttings and by grafting. Plants grown from seed may take up to 10 years before they flower.

Magnolia

ⓘ

Location: ◆ ☼ – ☼ ⚠
Care: ✽
Propagation: ∘°
Characteristics: ∞ ✿
Pests: scale insects
Flowering: early summer – autumn

New Zealand Christmas tree

Metrosideros excelsa

The New Zealand Christmas tree, a member of the *Myrtaceae* family, is as the name suggests native to New Zealand, where it flowers in December. The genus includes trees, shrubs and climbers. Container-grown specimens grow up to 6 ft 6 in high. The flowers are quite small and inconspicuous with numerous, long, crimson stamens grouped in dense clusters. This vigorous-growing shrub will grow in sun as well as partial shade. Water regularly but only with soft water. In addition, feed once a week with rhododendron fertilizer. Tip: dry conditions in early summer promote the production of flowers. Because it is very tender, well before the first frosts it should be moved indoors to a sunny place with a temperature of 41–50° F and taken outdoors again when there is no longer any danger of frost. Large specimens can be cut back after flowering. It is propagated from greenwood and semi-ripe cuttings from late winter to summer. It produces bushy shrubs more quickly when grown from seed.

Location: ◗ ☼ – ☼
Care: ⊞
Propagation: ₒᵒᵒ
Characteristics: ∞ ❀
Pests: scale insects
Flowering: spring – summer

Myrtus communis

Location: ◗ ☼ – ☼
Care: ⊞
Propagation:
Characteristics: ∞ ❀
Diseases: root rot
Pests: white fly, scale insects
Flowering: summer – autumn

Common myrtle

Myrtus communis

The common myrtlle, a member of the *Myrtaceae* family, is native to the Mediterranean, where it grows as a small, evergreen shrub. Grown in a container it can still reach a height of 6 ft 6 in. The lanceolate leaves produce an intense aroma when crushed. They are used as a medicinal herb in the form of myrtle oil, which is extracted from the leaves. The white flowers that are produced until autumn are also fragrant. Myrtles grow both in sun and partial shade and they need plenty of water in summer. Because they are lime-haters, they should only be watered with soft water or rain water. During the growing season, they should be given weekly applications of rhododendron fertilizer. They do not need pruning but can be trimmed into shape if necessary. In winter, they should be moved to a bright place with a temperature of 41–50° F. Greenwood cuttings taken in spring root easily.

Oleander

Nerium oleander

Oleanders are members of the *Apocynaceae* family. Because they immediately evoke, the Mediterranean, it is not surprising that these evergreen, bushy shrubs growing up to 10 ft high are so popular. The narrow, lanceolate leaves are as elegant as the beautiful flowers. There are numerous varieties, some of them fragrant, which flower profusely well into the autumn so long as the summer has been warm and sunny. This is why oleanders should be placed in the brightest, warmest place where they are also sheltered from the rain. In summer they should be watered freely, preferably in the stand in which the container is placed. In addition, they need weekly applications of fertilizer. Do not remove faded blooms because they can produce buds again in the following spring. Old branches can be cut back in spring. In winter, oleanders should be moved to light, well-ventilated place with a temperature of 41–50° F. Varieties can be propagated from cuttings taken in winter and allowed to root in water in a glass. Oleander can also be grown from seed. All parts of the plant are poisonous.

ⓘ

Location: ◗ ☼ ⚠
Care: ❄
Propagation: ⸰°
Characteristics: △ ✖ ∞ ❀
Diseases: sooty mould
Pests: scale insects
Flowering: autumn

Nerium oleander

Olive tree

Olea europea

ⓘ

Location: ◌ ☼
Care: ❄
Propagation:
Characteristics: △ ∞ ❀ ✿
Pests: scale insects, aphids
Flowering: summer

The olive tree (*Oleaceae*) is an evergreen native to the eastern Mediterranean. This gnarled tree with attractive green-green lanceolate leaves can grow up 40 ft high. In spring it can be trimmed to the desired shape and size. The yellowish-white flowers appear in summer and are later followed by the fruits or olives. When the plant is to be grown in a container it is best to choose self-pollinating varieties. The position should be as warm and sunny as possible. Olive trees will tolerate periods of drought but in summer they will benefit from regular watering. Good drainage is also very important. In addition, olive trees should be given applications of fertilizer every two weeks from spring until summer. In winter, they should be moved to a light place where the temperature is between 41–50° F. The quickest method of propagation is from cuttings of semi-ripe wood taken in summer. Young plants must be pruned several times to encourage them to branch out.

Osmanthus

Osmanthus

ⓘ

Location: ◖ ☼
Care: ❄
Propagation:
Characteristics: △ ∞ ❀
Flowering: spring – autumn

Most species of this genus, a member of the *Oleacea* family, are native to south and east Asia, where they grow as evergreen trees or shrubs 6–13 ft high. The white or yellowish flowers borne in clusters are very fragrant. The blue-black oval fruits are also very decorative as are the glossy, dark green leaves. *O. delavayi* flowers in spring while *O. heterophyllus*, which has holly-like leaves, flowers in autumn. The intensely fragrant flowers of *O. fragrans* appear in spring. Osmanthuses grow best in partial shade. They must be watered regularly but hate being waterlogged. They also benefit from weekly applications of fertilizer until the end of the summer. In the winter they should be moved to a bright, well-ventilated place with a temperature of about 41–50° F. It can be propagated from ripe wood cuttings in summer. Young plants should be pruned several times to give them a shape, but older specimens do not need pruning.

Passion flower

Passiflora

This tropical climber which is a member of the *Passifloraceae* family is famous for its exotic, fragrant flowers with stalked ovaries and striking corona of filaments. These filaments are often arranged in bands of different colors. The yellowish fruits are edible. The best-known ornamental varieties include *P. caerulea* with white to pink petals and *R. racemosa* with crimson flowers. Passion flowers thrive in a warm, sunny location where they are protected from direct midday sun. They should be watered according to the ambient temperature because they hate dry conditions as much as excessive moisture. They benefit from weekly applications of fertilizer until the autumn. In milder climates they can remain outdoors if protected against the cold. However, it is safer to move them to a bright, well-ventilated place where the temperature ranges between 41–50° F. Specimens trained against a trellis can be cut back before being taken indoors. Plants can be grown from seed in spring and propagated from semi-ripe cuttings in summer.

Location: 💧 ☼ ⚠
Care: ❄
Propagation: ⸰°°
Characteristics: ∞ ❀
Diseases: virus diseases
Pests: aphids and sucking
*   insects*
Flowering: summer

Passiflora

Date palm

Phoenix

ⓘ

Location: 💧 ☀
Care: ❄ 🏠
Propagation: ⊙
Characteristics: ∞ ❧
Diseases: leaf calluses, leaf spot
Pests: scale insects, spider mites,
  thrips

These evergreen palms with their attractive divided foliage are native to the tropical and sub-tropical regions of Africa and Asia. The Canary Island date palm (*P. canarensis*), the elegant and more tender *P. roebelinii* and the date palm *P. dactylifera* can all be grown as container plants. Members of the *Arecaceae* family, all date palms are fairly undemanding plants but they need a lot of space and plenty of sun. The root balls must be kept moist at all times although never waterlogged. Watering with very cold or hard water can lead to leaf spot. Fertilizer should be applied every two weeks until the beginning of autumn. Date palm seeds that can be planted in spring are available from specialist nurseries. They should left to soak in warm water for a few days before sowing. In winter, the plants should be moved to a bright place with a temperature of 41–50° F, although *P. roebelinii* needs a temperature of 50–59° F. When repotting more mature specimens, large root balls should be reduced with a knife. Watch out for scale insects.

New Zealand flax

Phormium

ⓘ

Location: 💧 ☀ — ☀
Care: ❄
Propagation: ✦
Characteristics: ∞ ❧
Pests: spider mites
Flowering: summer

These evergreen shrubs, members of the *Phormiaceae* family, are native to New Zealand. Their robust, sword-shaped leaves grow in tufts. The tubular flowers are borne in summer in panicles on leafless stems. There are also varieties with variegated leaves, green and white or green and yellow stripes. *P. cookianum* has yellow or reddish-brown tubular flowers and with its leaves 5 ft long it is slightly smaller than *P. tenax*, which has red flowers and leaves 10 ft long. Variegated varieties do best in full sun while those with green leaves also grow in the shade. In summer the soil must always be kept moist. They all benefit from weekly applications of fertilizer. New Zealand flax can over-winter in a light or dark place where the temperature must not exceed 50° F. During this period it should be watered sparingly. However, it will tolerate slight frost so that it may be left outdoors in a sheltered location in regions where the winter is mild. The rhizomes can easily be divided when repotting.

Black bamboo

Phyllostachys nigra

Black bamboo is native to China and a member of the *Poaceae* family. When grown in a container, it can reach a height of 10 ft. It is particularly popular for the striking colors of the jointed stems, which are green when they first develop, gradually turning brown, then finally shiny black. The pale green leaves contrast beautifully with the shiny black stems. These undemanding shrubs prefer a sunny, warm location where they are sheltered from the wind. In summer they need a lot of water. The soil must remain moist at all times but must never be waterlogged. A layer of mulch will prevent the soil from drying out too much. In addition, bamboos should be given weekly applications of a compound fertilizer until late summer. The young, decorative stems are more effective if the older stems are removed. The plants can be divided as soon the new shoots begin to develop. They can over-winter outdoors if protected against the cold or be moved to a light room with a temperature of 41–50° F.

Spruce

Picea

The pine family (*Pinanceae*) consists of a large number of species that can be found everywhere in the temperate regions of the northern hemisphere. Only slow-growing varieties that need no pruning should be grown in containers. *Picea pungens* "Glauca Globosa" (a form of Colorado spruce) has silvery blue needles and grows 39 in high. *P. orientalis* (Oriental spruce) has a particularly dense needle-like foliage and is therefore an excellent visual screen. *P. abies* "Acroncona" has an extraordinarily large number of cones, while the dwarf form "Pumila Glauca" forms cushion-like mounds. It combines beautifully with shrubs and grasses as does the spherical *P. omorika* "Nana," a dwarf form. They all prefer a sunny location with sandy, slightly acid soil, rich in humus. They will tolerate periods of drought if planted in a flowerbed but in a container they need regular watering and should be given conifer fertilizer every four weeks. *Picea* species can be grown from seed in spring or propagated from semi-ripe cuttings in summer. In winter the roots should be well protected against frost.

ⓘ

Location: 💧 ☀ ⚠
Care: ❄
Propagation: ✂
Characteristics: ∞ 🌿 ❄
Pests: slugs and snails

Picea

ⓘ

Location: 💧 ☀
Propagation: ⋄
Characteristics: ∞ 🌿 ❄
*Pests: spruce gall mite, aphids,
   spider mites*
Flowering: spring, summer

Pieris

Pieris japonica

ⓘ

Location: 💧 ☀️ – ☀️
Propagation: ⚬°
Characteristics: ✖ ∞ ❀ ❃ ❄
    with container protection
Diseases: leaf spot,
    Phytophthora-root rot
Flowering: spring

Pieris, a member of the *Ericaceae* family, is native to China and Japan, where it grows as an evergreen shrub with an upright, bushy habit that can reach up to 10 ft in height. The narrow, oval to lanceolate leaves are produced at the end of the shoots and are usually reddish when young. The white, bell-shaped flowers are borne in 8 in long, drooping panicles that appear in spring. The variety "Forest Flame" can reach a height of 5 ft and has brilliant red leaves when they first emerge. "Variegata" will light any dark corner with its decorative, white-yellow variegated leaves. Pieris thrives in moist, well-drained, acid soil and should be watered with soft water. Dead wood should be removed, otherwise there is no need for pruning. In winter the root balls should be protected against frost. It can be propagated from greenwood and semi-ripe cuttings in spring and summer. The leaves cause nausea if consumed.

Pieris japonica

Dwarf mountain pine

Pinus mugo ssp. Pumilio

Dwarf mountain pine belongs to the family of *Pinaceae* and is native to central and southern Europe, where it grows as multi-stemmed shrubs or small tree that can reach a height of 5 ft and spread of 10 ft. However, the varieties most suitable for growing in containers are the slow growing ones such as *P. mugo* "Gnom," a compact, densely branched form that in time can reach a height and spread of 10 ft, or "Mops," which has a rounded habit and can reach a height and spread of 6 ft 6 in. *P. contorta* or *P. leucodermis* make excellent visual screens. These pines thrive in sun or light shade, in sandy, moderately fertile soil. They will also benefit from an application of conifer fertilizer every 4 weeks. If the plant becomes too large, cut back the young, central shoots, leaving only the weaker side shoots to grow further. If growing from seed, the seeds should stored for three weeks in the refrigerator before sowing. Tip: ripe cones are light brown. Varieties and cultivars are grafted in late winter.

Location: ○ ☼ – ☼
Propagation: ⚬°
Characteristics: ∞ 🏵 ❄
Pests: spruce mite, aphids, tortrix caterpillars
Flowering: spring

Japanese white pine

Pinus parviflora

This evergreen pine tree is a member of the *Pinaceae* family and is native to Japan and the surrounding islands. However, many of its species are also found in gardens in many parts of the world, such as for instance the "Glauca" variety. Its irregular habit and blue-green foliage make it a particularly decorative tree. Also very beautiful are the Japanese variety "Negishii," a broad round-shaped bush, and the slow-growing, more compact variety "Adcock's Dwarf." The soil should not be too chalky, only moderately moist and well-drained. Like all pine trees the Japanese white pine does not mind periods of drought. It is hardy and frost-resistant and it can be pruned if necessary. If it becomes too large, the young central branches can be removed so that only the weaker side shoots continue to grow. Before sowing in spring the seeds should be stored in the refrigerator for three weeks. Tip: the cones are pale brown when ripe. Varieties and cultivars are grafted in late winter.

Location: 💧 ☼
Propagation: ⚬°
Characteristics: ∞ 🏵 ❄
Pests: spruce mites, aphids, tortrix caterpillars
Flowering: spring

Pittosporum

Pittosporum

Location: 💧 ☼ – ◐
Care: ❄
Propagation: ∘°
Characteristics: ∞ ❀
Pests: aphids, scale insects, ewoolly aphids
Flowering: spring – summer

The *Pittosporum* genus includes some 150 species that originate from Australia and New Zealand to Japan and China. They are small trees or shrubs with decorative evergreen foliage. The creamy-white to yellowish, delicately scented flowers of *P. tobira* are borne in summer and contrast beautifully against the background of the leathery, green leaves. The "Variegatum" variety has green leaves with white edges while *P. undulata* has narrow, oval, wavy-edged leaves. *P. tenuifolium* has red-brown flowers that appear in spring. They all grow in sun and partial shade and will even tolerate wind and periods of drought. They need fertile soil rich in humus, which must be kept moist during the growing season, and weekly applications of fertilizer. They can be trimmed to preserve the shape but will flower much less as a result. They can be propagated from cuttings taken in summer and grown from seed, although germination is uneven. In winter, they should be moved to a bright place with a temperature of 41–50° F. Scale insects and aphids can be a problem.

Pittosporum tobira "Variegatum"

Plumbago auriculata

Cape leadwort

Plumbago auriculata

Cape leadwort, a member of the *Plumbaginaceae* family, is native to South Africa. This species can reach a height of 6 ft 6 in. It grows upright when young before adopting a scrambling climbing habit. The pale blue flowers are borne in numerous clusters almost into the autumn. The "Alba" variety has white flowers. *Plumbagos* will even tolerate short periods of drought, nevertheless they should be watered regularly. In addition, they should be given weekly applications of fertilizer until the end of the summer and dead blooms should be removed regularly. These tender plants should be moved indoors well before the first frost and only taken out again after all danger of frost is past. They should be over-wintered in a bright place where the temperature is between 50° F. If the plants are kept in a dark place they should be cut back before being brought in. Otherwise, pruning, if it is necessary, should take place in spring. *Plumbago* can be grown from seed in spring and greenwood cuttings can be taken in June. If attacked by gall wasps, the shoots shrivel up and die off.

Location: ♦ ☼ – ☼ ⚠
Care: ❉
Propagation: ⸴⸰⸴
Characteristics∞ ❀
Pests: *gall mites, aphids, spider mites*
Flowering: *summer*

Cinquefoil

Potentilla fruticosa

ⓘ

Location: 💧 ☼ – ☼
Propagation:
Characteristics: ∞ ❀ ❄
Flowering: summer

The small shrub, a member of the *Rosaceae* or rose family, grows everywhere throughout the northern hemisphere and can reach a height of 4 ft. It is covered with a mass of large, saucer-shaped flowers from spring to autumn that come in a variety of colors depending on the variety: yellow ("Goldteppich," "Klondike"), red ("Red Ace"), orange ("Sunset," "Tangerine") or white ("Abbotswood"). *Potentillas* grow best in a sunny to partially shaded location. These frost-resistant, robust flowering shrubs are perfect for planting in the shrubbery or rock garden. They will not tolerate long periods of drought or chalky soil which is why they should be watered regularly with soft water. They need well-drained soil, and the application of a compound fertilizer every four weeks. If necessary, the plants can be cut back by one third every two years and older specimens can even be cut back to the ground. Propagation is by greenwood cuttings taken in late spring or semi-ripe cuttings in late summer.

Potentilla fruticosa "New Dawn"

Cherry laurel

Prunus lauroceraus

The evergreen cherry laurel, a member of the *Rosaceae* family, is native to eastern Europe as far as Asia. The 6 in long, glossy green leaves are particularly decorative. The fragrant, cup-shaped flowers are borne in dense, upright spikes in spring, followed by the poisonous black fruits in autumn. The compact variety "Otto Luyken" grows up to 5 ft high and makes an excellent screen. Like the spreading "Zabeliana" variety, it flowers a second time in autumn. It prefers a sunny to a partially shady location and fertile, not too chalky soil that should be moisture retentive but well-drained. An excessively chalky soil leads to chlorosis. Dead blooms and dead wood should be removed regularly. It can be propagated from semi-ripe cuttings taken in mid-summer, varieties and cultivars can be grafted. The root ball should be well protected in winter.

Location: 💧 ☼ — ☼
Propagation: ✦
Characteristics✘ ∞ ❀ ❦ ❄
  Diseases: spur blight
Pests: aphids, caterpillars
Flowering: spring, autumn

Prunus serrulata

Japanese cherry

Prunus serrulata

The wild form of this member of the *Rosaceae* family is native to Japan, where the shrubs and trees can grow quite tall. The numerous varieties vary in habit, depending on the variety: columnar ("Amanogawa" with whitish pink flowers), broadly spreading ("Shiro-fugen" with white flowers) or arching ("Kiku-shidare-zakura" with white flowers). The delicately fragrant, mostly double flowers appear in spring. Besides varieties with pink and white flowers, there are also some with yellow flowers. Some varieties such as "Kanzan" have striking autumn colors, as does the slow-growing, white-flowering *P. x cistena*. They need a very sunny location and well-drained soil. In summer they should be watered regularly and given regular applications of fertilizer during the flowering season. Unwanted, straggly or dead shoots can be removed in late winter to early spring. Japanese cherries can be propagated from semi-ripe cuttings in summer, varieties and cultivars are grafted. The root ball should be well protected in winter.

Location: 💧 ☼
Propagation:
Characteristics: ∞ ❀ ❄
Diseases: spur blight
Pests: aphids, caterpillars
Flowering: spring

Flowering almond

Prunus triloba

ⓘ

Location: 🌢 ☼ — ☼
Propagation:
Characteristics: ✖ ∞ ❁ ❋
Diseases: spur blight
Pests: aphids, caterpillars
Flowering: spring

This deciduous member of the *Rosaceae* family is native to China and is a real eye-catcher on balconies and terraces in spring. The pale pink double flowers are produced on the previous year's wood. This bushy, densely branched shrub grows up to 6 ft 6 in high and wide. It is usually trained as a strandard. By contrast, the pink-flowering dwarf variety *P. tenella* grows very erect. These both grow best in a sunny to partially shaded location. The rootballs must remain moist at all times. They need humus-rich, well-drained soil and regular applications of fertiliser during the flowering season. The tree or shrub is cut to a strong bud or young shoot every year after flowering. A round crown can be kept in the desired shape in the same way. Both can be propagated from softwood cuttings in summer. Standards are propagated by grafting. Fungus-affected branches should be removed. The roots should be well protected duting winter.

Pomegranate

Punica granatum

ⓘ

Location: 🌢 ☼ ⚠
Care: ❋
Propagation: ₀°
Characteristics: ∞ ❁
Diseases: root rot
Pests: aphids, spider mites
Flowering: summer

The Asian pomegranate, a member of the *Punicaceae* family, is native to the Mediterranean, where its fruit is much appreciated. Grown in containers, pomegrantes make densely branched shrubs with gnarled branches that can grow up to 6 ft 6 in in height. The pale green leathery leaves are copper coloured when they first come out. The striking flowers are scarlet, orange, yellow or white and may be single or double depending on the variety. They are followed by reddish-brown edible fruits. The dwarf form "Nana" flowers prolifically. Pomegranates love a sunny, warm location. In summer, they need plenty of water and an application of fertilizer every two weeks. They tolerate short periods of drought but not being waterlogged. Water only occasionally in winter. Large specimens can be cut back in autumn if necessary. Because pomegranates lose their leaves, they can over-winter in a dark place where the temperature is between 41–50° F or even cooler. Plants can be grown from seed all year round or propagated from semi-ripe cuttings during summer.

Punica granatum

Cork oak

Quercus suber

This evergreen tree, a member of the *Fagaceae* family, is native to the Mediterranean. But it is cultivated in many other parts of the world because of its corky bark. The thick, gnarled bark makes it a very decorative container plant. The male flowers are borne in hanging catkins in late spring while the female flowers are borne singly or in spikes. These develop into oval acorns. Cork oak thrives in warm, sunny location although it will also grow in partial shade. Although it needs a lot of water in summer, the soil should be allowed to dry out between waterings. It is best to use soft water or rainwater but it hates being waterlogged. It will benefit from weekly applications of fertilizer in spring and summer. In winter it should be moved to a light, frost-free place with a temperature of about 41° F. It can be cut back or thinned out in spring if necessary. Propagation is from seed.

Location: 🌢 ☼
Care: ❄
Propagation: ₀°°
Characteristics: △ ∞ 🦋
Diseases: root rot
Pests: scale insects, woolly aphids
Flowering: spring

Lady palm or Ground rattan

Rhapis

ⓘ

Location: 💧 ☀ — ☀ ⚠
Care: ❄ — ☼
Propagation: ✂✿
Characteristics: △ ∞ ✿
Diseases: blight
Pests: scale insects, woolly
  aphids

This decorative bamboo palm, a member of the *Arecaceae* or palm family, is native to China. The genus is made up of only two species: *Rhapis excelsa* and *Rhapis humilis*. The green leaves consist of 20 or more deep green lobes. The smaller *R. humilis* has denser, narrower lobes than those of *R. excelsa*. The numerous suckers develop into stems, an aspect that is very reminiscent of bamboos. If placed outdoors in summer, they require a warm, partially shaded location, not in direct sun, where they are protected from rain and wind. The root balls should be kept moist all year round but never waterlogged. The plant benefits from weekly applications of fertilizer during the growing season but only every four to six weeks during the winter. The brighter the place where they over-winter, the warmer the temperature, within the range 41–68° F. If the air is too dry, the tips of the leaves will turn brown. Lady palm can be propagated from suckers that can easily be detached when repotting the plant.

Rhododendron

Rhododendron

ⓘ

Location: 💧 ☀ ⚠
Care: ❄
Propagation: ⦿
Characteristics: ∞ ✿ ❄
Diseases: rot, bud drop
Pests: weevils, rhododendron
  lace bug, leafhoppers
Flowering: spring – summer

Varieties of *Rhododendron*, members of the *Ericaceae* family, grow everywhere in the world. Besides the evergreen hybrids with large flowers and the Yakushimanun varieties, the evergreen Japanese azaleas also make excellent container plants. All share a common feature in the beautiful, sometimes fragrant flowers that appear in spring. They mostly prefer shady locations but the "Gibraltar" and Klondyke" varieties in the Knaphill group will also grow in the sun. They need well-drained, acid soil that should be kept moist at all times. It is recommended to use a special rhododendron compost because excessive lime in the soil can lead to chlorosis. Rhododendrons will benefit from the application of a slow-release fertilizer. Dead blooms should be removed with care. It is best to put the containers in a place where they are sheltered from cold winds. Tender species should over-winter in a cool greenhouse. Plants can be propagated from semi-ripe cuttings taken in late summer, but varieties and cultivars are usually grafted.

Rhododendron

Palma christi

Ricinus communis

Ricinus communis is the only species of its genus. It is native from the Mediterranean to the tropics, where it grows as a shrub, semi-shrub or tree. It is usually cultivated as an annual because it can reach a height of 10 ft in just one year. Besides its amazingly vigorous habit, it also has magnificent, large, deeply lobed leaves that may be pale green to deep bronze depending on the variety. The spiny, red fruits are equally striking. The seed coats are extremely poisonous yet it is from the inner part of the seeds that castor oil is extracted. It grows best in a sunny, warm position where it is are sheltered from the wind and rain. The plants should be watered freely and fed generously every week during the growing season. Because they are cultivated as annuals, there is no need for over-wintering and pruning. They are raised from seed in spring. Germination can be speeded up by scratching the seeds. The plants are usually trouble-free. All parts of the plants, especially the seeds, are highly poisonous.

Ricinus communis

Location: 💧 ☼ ⚠
Care: ❋
Propagation: ⚬°°
Characteristics: ✖ ☉ ∞ ⚘
Pests: spider mites
Flowering: summer

Rosmarinus officinalis

ⓘ

Location: ○ ☀
Care: ❋
Propagation: ⚬°°
Characteristics: ∞ ❀ ⬚
Pests: aphids
Flowering: spring, early
summer

Rosemary

Rosmarinus officinalis

This evergreen shrub with needle-like aromatic leaves is native to the Mediterranean. A member of the *Lamiaceae* family, rosemary can grow up to 6 ft 6 in high. As well as being highly valued for its culinary and aromatic properties, it is appreciated for its medicinal qualities and also for its decorative appearance. The mauve to blue two-lipped flowers are borne in spring in terminal clusters. It thrives in warm, sunny conditions, so it should only be watered moderately even during the growing season. It does not mind periods of drought but will not tolerate being waterlogged. It grows best in well-drained, sandy soil, rich in humus and benefits from weekly applications of fertilizer until the end of the summer. It is easily propagated from semi-ripe cuttings taken in summer but it can also be grown from seed. In winter it shold be moved to light, cool place with a temperature of 41–50° F and watered sparingly. Young plants should be pruned regularly and older specimens rejuvenated by cutting back in spring.

Butcher's broom

Ruscus aculeatus

Location: ○ ☀ — ☀
Care: ❋
Propagation: ⚬°° ✂❀
Characteristics: ✖ ∞ ❀
Flowering: spring

This evergreen shrub, a member of the *Ruscaceae* family, is native from Madeira to the Mediterranean countires and as far as Iran. It owes its name less to the leaves, which are reduced to tiny scales, but more to the prickly short, leaf-like shoots known as cladodes. The greenish-white flowers are borne in spring on the underside of these cladodes. The flowers are succeeded by round, bright red, poisonous berries that remain on the tree well into the winter. But you will need both a female and male plant in order to have berries. This shrub grows up to 39 in high and is very undemanding, growing well in either sun or shade. Even in summer *Ruscus* does not need much water; in fact, the soil should be allowed to dry out before watering again. It needs feeding every week during the growing season. It is easily propagated by division of the rhizomes but growing from seed is a lengthier process because germination is quite slow. In winter, the plant must be moved to a light, airy place with a temperature of about 41° F. Old, straggly shoots can cut back to the base in spring.

Willow

Salix

These evergreen members of the willow or *salicaceae* family are native to Europe and Asia. Varieties such as *Salix caprea* "Pendula" are particularly suitable for growing in containers because of their elegant shape. The latter has silvery-grey, later yellow catkins that appear in spring before the foliage. *S. helvetica* only grows to a height of 39 in and is another excellent variety for growing in containers. Willows grow best in sun or partial shade. Standards should be protected from the wind. They need fertile soil, rich in humus, which should be kept moist at all times. In addition they should be fertilized regularly. The plants can be trimmed to keep them in shape or cut down to the ground to rejuvenate them. They can be propagated from greenwood cuttings in spring, from semi-ripe cuttings in summer and hardwood cuttings in winter. The roots should be well protected in winter.

Location: 🌢 ☼ – ☼ ⚠
Propagation:
Characteristics: ∞ ❄
Diseases: *rust fungus, willow scab*
Pests: *aphids, caterpillars*
Flowering: *spring*

Skimmia japonica

Skimmia

Skimmia japonica

The Japanese skimmia, a member of *Rutaceae* family, is native to the mountainous regions of Japan as its name suggests. This bushy shrub 5 ft high has lanceolate, dark green leaves that are not unlike those of a bay tree. The small, fragrant flowers are borne in spring in terminal trusses. They are usually white but often also tinged with pink or red and are followed by bright red berries that remain on the tree until winter. The male variety "Rubella" does not produce berries but has clusters of brown-red buds all winter, which open in spring. Skimmias love shade and acid to neutral soil that should kept moist at all times during summer. The plants benefit from regular feeding during spring and summer. Pruning is not necessary. New plants can be propagated in summer and autumn from semi-ripe and hardwood cuttings. They can also be grown from seed in autumn.

Location: 🌢 ☼
Propagation: ⟡
Characteristics: ∞ ❁ ❄
Pests: *scale insects*
Flowering: *summer*

Spiraea

Spiraea japonica

Location: 💧 ☼
Propagation:
Characteristics: ∞ ❀ ❄
Flowering: summer

Spiraea, a deciduous shrub and member of the *Rosaceae* family, is native to China and Japan. The prolific flowering, compact varieties of this species have become very popular in gardens and on balconies and terraces. One such variety is "Little Princess," which only reaches a height of 24 in and spread of 39 in. It bears a mass of pale pink flower heads in early summer. There are also white-flowering and crimson-flowering varieties such as "Anthony Waterer." Spiraeas need full sun, fertile soil and plenty of water during summer. They are not usually prone to attacks by pests and diseases and they are frost-resistant. Nevertheless, it is advisable to protect the roots against frost. The summer flowering varieties should be pruned hard in spring. This will help them to keep their shape, and varieties with colorful foliage such as "Goldflame" will continue to produce its yellow, to copper-coloured young foliage. Propagation is from semi-ripe cuttings taken in late summer.

Spiraea japonica

Bird of paradise

Strelitzia reginae

Strelitzia, a member of the *Strelitziaceae* family, is native to South Africa, where it grows as an evergreen herbaceous perennial 6 ft 6 in high. It takes its name from the exotic arrow-shaped, orange-red single flowers that emerge from the red to blue-violet bracts and are produced in succession throughout spring. The large, leathery leaves are reminiscent of those of banana trees. *S. reginae* is famous as a cut flower and container plant. *Strelitzias* need plenty of light and warmth, preferably a south-facing location. They should be watered freely during the growing period and given weekly applications of general fertilizer until the end of the summer. They thrive in well-drained, fertile soil. In winter they should be kept in a temperatuure of 50–59° F and watered very sparingly. The plants can be propagated by division in spring. They can also be grown from seed but this takes longer. Older leaves should be removed so that the plants have sufficient light and air. Leaf spots are a sign of infection.

ⓘ

Location: 💧 ☼ ⟁
Care: 🏠
Propagation: ˒° 🪱
Characteristics: ∞ ❀
Diseases: leaf spot
Pests: scale insects, spider mites
Flowering: spring – summer

Lilac

Syringa microphylla

Lilacs, a member of the *Oleaceae* family, are native to northern China. The "Super-ba" variety, a slender bush with arching branches that grows up to 5 ft high, is ideal for growing in containers. The fragrant, pink flowers are borne in small panicles in early summer and then again in autumn. This small, vigorous, frost-resistant shrub thrives in a warm, sunny location, sheltered from the wind. It needs fertile soil without too much lime. Make sure that the root ball remains moist at all times during the growing season but never allow it to become waterlogged. It benefits from monthly applications of fertilizer until the end of august. Remove faded flower heads but make sure you do not damage the new shoots that are developing underneath. Lilac can be propagated from greenwood cuttings in early summer, while varieties and cultivars may be grafted. Remove all damaged parts immediately.

ⓘ

Location: 💧 ☼
Propagation: ˒°
Characteristics: ∞ ❀ ❄
Diseases lilac blight, leaf spot,
*   mildew*
Pests: lilac leaf miners
Flowering: summer, autumn

Giant water gum

Sygyzium paniculatum

ⓘ

Location: 💧 ☼
Care: ❋
Propagation: ⚬°°
Characteristics: ∞ ❀ ❧
Pests: scale insects, spider mites
Flowering: summer

Giant water gum, a member of the *Myrtaceae* family, is native to Australia, where it grows as a tree or shrub 33 ft high. Its magnificent glossy, deep-green leaves alone make it a very attractive container plant. In addition, it has striking creamy-white flowers that are borne in summer in dense clusters, followed by rose-purple berries. The plants thrive in a sunny, warm location. In temperatures below 68° F, they do not grow as vigorously. They need plenty of water during summer and weekly applications of fertilizer, although in small doses. In winter, plants should be moved to a light, frost-free place where the temperature does not exceed 50° F. In summer, they can be propagated from semi-ripe cuttings or raised from seed in spring. The plants can be pruned into shape or cut back hard if necessary. Watch out for scale insects and spider mites.

Common yew

Taxus baccata

ⓘ

Location: ○ ☼ — ☀ ⚠
Propagation: ⚬°°
Characteristics: ✖ ∞ ❧ ❋
Diseases: root rot
Pests: weevils, tortrix
    caterpillars
Flowering: spring

Evergreen trees and shrubs, yews, members of the *Taxaceae* family, are native to Europe and Asia Minor. In the wild, yews can grow up to 33 ft high and wide. There are more compact growing varieties such as "Fastigiata" with dark green needles and a columnar habit that is ideally suited for growing in containers. Yews will thrive in a sheltered location in sun and partial shade and fairly high humidity. They need fertile, well-drained soil. They tolerate periods of drought but not being waterlogged, which leads to phytophthora, a fungal infection. They can be pruned to keep them to the desired shape. The seeds are enclosed in a fleshy, scarlet-red berry. Yews can be grown from seed but it a lengthy process. They can be propagated much more quickly from hardwood cuttings taken in autumn, treated with rooting powder and kept in a warm place. All parts of the plant are poisonous.

Taxus baccata

White cedar

Thuja occidentalis

These evergreen conifers add a touch of greenery to balconies and terraces all year round. This genus, which includes a large number of species, is native to North America. Several are slow-growing, cone-shaped bushes such as "Smaragd," up to 39 in high, whose needles remain bright green even in winter, or "Rheingold" and "Sunkist" of similar size but with gold-yellow needles. "Globosa" and "Little Champion" have a more rounded shape. They thrive in sun and partial shade, in light, fertile soil. During the growing season they should be watered generously and given an application of conifer fertilizer every four weeks. These frost-resistant conifers can be trimmed to the desired shape and size. They can be propagated from semi-ripe cuttings taken in summer and allowed to root at about 64° F. The erect, female cones contain the seeds which should be sown in spring. Young plants are particularly vulnerable to die-back of the branches. The needles can cause allergies.

Location: 💧 ☼ – ☼
Propagation: ⌀
Characteristics: ✖ ∞ ❄
Diseases: die-back
Pests: scale insects, aphids

Tibouchina urvilleana

❶

Location: ▮ ☼ ⚠
Care: ❆
Propagation:
Characteristics: ∞ ✿ ✾
Diseases: grey mould
Pests: spider mites, white fly,
    aphids
Flowering: summer – autumn

Glory bush

Tibouchina urvilleana

This climbing shrub which belongs to the *Melastomataceae* family, is native to tropical America. It has large, violet-blue flowers that stand out beautifully against the oval, deep-green leaves, which are velvety with prominent veins. The flowers that appear in summer only last one day but are produced uninterruptedly until autumn. The plants will thrive in a warm, sunny location and should be kept moist at all times during summer. If the soil is too chalky, the plant will suffer from chlorosis. This is why it is advisable to use soft water. It is also very important to feed the plants every week with a general liquid fertilizer during spring and summer. In winter, it should be moved to a bright place where the temperature ranges between 41–50° F. Grey mould may be a problem if the humidity of the air is too high. Young plants should be pruned regularly, otherwise only flowering shoots are cut back to within the next bud of the main branch each spring.

❶

Location: ◌ ☼–☼ ⚠
Care: ❆
Propagation:
Characteristics: ∞ ✾
Pests: scale insects
Flowering: summer

Chusan or Fan palm

Trachycarpus fortunei

This evergreen palm, a member of the *Arecaceae* family, can be found in the wild in China and Japan, where it grows to a slender tree 40 ft high. The large, mid-green, deeply-divided, fan-shaped leaves are particularly decorative. The trees bear male or female flowers so it is necessary to have both for the long panicles of small yellow flowers to be followed by the blue-black berries. The plants produce many more new leaves in a sunny location than in partial shade. Furthermore, they should be sheltered from the wind so that they do not get blown over. The root ball must remain moist at all times during summer but almost dry in winter. During the growing season the plants must be given a weak dose of fertilizer every week. This vigorous-growing palm can survive a temperature of 23° F. In regions with harsh winters, it should be moved to a dry, dark place with a temperature of 41–50° F. It can be grown from seed in spring and autumn.

Dutch Elm

Ulmus x hollandica

A member of the *Ulmaceae* family, this genus includes numerous species and varieties. Many are very popular with gardeners because of their beautiful golden-yellow autumn colors. The small, bell-shaped flowers are borne in spring in dense clusters, later followed by round, nut-like fruits. The group of Dutch elms includes many hybrids such as "Elegantissima" or "Jacqueline Hillier." The latter, a slow-growing branched shrub, only reaches a height of 6 ft 6 in in 10 years. Elms grow in sun and partial shade. They like well-drained, fertile soil and plenty of water in summer. They can be propagated from semi-ripe cuttings in summer. Unwanted or dead branches can be cut back in late winter or early spring, otherwise elms do not need pruning. The container should be protected against frost in winter. Some hybrids are less prone than others to Dutch elm disease.

Trachycarpus fortunei

ℹ

Location: 💧 ☼ – ◐
Propagation:
Characteristics: ∞ ❦ ❄
Diseases: elm die-back
Pests: aphids, leafhoppers, gall midges
Flowering: spring

Laurustinus

Viburnum tinus

This evergreen shrub, a member of the *Caprifoliaceae* family, is native to the subtropical regions of the earth. It can grow as high as 8 ft and owes its name "laurustinus" to its leaves, which are 4 in long and very similar to those of the bay laurel tree. The white, fragrant flowers, sometimes tinged with pink, are borne in terminal flat heads from autumn to spring and are later followed by black berries. *Viburnums* thrive in light, airy places, sheltered from direct sun. During the growing season they need a lot of water and even during winter the soil must never be allowed to dry out. In order to ensure early flowering, they should only be fed until the end of July. In winter, they should be moved into a light, airy place where the temperature should be about 41° F. *V. x burkwoodii* can remain outdoors during winter. Laurustinus can easily be propagated from greenwood cuttings taken in spring. Large specimens can be pruned hard after flowering.

ℹ

Location: 💧 ☼ – ◐
Care: ❄
Propagation:
Characteristics: ∞ ✿ ❦
Pests: leaf beetles, all kinds of aphids, white fly
Flowering: autumn, spring

Opposite page: Viburnum

Desert fan palm

Washingtonia filifera

This evergreen palm that belongs to the *Arecaceae* family is native to southern California. The almost round, fan-shaped leaves or fronds grow on grey-green stalks covered with thorns. The whitish bark fibers that surround the individual leaf segments are quite striking. Their relative *W. robusta* differs from *W. filifera* in that it has brownish leaf stalks and considerably fewer fibers. Desert fan palms need a lot space and a sunny, airy location protected from the wind. They grow best in well-drained soil, rich in humus. The latter should be kept moist at all times during summer while during winter the amount of watering depends on the temperature. The plants will benefit from a weekly small rose of organic fertilizer from spring until the end of the summer. In winter, it can be moved to a dark or light location with a temperature of 32–50° F. It can be grown from seed in spring when germination can take between four weeks and four months at a temperature of 77–86°. Watch out for spider mites, scale insects and woolly aphids.

Location: 💧 ☀ /▲\
Care: ❄
Propagation: ⋅ᵒᵒ
Characteristics: ∞ 🔲
Pests: spider mites, scale insects
   and woolly aphids

Weigela

Weigela florida

This frost-resistant, deciduous shrubs with arching branches covered with pink, bell-shaped flowers is a striking sight in spring. A member of the *Caprifoliaceae* family, weigela is native to the warm forests of east Asia, where it can grow up to 10 ft high and wide. Popular cultivated varieties are "Bristol Ruby" with ruby-red flowers, "Styriaca" with crimson-pink flowers and "Bouquet Rose" with crimson-pink flowers with a paler edge. They thrive in sun and partial shade in well-drained soil. They also need plenty of water and food. Each year weigelas should be cut back by one-third to a strong bud or new shoot immediately after flowering. Otherwise, prune hard to encourage new growth. It can easily be propagated from greenwood cuttings or semi-ripe cuttings from late spring to mid-summer.

Location: 💧 ☀ — ☀
Propagation:
Characteristics ∞ ❀ ❄
Diseases: leaf and bud drop
Flowering: spring

Roses

Opposite page:
Rosa "Eden 85"

Roses have long dominated our gardens but are now becoming increasingly common on balconies and terraces as well. Today there are many species and varieties that are ideal for growing on balconies and terraces, either in tubs, containers or lange hanging baskets. Roses add a wondeful touch to any balcony or terrace, whether they are repeat flowering, that is, flowering several times during the season, or just once but over a longer period. Scented English roses that flower from May till the first night frosts are particularly attractive. Standard roses are real eye-catchers and the fragrant flowers are at nose level, which is an additional bonus. They also look very good with other summer flowers planted at the base. Climbing roses trained as standards, so-called cascade roses, are quite unusual. Last but not least, there are climbing roses which will embellish any wall but need a support structure against which they can be trained.

Roses have deep roots. If roses are to be cultivated in tubs for several years, it is important to buy special rose containers. Dwarf roses need a container with a minimum depth of 10 in. When planting roses, the grafting point should be just less than 1 in below the surface. Use special potting soil. It is lighter and contains sufficient nutrients so that it does not need fertilizing later in the season. Over-fertilized plants develop weaker tissues and become more sensitive to frost as a result. On the subjet of over-wintering: roses can over-winter outdoors but the containers must be well insulated to protect them against frost. The grafting point, which is sensitive to frost, should also be protected. Pruning of container-grown roses should only consist of removing dead blooms. If you cut back a little too much because you wanted some cut flowers, move the plant out of full sun.

Rose pests and diseases and how to deal with them

Pest and diseases can strike even if you look after your roses well. But if treated early on, they can easily be contained and stopped. Information about diagnosis and treatment can be found in the chapter "Pests and Diseases" (see page 394)

Large rose aphids: *The leaves and shoots become stunted and deformed, honeydew leading to rose rust. The black eggs are easily identified in winter; they should be rubbed off the shoots with a brush and soap solution and the affected shoots removed at the latest when pruned in spring.*

Leaf-rolling sawflies: *After the eggs have been laid between the beginning of May and June, the larvae come out and eat the underside of the leaves. This leads to leaf curl when the the leaves turn yellow and die. Cut way affected leaves and burn them – do not compost them.*

Red spider mites and leafhoppers: *Their sucking causes small whitish spots on the leaves that in the case of spider mites are also covered with fine cobwebbing. The yellow-green leafhopper jumps away as soon as it is touched. A cold extract of stinging nettles can be helpful in discouraging them.*

True mildew: *The symptoms are a whitish deposit on the top surface of the leaves which then turn brown and die. If the attack is serious the whole plant may die.*

Rose rust: *Small, yellow to reddish spots appear on the top surface of the leaves while the underneath is covered with black spores. The leaves turn brown and die off.*

Downy mildew: *Dark blotchy spots develop on the leaves, which then turn yellow and drop off. Destroy as soon as possible to ensure the fungus does not survive.*

Small bush rose

Rosa "Alba Meidiland"

ℹ

Location: ◊ ☼
Care: ⚠
Propagation:
Characteristics: △ ∞ ❀
Flowering: summer – autumn

This small, compact bush rose that reaches about 12-15 in in height and spread is ideal for growing in pots on a balcony and terrace. It was first developed by the Meilland tree nursery in 1987. It is covered with small, dense, shiny green foliage. The large clusters of up to 20 flowers are in borne in summer and autumn on arching, overhanging branches. The pure white flowers are double and about 1.25 in across. Like many other roses "Alba Meidiland" is prone to pests, such as aphids and spider mites, and diseases, such as mildew and rust. To avoid fungal infections it is important not to wet the leaves when watering the plant. Outward-growing buds can be cut back in order to keep the plant in shape. Excessively dense lateral shoots can be cut back. It is generally propagated from cuttings, which should be planted in autumn.

Bedding rose

Rosa "Anabel"

ℹ

Location: ◊ ☼
Care: ⚠
Propagation:
Characteristics: △ ∞ ❀
Flowering: summer – autumn

This rose was created by the Kordes tree nursery in 1972. It has a bushy, branched habit and reaches a height of 20 in. The leaves are bronze-coloured when they first develop, turning moss-green with age. The flowers are borne throughout summer until autumn, developing from pointed round buds into loosely double, salmon orange blooms that are grouped in clusters on strong stems. These lightly fragrant roses also make excellent cut flowers. They can be left outdoors during the winter but they should be protected against hard frost with a loose covering of spruce brushwood. They prefer a sunny location. In order to make sure that the leaves can dry quickly, the plants should not be placed within reach of dripping water from other plants or gutters. It can also be combined with other plants to achieve a special effect. Combined with lavender, for instance, it produces a fascinating contrast of color and shape.

Climbing rose

Rosa "Blaze Superior"

This hybrid, developed in 1954 by growers Jackson and Perkins, belongs to the group of climbing roses. It reaches a height of 13 ft and must therefore be tied to a supporting framework. With its carmine-red, medium-sized flowers, grouped in small clusters, it is a beautiful eye-catching plant grown against a house or terrace wall. The single-densely double flowers have 25–30 petals. The slightly shiny leaves are light green. Like all roses, it prefers a sunny, sheltered location. During the growing period it needs plenty of water and a compound fertilizer. In the first two years only dead or diseased wood should be removed. Subsequently, the main branches can be cut back to the required length and the lateral shoots to three or four buds. It is propagated from cuttings.

Location: ◊ ☼
Care: ⚠
Propagation:
Characteristics: △ ∞ ❀ 🍃
Flowering: summer – autumn

Rosa "Blaze Superior"

Dwarf rose

Rosa "Daydream"

ℹ

Location: ○ ☼
Care: ⚠
Propagation:
Characteristics: △ ∞ ✿
Flowering: summer – autumn

Also known under the name "Len Turner" and "Dicjeep," this rose was first developed in 1984 in Northern Ireland. It is a member of the Floribunda group, which means that the flowers are grouped in dense clusters. This robust, hardy rose can withstand wet weather better than other types. It has a compact habit and reaches a height and spread of 20 x 20 in. Its beautiful soft pink flower with reddish rim appear in summer until autumn. They are usually undulate and when fully open, the flowers resemble those of a pompom dahlia. They prefer a sunny, sheltered location in fertile, moist but well-drained soil. Dead, diseased shoots and suckers should constantly be removed. Suckers appear from the rootstock, that is below the point where the rose was grafted. In late winter and early spring, the plant should be cut back to 3–6 in if grown in a flowerbed but if grown in a container, only dead blooms should be removed. It should not be pruned during periods of frost.

Dwarf rose

Rosa "Dresden Doll"

ℹ

Location: ○ ☼
Care: ⚠
Propagation:
Characteristics: △ ∞ ✿
Flowering: summer – autumn

This variety, that is member of the group of miniature or dwarf roses, was developed in 1975. Only reaching a height of 12–18 in, it is ideal for growing in pots and containers on balconies and terraces. Being the first miniature moss-rose, "Dresden Doll" is unique. Its numerous buds that look as if they are covered in moss develop into oyster-pink flowers with prominent stamens. This miniature rose prefers partial shade in order to prevent the flowers from fading too quickly. In addition, dead blooms should be removed regularly. In spring dead and weak branches should be cut back and excessively dense specimens should be thinned. If left outdoors, the plant must be protected against frost by a layer of spruce brushwood. The plant will over-winter without any problems in a frost-free but cool room.

*B*ush rose

Rosa "Eden Rose 85"

This repeat-flowering, fragrant rose created in 1985 belongs to the group of bush roses and is particularly popular with lovers of old-fashioned roses. It is a bushy rose with fragrant flowers and shiny green leathery leaves and can reach a height of 5 ft and is therefore ideal for growing on its own on balconies and terraces. The fat, round yellowish buds develop into large, rosette-shaped, densely-double flowers, 4 in across, which can have as many 70 petals. They are borne from summer till autumn on powerful stems. The flowers are dark pink in the centre and pale pink along the edge. This rose prefers a sunny, sheltered, well-aired location. Because it is repeat-flowering, the dead blooms should be removed regularly together with a short piece of stem in order to encourage repeat flowering.

Location: ◊ ☼
Care: /✳
Propagation:
Characteristics: △ ∞ ✲
Flowering: summer – autumn

Rosa "Eden Rose 85"

Bush rose

Rosa "Elveshörn"

The Kordes tree nursery launched this repeat-flowering variety onto the market in 1985. It is ideal for planting in groups in flowerbeds or hedges but it also makes a very good container plant for balconies and terraces. It has a broad, bushy habit and grows up to 39 in high. This is why it is best planted on its own in a container, which at the start should be chosen to be large enough. The bright red flowers with a light silvery bloom have a fragrance similar to that of wild roses and contrast beautifully against the slightly shiny, green foliage. The flowers are round, very full and quite large, being some 3 in across. They are borne in large clusters that should be removed as soon as they have died. The variety is extremely robust and able to withstand wet weather. It can be left outdoors during winter if protected adequately against frost. It should be repotted in spring, or at least the top layer should be replaced by new compost.

Modern shrub rose

Rosa "English Garden"

This variety belongs to the group of modern shrub roses and was first developed in 1987 by the British tree nursery Austin. The decorative, upright plant reaches a height of 35 in and is therefore ideal for growing in a container. The leaves are light green and the large, double, rosette-shaped flowers that are borne from summer till autumn are quartered in the manner of old roses. They are pale yellow in the center fading to ivory white along the edges. They tolerate wet weather but should be protected in winter. The application of a slow-release fertilizer in spring and summer or soil dressing in spring should be followed by regular applications of liquid fertilizer during the growing season. Dead blooms should be removed regularly.

Location: ◌ ☼
Care: ⚠
Propagation:
Characteristics: ⚠ ∞ ✿
Flowering: summer – autumn

Rosa "English Garden"

Location: ◌ ☼
Care: ⚠
Propagation:
Characteristics: ⚠ ∞ ✿
Flowering: summer – autumn

English rose

Rosa "Gertrude Jekyll"

This rose belongs to the sub-group of the English roses, which themselves are members of the modern shrub roses group. These vigorous, upright plants can grow up to 5 ft high and are ideal for growing on balconies and terraces. They are quite eye-catching with their large, double, cup-shaped, dark-pink flowers that can measure up to 4 in across. Their petals turn inward and are intensely fragrant. Another advantage is that "Gertrude Jekyll" is a repeat-flowering variety. The main flowering season is in summer, followed by a less prolific second flowering in autumn. The plant can be left outdoors in winter as long as it is protected against frost by spruce brushwood or jute sacks. It prefers a sunny, airy location but sheltered from strong, cold winds. Like all roses it can be propagated from cuttings taken in summer or grafting in autumn.

Location: ◊ ☀
Care: ⚠
Propagation:
Characteristics: △ ∞ ✸
Flowering: summer – autumn

Rosa "Gertrude Jekyll"

English rose

Rosa "Graham Thomas"

ℹ️

Location: ○ ☼
Care: ⚠
Propagation:
Characteristics: △ ∞ ❁
Flowering: summer – autumn

This fast-growing English rose was named after the leading expert in the field of old roses. Its shape is very reminiscent of that of the 19th century "Remontant" roses with their large flowers, except that these only came in red, pink or pastel colors. "Graham Thomas" was developed in Great Britain 1983 by the Austin rose nursery. It has yellow flowers that are borne from summer till autumn. They are quartered to cupped and are pleasantly fragrant. The long shoots are covered with glossy, light green leaves and they bend down under the weight of the blooms, especially after it has been raining. This variety grows up to 4 ft high and makes a very good container plant for the balcony or terrace. But make sure that the container is deep enough because the roots need plenty of room. It can propagated in autumn by grafting.

Rosa "Graham Thomas"

Dwarf rose

Rosa "Guletta"

This yellow-flowering, deliciously fragrant variety was developed in 1976 by the Ruiter rose nursery. It is also known under the name "Rugul" and "Tapis Jaune." Although the large, round buds are dark yellow when they first come out, the flowers fade considerably with time. They are saucer-shaped, semi-double and medium-sized, measuring 1.5–2 in across. The plant makes a bushy, densely branched shrub that grows about 14 in high. The brilliant yellow effect of the flowers is especially striking when planted in a group. They are ideal for edging or growing in containers. They should be planted at an interval of 14 in. Grafted on a standard, they look quite stunning in containers. Miniature roses are usually grafted on stocks from 16 to 24 in high. They make an ideal gift for anyone who has a terrace or a balcony because they take up so little space.

ⓘ

Location: ◊ ☼
Care: /❋
Propagation:
Characteristics: △ ∞ ❀
Flowering: summer – autumn

Bedding rose

Rosa "Heidelinde"

This rose created by the German tree nursery Kordes was launched in 1991. It grows up to 28 in high and has a broad, bushy, arching habit. It is an ideal plant for growing in a pot or container on a balcony or terrace. The small, glossy, dark-green leaves contrast beautifully with the old rose, delicately fragrant flowers that are borne in profusion in dense clusters. They are cupped and wide open with undulate petals. The plant must be watered freely and fed regularly during the growing season. Roses that rest during winter can be left outdoors during winter but the container must be protected against the frost by wrapping it, in bubble wrap for example, and the graft point should be protected with peat, bark straw or brushwood. If brought indoors, it must be placed in a cool, frost-free room. It is propagated by grafting.

ⓘ

Location: ◊ ☼
Care: /❋
Propagation:
Characteristics: △ ∞ ❀
Flowering: summer – autumn

Small bush rose

Rosa "Heidetraum"

ⓘ

Location: ◊ ☼
Care: /⚹\
Propagation:
Characteristics: △ ∞ ✿
Flowering: summer – autumn

This very successful variety developed by the Noack tree nursery in 1988 has greatly enriched the range of roses. This undemanding broad-bushy shrub is also excellent ground cover. But with its elegant arching branches, it also makes a beautiful container plant for balconies and terraces. It grows up to 32 in high with a spread of 48 in. This vigorous-growing shrub is covered with a dense, glossy, light green foliage. The double, cupped pink-red flowers are borne from summer till autumn and are grouped in clusters of up to 25 blooms. Like all roses with a deep-growing root system it requires a very deep container. It needs a very sunny, airy location that also provides shelter from rain and becoming waterlogged. After applying a top soil dressing, it is recommended to feed the plant with a weak dose of fertilizer once a week.

English Rose

Rosa "Heritage"

ⓘ

Location: ◊ ☼
Care: /⚹\
Propagation:
Characteristics: △ ∞ ✿
Flowering: summer – autumn

This variety was developed in 1984 by the British grower David Austin. It has dark green, slightly glossy leaves that contrast beautifully with the light pink flowers. The very full globular flowers that are borne singly are very large with a diameter of about 4 in. They have up to 40 undulate petals and are intensely fragrant. This repeat-flowering rose has an upright shrubby habit and can reach a height of 4 ft. That is why it is an ideal container plant for balconies and terraces. It should be given a special place that emphasizes its beauty. It needs a sunny, airy location where it is protected from the rain. Dead-heading regularly will encourage a second flowering. It can remain outdoors in winter if protected against frost but in very cold parts of the country it can be placed indoors in a bright, cool, frost-free room.

Bedding rose

Rosa "Leonardo da Vinci"

This variety which was created in 1993 is a repeat flowering rose that belongs to the group of ground cover roses. Because of its compact, branched habit and the fact that it only grows up to 24 in high, it is ideal as a container plant for balconies and terraces. It has a dense, dark-green, leathery foliage. But its most striking feature are the dark pink, very full flowers, reminiscent of old-fashioned roses. The quartered, rosette-shaped flowers that have more than 60 petals are borne in numerous clusters of 3–5 blooms and are delicately fragrant. Their effect is particularly striking when combined with blue-flowering shrubs. The plant needs a sunny, airy and sheltered place and regular applications of fertilizer during the growing period. This can be in the form of a slow-release fertilizer in spring and summer or a liquid fertilizer every two to three weeks. Make sure that the containers are deep enough.

Location: ◊ ☼
Care: /❄\
Propagation:
Characteristics: △ ∞ ❀
Flowering: summer – autumn

English rose

Rosa "Little Flirt"

This little rose was created in 1961. It is a small, vigorous-growing shrub that reaches a height of just 12 in. It is an ideal container plant that will be a great addition to any balcony or terrace. The small, double, delicately fragrant flowers are orange-red in the center and gold-coloured on the back of the petals. Like all roses, this variety is prone to fungal infections such as mildew. The greyish white, furry coating affects mainly the young shoots, flower stems and leaves. They need an airy location in order to prevent fungal infections. It is important that the plants should dry out quickly after rain. Regular thinning is also important to prevent fungal attacks. If mildew develops in spring or summer, the diseased parts should be removed immediately. Mildew that develops in autumn will not cause much damage because the resting period will have already started by then.

Location: ◊ ☼
Care: /❄\
Propagation:
Characteristics: △ ∞ ❀
Flowering: summer – autumn

Dwarf rose

Rosa "Louise Odier"

Location: ◊ ☼
Care: ⚠
Propagation:
Characteristics: △ ∞ ✿
Flowering: summer – autumn

This Bourbon rose was developed by the French grower Margottin in 1851 and it is a real gem. It is beautiful container plant that will add a romantic note to any balcony or terrace. It is a real treat to the eyes and nose because its rosette-shaped, pink flowers are intensely fragrant. The elegant flowers that are very double measure about 2 in across. "Louise Odier" has a bushy habit and grows up to 5 ft high. Its delicate branches sometimes arch under the weight of the flowers. This is why it is advisable to tie the branches together to give them some support. You must take the size of the plant into account when selecting a container. Make sure you choose a sufficiently large container so that the deep-growing roots have enough room. Apply a slow-release fertilizer so that you do not need to feed the plant during the first year. It will thrive in a sunny, warm location where it is protected from the rain.

Rosa "Louise Odier"

Dwarf rose

Rosa "Maidy"

This variety which has a compact bushy habit was developed in 1984 by the Kordes rose nursery. With a height of 12 in it is an ideal container plant. The distance between each plant should be 10–12 in and there should be no more than 10 plants per square metre (1 plant per square foot). The oval pink buds appear throughout summer till autumn and develop into double, saucer-shaped flowers, about 2.5 in across, whose outer petals have rolled back edges. They are blood-red inside and silvery-white outside. The dense, moss-green foliage is slightly glossy. It prefers a very sunny, open, airy location but it must be protected against the strong midday sun. Rain can also damage the flowers. The soil should always be moist but waterlogging must be avoided at all cost. Regular dead-heading will encourage the production of new blooms.

Location: ○ ☼
Care: /✳\
Propagation:
Characteristics: △ ∞ ✿
Flowering: summer – autumn

Small shrub rose

Rosa "Mainaufeuer"

This rose, created in 1991 by the Kordes rose nursery, belongs to the group of small shrub roses. This compact, bushy shrub with arching branches grows to a height of about 20 in. The deep green leaves are very glossy. The oval red buds appear throughout summer till autumn and develop into double flowers with undulate petals, grouped in clusters of several blooms. The blood-red flowers have prominent gold-yellow stamens. The plant thrives in a sunny, airy location but it must be protected from dripping water and fierce sun. The soil must be kept moist during the growing period but never waterlogged. It needs regular applications of compound fertilizer every two or three weeks or the application of a slow-release fertilizer twice a year. This will encourage vigorous growth and prolific flowering. After the flowering season, the main shoot can be trimmed back lightly and the side shoots more vigorously.

Location: ○ ☼
Care: /✳\
Propagation:
Characteristics: △ ∞ ✿
Flowering: summer – autumn

Rosa "Mandarin"

Location: ◌ ☼
Care: /☀
Propagation:
Characteristics: △ ∞ ❀
Flowering: summer – autumn

Miniature rose

Rosa "Mandarin"

This miniature rose created by the Kordes tree nursery in 1987 only grows to a height of 10 in. This handsome, compact, bushy shrub is therefore ideal as a container plant for balconies and terraces. The small, green leaves are slightly glossy. The two-tone flowers whose colors range from salmon-pink to orange-yellow are borne in loose clusters grouping several blooms. The large, semi-double flowers are 4 in across. Containers combining miniature roses and summer flowering plants are particularly eye-catching. This rose looks very good with lavender, campanulas and candytuft, for instance. Make sure that the plant is not in the sun throughout the day and that the soil does not dry out. In winter, the plants are moved close together and protected against the cold with spruce brushwood or something similar.

Rosa "Orange Meidiland"

Location: ◌ ☼
Care: /☀
Propagation:
Characteristics: △ ∞ ❀
Flowering: summer – autumn

Small shrub rose

Rosa "Meidiland"

This rose belongs to the group of small shrub roses that are very popular as ground cover roses in flowerbeds or as container plants on balconies and terraces. Depending on the form, it has a spreading, bushy habit with arching branches or a shrublike growth with long shoots, reaching a height of 20 in. The flowers are saucer-shaped, single or double and are usually borne in loose clusters grouping numerous blooms. The "Red Meidiland" form has single, carmine-red flowers with a white centre and yellow stamens; "Magic Meidiland" (which was awarded the ADR seal of the All-German Rose Innovation Control Board) has double, dark-pink flowers. "Pink Meidiland" has single, pink flowers. The flowers of these robust forms are less sensitive to rain than many others and are also relatively frost-hardy. It is important that dead blooms should be removed regularly.

Bedding rose

Rosa "Mother's Day"

The variety was originally launched as "Muttertag" in 1950. It is known as "Mother's Day" in English-speaking countries and "Fête des Mères" in France. The bushy, branched shrub has an upright growth and reaches a height of 16 in. Because it grows very slowly, it is an ideal container plant for balconies and terraces. It also looks very good in flowerbeds planted at intervals of 12 in. When the leaves first come out they are reddish, but turn later a glossy, light green. The globular, semi-double raspberry-red flowers are grouped in large clusters. They are very small, measuring only 1.25 in across, and fade dramatically with time. This variety is an excellent repeat-flowerer, meaning that it flowers several times a year, the first flowering being much more prolific than subsequent ones.

Rosa "Mother's Day"

Location: ◊ ☼
Care: /⁂
Propagation:
Characteristics: △ ∞ ✿
Flowering: summer – autumn

Climbing rose

Rosa "New Dawn"

This vigorous growing variety that can grow to a height of 13 ft was first introduced in 1930 by a rose nursery in the United States. This frost-hardy variety is distinguished by its extremely flexible arching branches so that it is particularly versatile in its uses, depending on the location. It can be trained on frames of all kinds, such as trellises against walls, arches and pergolas. It combines very beautifully with clematis. As a standard, it makes a very decorative weeping rose. The glossy, dark green leaves are light green when they first come out. The large, double flowers are a very delicate light pink and are very elegant. They are lightly fragrant and fade with time to almost white with just a pinkish bloom. They appear uninterruptedly until the first frosts. If you cannot plant the rose directly in the ground against a house wall, you must use a very deep container and it must be protected against frost in winter.

Rosa "New Dawn"

Location: ◊ ☼
Care: /⁂
Propagation:
Characteristics: △ ∞ ✿
Flowering: summer – autumn

Climbing rose

Rosa "Parade"

Location: ○ ☼
Care: /⋇\
Propagation:
Characteristics: △ ∞ ❀
Flowering: summer – autumn

This still young, robust climbing rose flowers uninterruptedly throughout the year. The large, dark pink double blooms have a distinctive, old-fashioned charm. The intensely fragrant flowers are borne in dense clusters. They are excellent climbers and their old-fashioned charm make them ideal for galvanized steel rose arbours, obelisks or pyramids. But you will have to be patient because it will take two to three years before the trellis or wall is concealed by greenery. Climbing roses are very undemanding. All you need to do is remove dead wood or thin the plants if necessary. Repeat-flowering varieties are pruned in spring while those that only flower once are pruned immediately after flowering. It is important to choose a very deep container and use humus-rich soil with the addition of an organic fertilizer. This will save you the trouble of further applications of fertilizer later in the year.

Rosa "Parade"

Dwarf rose

Rosa "Pink Symphonie"

The pink flowering "Pink Symphonie" was launched in 1987. Although the flower buds are red when they first appear they develop into pink, round, double flowers that fade to pale pink with time. The outer, turned-back petals are quite conspicuous. It has a dense, bushy habit and reaches a height of 16 in. It is suitable for growing in containers and planting in groups in a flowerbed. It is extremely decorative as a standard in a container. Dwarf roses are usually grafted on 16 in high stocks or wildlings. It is a good idea to plant shrubs or summer flowering plants in the container together with the standard. "Pink Symphonie" standards combine beautifully with campanulas, cat mint, Michaelmas daisies, amellus starwort, lady's mantle, candytuft or veronica. This has the added advantage that the soil dries out less quickly. Wicker baskets also look very good with roses. But make sure that you line them and make drain holes.

Wild rose

Rosa "Pur Caprice"

This elegant wild rose was created by the French grower Delbard. It produces wonderful, semi-double blooms with irregularly fringed petals. When the flowers first appear they are yellow but gradually fade to pink and finally very pale green. The stamens are quite prominent. The handsome flowers are followed by very decorative hips if the dead blooms are not removed. "Pur Caprice" is a vigorous-growing variety that can grow up to 32 in high. It is used mainly in borders or as ground cover. But it also looks very attractive as a container plant on terraces and balconies. Roses grown in containers will ensure an amazing array of magnificent flowers on balconies and terraces in a very short time. They can be planted almost throughout the year, except during periods of frost.

Location: ○ ☼
Care: /☀
Propagation:
Characteristics: △ ∞ ❀
Flowering: summer – autumn

Rosa "Pur Caprice"

Location: ○ ☼
Care: /☀
Propagation:
Characteristics: △ ∞ ❀
Flowering: summer – autumn

Modern Shrub rose

Rosa "Romanze"

Location: ○ ☼
Care: ⚠
Propagation:
Characteristics: △ ∞ ❀
Flowering: summer – autumn

This repeat-flowering shrub rose, launched in 1984, comes from the German rose nursery Roses Tantau. With a height of 5 ft and spread of 32 in, it needs a little more room than the decorative dwarf roses and is best planted on its own. With its profusion of magnificent flowers it is a wonderful eye-catcher. Its pink, double, saucer-shaped flowers with slightly wavy petals appear throughout the summer and well into the autumn until the first frost. The flowers are very large, measuring up to 4–5 in across. Roses usually prefer a sunny location but "Romanze" is one of the few that also do well in partial shade. But make sure that the shade is indeed partial and that they are in the sun for a few hours of the day. It is also important not to plant roses directly under trees because the drops of rain that would continue to drip on the roses after a shower would lead to fungal infection.

Climbing rose

Rosa "Rosarium Uetersen"

Location: ○ ☼
Care: ⚠
Propagation:
Characteristics: △ ∞ ❀
Flowering: summer – autumn

Opposite page:
Rosa "Rosarium Uetersen"

This slow-growing climbing rose that can reach a height of 8 ft was developed by the Kordes tree nursery. It is densely branched, ideal for concealing walls, and it will grow on any kind of support. When grafted on a stock, it produces a decorative cascade of flowers. The rosette-shaped, very double, pink flowers with silvery sheen are produced uninterruptedly throughout the summer. They are delicately fragrant, weather-resistant and relatively large with a diameter of 2.5–3.5 in. The blooms, which fade strongly with time, form a beautiful contrast with the glossy green leaves, which are reddish when they first come out. Although it is frost-resistant, it is best to protect it in winter when grown in a container. The branches that grow on trellis or other support frames should be protected by covering them with spruce brushwood.

Dwarf rose

Rosa "Rosmarin 89"

ⓘ

Location: ◌ ☼
Care: ⧸⃰
Propagation:
Characteristics: △ ∞ ✾
Flowering: summer – autumn

The ancestors of the dwarf roses originate from China where they were well adapted to their habitat. They have a compact, densely branched habit and thick foliage and are frost-resistant. Like "Rosarium Uetersen," "Rosmarin 89" was developed by the Kordes rose nursery and was launched onto the market in 1989. The deep pink, medium-sized, rosette-shaped blooms are double, very full and grouped in dense clusters. The dark green leaves are very decorative. This variety is extremely compact, densely branched and barely reaches 8 in in height, which makes it ideal for balconies and terraces. It is also excellent as edging along paths. Dwarf roses combine beautifully with slow-growing, cushion rock-plants or summer flowering plants. The combination with vigorous-growing neighbours would deprive it of light and nutrients. Make sure there is an interval of 8 in between the plants.

Rosa "Rosmarin 89"

Rosa "Schneewittchen"

Modern shrub rose

Rosa "Schneewittchen"

Also known as "Iceberg," "Schneewittchen" means "Snow White" and as expected, it has medium-sized, double, pure-white flowers that are produced throughout the summer until the first frost. The handsome, delicately fragrant flowers that are borne in large clusters become saucer-shaped when fully open. The narrow leaves are glossy, mid-green. This vigorous-growing, long-flowering rose flowers grows to a height of 5 ft and spread of 32 in. The slender, arching, flowering shoots give this variety a particular romantic charm. In 1983, "Schneewittchen" was chosen as the most beautiful white variety or "world rose." With its profusion of white flowers, it is ideal for brightening up herbaceous borders and other bedding roses. It also looks very good planted on its own in large container. It is very resistant to leaf diseases. In regions with harsh winters, it is very important to protect the plant against frost.

Location: ◌ ☼
Care: ⚺
Propagation:
Characteristics: △ ∞ ❁
Flowering: summer – autumn

Rosa "Sea Foam"

ⓘ

Location: ◊ ☼
Care: /*\
Propagation:
Characteristics: △ ∞ ✿
Flowering: summer – autumn

Small shrub rose

Rosa "Sea Foam"

This attractive variety has a bushy habit and grows 20 in high. The arching, subsequently prostrate shoots can reach 5 ft in length. Planted as ground cover, they soon form a magnificent carpet of flowers but they are also ideal in hanging baskets. The small, shiny green leaves contrast beautifully with the round, white flowers delicately flushed with pink. They are slightly fragrant and grouped in clusters. The variety is frost-resistant but when grown in a container, it needs to be well protected against frost so that the roots do not freeze. They can tolerate frost in nature where the roots freeze slowly and can "thaw out" again slowly. Frost damage results in wavy leaves with brown edges and spots. These must be removed in spring and the plant usually develops new leaves again. Make sure the leaves do not get spattered when you water the plant because this could lead to fungal infections.

Dwarf rose

Rosa "Sonnenkind"

ⓘ

Location: ◊ ☼
Care: /*\
Propagation:
Characteristics: △ ∞ ✿
Flowering: summer – autumn

Like all dwarf roses, this variety is ideal as a container plant for balconies. It is also perfect for rock gardens and edging for paths and borders. "Sonnenkind" has a bushy, densely branched habit and remains very compact, reaching only 14 in in height. It owes its name to the golden-yellow, medium-sized, very full, double flowers that cover the plant almost entirely. The petals are tightly bunched up and the glossy, dark-green leaves almost disappear under the mass of flowers. Dwarf roses are not always the most robust of plants and this is why it is important to place "Sonnenkind" in a sunny, airy location. The roots must be protected well before the first frost so that they do not freeze suddenly. Either you can insulate the container and protect the parts of the plant above ground with brushwood or bring the plant indoors in a bright, cool room.

Dwarf rose

Rosa "Stars 'n' Stripes"

This striking miniature rose that has red and white striped, saucer-shaped flowers is perfect for those who love unusual plants. It grows up to 16 in high and is highly recommended for the small garden, balconies and window boxes. The larger the container, the happier the plant will be because it has a deep-growing root system. Containers used for miniature rose should be at least 10 in deep. If you are planning to combine it with other plants, choose them very carefully. They should be slow-growing, cushion rock plants or summer flowering plants which will not overpower the roses and deprive them of light. Campanulas or candytuft, speedwell, sage or lavender are all perfect partners. Dwarf varieties of conifers, junipers or cypresses that are suitable for window boxes combine very well with roses, as do ornamental grasses.

Climbing rose

Rosa "Super Dorothy"

"Super Dorothy" is an ideal choice if you wish to conceal an unsightly wall or pergola very quickly. Like all rambling roses, this variety has slender, soft shoots that can grow up to 13 ft long, which can easily be tied to support frames. They also look very good in hanging baskets. Grafted on a standard, they make decorative container plants producing beautiful cascades of flowers. If left untied, they can be used as ground cover on slopes where they are perfect for protecting the soil from erosion. The large, reddish buds develop into pink, very full, pompom-like blooms. After the main flowering in summer when clusters can be made up of as many as 20 blooms, the plant continues to produce flowers well into the autumn. With its deep-growing root system, it needs additional watering on hot summer's days. Avoid getting the leaves wet when watering the plants because this could lead to fungal infections.

Location: ◊ ☀
Care: /⋇
Propagation:
Characteristics: △ ∞ ❁
Flowering: summer – autumn

Rosa "Super Dorothy"

Location: ◊ ☀
Care: /⋇
Propagation:
Characteristics: △ ∞ ❁
Flowering: summer – autumn

Climbing rose

Rosa "Super Exelsa"

ℹ️

Location: ◊ ☼
Care: /⁂\
Propagation:
Characteristics: △ ∞ ✿
Flowering: summer – autumn

This variety which was also developed by rose grower Hetzel was launched in 1986 and is the color counterpart of its sister "Super Dorothy." The blooms are carmine-red with white stripes in the middle, fading to violet with time. The small, very full flowers are grouped in dense clusters and are produced uninterruptedly well into the autumn. "Super Exelsa" grows fast and will soon cover trellises and pergolas. It also looks good in hanging baskets and as a standard in a container. In addition, it is an ideal ground cover that will soon cover banks and slopes. Roses need plenty of food. It is therefore recommended to give the plants a slow-release fertilizer in spring and summer to ensure a profusion of flowers. This will spare you the trouble of regular feeding with liquid fertilizer throughout the growing season. If you have worked an organic fertilizer into the soil after planting the rose, it will not need further feeding during that year.

Small shrub rose

Rosa "Swany"

ℹ️

Location: ◊ ☼
Care: /⁂\
Propagation:
Characteristics: △ ∞ ✿
Flowering: summer – autumn

"Swany" has a spreading habit and grows 20 in high and 32 in wide. It is a vigorous grower that quickly forms a thick ground cover. But this ground cover rose is extremely versatile. Its partly prostrate shoots make it an ideal plant for hanging baskets and containers. When grown as medium-sized standard grafted on a stock 24 in tall, it is a real eye-catcher. It combines beautifully with blue-flowering plants such as lavender, sage and campanulas, whose colors contrast very pleasantly with that of the roses. "Swany" also looks very good with white-, pale blue- and pale pink flowering plants. The small, pinnate leaves are copper-coloured when they first come out and turn glossy dark-green with time. They form an attractive, contrasting background with the white, rosette-shaped, very full blooms that are grouped in wide, dense clusters. Remove only the dead blooms without reducing the mass of leaves.

Opposite page:
Rosa "Super Exelsa"

Rosa "Sweet Dream"

ℹ

Location: ◊ ☼
Care: /∗\
Propagation:
Characteristics: △ ∞ ✿
Flowering: summer – autumn

Rosa "The Fairy"

ℹ

Location: ◊ ☼
Care: /∗\
Propagation:
Characteristics: △ ∞ ✿
Flowering: summer – autumn

Patio rose

Rosa "Sweet Dream"

This bushy, upright patio rose is a real little gem. It is taller and more vigorous than many miniature roses as well as relatively frost-resistant. The very full, apricot-coloured, delicately fragrant blooms flower uninterruptedly throughout summer until autumn, contrasting beautifully with the shiny green leaves. It is ideal for growing in containers and window boxes and it is recommended that a special container potting soil is used, as you would do for all container-grown plants. This compost already contains fertilizer so that you not need to apply any fertilizer during the first year. Indeed, it is important not to over-fertilize roses because this would lead to weak shoots that would be prone to attacks by aphids and other pests. The shoots must be able to mature fully, in other words become woody, so that they are able to withstand frost without suffering serious damage. Slow-release or organic fertilizer releases nutrients gradually so that the sensitive roots do not become scorched.

Bedding rose

Rosa "The Fairy"

This old rose is experiencing a renaissance. It was first developed in 1932 and is still as popular today as it was all those years ago. It has a shrub-like, bushy habit and yet is very compact with prostrate to arching shoots. It can reach a height of 35 in and a spread of 28 in. Because it is fast-growing, it is often used as ground cover, hedging, in hanging baskets or as standard in a container. The pink, very full, rosette-shaped blooms that are saucer-shaped when fully open are particularly graceful. They are quite small, between 0.75 and 1 in, and they are borne in dense clusters throughout the summer. The leaves are small and glossy green. "The Fairy" looks wonderful combined with herbaceous perennials such as lavender, for instance, which will make up for the fragrance that this rose lacks. "The Fairy" is very robust and resistant.

Miniature rose

Rosa "Yellow Doll"

This miniature rose is a vigorous, bushy plant that grows only 12 in high. Its small, full, pale yellow, slightly fragrant flowers are absolutely enchanting. "Yellow Doll" will bring the magic of roses to even the smallest terrace or balcony. The only condition is that it should be sunny and airy. They can be grown in pots or window boxes and look particularly attractive in terracotta pots. Terracotta adds a Mediterranean charm and has the further advantage that it is also very good for the plant. The soil dries quickly and there is little danger of waterlogging, which roses hate. Dead blooms must be removed regularly to encourage more flowers. This rose is easily propagated from semi-ripe cuttings in summer and hardwood cuttings in late autumn. For further information, see the chapter on "Propagation".

Location: ◊ ☼
Care: /⚹\
Propagation:
Characteristics: △ ∞ ✿
Flowering: summer – autumn

Miniature rose

Rosa "Zwergkönig 78"

"Zwergkönig 78" with its brilliant red blooms was created in 1978, which explains the number in its name, the rest of which means "dwarf king." The medium-sized blooms are loosely full, long-lasting and weather-resistant. Their appearance remains unchanged even when fading. The dark green leaves contrast beautifully with the bright red blooms. The plant has a bushy yet compact habit. With a height of 20 in, it is ideal for growing in a container but it can also be used for low hedging, edging and borders. There should be a distance of 12 in between plants when planted in a container, while you should allow for about 1 plant per square foot if planted out. This rose is frost-resistant but when grown in a container it should be protected in winter. It has a counter-part that was created in 1982, "Zwergkönigin 82" with pink blooms. It is as robust and weather-resistant as its partner but in addition has a delicate fragrance.

Location: ◊ ☼
Care: /⚹\
Propagation:
Characteristics: △ ∞ ✿
Flowering: summer – autumn

Climbing plants

Opposite page: Lathyrus

Climbing plants are good all-rounders. While annual climbers surprise you every year with unexpected delights, perennials offer an ideal visual screen against prying eyes. Grapevines, scarlet runner beans or ornamental pumpkins will also produce fruit or vegetables. Plants native to cooler regions such as clematis or wisteria can over-winter outdoors while the exotic Mandavilla needs a frost-free place.

Self-clinging climbers such as ivy, Russian vine or climbing hydrangeas do not need any climbing support because they have holdfasts that enable them to cling to walls. However it is important that there are no cracks in the walls or plaster because this would allow the roots to get into the wall and possibly damage it. When the plants have reached the desired height, they can be pruned every year. Climbers such as clematis and jasmine need a climbing support because they climb by twisting the stalks or petioles of their leaves round a support. Twining climbers such as knot-grass and honeysuckle climb by twining themselves around the climbing support. All they need is a vertical support such as a pole or a vertical wire. Climbing roses and bougainvillea are scrambling climbers that in nature grow over other plants. They need to be trained against a climbing support to which they should be tied. It is recommended that the climbing support be placed 2–4 in from the wall of the house. When selecting a climbing support for a container-grown plant, it is advisable to choose a sufficiently large and stable one because it is likely to be difficult to change it later. Supports made from treated wood or metal are ideal because they do not rot.

Remember when choosing a site for your climbing plant that species and varieties with large, tender leaves need a place where they are sheltered from the wind. When selecting a container, choose one that is large enough so that the plant can remain undisturbed for several years. Apply a slow-release fertilizer when planting.

*A*ctinidia

Actinidia kolomikta

Actinidia kolomikta

Location: ◗ ☼ ⚠
Propagation: ₀°°
Characteristics: ∞ ❀ ⚘ ❄
Flowering: spring – summer

This deciduous, woody-stemmed twining climber, a member of the *Actinidiaceae* family, is native to Japan, Korea and China. It can climb to a height of 10 ft and grows considerably slower than its relatives *A. arguta* and *A. chinensis*, Chinese gooseberry and kiwi. Low supports on house-walls or placed in containers are quite sufficient. The white fragrant flowers appear in early summer, followed in female plants by gooseberry-like, edible fruits. However, to produce fruit, you need a male and a female plant. The leaves of the male plant are very striking, green at first then, starting at the point, turning white, then pink to reddish-violet. It needs a warm, sunny, sheltered place, especially in winter. It also needs plenty of water and monthly applications of liquid fertilizer. It is propagated from semi-ripe cuttings in summer or from seed immediately after the seed has ripened. The plant can be trimmed into the desired shape in early spring.

*A*kebia

Akebia quinata

ℹ

Location: ◌ ☼ – ☼ ⚠
Propagation: ₀°°
Characteristics: ∞ ❀ ❄
 Flowering: spring

This deciduous climber which belongs to the *Lardizabalaceae* family is native to East Asia. The deep-green leaves that consist of 5 rounded leaflets quickly form a dense foliage. The unisexual, brownish-purple flowers that appear in early spring are borne in drooping flower heads that emanate a delicate vanilla fragrance. The strikingly large, brownish-purple fruits develop in September after a warm summer. Akebias will grow in sun or partial shade, in any fertile, well-drained soil. They tolerate temperatures of 5° F, so normal late frosts will only damage the flowers. An akebia can easily reach a height of 26 ft so it should be planted against a house or terrace wall, supported by trellis or a similar support structure. It is advisable to prune after flowering to promote vigorous growth. It can be grown from seed in spring and from cuttings in summer or runners in winter.

Blueberry climber

Ampelopsis brevipedunculata

This deciduous climber, a member of the *Vitaceae* family, is native to China, Japan and Korea. The smooth, dark-green leaves are divided into 3 to 5 lobes. The rather inconspicuous green flowers appear in summer, followed in autumn by small, attractive berries that are pink-purple at first, becoming deep blue later. This vigorous climber can grow up to 16 ft and is ideal for growing against a terrace wall but it will need the support of a trellis or similar support frame. By cutting it back in spring, *Ampelopsis* can be kept to the desired height. Although it will grow well in partial shade, it needs sun to produce fruit. It thrives in loamy, moist soil and benefits from monthly applications of a compound fertilizer. It can be grown from seed in spring and semi-ripe cuttings in summer. In winter it must be placed in a frost-free place.

Location: ◆ ☼—☀ ⚠
Care: ❄
Propagation: ₀°°
Characteristics: ∞ ❀
Flowering: *summer*

Dutchman's pipe

Aristolochia macrophylla

This variety, a deciduous twining climber that is also known as *A. durior* and *A. sipho*, belongs to the birthwort family (*Aristolochiaceae*) and is native to North America. The heart-shaped leaves 12 in long are dark green with paler, downy undersides and arranged in such a way that they overlap. The single, round lobed flowers, purple to brown inside and yellow-green outside, appear in summer, concealed among the foliage. Supported by a trellis, Dutchman's pipe makes an excellent visual screen or protection against the sun on terraces. Pinching out the tips of shoots during growth period promotes branching. It prefers partial shade and needs plenty of water and fertilizer during summer. It winter it needs some protection against frost. It can be grown from seed or propagated from greenwood cuttings in spring.

Aristolochia macrophylla

Location: ◆ ☼—☀ ⚠
Care: ⚠
Propagation: ₀°°
Characteristics: ∞ ❀ ❀
Flowering: *summer*

Creeping snapdragon

Asarina barclaiana

Location: ◑ ☼ △
Care: ❄
Propagation: ⊙°
Characteristics: ⊙ ✿
Flowering: summer – autumn

Creeping snapdragon, a member of the brownwort or *Scrophulariaceae* family, is native to Mexico. It has kidney-shaped leaves 1.5 in long and bears flowers 1.5–3 in long, tubular with white or greenish throat and purple-red, pink-red, lilac or white tipped petals, depending on the variety. Growing to a height of 10 ft, creeping snapdragons are ideal container plants for balconies and terraces. They cling to their support, which may be wire or rope, by means of twining leaf and flower stems. They grow best in the sun, sheltered from the wind, in fertile, well-drained soil. Although perennial in nature, they are usually cultivated as annuals because of their sensitivity to frost. If moved indoors in autumn, they will flower for a few more weeks. The plant is best grown from seed or propagated from cuttings in spring.

Trumpet flower

Bignonia capreolata

Location: ◑ ☼ △
Care: ❄
Propagation:
Characteristics: ∞ ✿
Pests: spider mite, aphids
Flowering: spring–summer

This climber, a member of the trumpet tree family (*Bignoniaceae*), is native to forests of the south-eastern United States. Although it can be grown in the garden, terrace or balcony in temperate zones, it must be moved indoors during winter because it is not frost-resistant. The evergreen leaves 7 in long consist of 2 oblong, dark green leaflets and are arranged in opposite pairs. The funnel-shaped, orange-red flowers that appear in summer are followed in autumn by pea-pod shaped fruits. This robust, vigorous growing climber can reach a height of 33 ft. It prefers a very sunny position and fertile, moist but well-drained soil. It must fed every week during the growing season. In winter it must be moved to a light place with a temperature of 41–50° F. The plant can be cut back after flowering. In spring it should be repotted or the top soil renewed. It can be propagated from semi-ripe or ripe wood cuttings in summer and autumn and from runners in winter.

Trumpet vine

Campsis radicans

This perennial climber belongs to the *Bignoniaceae* family and is native to North America. Its English name refers to the striking orange to red, trumpet-shaped flowers that appear in late summer till autumn. The light green, pinnate leaves are 10 in long and Trumpet-shaped flowers are grouped in drooping clusters. The trumpet vine uses aerial roots to climb with and can reach a height of 33 ft by this means. If there is enough space on the terrace, this frost hardy climber is ideal for concealing walls or covering facades with greenery. If trained against a very smooth surface it is advisable to provide some support for the aerial roots to cling to. It needs a warm, sunny location where it is sheltered from the wind. The roots should be in the shade. In summer it needs plenty of water and food. The previous year's wood is cut back in late winter or early spring. It is propagated from cuttings or runners.

Campsis radicans

ⓘ

Location: ◗ ☼ ⚠
Propagation:
Characteristics: ∞ ✿ ❄
Diseases: leaf spot
Pests: mildew, scale insect,
    mealy bug, white fly
Flowering: summer – autumn

Balloon vine

Cardiospermum halicacabum

This evergreen climber, a member of the *Sapindaceae* family, is native to tropical Africa, India and North, Central and South America. It is mainly grown for its attractive fern-like foliage and balloon-like fruits. The tiny, greenish-white flowers that are borne in summer are followed by oval fruits 1.25 in long that are light green when they first develop and later ripen to reddish brown. This climber grows up to 13 ft high and is usually sold as an annual or biennial. It is sensitive to frost and should therefore be moved indoors during winter if it is grown as a biennial. It grows best in full sun and needs plenty of water and monthly applications of liquid compound fertilizer. Remove the dried parts in early spring. It can be propagated from seed or semi-ripe cuttings in summer.

ⓘ

Location: ◗ ☼ ⚠
Care: ⌂
Propagation: ⠐
Characteristics: ⊙/∞ ✿
Pests: aphids, white fly
Flowering: summer – autumn

Clematis, the star climber

Clematis should always be given a special place, for instance near a seat on the terrace or balcony or near the front door. Clematis needs moist, humus-rich soil and likes to keep its roots cool. The root area should therefore always be in the shade, whether grown in a container or directly in full garden. When growing clematis in a container, planting smaller plants such as lavender, pinks and campanulas around the base is helpful to provide the necessary shade.

By carefully selecting the varieties of clematis you can prolong the over-all flowering period. The small-flowered Clematis montana with its fragrant varieties "Pink Perfection" or "Elizabeth" and C. macropetala mark the beginning of the flowering season in spring. Clematis hybrids such as "Nelly Moser" and the Alpine clematis C. alpina flower from May onward with a repeat flowering in summer. C. viticella flowers in July with numerous, small flowers in shades of blue-violet. Large-flowered hybrids such as "Jackmanii" with its dark violet blooms and "Ernest Markham", which produces wine-red blooms, flower uninterruptedly from early summer until autumn. Clematis come in the most delightful colors that combine beautifully and produce a wonderful effect. Planting several different varieties of similar color can also be succesful.

Roses and clematis go very well together but you must make sure that their growing strength is about the same. They will then live happily together in the same container for several years. Repeat-flowering varieties like "Super Dorothy" or "New Dawn" and the summer flowering clematis such as C. viticella are ideal combinations.

Young plants should be cut down to 4 in from the ground to ensure a bushy growth. Spring-flowering varieties should be pruned immediately after flowering. Larger specimens can be thinned after flowering, while summer flowering varieties should be cut back vigorously in late autumn.

Alpine clematis

Clematis alpina

ℹ

Location: ●☀ ⚠
Propagation: ₀°°
Characteristics: ∞ ✿ ❄
Diseases: clematis wilt
Pests: aphids
Flowering: spring – early spring

This early-flowering clematis, a member of the *Ranunculaceae* family, is native to the mountainous regions stretching from the Alps to Siberia. A slow-growing climber, it can reach a height of 6 ft 6 in. The mid-green leaves consist of 3 lanceolate to broad-oval leaflets. The bell-shaped flowers 1.5 in long, appear in spring. Besides the original blue with a white center, the flowers also come in pink and mid-blue. The fluffy fruits develop in late summer and autumn. This robust, undemanding clematis is ideal for covering walls and trellises on balconies and terraces. It is hardy and grow best in the sun or partial shade but it is important that the roots should be shaded. It needs plenty of water and nutrients during the growing season and will benefit from light thinning. It can be propagated from seed or cuttings.

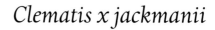
Clematis x jackmanii

ℹ

Location: ●☀–☀ ⚠
Propagation: ₀°°
Characteristics: ∞ ✿ ❄
Diseases: clematis wilt
Pests: aphids
Flowering: summer

Large-flowered clematis

Clematis x jackmanii

This clematis hybrid, a member of the *Ranunculaceae* family, is a magnificent sight on any balcony or terrace. A late-flowering, large flowered climber, it blooms throughout summer and can reach a height of 10 ft. The single flowers that measure 3–4 in across are deep purple when they first come out, later turning violet. The plant grows well both in sunny and shady location and is completely frost-resistant. Unlike the leaves and flowers that prefer sun, the roots must be kept cool and shaded. It is therefore recommended to plant low-growing herbaceous perennials around it. It needs wire or trellis to climb. Late-flowering varieties need severe pruning. In early spring, cut above a pair of upward pointing buds just above the base to promote growth and prolific flowering. Clematis are prone to clematis wilt; an apparently completely healthy plant affected by it can die within just a few days.

Clematis montana

Clematis montana "Rubens"

Clematis montana, a member of the *Ranunculaceae* family, is native to China. The leaves of this early-flowering climber have three, long, coarsely-toothed leaflets, flushed with purple. The single, deep pink flowers with cream-coloured stamens appear in early summer. Sometimes the plant flowers again until the autumn. It is an extremely vigorous growing clematis tht can reach a height of 26 ft or more and is therefore ideal for growing against facades and terrace walls. It prefers a sunny to partially shaded location but it is important that the roots should be in the shade. If the plant must be cut back because of space reasons, it should be trimmed in summer, that is immediately after flowering. Like most clematis, it is usually propagated from cuttings. In regions with harsh winters, it is advisable to protect them against frost during winter.

Location: ◦ ☀—☀ ⚠
Propagation: ◦°
Characteristics: ∞ ❀ ❄
Diseases: clematis wilt
Pests: aphids
Flowering: early summer

Clematis hybrid "Multiblue"

Large-flowered clematis

Clematis hybrid "Multiblue"

This unusual clematis, a member of the large-flowered group, is a great eye-catcher on balconies and terraces with its impressive, colourful flowers. What makes this clematis so extraordinary are the flowers, which are dark-blue, very full and could almost be confused with dahlias. They are quite large, measuring 3-4 in across. The main flowering period is in early summer, followed by a repeat flowering in late summer or autumn. Supported by wires, the plants will soon cover walls and pergolas, reaching a height of 8 ft. This frost-resistant plant remains outdoors in winter. It prefers a sunny to partially shady location and needs plenty of water during the growing period. However, the roots must never be waterlogged. The flowers are borne on new wood, which is why it must be cut back to 20 cm (8 in) in autumn. The shoots should be trimmed lightly after the first flowering. It is propagated from cuttings or grown from seed.

Location: ◦ ☀—☀ ⚠
Propagation: ◦°
Characteristics: ∞ ❀ ❄
Diseases: clematis wilt
Pests: aphids
Flowering: early summer,
    autumn

Large-flowered clematis

Clematis hybrid "Nelly Moser"

ⓘ

Location: 💧 ☼–☼ ⋀
Propagation: ⋅°°
Characteristics: ∞ ❀ ❅
Diseases: clematis wilt
Pests: aphids
Flowering: early summer,
  autumn

This deciduous member of the *Ranunculaceae* family belongs to the group of the large-flowered clematis hybrids. It grows up to 10 ft high with a rather compact habit and is a real eye-catcher as a container plant on balconies and terraces. The single, very large flowers measure up to 6 in across and are pale pink with red stripes in the middle and prominent, dark red stamens. The flowers appear in early summer. Like most clematis, this hybrid prefers a bright to partially shaded location whereby the flowers are in the sun and the roots in the shade. It needs plenty of water during the growing period but does not tolerate being waterlogged, which can lead to wilt. In early spring, cut back weak and dead shoots as well old leaves. If necessary, the plant can be cut back to 16-24 in. It is propagated from seed or cuttings.

Large-flowered clematis

Clematis-hybrid "Ville de Lyon"

ⓘ

Location: 💧 ☼–☼⋀
Propagation: ⋅°°
Characteristics: ∞ ❀ ❅
Diseases: clematis wilt
Pests: aphids
Flowering: summer, autumn

This large-flowered clematis which belongs to the *Ranunculacea* family is a striking plant and a magnificent addition to any balcony or terrace. Supported by trellis or wires it will soon reach a height of 10 ft on a balcony, terrace or roof garden. It is very sensitive to rain and should therefore not be placed under a gutter where it could be dripped on. The deep carmine-red flowers with dark edges and yellow stamens appear in late summer. During the growing they need plenty of water and monthly applications of a compound fertilizer. The container should be deep enough so that the root ball are at least 4 in below the surface. They can remain outdoors during winter but young plants should be protected against frost. The previous year's shoots should be cut back drastically. It is propagated from seed or cuttings.

*P*urple clematis

Clematis viticella

This late-flowering clematis, a member of the *Ranunculaceae* family, was already known and cultivated as a garden plant in the 16th century. There are many varieties besides the wild species, which is native to central-southern Europe. This elegant plant that can reach a height of 13 ft is ideal for covering walls, railings, trellises and walls on terraces and balconies. Those who are in a hurry should plant three specimens in one container about 20 in diameter. The plants will also need a support. The wild species has violet, bell-shaped flowers with four petals that are produced from July until September. There are new varieties that come in other colors such as various shades of blue, purple-red or pink. These frost-hardy plants can remain outdoors in winter. They need severe pruning in early spring.

Location: ♦ ☼ — ☀ ⚠
Propagation: ₒ°°
Characteristics: ∞ ❀ ❆
Diseases: clematis wilt
Pests: aphids
Flowering: summer

Clematis viticella "Kermesina"

Cobaea

ℹ

Location: ◊ ☼–☼ ⚠
Care: 🛈
Propagation: ⸬
Characteristics: ☉ ❀
Pests: aphids
Flowering: summer – autumn

Cup-and-saucer vine

Cobaea scandens

This evergreen woody-stemmed tendril climber, a member of the *Cobaeaceae* family, is native to the mountainous regions of Mexico. In temperate regions it is cultivated as an annual and grows to a height of 16 ft. The deep green leaves consist of 4 to 6 oval leaflets. It climbs by means of tendrils that develop at the end of the leaves. The cup-and-saucer vine takes its name from the large, bell-shaped fragrant, yellowish green flowers that turn purple with age and are produced from mid-summer to the first frost. When cultivated in a container, this can be moved outdoors on the balcony or terrace from May onwards where it should be placed in a sunny location. The plant needs plenty of water and weekly applications of fertilizer. Because it is such a vigorous grower, plants make ideal visual screens and provide excellent protection against wind and sun. When cultivated as an annual, it is propagated from seed in spring.

Chilean glory vine

Eccremocarpus scaber

ℹ

Location: ◊ ☼ ⚠
Care:
Propagation: ⸬
Characteristics: ⚠ ☉/∞ ❀
Pests: spider mite
Flowering: summer – autumn

The fast-growing, evergreen member of the *Bignoniaceae* family is native to the high mountain ranges in Chile. In temperate regions, it is often cultivated as an annual or biennial. Chilean glory vine is a densely branched tendril climber which can reach a height of 10 ft. The leaves are bipinnate and the tubular, orange-red flowers are borne in racemes 4–6 in long from late spring to autumn. The fruits are inflated fruit pods 1.5 in long. When grown in a container Chilean glory vine thrives best in a sunny, sheltered location and needs wire or trellis for support. Rain and low temperatures can seriously affect growth and the production of flowers. During the growing period it needs plenty of water and weekly applications of fertilizer. Only in the mildest regions can *C. scandens* over-winter outdoors. Ideally it should be moved to a bright place with a temperature of 41–50° F. It is propagated from seed in spring.

Russian vine

Fallopia baldschuanica

Russian vine, a member of the polygonum or *Polygonaceae* family that is native to south-east Russia, is today one of the most popular climbers. It is also known as *Bilderdykia baldschuanica* and *Polygonum baldschuanicum*. This deciduous climber has dark green, heart-shaped leaves and tiny, fragrant, funnel-shaped white flowers, flushed with pink, borne in drooping sprays in summer and autumn. The small fruits are triangular and pale pink. This undemanding twining climber is ideal for covering, facades, pergolas and walls. If grown on balconies and terraces, it needs to be trimmed back several times a year in order to keep it in check. It is rampant and can grow 10–13 ft a year. It is important to give it a strong support. It can easily be propagated from semi-ripe cuttings take in summer.

Location: ◗ ☼ – ☀
Propagation:
Characteristics: ⊔ ∞ ❀ ❄
Pests: leaf mine
Flowering: summer – autumn

Fallopia baldschuanica

Common ivy

Hedera helix

ℹ

Location: 💧 ☀—☀
Propagation: ✿✿
Characteristics: 🪣 ✖ ∞ 🏵 ❄
Diseases: leaf spot
*Pests: spider mite, scale insect,
   aphids*
Flowering: autumn

This species of ivy, a member of the *Araliaceae* family, is native to Europe and includes numerous varieties, some of them with variegated foliage. This robust, evergreen, frost-hardy, self-clinging climber can reach a height of 33 ft or more and will grow against any kind of support. It is easily grown in containers on balconies and terraces. Being evergreen, it also provides welcome greenery in winter. Its leaves are 3- to 5-lobed, oval to triangular depending on the variety. After about ten years umbels of small, green flowers are produced in autumn. The pea-like, black berries are very popular with birds. Ivy tolerates severe pruning and prefers shade. Young plants are relatively tender. It can easily be propagated from seed, cuttings or runners, but seedlings are thought to climb better. The consumption of ivy can cause severe nausea.

Hedera helix

Japanese hop

Humulus japonicus

This herbaceous, twining climber, a member of the *Cannabaceae* family and native to Asia, is usually cultivated as an annual because it is sensitive to frost. It will soon grow to a height of 20 ft and will quickly cover balcony railings and terrace walls. The 5- to 7-lobed, palmate, dark green leaves covered with coarse hairs are very decorative. There are male and female plants but some are also dioecious. In mid to late summer female plants produce oval clusters of tiny, green flowers. Japanese hop will do well both in sun and partial shade. The soil must be moist but well-drained. It can be propagated from seed but the seedlings should only be planted out in late spring after all danger of frost has passed.

Location: 💧 ☼ — ☼ ⚠
Propagation: ⸰°°
Characteristics: ☉ ⚘
Diseases: verticillium wilt
Flowering: summer

Climbing hydrangea

Hydrangea anomala ssp. Petiolaris

This root climber, a member of the *Hydrangeaceae* family, is native to Japan, Korea and Taiwan. It is a woody-stemmed, deciduous plant with dark green, heart-shaped leaves that turn a brilliant yellow in autumn and can very quickly reach a height of 33 ft. But the main attraction are the fragrant flowers, which are borne in flat heads in early summer. They are creamy-white and the heads are up to 10 in across. Climbing hydrangea's dense, vigorous growth makes it ideal for covering balcony and terrace walls. It needs partial or complete shade and plenty of water and food. The soil should be low in lime and well-drained. Being frost-hardy it can remain outdoors all year round. *H. petiolaris* can be propagated from cuttings or runners. Consumption of any part of the plant can cause slight stomach upsets.

Location: 💧 ☼ — ☼ ⚠
Propagation:
Characteristics: ✖ ∞ ⚘ ❄
Diseases: hydrangea virus,
    mildew, leaf spot, grey mould
Pests: aphids, spider mite, scale
    insect, weevils, leaf bugs
Flowering: summer

Opposite page: Ipomoea

Red morning glory

Ipomoea coccinea

Location: 🌢 ☼ ⚠
Propagation: ₀°
Characteristics: ✖ ☉ ✿
Diseases: mildew, viruses
Pests: spider mite
Flowering: summer – autumn

This annual, twining climber that belongs to the *Convolvulaceae* family is native to the south-east of the United States and is also known as *Quamoclit coccinea*. With the help of support it can reach a height of 13 ft and is a spectacular sight on any balcony or terrace. The oval leaves over 5 in long are mid- to deep-green. The small, fragrant, scarlet flowers with yellow throat are borne in summer in clusters of 3 to 8 blooms. The plant needs a very sunny location, sheltered from the wind. It requires plenty of water and weekly applications of fertilizer to encourage growth and the production of flowers. But it does not tolerate being waterlogged at all. It can be raised from seed in spring indoors, sowing several seeds per pot. The tender seedlings must be gradually accustomed to cooler temperatures. The seeds are very poisonous if swallowed.

Morning glory

Ipomoea lobata

Location: 🌢 ☼–☼ ⚠
Propagation: ₀°
Characteristics: ✖ ☉ ✿
Diseases: mildew, viruses
Pests: spider mite
Flowering: summer – autumn

Also known as *I. versicolor*, *Mina lobata* and *Quamoclit*, this well-known climber is a member of the bindweed or *Convolvulaceae* family. Although cultivated as an annual in temperate zones because it is frost tender, it is a herbaceous perennial in its native country of Mexico. The shoots and leaf-stalks of this species are tinged with carmine red. The serrated, mid-green leaves are usually 3-lobed. The short-lived, dark red flowers that later fade to orange, yellow and finally white, are borne in one-sided racemes that appear in summer. It is best to plant several specimens together and provide some climbing support. The plants needs a sunny to partially shady location, sheltered from the wind and sandy, well-drained soil. They also require plenty of water and weekly applications of fertilizer during the growth period. It is propagated from seed in spring. The seeds are very poisonous.

Common morning glory

Ipomoea purpurea

ⓘ

Location: 💧 ☀ ⚠
Propagation: ⸪
Characteristics: ✖ ⊙ ❀
Diseases: mildew, viruses
Pests: spider mite
Flowering: summer

The wild form of this well-known climber that is also known as *Convolvulus pur-pureus* and *Pharbitis purpurea* is probably native to Mexico. This species is cultivated as an annual in temperate zones and has slender, hairy shoots and large, heart-shaped, mid-green leaves. The wide-open, trumpet-shaped flowers appear in summer and may be pink, red, purple-blue or white, striped, three-coloured or full, depending on the variety. Morning glory can reach a height of 10 ft, quickly covering trellises, wires, walls and pyramids on balconies and terraces. The plant needs a very sunny location and will not tolerate cold, wet weather or draughts. It needs plenty of water and weekly applications of fertilizer to ensure abundant flowering. It is propagated from seed, sown in spring, either early in spring under glass or in May directly in pots or containers. The seeds are very poisonous.

Morning glory

Ipomoea tricolor

ⓘ

Location: 💧 ☀ ⚠
Propagation: ⸪
Characteristics: ✖ ⊙ ❀
Diseases: mildew, viruses
Pests: spider mite
Flowering: summer

This species of morning glory, also a member of the *Convolvulaceae* family, is native to tropical America and has been cultivated as a garden plant for centuries. In temperate zones this floriferous, herbaceous, perennial, twining climber is cultivated as an annual. Trained along wires or a trellis it can soon reach a height of 10 ft. With its numerous heart-shaped leaves and striking, trumpet-shaped flowers that are produced in profusion throughout the summer, this morning glory is ideal for providing luxuriant greenery on balconies and terraces. When cultivated in pots or containers, it is best to plant several of them together. It takes its botanical name *tricolor* from the flowers, which are purple when they first come out, then fade to pale blue with a white throat. Morning glories need a sunny location where they are also sheltered from the wind. In summer, they need regular watering and weekly applications of fertilizer. It is grown from seed in spring. The seeds are very poisonous if ingested.

Winter jasmine

Jasminum nudiflorum

This spreading shrub that belongs to the *Oleaceae* family is native to Western China. This scrambling climber can reach a height of to 10 ft when trained against a support. It is an ideal container plant for a balcony or terrace. Placed in a sunny to partially shaded location, sheltered from the wind, it already starts flowering in early spring. It will also benefit from monthly applications of a compound fertilizer. The pinnate leaves are only 1.25 in long. In temperate regions it is rare that the flowers ever to develop into fruits. The flowering shoots must be cut immediately after the blooms have faded so that the plant does not become too dense and to encourage it to flower again. Winter jasmine can stay outdoors all year round; only in regions with extremely cold winters will it need some protection. It is propagated from cuttings in summer.

Location: 💧 ☼–☼ ⚠
Propagation:
Characteristics: ∞ 🏵 ❄
Pests: aphids, mealy bug
Flowering: spring

Lonicera

Evergreen honeysuckle

Lonicera henryi

This woody-stemmed, evergreen honeysuckle, a member of the *Caprifoliaceae* family, is native to western China. Its dense, vigorous habit, elegant, lanceolate leaves and fragrant flowers make it an ideal container plant for balconies and terraces where it will provide an excellent visual screen and protection against the wind. However, it needs the help of a support to climb. In autumn the yellow-red flowers develop into round, black-blue berries which are not edible. Honeysuckle needs a sunny to partially shady location, plenty of water and monthly applications of fertilizer during the growth period. It should be cut back after flowering so that it does not become bare at the base. It needs protection in winter if left outdoors. It is propagated from cuttings in early summer.

Location: 💧 ☼
Care: ⚠
Propagation:
Characteristics: ⊔ ✖ ∞ 🏵
Pests: aphids
Flowering: summer

Lathyrus odoratus

ⓘ

Location: ●● ☼ ⚠
Propagation: ₒ°°
Characteristics: ✖ ☉ ✿
Diseases: mildew, stem and root
rot, fusarium wilt, viruses
Pests: aphids, slugs and snails,
thrips
Flowering: summer – autumn

Sweet pea

Lathyrus odoratus

This annual papilionaceous annual, a member of the *Fabaceae* family, is ideal for bringing delicate colour to your balcony or terrace. Trained along wires, it will soon cover walls and railings. For window boxes and containers, it is best to choose bushy or dwarf varieties that only grow 20 in high. The leaves are small, pinnate and oval. The fragrant flowers 1.25 in across come in white, pink, violet and blue, depending on the variety, and are borne in clusters throughout the summer until early autumn. They are followed in autumn by oblong, pod-like capsules. This undemanding plant requires a warm, sunny location, protected from wind and the midday sun. It needs plenty of food and regular watering. Faded flowering shoots must be removed in order to encourage further flowering.

Chilean jasmine

Mandevilla laxa

ⓘ

Location: ●● ☼ ⚠
Care: 🏠
Propagation: ₒ°°
Characteristics: ⚠ ∞ ✿
Pests: aphids, spider mite,
mealy bug, white fly
Flowering: summer – autumn

The wild form of this woody-stemmed twining climber that belongs to the dogbane family (*Apocynaceae*) is native to Bolivia and Argentina. Trained against a suitable support on a balcony or terrace it can reach a height of 16 ft. In summer it needs plenty of water and nutrients. The glossy green, oval leaves, heart-shaped at the base, are shed in winter. The white, tubular-shaped flowers are borne in large, loose clusters throughout the summer till autumn. Their intense fragrance can cause headache in some people. All parts of the plant can cause nausea if ingested. The milky sap can cause skin irritation. If placed in a dark place during winter, it loses its leaves and is therefore cut back vigorously beforehand. It is best propagated from cuttings in late summer.

Virginia creeper

Parthenocissus

This woody-stemmed, deciduous tendril climber that includes several varieties is native to North America and East Asia. The leaves consist of oval, pointed leaflets and they turn a brilliant red in autumn, adding great colour to the balcony or terrace. The inconspicuous white-greenish flowers that appear in summer concealed among the foliage are followed in autumn by dark-blue or black berries, which are very popular with birds. This undemanding plant, which in nature can reach a height of 40 ft or more, does best in a sunny to partially shady location. It is important to choose a sufficiently large container and to provide young plants with a support. This quick-growing climber must be cut back in early winter and, if necessary, again in summer. It is propagated from semi-ripe cuttings in late summer or hardwood cuttings in late autumn.

Scarlet runner bean

Phaseolus coccineus

This fast-growing papilionaceous climber (*Fabaceae*) is native to South America and is closely related to the garden bean. It is a vigorous-growing plant that does well even in cool, rainy summers and with its dense foliage, it is an ideal wind and sun-screen on balconies and terraces, where it can reach a height of 10 ft. The numerous, small red flowers that give the plant its name are borne on long-stemmed clusters from June to September. Varieties such as "Désirée," "Weisse Riesen" and "Bicolor" have white or white-red flowers. The firm, pod-like fruits are a delicious vegetable when cooked, but the raw beans are poisonous. The scarlet runner bean grown as an annual is quite undemanding. The soil must not be allowed to dry out and they must not stand in full sun. It needs weekly applications of fertilizer during the growing period. It can be propagated from seed in May by sowing directly in the container at intervals of 2.5 in.

Location: 🌢 ☼–☼
Propagation:
Characteristics: ⊔ ∞ ▨ ❋
Flowering: summer

Phaseolus coccineus

Location: 🌢 ☼–☼
Propagation: ∘°
Characteristics: ⚠ ☉ ❀
Diseases: root rot
Pests: black bean aphid
Flowering: summer – autumn

*P*urple bell vine

Rhodochiton atrosanguineus

🛈

Location: 💧 ☼ ⛰
Propagation: ⸪
Characteristics: ☉ ❀
Pests: spider mite, white fly
Flowering: summer-autumn

This climbing semi-shrub is native to Mexico and is a member of the brownwort family (*Scrophulariaceae*). It is grown as an annual in temperate zones and reaches a height of 10 ft, clinging to any suitable support with its leaf-stalks. It has heart-shaped leaves and flowers profusely throughout summer until autumn, which makes it an ideal plant for balconies and terraces. The tubular, black to reddish-purple blooms surrounded by cup-shaped calixes are borne on long drooping flower-stems. *Rhodochiton* grows best in a sunny, sheltered location in fertile soil, rich in humus and well-drained. It needs generous watering and weekly applications of fertilizer during the growing period. It is propagated from seed in early summer immediately after the seeds have ripened or in early spring. The first blooms appear only five months later. It is prone to attacks by spider mites and whitefly.

Rhodochiton atrosanguineus

Cape honeysuckle

Tecomaria capensis

This evergreen, shrubby, climbing scrambler is a member of the *Bignoniaceae* family, whose wild form can be found in South Africa. It has a loose, bushy habit and can reach a height of 23 ft. Because of its showy flowers and vigorous growth, it is an ideal plant for covering facades, terrace walls and balcony walls with greenery. It also looks very good trained along an arch. The mid- to dark green, pinnate leaves can be as long as 6 in and consist of 5 to 7 leaflets. The orange to red, tubular flowers are borne in terminal clusters. Cape honeysuckle does best in full sun, sheltered from the wind. It requires a lot of water and monthly applications of a compound fertilizer during the growth season. Although it tolerates temperatures of 23° F it should be moved to a frost-free place in winter, which may either be light with a temperature of 50° F or darker and cooler. It can be cut back in early spring. It is best propagated from cuttings or runners.

Location: ♦ ☼ ⚠
Care: ❀ 🌡
Propagation: ⸱°°
Characteristics: ∞ ❀
Pests: *spider mite, white fly*
Flowering: *summer*

Black-eyed susan

Thunbergia alata

This popular, annual, twining climber belongs to the acanthus family (*Acanthaceae*) and is native to tropical Africa. Because it is frost tender it is best grown from seed, which is easy to do, and it already flowers during the first year. So it is grown as an annual in temperate zones. Trained against trellis or other similar support, it grows 3–6 ft high and is ideal for planting together with large container plants and hanging baskets. The bright orange-yellow, often creamy-white flowers with black-brown center that are produced throughout summer till autumn are quite striking. It needs a warm, sunny location where it is sheltered from the wind. In cold, rainy weather it hardly flowers. It needs plenty of water but does not tolerate being waterlogged. It must be fed every week during the growing season. It is grown from seed in spring at a temperature of 65–68° F. The seedlings must be pricked out and staked from the very beginning.

Thunbergia alata

Location: ♦ ☼ ⚠
Propagation: ⸱°°
Characteristics: ⊙ ❀
Pests: *aphids, spider mite, white fly*
Flowering: *summer – autumn*

Blue trumpet vine

Thunbergia grandiflora

Location: ◗ ☼ ⚠
Propagation: ∘°
Characteristics: ⊙ ❀
Pests: aphids, spider mite, white fly
Flowering: summer – autumn

This evergreen, woody-stemmed twining climber that belongs to the *Acanthus* family (*Acanthaceae*) is native to north India. Unlike Black-eyed Susan, its better known relative, it can reach a height of 33 ft. Its serrated, lobed, hairy, dark green leaves are also much longer, measuring up to 4–8 in. The trumpet-shaped blooms 3 in long, appear singly or in hanging clusters throughout summer. They are lavender to violet-blue, sometimes white, with a yellow throat. This species is grown as an annual in temperate zones. It is propagated from seed indoors in early spring. The young plants are only planted out when all danger of frost has past. In order to ensure robust plants, sow several in one pot and prick out. Blue trumpet vine needs plenty of sun and warmth. It does not tolerate wind or being waterlogged.

Canary creeper

Tropaeolum peregrinum

Location: ◗ ☼ – ☼ ⚠
Propagation: ∘°
Characteristics: ⊙ ❀
Pests: flea beetle, aphids, caterpillars
Flowering: summer – autumn

This species, which is also known under the botanical names of *T. canariense* and *T. aduncum,* is a member of the *Tropaeolaceae* family. This herbaceous leaf-stalk climber is native to the mountainous regions of Peru and Ecuador but in temperate zones it is grown as an annual because of its frost tenderness. The palmate leaves with 5 to 7-lobes, are fresh-green on top and grey-green underneath. The delicate, decorative lemon-yellow flowers appear throughout summer until autumn. Supported by stakes or wires, it can reach a height of 6 ft 6 in and provide an attractive, colourful visual screen on balconies and terraces. It does best in warm, sunny to partially-shaded location, sheltered from the wind. It needs plenty of water and should be fed at least twice a month with a weakly-dosed fertilizer. In can be grown from seed indoors in spring with four seeds being sown in each pot.

Grape vine

Vitis vinifera

The grape vine, which belongs to the *Vitaceae* family, has been cultivated for the production of wine since antiquity. It is native to the regions of the temperate northern hemisphere. If it is not pruned regularly in winter or summer to keep it size under control, it can easily reach a height of 23 ft. It needs a lot of space and should be placed in a sunny, sheltered location along the edge of the terrace. The 3- to 5-lobed leaves 6 in long turn brown-red in autumn. The inconspicuous greenish flowers develop into grapes in autumn that, depending on the variety, are pale green, yellow or black. To ensure a good yield of grapes, the plant needs the application of a slow-release fertilizer or organic fertilizer once a year. It is propagated from hardwood cuttings in late autumn. It is susceptible to mildew and honey fungus.

Location: ◆◦ ☼—☀ ⚠
Propagation:
Characteristics: ∞ ✿ ❄
Pests: mildew, honey fungus
Flowering: summer

Vitis vinifera

Japanese wisteria

Wisteria floribunda

ℹ

Location: 💧 ☼—☀ ⚠
Propagation:
Characteristics: ✖ ∞ ❀ ❄
*Diseases: leaf spot, honey
    fungus, scab*
Pests: aphids
Flowering: summer

This deciduous, woody-stemmed twining climber that belongs to the papilionaceous or *Fabaceae* family is native to East Asia and has been a popular garden plant for many centuries. This fast-growing climber can reach a height of 33 ft and is suitable for growing against any type of support such as terrace walls, porches and pergolas. It is very popular not only for its magnificent show of flowers, borne in drooping racemes in early summer, but also for its attractive feathery leaves that can be 14 in long. The fragrant blooms can be violet-blue, purple, pink or white, depending on the variety, and they flower one after the other from the top of the raceme to the tip. They are followed by long, bean-like pods. Wisterias thrive in warm, sunny places but it will also grow in partial shade. Although it can be propagated from semi-ripe cuttings taken in late summer and autumn, wisteria is generally propagated by grafting. Seedlings usually have flowers of poor colour and form. The seeds are very poisonous.

Right and opposite page:
Wisteria floribunda

Herbs

Every garden or terrace should have its herb garden, whether for decorative purposes, because of their fragrance, for culinary or even medicinal use. In addition, they bring nature to your doorstep because their delicious fragrance attracts bees and butterflies even to the highest balcony.

Special terracotta herb pots with holes on the sides in which you can plant the herbs are both very practical and decorative. They enable you to have a wide variety of plants in a very small area. These large herb pots have the advantage that they can easily be brought in the house during winter. Mediterranean herbs such as thyme, basil, oregano, and sage will provide all the traditional herbs used in the preparation of those delicious Italian dishes while creating a southern atmosphere.

Herbs thrive and develop their aroma best in a sunny, warm location in full sun. Apart from this they need very little care. Some herbs, like parsley, will also grow in shade. However, it is important not to water too much because herbs will survive dry conditions much better than excessive watering. They are best harvested before they begin to flower and consumed fresh. By drying or freezing them, you will also have herbs throughout winter.

There is a great choice of herbs for growing in pots. These can be bought either on the market or in specialist stores. If you have sufficient space and time you can also raise your herbs from seed. More tender species should be grown in the house for a while before planting them out. You must remember, however, that many plants that are frost-hardy planted in full earth in the garden are not as hardy when grown in a pot. This is why they should be protected with bracken or similar material or brought indoors to over-winter in a light, frost-free room.

Chives

Allium schoenoprasum

ℹ

Location: 💧 ☼–☀
Care: ❄
Propagation: ∘° 🐝✿
Characteristics: ∞ ❄
Diseases: white rot, downy mildew
Pests: onion flies, aphids
Harvesting: spring – summer

This member of the *Alliaceae* family is a bulbous perennial, much used in cooking, that grows throughout Europe, in Asia from Siberia to China and in North America. Chives are hardy perennials and grow in sun and partial shade in fertile, calcareous soil that should be kept evenly moist but not waterlogged. Chives benefit from feeding every two weeks. The rootstock can be divided in spring and autumn. The dark green, tubular hollow leaves grow uninterruptedly and are used to flavour and garnish dishes such as salads, soups, butter and dips. They are very rich in vitamin C and also stimulate the appetite and digestion. The pink to lilac flowers, borne in umbels, are produced throughout summer. It can be sown indoors from February onward and directly in the window box from the end of March. They can be harvested from spring onward. Container-grown chives should be moved to a frost-free place in winter.

Allium schoenoprasum

Dill

Anethum graveolens

Dill, a member of the *Umbelliferae* family, is an annual with fine, feathery, blue-green leaves from which the flat yellow flower heads emerge in summer, followed by flat, oval seeds whose taste is reminiscent of caraway. Dill needs light, moist soil and a sunny, sheltered location. Sow dill from spring until late summer at intervals of 3 to 4 weeks to ensure a constant supply. They should be planted at least 8 in deep. Dill is used to flavour salads, dips, fish and meat dishes and in pickled gherkins. Because the leaves and seeds contain ethereal oils they are also used for medicinal purposes, to relieve flatulence and colic and as a diuretic.

Location: ◍ ☼ ⚠
Propagation: ⠿
Characteristics: ☉
Harvesting: summer – autumn

Anethum graveolens

Garden chervil

Anthriscus cerefolium

ⓘ

Location: ◐ ☼ – ☀
Care: ❄
Propagation: ⠄°°
Characteristics: ⊙
Diseases: powdery mildew
Pests: slugs and snails,
*   caterpillars*
Harvesting: summer – winter

Garden chervil, a member of the *Umbelliferae* family, is a popular annual plant native to Europe and western Asia. The bright green, very aromatic leaves have an aniseed-like fragrance much used in cooking. The leaves should be picked before the white flower umbels appear in summer. Chervil is sown from the end of March onward until mid-summer at intervals of 3 to 4 weeks to give a continuous supply and it can be harvested from May until September. Chervil grows best in rich, well-drained soil in shade or partial shade. In summer, it needs regular watering. If you want to enjoy chervil in winter, you can grow it indoors at a temperature of 45–50° F. Chervil is used in salads, dips, herb butter, egg dishes, fish sauces and the famous creamy chervil soup. The leaves can be frozen but not dried because the leaves loose their distinctive taste, as they also do when cooked for a long time.

Tarragon

Artemisia dracunculus

ⓘ

Location: ◐ ☼ ⚠
Care: ⚠
Propagation: ⚘⚘
Characteristics: ∞
Harvesting: spring – autumn

Artemisia dracunculus, a member of the *Compositae* family, is native to Asia and North America. Its distinctive, fine aroma make it an excellent plant for balconies and terraces. A perennial but frost-sensitive plant, tarragon develops underground runners that produce leafy stems with terminal panicles of inconspicuous, yellow-brown flower heads. The bright green, fragrant leaves are harvested from spring until late autumn. Tarragon loses much of its aroma when dried. It grows best in a sunny, sheltered location in calcareous, humus-rich soil. The root ball must always be kept moist. In winter it should be covered to protect it from the cold and in spring it must be cut back to the top edge of the pot. It is propagated from runners or by division. Its leaves are used to flavoured salads, vinegar, the braised beef dish called sauerbraten, poultry and game dishes. Tarragon promotes digestion and has diuretic properties.

Borage

Borago officinalis

These annual plants of the *Boraginaceae* family are grown not only for culinary purposes but also for their very elegant, star-shaped blue flowers. Borage was first introduced into Spain by the Arabs from where it spread to the rest of Europe. It is sown from April until June, the seeds covered with a generous layer of sowing soil. As soon as the flower buds begin to emerge, the plant must be fed every two weeks. It needs sun and moist, well-drained, fertile soil. The stems and leaves that are covered with rough hairs can cause skin irritation and allergies. It is therefore advisable to wear gloves when handling borage. The leaves are rich in minerals and taste a little like gherkins. They stimulate the metabolism and are used in salads and soups. The flowers may be white or pink depending on the species and they are edible too. Borage tea has blood-cleansing and expectorant properties.

Location: ◆ ☼ – ☼
Propagation: ॰°°
Characteristics: ⊙
Diseases: powdery mildew
Pests: aphids
Harvesting: spring – summer

Borago officinalis

Melissa officinalis

ⓘ

Location: 💧 ☼ ⚠
Care: ⚠
Propagation: ∘°° ✄
Characteristics: ∞
Harvesting: spring – autumn

Lemon balm

Melissa officinalis

This herbaceous perennial that is native to southern Europe and Asia Minor takes its name from the strong lemon scent exuded by the leaves. The aroma is very volatile, which is why this herb should only be used fresh and never be cooked. A member of the *Labiatae* family, it grows 20 in high and prefers a warm, sheltered location and fertile, well-drained soil. It must be kept moderately moist and fed only sparingly. The easiest way to propagate is by division and from cuttings. It can also be raised from seed from April onward. For use as a condiment, the young stems and leaves are gathered between spring and late autumn. To make tea, the leaves should be cut shortly before the stems bear flowers and dried. Lemon balm is used to flavour salads, game and mushroom dishes. Its ethereal oil is used to alleviate fatigue, lack of appetite and nervous disorders.

Green mint

Mentha spicata

ⓘ

Location: 💧 ☼ ⚠
Care: ⚠
Propagation: ∘° ✄
Characteristics: ∞
Diseases: powdery mildew, rust fungus
Harvesting: spring – autumn

Green mint, also known as spearmint, is a spreading herbaceous perennial with lanceolate, serrated, sometimes hairy leaves. Like all the other types of mint, it is a member of the *Labiatae* family. In summer it produces pink, lilac or white flowers, depending on the variety. It can be grown from seed or by division; the best time to do this is in spring. Growing green mint in a pot is ideal because it is so invasive in an ordinary bed in the garden. Like most other mint species it need, moist soil and plenty of sun but it does not require much feeding. The leaves are used as decoration or as a condiment, for instance in mint sauce. It is also used in the preparation of herbal teas and iced drinks. It alleviates digestive problems, colic and flatulence. Its ethereal oil is used in the manufacturing of toothpaste, mouth rinses and chewing gum.

Apple mint

Mentha suaveolens

This species of white or pink-flowering mint is native to western and southern Europe. It has serrated, woolly leaves, often with a wavy or rolled-in margin. The "Variegata" variety has mid-green leaves with splashes of cream which exude a strong fruity scent. They taste like *Mentha spicata* and are also used in cooking. Because the mature leaves are woolly they are rarely used fresh but they are ideal for crystallizing. Like the other species of mint, the young aromatic leaves can be harvested throughout the growing season and used fresh. They also make very decorative foliage plants in window boxes and hanging baskets. Cultivation and propagation are the same as for green mint but apple mint prefers light shade rather than direct sun.

Location: 💧 ☼ — ☼
Propagation: ✂🌱
Characteristics: ∞ 🐞 ❄
Diseases: powdery mildew, rust fungus
Harvesting: summer

Mentha x piperita

Peppermint

Mentha x piperita

Peppermint is the result of the crossing of several wild species and can be found throughout Europe. This bushy, herbaceous perennial has dark green, serrated leaves that exude an ethereal oil containing menthol. If the plant is not entirely picked bare, the stems will continue to grow up to 20–32 in high and will bear terminal spikes of pink to violet flowers throughout the summer. Peppermint is used for both medicinal and culinary purposes. Peppermint tea has been used since time immemorial to alleviate pain, colds, nausea and cramp. The number of species and varieties is very large because of the many crossings. English mint (*M. x piperita* "Mitcham") and Eau-de-Cologne mint (*M. x piperita* "Citrata") are very popular. Peppermint has dark green leaves with purple margins. Cultivation and care are the same as for green mint.

Location: 💧 ☼ ⚠
Propagation: ✂🌱
Characteristics: ∞ ❄
Diseases: powdery mildew, rust fungus
Harvesting: spring – autumn

Basil

Ocimum basilicum

i

Location: ◗ ☼ ⚠
Propagation: ₀°
Characteristics: ⊙
Diseases: powdery mildew
Pests: aphids, slugs and snails
Harvesting: summer

Basil belongs to the *Labiatae* family and came from India through Persia and Greece to Italy and the rest of Europe. It is now an indispensable ingredient of western cuisine. The aromatic leaves and young shoots are harvested throughout summer until the plant begins to flower. Besides its culinary uses, basil is used in alternative medicine because of its diuretic and anti-spasmodic properties. The ethereal oils are also used in the perfume industry and in the manufacture of herb-based liqueurs. Basil is a sub-tropical plant and is sown in spring in sandy, well-drained soil, rich in humus, in a sunny location, sheltered from the wind. The soil must be kept moist at all times and the plant fed occasionally. There are many varieties that vary in size, aroma and leaf color. "Opal" and "Genoveser" have dark red leaves, the "Lemon" variety has a lemon fragrance. The green-leaved varieties are the most robust.

Marjoram

Origanum majorana

i

Location: ○ ☼ ⚠
Care: ❋
Propagation: ₀°
Characteristics: ⊙/∞
Pests: aphids, spider mites
Harvesting: spring – winter

In the warm regions of southern Europe marjoram grows as a herbaceous perennial but in temperate zones, this member of the *Labiatae* family is cultivated as an annual or biennial. It is sown indoors in early spring in light, humus-rich, calcareous soil. The young plants should only be moved outdoors when all danger of frost has passed. The need a sunny, sheltered location. Unlike older specimens, young plants should be watered constantly but never be allowed to become waterlogged. Marjoram can be harvested after about 6 weeks. To have a fresh supply of marjoram in winter, sow again in summer but do not forget to bring the plants indoors before the first frost. The leaves of the first crop can also be dried for use in winter. The intensely aromatic leaves can be used fresh or dried in stews and potato dishes. It is also used for medicinal purposes, namely to alleviate rheumatism and digestive problems as well as to stimulate the appetite.

Oregano

Origanum vulgare

This highly aromatic culinary and medicinal herb, a member of the *Labiatae* family, is mainly known as the condiment used to flavour pizza. Common marjoram or oregano can be found throughout Europe where it grows as a perennial. It is easily propagated by division, otherwise it can be grown from seed in spring in humus-rich, well-drained soil in a sunny position. The delicious twigs can be harvested throughout summer until the beginning of winter. To make herbal tea and to dry, the leaves should be gathered during the flowering period. Oregano is also used in alternative medicine as an anti-spasmodic and nerve tonic. Oregano is a decorative foliage plant that looks very attractive among brightly coloured summer flowering plants. It should be watered sparingly and only fed after the growing season. Although oregano is a perennial it is only half-hardy and does not tolerate severe frost. In winter it should therefore be protected against the cold or moved indoors. Older specimens should be cut back vigorously in spring in order to encourage new growth.

Parsley

Petroselinum

Parsley, a biennial that belongs to the *Umbelliferae* family, is native to the Mediterranean. In the first year it develops a leaf rosette from which clusters of flowers emerge in the second year. Parsley is no longer edible by the time it has started flowering. The whole plant is intensely aromatic but only the fresh leaves, harvested from the outside inward, are used. Parsley can be dried or frozen so that it can be used throughout the winter. There are many varieties, including a flat-leaved one. The fleshy roots of the Hamburg or root parsley are used to flavour soups. Parsley is sown from March onward in fertile, humus-rich soil. The plants can be placed outdoors at the end of April and should be kept moist at all times but never allowed to become waterlogged. Parsley grows best in sun or partial shade and will benefit from weak solutions of fertilizer every two weeks. It should only be harvested when the leaves are 4 in high without damaging the heart or leaves in the middle of the plant.

Location: ○ ☼ ⚠
Care: ⚠ ❄
Propagation: ∴ ✀
Characteristics: ∞
Pests: aphids, spider mites
Harvesting: spring – winter

Petroselinum crispum

Location: ◖ ☼ – ☼ ⚠
Characteristics: ∞
Diseases: leaf spot, virus
  diseases
Pests: carrot flies, celery flies,
  aphids
Harvesting: spring – autumn

Rosemary

Rosmarinus officinalis

ⓘ

Location: ◊ ☼ ⚠

Care: ❄

Characteristics: ∞

Pests: aphids

Harvesting: all year

This evergreen shrub with aromatic, needle-like leaves is native to the Mediterranean. A member of the labiate or *Lamiaceae* family, rosemary can grow up to 6 ft 6 in high and it is valued not only as culinary and aromatic plant but also for its medicinal qualities. The mauve to blue 2-lipped flowers are borne in spring in terminal clusters. Rosemary thrives in warm, sunny conditions and it should therefore only be watered moderately even during the growing season. It does not mind periods of drought but will not tolerate being waterlogged. It grows best in well-drained, sandy soil rich in humus and it benefits from weekly applications of fertilizer until the end of the summer. It is easily propagated from semi-ripe cuttings taken in summer but can also be grown from seed. Because it will only survive short periods of frost it must be moved to a bright, cool place (41–50° F) during winter, when it must be watered sparingly. Young plants should be pruned regularly and older specimens can be rejuvenated by cutting back in spring.

Rosmarinus officinalis

Salvia officinalis

Sage

Salvia

This decorative, herbaceous perennial is native to the Mediterranean and like many herbs, it belongs to the *Labiatae* family. The young shoots and leaves of this strongly aromatic plant can be harvested throughout the summer and are used for flavouring food. The leaves intended for making tea should be harvested shortly before flowering. The leaves can also be frozen or dried. Muscatel-sage is even more intensely aromatic and is used in the cosmetic industry as well being grown as an ornamental plant. Sage thrives in dry, well-drained soil in a very sunny location, sheltered from the wind. The soil is kept dry and the plant only fed once a month. It is propagated from seed, cuttings or by division. It must be cut back vigorously in spring. In antiquity, sage was used as a universal remedy to treat inflammation and healing wounds. It takes its name from this use: the Latin name *salvere* means "to be in good health."

Location: ◊ ☼ ⚠
Propagation: ⚬°° ✃
Characteristics: ∞
Diseases: root rot
*Pests: slugs and snails, aphids,
    spider mites, white fly*
Harvesting: summer

Savory

Satureja hortensis

ⓘ

Location: ◊ ☼ – ☀ ⚠
Propagation: ∴ ✄
Characteristics: ⊙/∞
Harvesting: all year

Savory, a bushy herbaceous annual that belongs to the *Labiatae* family, is native to the Mediterranean. It can be harvested up to the beginning of winter and is used to flavour stews, pulses and meat dishes. The juice extracted from the stems is believed to have blood-cleansing and diuretic properties. Savory is sown in April under glass in light, chalky soil and placed outdoors in sun or partial shade after all danger of frost has passed. It should be watered very sparingly and should never be allowed to become waterlogged. It benefits from an application of fertilizer at the beginning of the summer. Savory should be harvested just before flowering and can be frozen or dried. *Satureja montana* or winter savory is more robust and can be harvested all year round. Savory is also very suited for growing in containers and window boxes. It must be cut back vigorously in spring and can easily be propagated by division.

Satureja hortensis

Common thyme

Thymus vulgaris

This dwarf evergreen shrub, native to the Mediterranean, has a pungent aroma. The sprigs can be used fresh or dried to flavour a variety of dishes. Thyme is also used in natural medicine and natural plant-based cosmetics. The seeds are sown in April in loamy, humus-rich soil. In May the young plants can be placed outdoors in a sunny location. Watering is hardly necessary and a one-off application of fertilizer is sufficient. Thyme can be harvested until it begins to flower. The amount of ethereal oils is highest at midday, which is therefore the best time to cut the sprigs, leaving about 3 in on the plant. Vigorous pruning in the second year will encourage a bushy growth. Remember when buying thyme seeds that only winter thyme is frost-hardy while French summer thyme is not.

Location: ○ ☀ ⚠
Propagation: ₀°°
Characteristics: ∞ ❋
Harvesting: summer

Thymus vulgaris

Vegetables

Do you want to eat healthily? Then what better than vegetables! The trend towards mini-vegetables and their popularity is very appropriate for balcony gardening. Possibilities include cauliflower, carrots, cucumbers and tomatoes – there is something for everyone. Growing in this way and harvesting when needed has the advantage of always providing the right amount at the right time so that there is no longer any need to store large amounts of vegetables in the refrigerator, which only dry out in the end. One important tip: vegetables are much more tender when picked early in the season.

But it would be a shame to only eat the vegetables. The bright red stalks of Swiss chard, the purple-red pods of scarlet runner beans, yellow zucchini, colorful lettuces or the interesting "Romanesco" cauliflower are but a few of the very decorative vegetables available. Because of their shape, color and structure vegetables combine very successfully with summer flowers. For instance, an ideal combination could be snapdragon, marigold, grass-of-Parnassus and different varieties of sage.

For growing in containers it is important to select vegetables that do not need a lot of feeding. Smaller species are more suitable for containers, which should be at least 8 in deep and wide. Larger specimens will need a volume of soil equal to about 2–2.5 gallons and a container with a minimum depth of 12 in. You can use ordinary potting compost and an application of slow-release fertilizer at the time of planting.

Combine vegetables that will not compete for the same nutrients. The growing strength should also be taken into account so that none of the plants overshadow the others. The following plants go very well together: beans and strawberries, cucumbers and head lettuces, lettuces and cabbages, carrots and lettuces. On the other hand, tomatoes and cucumber or onions and radishes must never be planted together.

Cucumber

Cucumis sativus

ⓘ

Location: ◗ ☼ ⚠
Propagation: ⸖
Characteristics: ☉
Diseases: mildew, grey mould,
  cucumber mosaic virus
Pests: aphids, spider mites,
  white fly
Harvesting: summer – autumn

Cucumbers on your terrace or balcony? Not impossible provided you have large containers, trellises or other climbing support and a sheltered location where they can grow. Scrambling and climbing cucumbers are most suitable. All cucumbers need warmth to develop properly. Sow the cucumbers indoors from April onward in humus-rich, fertile soil and plant out after all danger of frost has passed. The young plants should be fed twice while the fruits develop, but regular watering with water that is not too cold is a prerequisite because cold water would hinder the production of fruit. Pinch out the growing tip after five or six leaves have developed on the main shoot in order to encourage the production of side shoots.

Green beans

Phaseolus

ⓘ

Location: ◗ ☼ ⚠
Propagation: ⸖
Characteristics: ✖ ☉
Diseases: bean mosaic virus,
  grey mould
Pests: aphids, bean seed flies
Harvesting: summer – autumn

Most European bean species, members of the *Leguminosae* family, originate in the sub-tropical regions of America – hence their great need for warmth. The best varieties for growing in containers are *Phaseolus vulgaris* and the robust, wind-resistant *P. coccineus*. It does not only develop fruits but produces a profusion of attractive, bright red flowers. Both varieties need humus-rich, well-drained soil and a warm, sunny, sheltered location protected from the wind. It is important to give the plant an appropriate support structure. It is sown indoors in April but can only be placed outdoors when all danger of frost has passed. It needs plenty of water (at abut room temperature) during the growing season and weekly feeding. However, the soil must never be allowed to dry out. As a rule of thumb, the beans can be harvested 40 days after sowing. Pick the beans carefully so as not to damage the plants. Uncooked beans are poisonous.

Phaseolus

*F*ennel

Foeniculum vulgare var. azoricum

Fennel belongs to the *Umbelliferae* family. Sometimes yellow flower heads are produced after long, hot summer days which, however, must be removed to enable the bulbs to develop. There are now special varieties that can be sown indoors in spring in sufficiently large pots or containers. If the containers are not protected with a thin sheet of plastic, they should only be placed outdoors when all danger of frost has passed. Harvesting can start three or four months later. Fennel must be watered regularly because otherwise the bulbs become woody. Fennel needs fertile, well-drained soil and a sheltered, sunny location but should be fed only sparingly to ensure the development of the bulb. The bulbs can be served raw as a salad or braised, while the tender leaves are used as a condiment. Stored in moist sand, in a dark, cool place, the bulbs will keep till the following year.

Foeniculum vulgare

Location: 💧 ☼ ⟁
Propagation: ⦁°°
Characteristics: ☉
Diseases: mildew
Pests: aphids, slugs and snails
Harvesting: summer – autumn

Carrots

Daucus carota ssp. Sativus

Location: ◗ ☼ ⚠
Propagation: ⠐⠐
Characteristics: ☉
Diseases: *leaf spot*
Pests: *carrot flies*
Harvesting: *summer – autumn*

This popular vegetable is a member of the *Umbelliferae* family. Short, stump-rooted or wedge varieties are better suited for growing on balconies and terraces because the long, cylindrical varieties need very deep containers. Sow from March until June in humus-rich, well-drained soil, starting with an early variety, followed by a medium and a late variety, to ensure a constant supply of carrots from the beginning of summer until late autumn. Carrots need plenty of water and very little fertilizer. However, they do not tolerate being waterlogged. Cover the heads that protrude from the soil with soil immediately to prevent them from going green. Carrots harvested when young are particularly tender; late varieties should be harvested shortly before the first frost. Stored in a cool place, they will keep for months. Carrot fly can be a serious problem because their larvae penetrate the fruit, but all you need to protect the carrots is a special net.

Kohlrabi

Brassica oleracea – Gongylodes group

Location: ◗ ☼ ⚠
Propagation: ⠐⠐
Characteristics: ☉
Pests: *slugs and snails, flea beetles*
Harvesting: *summer*

This vegetable is a member of the *Brassicaceae* family. Like all other types of cabbage, it is descended from the wild cabbage. There are white sorts with bright green "bulbs," leaves and stalks and blue sorts with blue-violet "bulbs." The plants are grown indoors on a window-sill from February onward and they are then planted in mid-spring. The distance between the young plants should be 16 in. Kohlrabi grows best in humus-rich, calcareous soil in a sunny position. It needs moderate but regular watering and feeding. If these conditions are fulfilled, you should be able to harvest delicious, tender bulbs of 2.5–3.5 in in diameter after about two months. It is important not to leave them any longer because the bulbs become woody and lose much of their flavour.

Swiss chard

Beta vulgaris

This vigorous-growing biennial, a member of the *Chenopodiaceae* family, is a useful and a decorative addition to balconies and terraces. Sown in spring, Swiss chard will develop attractive, upright leaves with striking stalks that are creamy white or bright red depending on the variety. Spinach beet, which is a kind of Swiss chard with smaller stalks, can be harvested two months after sowing, and ordinary Swiss chard three months after sowing. If allowed to over-winter, Swiss chard will complete its growing cycle by flowering in the summer of the second year. The leaves of both varieties can be cooked like spinach while in the case of the ordinary Swiss chard both the leaves and the stalks are used separately in cooking. When growing Swiss chard in a container, remember that when cultivated in the garden they are planted 16 in apart, so they need plenty of space. They grow best in humus-rich soil in a sheltered, sunny or partially shaded location with moderate but regular watering and feeding.

Location: ◗ ☼ – ☀ ⚠
Care: ⚝
Propagation: ⦁°°
Characteristics: ☉ / ∞ ⚘
Diseases: downy mildew
Harvesting: summer

Beta vulgaris

Capsicum annuum

ⓘ

Location: 💧 ☀ ⚠
Propagation: ⸰ᵒᵒ
Characteristics: ✖ ⊙
Diseases: wilt, powdery mildew,
    virus diseases
Pests: spider mites, aphids
Harvesting: summer – autumn

*P*epper

Capsicum annuum

Peppers, like their relatives the aubergines or eggplants and tomatoes, are members of the *Solanaceae* family and need more warm weather to develop fully than any other vegetable. In temperate zones they will only mature properly if they are in a warm, sheltered location and the summer is very sunny. These annual plants, grown for culinary and decorative purposes, can be bought in nurseries until late autumn. There are also low varieties with small fruits that have been especially developed for balconies and you must grow these from seed yourself. The production of fruit is encouraged by pinching out the first flower in the centre of the plant. Because pepper plants grow up to 4 ft high, they need to be staked. If the conditions are favourable, the first green fruits can already be harvested in August. As they ripen further they turn yellow and red. Peppers are very rich in vitamin C. The leaves are poisonous.

*R*adish

Raphanus sativus

ⓘ

Location: 💧 ☀ ⚠
Propagation: ⸰ᵒᵒ
Characteristics: ⊙/∞
Diseases: downy mildew
Pests: aphids, vegetable flies
Harvesting: spring – summer

This spicy, root vegetable that belongs to the *Brassicaceae* family is very quick and easy to grow. All that radishes need is full sun, light soil rich in humus, and regular watering. After about a month, they are ready to be harvested. It is possible to sow radishes from the beginning of spring until mid-summer. The harvest can be prolonged by sowing early and late varieties. Besides the traditional red radishes, there are also red and white varieties and all white ones with cylindrical roots. Like lettuce they are ideal for filling gaps in window boxes and containers. Radishes should be harvested constantly because they become woody and hollow if they are left too long in the soil. They owe their spicy, hot taste to the presence of mustard oil.

*L*ettuce

Lactuca sativa

Lettuce, a member of the *Compositae* family, can be used in many ways in the kitchen and garden. Besides the well-known butterhead lettuces, there are also crisp heads or Icebergs and loose-leaf varieties. You will need very large containers to grow lettuces on balconies and terraces because both the roots and the heads need a lot space. Loose-leaf varieties like "Lollo rosso," "Lollo bionda" and red oak-leaf lettuce such as "Red Salad Bowl" are particularly decorative on balconies and terraces. They require a sunny location, well-drained, light soil and regular watering to develop properly. They should only be fed sparingly, just before sowing or planting. Loose-leaf types that can be cut and left to regrow, should be fed again after the first harvest. Lettuce is sown indoors from January onward and only planted out when all danger of frost has passed. Harvest time can be prolonged by selecting early and late varieties.

Location: ◕ ☼
Propagation: ⸳°
Characteristics: ☉
Diseases: grey mould
Pests: slugs and snails, aphids
Harvesting: summer

Lactuca

Lycopersicon esculentum

ⓘ

Location: 💧 ☼ ⚠
Propagation: ⣀
Characteristics: ✖ ☉
Diseases: root rot, grey mould
*Pests: white fly, spider mites,
  aphids*
Harvesting: summer – autumn

Tomato

Lycopersicum esculentum

Tomatoes belong to the *Solanaceae* family. They are a delicious, very healthy fruit that has been used in cooking for a long time. The small bush varieties that have been developed especially for growing in containers on balconies and terraces have particularly aromatic fruits. However, even the plants of small fruited varieties such as cherry or cocktail tomatoes can reach a height of 6 ft 6 in. It is therefore important to check the ultimate height of the plant when choosing the variety if space is at a premium. Tomatoes can be sown indoors in spring or bought as seedlings that are planted out after all danger of frost has passed. They need a very sunny, warm location where they are protected from the rain and wind and fertile soil, enriched with fertilizer. They need plenty of water and weekly applications of fertilizer while the fruits develop. To ensure a good yield, it is important remove the side-shoots. Green fruits and other parts of the plant contain poisonous alkaloids.

Zucchini

Cucurbita pepo

ⓘ

Location: 💧 ☼ – ☼ ⚠
Propagation: ⣀
Characteristics: ☉ ❀
*Diseases: mildew,
  wilt*
Harvesting: summer

Zucchini, a cucumber-like member of the *Cucurbitaceae* family, is a popular vegetable that is much easier to grow than cucumbers. It can be grown in almost any kind of climate. All it needs is a sheltered location in full sun, well-drained, fertile soil and plenty of water and food. If these conditions are fulfilled you will be rewarded with a good crop of vegetables that can be harvested from early summer until autumn as well as extremely decorative, yellow star-shaped flowers. Sow them indoors from April onward and plant the seedlings out at the end of May. When choosing a container, remember that zucchini needs a lot of space – 10 sq ft – because the leaves grow very large. In the past, many a gardener's ambition was to grow the largest zucchini possible. Today, people prefer to eat smaller zucchini, which are produced in larger numbers on the plant and have much more flavour.

Cucurbita pepo

*P*eas

Pisum sativum

Pisum sativum

Peas are members of the *Leguminosae* family. Three types of varieties are particularly suited for growing in containers: green or marrowfat round-seeded peas, sugar peas or mangetout, and petits-pois. Several low-growing varieties have been developed from the green pea, which is the best-known type. These low-growing forms do not need any support structure. Green or split peas are used to make pea soup. Nowadays there are also low-growing varieties of sugar peas which can be eaten with the pod. Peas can be sown indoors from February. Sugar peas or mangetout can already be sown outdoors at the beginning of April, while green peas and petits-pois can only be sown after all danger of frost has passed. Peas grow best in well-drained, humus-rich soil in a sunny, airy location. They need watering regularly and weekly feeding. Except for the low-growing varieties, all peas will require a supporting structure. Mangetout peas should be picked before they go yellow. Green peas and petits-pois also taste better when young.

Location: ◖ ☀
Propagation: ˳°˳
Characteristics: ☉
Diseases: mildew
Pests: aphids, pea thrips
Harvesting: summer

Fruit

"A land of plenty" on your balcony or terrace is not difficult at all. There is always room for strawberries even on the smallest balcony and there is no longer any need for even fruit trees to reach for the sky any longer. There is a wide choice of dwarf fruit trees, developed for growing in containers, that need very little soil. It is vital that the tree be grafted on a slow-growing rootstock such as, for instance, the "Ballerina" apple.

Gooseberries and currants trained as standards need very little space; they make picking the fruit easier and, in addition, they provide space for planting summer flowers at the base of the standards. Fig trees not only provide delicious fruit but their foliage is also particularly attractive.

Containers for berry bushes should be able to contain about 2 to 3 gallons of soil. Clay and terracotta pots are the best. These do not warm up as quickly as the black plastic containers and they create a natural water balance. But the root balls should never be allowed to dry out. You can either buy special container soil from a garden center or mix your own with compost, garden soil and sand in equal parts. Do not forget to add a slow-release fertilizer.

In order to ensure that the tree or shrub produces fruit, plant those species that need warmth in a sunny, sheltered location. Tender species such as figs and peaches should over-winter in a frost-free room. Apple and cherry-trees as well as berry bushes should be placed against a wall where they are protected from direct sun. The containers should be insulated as with all other container grown plants. It is important that the soil be kept moist even in winter.

*A*pple

Malus

ℹ️

Location: 💧 ☀️ ⚠️
Characteristics: ∞ ❄️
Diseases: canker, apple scab, fire blight, mildew
Pests: aphids, spider mites, caterpillars
Harvesting: summer – autumn

Apple trees are members of the *Rosaceae* family. They always remain real trees even when they are grown in a large container, like the small "Ballerina" apple. But even this can grow to a height of 6–10 ft high. Because apple trees can spend the winter outdoors, it is important to select a frost-resistant container. Black plastic pots are not very suitable because the roots get very hot in the sun. "Ballerina" varieties are grafted on slow-growing stock and only develop a trunk and small fruiting shoots but not side-shoots. However, if the tree develops a lateral branch, it can be cut back to two or three buds. Two very reliable varieties are "Waltz," whose flavour is reminiscent of that of "Golden Delicious," and "Bolero," which tastes rather like "James Grieve." Apples need fertile, well-drained soil in a sunny location. They also need regular watering and feeding and will benefit from winter pruning.

Malus "Red Ellison"

Prunus persica

Peach

Prunus persica

This early-flowering member of the *Rosaceae* family, famous for its delicious fruit, is native to northern and central China. This explains why it needs a warm, sunny place to do well, and in temperate zones, the peach, like the nectarine, will only bear a good crop of fruit when the conditions are absolutely perfect. Balconies and terraces are ideal micro-climates. There are now excellent dwarf varieties that look like small palms but whose fruit is just as good that of their larger siblings. There is another advantage: they do not need pruning. With their beautiful blossoms – which must however be protected from late frosts – peaches are extremely decorative. They need well-drained, fertile soil, regular watering and applications of fertilizer every two weeks. The pollen can be transferred from flower to flower with a brush to ensure fertilization.

Location: ● ☼ ⚠
Care: ❄ – 🌡
Propagation: ∘°°
Characteristics: ∞
Diseases: bacterial canker,
    peach mildew, peach leaf curl
Pests: aphids, scale insects,
    caterpillars
Harvesting: summer

Opposite page: Fragaria x ananassa

Sweet cherry

Prunus avium

ℹ

Location: ◆ ☼ ⚠
Characteristics: ∞ ❄
Diseases: *Bleiglanz, spur blight*
Pests: *aphids, caterpillars, birds (bullfinches)*
Harvesting: *summer*

Prunus avium is native to Europe and belongs to the *Rosaceae* family. Recently new, slower-growing forms of have been developed that are ideal for growing in containers. Although sweet cherries are hardy, the blossoms are vulnerable to spring frost. It grows best in well-drained, fertile soil. It must be watered regularly and fed every two weeks during the growing season. It is very important that it should be placed in a sunny location. The soil should never be allowed to dry out because the plants cannot get any more water from the ground. Neither should they be overshadowed by other trees because this would diminish the yield and aroma. Sweet cherries are pruned to the desired shape when young although not too early on. Its is advisable to protect the tree from the birds while the fruit is developing by covering it with a net. It is propagated by grafting, a skill that is best left to experts.

Strawberry

Fragaria x ananassa

ℹ

Location: ◆ ☼ ⚠
Propagation: ✂ runners
Characteristics: ∞ ❄
Diseases: *grey mould*
Harvesting: *summer*

There is always room for strawberries on a balcony and terrace. The wild form of this member of the *Rosaceae* family can be found throughout Europe. There are a number of varieties that will also grow very well in hanging baskets and containers. In order to develop fruit, strawberry plants need plenty of sun and regular watering. They should be protected from the wind and rain. Plant in spring in potting soil to which a slow-release fertilizer has been added. The container should be large enough for the roots to develop. Put straw around the plant so as to cover the soil. This will prevent the fruit from rotting. By choosing varieties that ripen at different times, you can prolong the harvest. Repeat-fruiting varieties will produce fruit throughout summer until the autumn. They can be propagated from runners in late summer.

Pears

Pyrus communis

ⓘ

Location: 💧 ☼ ⚠
Care: ⚠ – ❄
Characteristics: ∞
Diseases: brown rot, powdery mildew, scab
Pests: pear leaf blister mite, aphids, weevils
Harvesting: autumn

Pears have been cultivated for many centuries but they have never acquired the importance of their relatives, the apples. The reason is that their storage capability is not as good and the fact that the trees need more care and attention. A pear tree requires fertile, humus-rich soil and a sunny, warm location sheltered from the cold. In addition, it does not tolerate low temperatures or being waterlogged. The blossom is particularly vulnerable to late frosts. Early varieties are more robust than late ones. The best varieties are grafted on slow-growing stocks such as the "Conference" dessert pear or the autumn variety "Köstliche von Charneu." Most of these are available as container plants. The fact that most pears have a French name is because many varieties were developed in France and Belgium between 1700 and 1900. Being self-pollinating, the plants benefit from an extra boost of hand-pollination.

Pyrus communis

Ribes

Currant

Ribes

These shrubs with their delicious red, black or white berries are members of the *Grossulariaceae* family and are ideal for growing in containers. Although hardy, the flowers are frost-sensitive, which is why the plants should be protected against frost or moved indoors until all danger of frost has passed. Currants are best planted in autumn in well-drained, humus-rich soil. Prune vigorously during the rest period in order to encourage the formation of fruit for the following year. They need plenty of water and food during the entire growing season in late spring. There are slow-, medium- and fast growing varieties of red and white currants but not of black currants. It is important to cut back whole branches to let the light in. It is easier to pick the fruit from standards.

ⓘ

Location: 💧 ☀ ⚠
Propagation:
Characteristics: ∞ ❄
Diseases: powdery mildew, rot
Pests: aphids, gall mites
Harvesting: summer

Blackberry

Rubus

ℹ

Location: 💧 ☼ – ☼ ⚠
Care: ⚠
Propagation: ✂
Characteristics: ∞
Diseases: botrytis, root rot
Pests: maggots
Harvesting: summer – autumn

Blackberry, a woody, rambling shrub, belongs to the *Rosaceae* family. It is best to choose thornless varieties for growing in containers because the fruit is easier to pick. The black fruit is ready to pick from late-summer to early autumn. Before filling the container with fertile, well-drained soil, line the bottom with a layer of drainage material such as pieces of broken clay pots. Blackberries grow best in sun or partial shade sheltered from cold winter winds. They need plenty of water and weekly applications of fertilizer during the growing season. Cut the shrub back to 12–16 in after planting. Blackberries produce fruit on the previous year's canes. This is why all the canes that have produced fruit are cut back after fruiting. Blackberries usually need some kind of support and if left outdoors during winter, they must be well protected against the cold.

Rubus

Highbush blueberry

Vaccinium corymbosum

The robust blueberry, native to North America, is a member of the *Ericaceae* family. Like the cranberry, it will only produce a good crop of fruit if it grows in acid, very moist soil in a sunny, sheltered location. This bushy, slow-growing plant can also be grown in a container, where it can reach a height of 39 in. It needs large amounts of water and regular feeding especially during the growing season. Because they only produce fruit on one-year-old wood, it is hardly necessary to prune or trim blueberries to keep them to the desired size or shape, although they should be cut back to rejuvenate them after a few years. They are propagated from cuttings or by division of the rootstock. The vigorous-growing "Bluecrop" and "Goldtraube," the frost-hardy "Patriot" and the compact "Top Hat" are among the most popular varieties. Blueberry is not prone to diseases and pests.

Location: 💧 ☀ ⚠
Propagation: ✂🌱
Characteristics: ∞
Diseases: root rot
Harvesting: summer

Vaccinium corymbosum

The year's tasks

In spring...

At last it is time to begin. After the long winter period with nothing to do, work begins in March and increases rapidly:

• Sow seed of summer annuals, herbs and vegetables, either in the house or directly in seed trays on the balcony or terrace, depending on temperature.

• Cut back plants in containers and at the same time take cuttings to root and make new ones.

• Divide plants such as periwinkles, echinaceas, astilbes, day lilies, bergenias and thyme.

• Your "green room" can already be beautiful with colourful spring-flowering bulbs and tuberous plants, herbaceous perennials and early-flowering biennials.

• Cut back perennials and other woody plants.

• Cut back bedding roses.

• Repot container plants. As a rule of thumb: younger plants should be repotted after 2 to 3 years and older ones after 5 to 6 years.

• Do not forget to air the greenhouse well in warm sunny weather, so that the temperature does not get too high. Vegetable seedlings in particular resent this. Small greenhouses for use on a balcony and terrace to provide some protection in the winter are available from garden centers and garden mail order firms.

• From April give container plants that have not been repotted a light feeding for example with organic liquid fertilizer. Alternatively, remove the upper layer of soil and replace with a mixture of compost and fresh soil. This method is particularly good for bay trees.

• Hardy container plants should be slowly accustomed to warmer conditions in the open air, but they must still be protected from excessive sun and late frosts.

• Now it the time to prepare fruits such as blueberries and raspberries, so that the fruits will be ripe in midsummer. With raspberries, all shoots should be cut back in December to soil level, because fruits only develop on new shoots.

- Formal bushes and hedges such as box, privet or euonymus should be clipped to shape and fertilized as required, ideally with long working garden fertilizers. The clippings of box can be planted as cuttings to increase your stock of plants further.

- Summer-flowering bulbs can be brought out of storage and planted out.

- From mid-May, or depending on your local conditions, all frost-sensitive plants can be put outside. The summer flowering season begins.

- With warmer weather the time of garden pests begins: aphids, spider mites and snails may become troublesome from May onwards. Check your plants regularly. Roses may suffer from powdery mildew, rose rust or black spot.

- Cut off suckers from rose rootstocks.

In summer...

... many regular tasks need to be done.

- Remove dead flower heads and wilted foliage immediately, as well as dry or dead branches.

- Remove bulbs when the leaves have died down. Plant autumn-flowering bulbs and tubers at the same time.

- Make sure everything has enough water.

- If you have used soil with fertilizer when potting new plants in the spring, June is the time to add more fertilizer because the initial amount is usually exhausted after 4 to 6 weeks. Conifers need fertilizers containing magnesium.

- Give a summer pruning to all roses after repeat flowering, whether they are bedding, climbers or standards. Cut off any old shoots and cut back flowering shoots. At the same time give the plants some special rose fertilizer.

- Feed tomato plants regularly with tomato fertilizer and pinch out any side shoots that appear.

- From July remove strawberry runners and fasten them down in soil in the open or in pots. Water well and cover with fleece.

- Start harvesting herbs, vegetables and fruit as they become ready, according to type and kind.

- In late summer harvest seed from annual and perennial flowers, shrubs and grasses.

- Sow seeds of biennial plants.

- Take cuttings of pelargoniums, chrysanthemums, fuchsias and some woody plants.

- Make arrangements for your plants to be looked after while you are on vacation.

- In late summer protect tomatoes, paprika, aubergines or eggplants and other warmth-loving vegetable varieties with foil to encourage ripening.

In autumn...

... the time for tidying up and protecting

- Replace faded summer flowers with autumn plantings. At the same time plant shrubs and hardy perennials.

- Fertilize Mediterranean container plants, perennial herbs and shrubs before winter dormancy or the shoots will not ripen.

- Move tender and half-hardy perennials into their winter quarters before the first frost.

- At the same time protect hardy perennials and shrubs in containers from hard frosts.

- Cover the blooms of autumn-flowering perennials to protect them from night-frosts, for example with fleece.

- Now is the time to plant bulbs for next spring in pots, bowls or containers. They must spend the winter in a protected place, either covered with brushwood or buried under a layer of soil.

- Protect fruit plants from birds with netting.

- This is the best time to plant clematis.

- If the depth of water in your pond is less than 32 in, over-winter any tender water plants such as waterlilies in a vessel filled with water and keep in a cool, dark and frost-free place.

- In October or November dig up dahlia and canna tubers, clean them, wrap in newspaper and store in a cool, frost-free place for the winter.

- Take cuttings of scented pelargoniums and herbs such as rosemary, sage and lemon verbena and root them in a tray of soil on the window-sill under foil.

In winter...

... there's no time to be lazy

- There is no need give up the pleasure of a decorative balcony during the cold season. Pots and containers can be decorated with branches of Tree of life, yew, boxwood, fir or spruce. Branches with fruits such as rowan, cotoneaster sloe and ilex are just as popular with birds as commercial bird-seed.

- If wet snow settles on plants, gently brush it off the plants. Do this carefully, because frozen stems can break easily. But a blanket of loose snow holds warmth.

- Protect evergreen perennials such as Christmas roses and cyclamens with a covering of twigs or dry foliage during long period of frost.

- Check container plants in their winter quarters once a week for pests and diseases. Water if necessary and keep well ventilated.

- Keep bags of potting soil and watering cans indoors, so that they do not freeze and even burst. Turn off any water connections.

- On frost-free days from January onwards, put Mediterranean plants such as rosemary or bay in wind-protected positions outside. This will harden them off and make them more resistant to attack from pests. But don't forget to bring them in again.

- From mid-January sow seeds in trays on the window-sill of early vegetables, annuals and container plants, for example salads, pelargoniums, begonias, fuchsias, palms, strelitzias and bananas.

- Don't give up on vitamins during the winter. With bean sprouts and green herbs in bowls or glasses this is easily done. Chives can be grown on the window-sill and picked when needed.

- In February cut back summer-blooming shrubs on frost-free days, including forsythia, weigela, whistle-shrub, guelder rose and deutzia. Spring-flowering shrubs on the other hand should only be pruned after flowering.

- Even in winter evergreen plants need watering on frost-free days. During winter remove under-trays from containers to avoid the soil becoming waterlogged.

What thrives where?

Besides taking the regional climate into account, it also important to choose the right place on the balcony or terrace to ensure the plants' well-being. Do the plants tolerate direct sun and warmth? Which plants will grow against a badly lit, cool, north-facing wall? You will find the answers to all these questions in these tables.

Key:
Flowering: S = Summer, Sp = Spring, A = Autumn, W = Winter

Temperature conversion

32° F = 0° C	50° F = 10° C
41° F = 5° C	59° F = 15° C

Annual and biennial plants ...

... for locations in full sun

Botanical name	Common name	Flowers/fruit	Characteristics / Watering
Aeonium	Pinwheel	Sp-S	Architectural / moderate
Amaranthus caudatus	Love-lies-bleeding	S	Flowering / generous
Asteriscus maritimus	Asteriscus	S	Flowering / little to moderate
Bassia scoparia	Summer cypress	S	Architectural / moderate
Bidens ferulifolia	Tickseed	S	Flowering / generous
Briza maxima	Greater quaking grass	S	Architectural / generous
Callistephus chinensis	China ster	S	Flowering / little to moderate
Calocephalus brownii	Wire mesh plant		Architectural / moderate
Capsicum annuum	Ornamental pepper	S, fruit A	Fruit / generous
Celosia spicata	Cockscomb	S	Flowering / generous
Centaurea cyanus	Cornflower	S	Flowering / moderate
Cleome spinosa	Spider flower	S	Flowering / generous
Clianthus punicus	Parrrot's bill	S	Flowering / generous
Convolvulus sabatius	Ground blue convolvulus	S	Flowering / generous
Crassula coccinea	Crassula	S	Flowering / moderate
Crocus	Crocus	Sp or A	Flowering / generous
Cucurbita pepo	Ornamental squash	S, fruit A	Fruit / generous
Curcuma	Turmeric	S	Flowering / generous
Dahlia	Dahlia	S	Flowering / generous
Dianthus	Pink	S, scent	Flowering / moderate
Diascia	Diascia	S	Flowering / moderate
Dorotheanthus bellidiformis	Livingstone daisy	S	Flowering / moderate
Echeveria	Echeveria	A	Flowering / moderate
Euphorbia marginata	Snow-on-the-mountain	S	Flowering / generous
Felicia amelloides	Blue marguerite	S	Flowering / moderate
Gazania	Treasure flower	S	Flowering / moderate
Gerbera jamesonii	Gerbera	S	Flowering / little to moderate

Botanical name	Common name	Flowers/fruit	Characteristics / Watering
Helianthus annuus	Sunflower	S	Flowering / generous
Helichrysum bracteatum	Straw flower	S	Flowering / moderate
Helichrysum subulifolium	Straw flower	S	Flowering / moderate
Heliotropium arborescens	Cherry pie	S, scent	Flowering / little to moderate
Hordeum jubatum	Foxtail barley	So	Architectural / moderate
Hymenostemma paludosum	Dwarf marguerite	S	Flowering / little to moderate
Iberis saxatilis	Candytuft	Sp-S, scent	Flowering / moderate
Iris	Iris	Sp	Flowering / little to moderate
Lagurus ovatus	Hare's tail grass	S	Architectural / moderate
Lampranthus	Ice plant	S	Flowering / moderate
Laurentia axillaris	Rock isotome	S	Flowering / little to moderate
Limonium sinuatum	Sea lavender	S	Flowering / moderate
Linaria maroccana	Toadflax	S	Flowering / moderate
Lobularia maritima	Sweet alyssum	S, scent	Flowering / moderate
Lotus	Parrot's beak	S	Flowering / little to moderate
Lupinus nanus	Dwarf lupine	S	Flowering / little to moderate
Matthiola incana	Brompton stock	S, scent	Flowering / little to moderate
Mesembryanthemum crystallinum	Mesembryanthemum	S	Flowering / moderate
Molucella laevis	Shellflower	S	Flowering / moderate
Muscari	Grape hycinth	Sp	Flowering / moderate
Nemesia	Nemesia	S	Flowering / little to moderate
Nicotinia	Tobacco plant	S, scent	Flowering / little to moderate
Nigella	Love in a mist	S	Flowering / moderate
Osteospermum	Osteospermum	S	Flowering / moderate
Papaver	Poppy	Sp-S	Flowering / generous
Pennisetum setaceum	African fountain grass	S	Architectural / generous
Phlox drummondii	Annual phlox	S	Flowering / little to moderate
Pogonatherum paniceum	Miniature bamboo		Architectural / generous
Portulaca grandiflora	Sun plant	S	Flowering / moderate
Salpiglossis sinuata	Painted tongue	S, scent	Flowering / generous
Salvia	Salvia	S	Flowering / generous
Sanvitalia procumbens	Creeping zinnia	S	Flowering / moderate
Schizanthus x wisetonensis	Poor man's orchid	S	Flowering / generous
Senecio cineraria	Cinerarie	S	Architectural / moderate
Solanum melongena	Aubergine, Eggplant	S, fruit S-A	Fruit / generous
Verbena	Garden verbena	S	Flowering / little to moderate

... for locations in sun to partial shade

Botanical name	Common name	Flowers/fruit	Characteristics / Watering
Ageratum houstonianum	Flossflower	S	Flowering / generous
Antirrhinum majus	Snapdragon	S	Flowering / moderate
Bellis perennis	Common daisy	Sp	Flowering / little to moderate

Botanical name	Common name	Flowers/fruit	Characteristics / Watering
Brachycome	Swan River daisy	S	Flowering / generous
Browallia speciosa	Bush violet	S	Flowering / moderate
Calceolaria integrifolia	Slipper flower	S	Flowering / generous
Calendula officinalis	Pot marigold	S, scent	Flowering / generous
Campanula	Bellflower	S	Flowering / moderate
Chlorophytum comosum	Spider plant	S	Architectural / little to moderate
Clarkia	Clarkia	S	Flowering / generous
Cosmos	Cosmos	S	Flowering / generous
Cyperus papyrus	Papyrus	S-A	Architectural / generous
Dendranthema indicum	Autumn chrysanthemum	A, scent	Flowering / moderate
Eustoma grandiflorum	Eustoma	So	Flowering / generous
Exacum affine	Persian violet	S	Flowering / generous
Fuchsia	Fuchsia	S	Flowering / generous
Helichrysum petiolare	Silver bush everlasting flower	S	Architectural / generous
Hyacinthus	Hyacinth	Sp, scent	Flowering / moderate
Justicia brandegeana	Shrimp plant	Sp-A	Flowering / generous
Lantana camara	Shrub verbena	S, scent	Flowering / generous
Lobelia	Lobelia	S	Flowering / little to moderate
Lysimachia congestiflora	Loosestrife	S	Flowering / little to moderate
Melampodium paludosum	Melampodium	S	Flowering / little to moderate
Myosotis	Forget-me-not	Sp	Flowering / generous
Narcissus	Daffodil	Sp, scent	Flowering / moderate
Nierembergia hippomanica	Cupflower	S	Flowering / little to moderate
Nolana paradoxa	Chilean bellflower	S	Flowering / moderate
Pelargonium varieties	Pelargonium, geranium	S	Flowering / Architectural / Scent; according to variety / moderate
Pentas lanceolata	Egyptian star	S, scent	Flowering / moderate
Pericallis cruentus	Cineraria	Sp	Flowering / generous
Petunia	Petunia	S, scent	Flowering / generous
Primula malacoides, P. obconica	Fairy primrose	Sp	Flowering / little to moderate
Ranunculus asiaticus	Persian buttercup	Sp	Flowering / little to moderate
Rudbeckia hirta	Black-eyed Susan	S	Flowering / generous
Scaevola saligna	Fan flower	S	Flowering / generous
Scilla sibirica	Scilla	Sp	Flowering / moderate
Sparmannia africana	African hemp	Sp-S	Flowering / generous
Sutera	Sutera	S	Flowering / generous
Tagetes	Marigold	S, scent	Flowering / little to moderate
Torenia fournieri	Wishbone flower	S	Flowering / generous
Tropaeolum	Nasturtium	S	Flowering / generous
Tulipa	Tulip	Sp	Flowering / moderate
Viola wittrockiana	Pansy	Sp, A	Flowering / little to moderate
Zantedeschia aethiopica	Arum lily	Sp, S	Flowering / generous

... for locations in partial shade to full shade

Botanical name	Common name	Flowers/fruit	Characteristics / Watering
Acalypha hispida	Red-hot cat's tail	S	Flowering / generous
Begonia	Begonia	S	Flowering / generous
Catharanthus roseus	Madagscar periwinkle	S	Flowering / moderate
Cyclamen	Cyclamen	Sp, scent	Flowering / moderate
Fuchsia	Fuchsia	S	Flowering / generous
Hypoestes phyllostachya	Polka dot plant	S	Architectural / generous
Impatiens walleriana	Busy lizzie	S	Flowering / generous
Impatiens New Guinea hybrids	Busy lizzie	S-A	Flowering / generous
Mimulus	Monkey flower	S	Flowering / generous
Plectrantus forsteri	Swedish ivy	S	Architectural / generous
Sinningia	Gloxinia	Sp, S	Flowering / little to moderate
Solenostemon scutellarioiedes	Coleus	S	Architectural / generous

Perennial container plants ...

... for locations in full sun

Botanical name	Common name	Flowers/fruit	Characteristics / Watering
Achillea	Achillea	S, scent	Flowering / moderate
Ajania pacifica	Ajania	A	Flowering / moderate
Alyssum	Alyssum	Sp, scent	Flowering / moderate
Arabis caucasia	Wall rock cress	Sp	Flowering / moderate
Armeria maritima	Thrift	Sp-S	Flowering / little to moderate
Artemisia	Wormwood	S	Flowering / generous
Aster dumosus	Aster	A	Flowering / moderate
Aster novi-belgii	Aster	A	Flowering / moderate
Aubrieta	Aubrietia	Sp	Flowering / moderate
Calluna vulgaris	Scotch heather	S, A	Flowering / moderate
Campanula capartica	Bellflower	S	Flowering / moderate
Carex buchananii	Goldband carex	S	Architectural / generous
Centranthus ruber	Red valerian	S	Flowering / moderate
Delphinium grandiflorum	Delphinium	S, scent	Flowering / little to moderate
Echinacea purpurea	Coneflower	S	Flowering / generous
Erigeron karvinskianus	Mexican fleabane	S, A	Flowering / generous
Gaillardia pulchella	Blanket flower	S	Flowering / moderate
Gypsophila	Baby's breath	S	Flowering / generous
Hebe	Shrubby veronica	S	Flowering / moderate

Botanical name	Common name	Flowers/fruit	Characteristics / Watering
Iberis	Candytuft	Sp-S	Flowering / moderate
Jovibarba sobolifera	Hens and chickens houseleek	S	Flowering / moderate
Kniphofia	Red-hot poker	S	Flowering / little to moderate
Liatris spicata	Blazing star	S	Flowering / moderate
Limonium	Sea lavender	S	Flowering / moderate
Linum	Flax	S	Flowering / little to moderate
Lupinus polyphyllus	Large-leaved lupin	S, A	Flowering / generous
Lychnis	Rose campion	S	Flowering / moderate
Nepeta X faassenii	Catmint	S, scent	Flowering / moderate
Oenothera	Evening primrose	S, scent	Flowering / moderate
Origanum laevigatum	Oregano	S, scent	Flowering / moderate
Panicum virgatum	Swtich grass	S	Architectural / little to moderate
Pennisetum alopecuroides	Chinese fountain grass	S, A	Architectural / moderate
Phlox	Phlox	Sp	Flowering / generous
Platycodon grandiflorus	Balloon flower	S	Flowering / generous
Primula veris	Cowslip	Sp	Flowering / moderate
Salvia nemorosa	Salvia	S, A, scent	Flowering / moderate
Salvia officinalis	Sage	S, scent	Flowering / moderate
Santolina chamaecyparissus	Lavender cotton	S, scent	Architectural / moderate
Scabiosa	Scabious	S	Flowering / moderate
Sedum telephium	Stonecrop	S-A, scent	Flowering / moderate
Sempervivum	Houseleek	S	Flowering / moderate
Stachys byzantina	Lamb's ears	Sp-S	Architectural / moderate
Stipa	Stipa	S-A	Architectural / moderate
Tanacetum parthenium	Feverfew	S, scent	Flowering / moderate
Thymus	Thyme	S, scent	Flowering / moderate

... for locations in sun to partial shade

Botanical name	Common name	Flowers/fruit	Characteristics / Watering
Acorus gramineus	Slender sweet flag	Sp-S	Architectural / generous
Agastache	Mexican giant hyssop	S, scent	Flowering / generous
Alchemilla mollis	Ladies' mantle	S	Flowering / moderate
Aquilegia	Columbine	Sp	Flowering / little to moderate
Aster alpinus	Alpine aster	Sp-S	Flowering / moderate
Bergenia	Bergenia	Sp	Flowering, Architectural / generous
Briza media	Quaking grass	Sp-S	Architectural / moderate
Campanula persicifolia	Narrow-leaved bellflower	S	Flowering / moderate
Campanula pyramidalis	Steeple bellflower	S	Flowering / moderate
Cerastium tomentosum	Snow-in-summer	Sp-S	Flowering / moderate
Dianthus plumarius	Common pink	Sp-S, scent	Flowering / moderate
Erica	Heather	S-A, W (acc. to variety)	Flowering / generous
Festuca	Fescue	S/Sp-W	Architectural / moderate

Botanical name	Common name	Flowers/fruit	Characteristics / Watering
Fragaria	Wild strawberry	So	Fruit / little to moderate
Gentiana	Gentian	S	Flowering / moderate
Geum	Avens	S	Flowering / generous
Hakonechloa macra	Golden Japanes forest grass	S-A	Architectural / generous
Heuchera micrantha	Alumroot	S	Flowering, Architectural / little to moderate
Linaria purpurea	Purple toadlflax	S	Flowering / moderate
Lobelia x speciosa	Lobelia	S	Flowering / generous
Lysimachia punctata	Dotted lossestrife	S	Flowering / generous
Malva moschata	Musk mallow	S	Flowering / little to moderate
Meconopsis	Meconopsis	S	Flowering / generous
Mimulus	Monkey flower	S	Flowering / generous
Molinia caerulea	Purple moor grass	S	Architectural / generous
Monarda	Bergamot	S, scent	Flowering / moderate
Oxalis	Sorrel	Sp	Flowering / generous
Papaver nudicaule	Iceland poppy	S	Flowering / moderate
Pulsatilla	Paque flower	Sp	Flowering / moderate
Pyracantha	Firethorn	Sp, S	Flowering / moderate
Trollius chinensis	Globeflower	S	Flowering / generous
Viola cornuta	Horned vilet	Sp-A	Flowering / moderate

... for a locations in partial shade to full shade

Botanical name	Common name	Flowers/fruit	Characteristics / Watering
Adiantum	Midenhair fern		Architectural / little to moderate
Ajuga reptans	Bugle	Sp	Flowering / generous
Anemone blanda	Windflower	Sp	Flowering / little to moderate
Aruncus	Goat's beard	S	Flowering / generous
Asplenium	Maidenhair spleenwort		Architectural / moderate
Astilbe	Astilbe	S-A	Flowering / generous
Calamintha nepetoides	Lesser calamint	S, scent	Flowering / generous
Campanula glomerata	Clustered campanula	S	Flowering / moderate
Campanula portenschlagiana	Wall harebell	S-A	Flowering / moderate
Campanula poscharskyana	Trailing bellflower	S	Flowering / moderate
Carex morrowii	Goldband carex	Sp	Architectural / generous
Dicentra spectabilis	Bleeding heart	Sp-S	Flowering / little to moderate
Dryopteris	Male fern		Architectural / generous
Geranium	Cranesbill	S	Flowering / moderate
Glechoma hederacea	Ground ivy	S	Architectural / generous
Helleborus	Hellebore	W, Sp	Flowering / generous
Hosta	Plantain lily	S	Architectural / generous
Houttuynia cordata	Houttuynia	S	Architectural / generous
Kirengeshoma palmata	Kirengeshoma	S	Flowering / generous

Botanical name	Common name	Flowers/fruit	Characteristics / Watering
Lamium maculatum	Striped dead nettle	S	Architectural / generous
Lewisia cotyledon	Bitterwort	S	Flowering / moderate
Mentha suaveolens	Apple mint	S	Architectural / generous
Ophiopogon	Snake's beard	Sp	Architectural / generous
Osmunda	Royal fern		Architectural / generous
Polystichum	Soft shield fern		Architectural / generous
Primula denticulata	Drumstick primrose	Sp, scent	Flowering / generous
Primula japonica	Japanische candelabra primrose	S	Flowering / generous
Primula vulgaris	Common primrose	Sp, scent	Flowering / generous
Pritzelago alpina	Chamois cress	Sp-S	Flowering / moderate
Saxifraga	Saxifrage	Sp	Flowering / little to moderate
Vinca minor	Periwinkle	Sp	Flowering / generous

Container plants ...

... for locations in full sun

Botanical name	Common name	Flowers/fruit	Over-wintering (guide only)
Abutilon megapotanicum	Chinese lantern	S-A	Light, 50-59 °F
Acacia	Acacia	Sp-A	Light, 41-59 °F
Agave	Agave	Flowers after 10 to 15 years,	Light, 41-59 °F; dark to 41 °F plants die after flowering
Anigozanthus	Kangroo paw	Sp-S	Light,
Argyranthenum frutescens	Paris daisy	S-A	Light, 41-59 °F
Asclepias curassavica	Blood flower	S	Light, 50-59 °F;
Bougainvillea glabra	Bougainvillia	S-A	Light, 50-59 °F; Dark 41-50 °F
Callistemon citrinus	Bottlebrush	S	Light, 41-50 °F
Canna indica	Canna	S	Dark (tubers), 50-59 °F
Cassia	Cassia	S-A	Light to 50 °F; Dark to 41 °F
Caryopteris x clandonensis	Caryopteris	S-A	Winter protection
Chamaerops humilis	European fan palm		Light, 41-59 °F; dark to 41°F
Cistus	Rock rose	S	Light, 41-59 °F; in winegrowing climate planted outside with winter protection
Citrus	Lemon	Sp-S, scent	Light, (41) 50-59 °F
Cotinus coggyria	Smoke bush	Sp-S, conspicuous fruit	In open
Cupressus macrocarpa	Monterey Cypress		Light, 41-59 °F
Cytisus decumbens	Broom	Sp	In open
Cytisus x racemosus	Genista	Sp, scent	Light, 41-59 °F

Botanical name	Common name	Flowers/fruit	Over-wintering (guide only)
Dracaena draco	Dracaena palm	Sp	Light,
Echium wildpretii	Echium	S	Light, 41-50 °F
Erica	Heather	Sp	Light, 41-50 °F
Erythrina crista-galli	Cockspur coral tree	S	Light-dark, 41-50 °F
Eucomis bicolor	Pineapple flower	S	Without leaves (bulb) Dark, 41-50 °F
Euryops	Resin bush	S-A	Light, 41-59 °F
Ficus carica	Common fig	Sp	Light-dark, 1-50 °F, in winegrowing climate planted out with winter protection
Genista maderensis	Broom	Sp	Light, 41-50 °F
Genista tintoria	Dyer's greenweed	S	In open
Hedychium	Kahli ginger	S	Light, 41-50 °F
Hibiscus rosa-sinensis	Hibiscus	S-A	Light; in conservatory to 68 °F; in the open with with winter protection
Hibiscus syriacus	Common hibiscus	So	
Jasminum officinale	Jasmine	S-A, scent	Light, 41-50 °F; in winegrowing-climate planted out with winter protection
Juniperus squamata	Blue star juniper		In open
Lagerstroemia indica	Crepe myrtle	S-A	Light 50-59 °F; Dark 41-50 °F
Lantana camara	Shrub verbena	S-A, scent	Light, 50-59 °F; Dark to 41 °F
Lavandula	Lavender	S-A, scent (also leaves)	Light, 41-59 °F
Lavatera thuringiaca	Garden tree mallow	S	In open
Lavatera arborea, L. olbia	Tree mallow	S	Light, 41-50 °F
Leptospermum scoparium	Tea tree	Sp-S	Light, 41-50 °F
Magnolia grandiflora	Southern magnolia	S, scent	Light, 41-50 °F
Nerinum oleander	Oleander	S-A, scent	Light, 41-50 °F
Olea europaea	Olive tree	S, fruit A	Light, 41-50 °F; in winegrowing climate planted out with winter protection
Passiflora	Passion flower	S, scent	Light, 41-50 °F °C
Phoenix	Date palm	S	Light, 41-50 °F
Phormium cookianum, P. tenax	New Zealand flax	S	Light (dark), 41-50 °F; in winegrowing climate planted out with winter protection
Picea pungens	Spruce	Sp, hanging cones	In open
Pinus parviflora	Japanese white pine	Sp, brown-red cones	In open
Prunus serrulata	Japanese cherry	Sp	In open
Punica granatum	Pomegranate	Sp-S, fruit S-A	Light- dark, 41-50 °F
Ricinus communis	Palma christi	S-A	Light, 41-50 °F; usually grown as an annual

Botanical name	Common name	Flowers/fruit	Over-wintering (guide only)
Rosmarinus officinalis	Rosemary	S, scent	Light, 41-50 °F; in winegrowing-climate planted outside with winter protection
Spiraea japonica	Spiraea	S	In open
Strelitzia reginae	Bird of paradis	Sp-S	Light, 50-59 °F
Syringa microphylla	Lilac	S, A	
Tibouchina urvilleana	Glory bush	S-A	Light, (50) 50-59 °F
Washingtonia filifera	Desert fan palm		Light (dark), 41-50 °F

... for locations in sun to partial shade

Botanical name	Common name	Flowers/fruit	Over-wintering (guide only)
Acer negundo	Ash-leaf maple	Sp	In open; autumn color
Acer palmatum	Japanese maple	Sp	In open; autumn color
Acer platanoides	Norway maple	Sp, scent	In open; autumn color
Agapanthus	Agapanthus	S	Light (dark), 41-50 °F
Albizia	Silk tree	S	Light, 41-50 °F
Aloysia triphylla	Lemon verbena	S (scented leaves)	Light, 41-50 °F
Anisodontea capensis	Cape mallow	S-A	Light, 50-59 °F
Berberis thunbergii	Berberis	Sp	In open
Brugmansia	Angel's trumpet	S-A, scent	Light; dark 41-50 °F
Cestrum elegans	Poisonberry	S	Light, 50-59 °F dark 41-50 °F
Chamaecyparis lawsoniana	Lawson cypress	small, round fruit	In open
Chamaecyparis pisifera	Sawara cypress	small, round cones	In open
Choisya ternata	Mexican orange blossom	Sp-S, scent	Light, 41-50 °F
Cordyline australis	Cabbage palm	inconspicuous	Light, 41-59 °F
Cotoneaster	Cotoneaster	Sp, berries S	
Eucalyptus	Eucalyptus, Gum	A-W	Light, 41-59 °F; in winegrowing climate planted out with winter protection
Euonymus alatus	Burning Bush	Sp	In open; autumn color
Exochorda macrantha	Exochorda	Sp	In open
Gingko biloba	Ginkgo	Sp	In open
Grevillea robusta	Silky oak	Flowers first after 10–15 years	Light, 50-59 °F; dark 41-50 °F
Hemerocallis	Day lily	S	In open with winter protection
Kalmia angustifolia	Sheep laurel	S	In open
Laurus nobilis	Bay, Bay laurel	Sp (scented leaves)	Light, 34-41 (50) °F
Lilium	Lily	4-5 Monate nach der Pflanzung; scent	In open, with winter protection
Lycianthes rantonetti	Blue potato bush	Sp-A	Light to 50 °F, dark to 41° F
Metrosideros excelsa	New Zealand Christmas tree	Sp-S	Light, 41-50 °F
Myrtus communis	Common myrtle	S-A, scent (also leaves)	Light, 41-59 °F

Botanical name	Common name	Flowers/fruit	Over-wintering (guide only)
Pinus mugo subsp. pumilio	Dwarf mountain pine	Sp, oval cones	In open
Pittosporum	Pittosporum	Sp-S, scent	Light, 41-50 °F
Plumbago auriculata	Cape leadwort	S-A	Light, 41-50 °F; dark 38-41 °F
Potentilla fruticosa	Cinquefoil	Sp-A	In open
Prunus laurocerasus	Japanese cherry	Sp, later round fruit	In open
Prunus triloba	Flowering almond	Sp	In open
Quercus suber	Cork oak	unspectacular	Light, 41-50 °F
Ruscus aculeatus	Butcher's broom	Sp	Light, 41-50 °F
Salix	Willow	Sp, catkins	In open
Syzygium paniculatum	Giant water gum	S	Light, 41-50 °F
Taxus baccata	Common yew	Sp, seeds in red berries	In open
Thuja occidentalis	Northern white cedar	Sp, oval cones	In open
Trachycarpus fortunei	Chusan fan	S	Light (dark), 41-50 °F
Ulmus x hollandica	Dutch elm	Sp	In open
Viburnum tinus	Laurustinus	Sp, A, scent	Light, 41-50 °F

... for locations in partial shade to full shade

Botanical name	Common name	Flowers/fruit	Over-wintering (guide only)
Aspidistra elatior	Aspidistra	Sp, unspectacular	Light, to 50 °F
Aucuba japonica	Aucuba	Sp, unspectacular	Light, 41-50 °F; in open with winter protection
Bambusa	Bamboo	S	with winter protection in open, indoors 41-50 °F and light
Buxus sempervirens	Box	Sp, unspecatcular	In open
Camellia japonica	Camellia	W-Sp	Light, 41-50 °F
Cleyera japonica	Japanese cleyera	Sp, berries S	Light, 41-49 °F
Corokia cotoneaster	Wire netting brush	Sp, scent	Light, 41-50 °F
Cornus alba	Red-barked dogwood	Sp	
Cycas revoluta	Sago palm		Light, (41) 50-59 °F
Euonymus japonica	Evergreen euonymus	S	Light, 41-50 °F; hardy to -41 °F
Fatsia japonica	Castor oil plant	S-A, small	Light, 41-50 (59) °F
Fuchsia	Fuchsia	Sp-A	Light-dark, 41-50 °F
Gardenia jasminoides	China flower, Gardenia	S-A, scent	Light,
Howeia belmoreana, A. forsteriana	Kentia palm		Light, (41) 50-59 °F
Hydrangea macrophylla	Hydrangea	S	Dark, 41-50 °F
Ilex	Holly	Sp	In open
Ligustrum indicum, L. lucidum	Privet	Sp-S, scent	Light, 41-50 °F
Osmanthus heterophyllus, O. delavayi	Osmanthus	Sp, scent	Light, 41-50 °F

Botanical name	Common name	Flowers/fruit	Over-wintering (guide only)
Phyllostachys nigra	Black bamboo		With winter protection in open or light, 41-50 °F
Pieris japonica	Pieris	Sp	In open
Rhapis humilis, R. excelsa	Lady palm	Sp (unspectacular)	Light, 41-68 °F depending on light
Rhododendron	Rhododendron	Sp	In open
Skimmia japonica	Skimmia	Sp, round red fruits	In open

Important tip: It is recommended to insulate the root balls – or rather the container – of all container plants that are left outdoors in winter. This is especially important in colder regions where there are prolonged periods of frost.

Climbing plants...

... for locations in full sun

Botanical name	Common name	Flowers/fruit	Type / Over-wintering
Actinidia arguta, A. kolomikta	Actinida	Sp-S, small fruit	Perennial, hardy
Akebia quinata	Akebia	Sp, scent	Perennial, hardy
Asarina barclaiana	Creeping snapdragon	S	Cultivated as annual, tender
Bignonia capreolata	Trumpet flower	Sp-S	Perennial
Campsis radicans	Trumpet vine	S	Perennial, hardy
Cardiospermum halicacabum	Balloon vine	S	Annual
Cobaea scandens	Cup-and-saucer vine	S-A	Annual
Convolvulus tricolor	Tricolor convolvulus	S	Annual
Eccremocarpus scaber	Chilean glory vine	S-A	Annual, perennial
Ipomoea coccinea	Red morning glory	S-A, scent	Annual
Ipomoea purpurea	Common morning glory	S	Annual
Ipomoea tricolor	Morning glory	S-A	Annual
Lathyrus odoratus	Sweet pea	S, scent	Annual
Mandevilla laxa	Chilean jasmine	S, scent	Light or dark, 41-50 °F
Phaseolus coccineus	Scarlet runner bean	S, large beans	Annual
Rosa	Climbing rose	S-A, scent,depending on variety	Perennial, hardy
Tecomaria capensis	Cape honeysuckle	S-A	Light, 50-59 °F; dark max. 50 °F
Thunbergia alata, Th. grandiflora	Black-eyed Susan	S-A	Annual
Wisteria floribunda	Japanese wisteria	Sp, S	Perennial, hardy

... for locations in sun to partial shade

Botanical name	Common name	Flowers/fruit	Type / Over-wintering
Ampelopsis brevipedunculata	Blueberry climber	S	Perennial
Clematis montana	Clematis montana	Sp-S, scent	Perennial, hardy
Clematis varieties (hybrids)	Large-flowered clematis	Sp-A, according to variety	Perennial, hardy
Humulus japonicus	Japanese hop	S, unspecatcular	Annual
Hydrangea anomala supsp. petiolaris	Climbing hydrangea	S	Perennial, hardy
Ipomoea lobata	Morning glory	S-A	Annual
Jasminum nudiflorum	Winter jasmine	Sp	Perennial
Rhodochiton atrosanguineus	Purple bell vine	S-A	Annual
Tropaeolum peregrinum	Canary creeper	S-A	Annual
Vitis vinifera	Grape vine	S	Perennial, hardy

... for locations in partial shade to full shade

Botanical name	Common name	Flowers/fruit	Type / Over-wintering
Aristolochia macrophylla	Dutchman's pipe	S	Perennial, hardy
Clematis alpina	Alpine clematis	Sp, S	Perennial, hardy
Fallopia baldschuriana	Russian vine	S	Perennial, hardy
Hedera helix	Common ivy	S, black berries, poisonous	Perennial, hardy
Humulus japonicus	Japanese hop	S, unspectacular	Annual
Lonicera	Honeysuckle	S, scented depending on variety	Perennial, hardy
Parthenocissus	Virginia creeper	S, blue-black berries, poisonous autumn color	Perennial, hardy

Important tip: Climbers, especially those with delicate leaves, need to be placed in a sheltered location protected from the wind. The root area should be covered against frost. If the plants are grown in containers, these should be protected.

Herb, vegetables, fruit

Most herbs, vegetables and fruit-trees need a sunny location in order to develop their full aroma. A few will also grow in the shade.

Herbs for partial shade and full shade:
Chives, chervil, tarragon, borage, melissa, curly-leaved mint, pineapple mint. peppermint, parsley
Vegetables and fruit for sunny to partially shaded places:
Beans, carrots, kohlrabi, chard, lettuce, courgettes
Strawberries, apples, peaches, sweet cherries, pears, currants, blackberries, blueberries

Pests and diseases

Prevention and treatment

To enjoy the beauty of your plants and flowers for as long as possible, you must adopt the same motto for your terrace and balcony as for your garden: "Prevention is the best medicine." The first step has already been made if you make sure that you select healthy specimens when you plant your plants. Naturally, quality has its price but the investment is worth it because healthy plants are more resistant than weaker specimens.

Equally important for good development is choosing the right location and treating plants with care. Planting too close together or in too dark, damp places will encourage pests and diseases, as will excessive or insufficient watering and feeding. If the plants stand in too much water, they will rot and enable fungal diseases to attack the plant. If given too much fertiliser, the plant tissues will become too soft and thus become easy prey to sucking insects such as aphids. Make sure that the plants are not placed too close together and that they can dry quickly after the rain to avoid fungal diseases.

Check your plants regularly for pests and diseases so that you can start treatment as early as possible if it should be necessary.

But you can also have useful insects on your balcony or terrace, which can exercise biological control of pests. The condition is that you do not use any chemical products to get rid of pests, since they may destroy benign insects as well. Ladybirds, wasp flies, green lacewing and other insects will come to establish themselves on your balcony or terrace of their own accord and often can work wonders by feeding off pests. Allow spiders to make their home among your plants because they eat aphids, midges and flies. Install nestboxes and put water for birds or hidingplaces for toads because they too are great consumers of pests.

The plants themselves will tolerate a certain number of pests without being damaged by them, so it is not necessary to be obsessive about destroying every pest. If there are enough natural enemies around and the biological balance is correct, you will not need to use chemical products. Sometimes, however, chemical pesticides will be the the only solution. In this case use products that will not kill useful insects. It is particularly important in treating flowering plants to make sure that the products you use will not be dangerous to bees.

Herbal preparations such as teas, decoctions and liquid manure, also available as pre-prepared products, are strongly recommended because of their preventive, plant fortifying and insect-repelling properties. You can make these yourself very easily. As a rule of thumb, you should use 2 lb of fresh or 6 oz of dried plants to 2 gallons of water. The teas are made as you would normally for the tea you drink and left to steep for a little while, while decoctions should be boiled after 24 hours. Both should be cooled before using. Liquid manure should be allowed to ferment for about 14 days until it no longer foams and be diluted before spraying

---

Fighting pests and diseases with liquid manure, teas and decoctions:

Use 2 lb fresh or 7 oz dried nettles for 2 gal water. If the smell of fermentation on the balcony or terrace bothers you, you can make a cold water nettle decoction, leaving the nettles to stand in water for 1–2 days and then spraying it undiluted on the plants.

Horsetail tea for combating mildew, rust and scab as well as red spider mites: boil 2lb fresh or 5 oz dried horsetail with 2 gal water for 30 minutes, then drain. Dilute one part with five parts of water and spray onto the plants. Garlic tea is also very effective: 3 oz crushed garlic with 2 gals water. This tea can be used undiluted.

Parsley fern decoction for combating aphids and fungal diseases: 10 oz fresh or 1 oz dried plants are left to macerate in 2 gals water for 24 hours. They are then boiled for 20 to 30 minutes and left to cool down before spraying on the plants.

---

onto the plants. This is best done in the evening.

Pests

Aphids: These wide-spread pests can affect almost any kind of plant. The typical symptoms are deformed, puckered, curled up leaves and stunted shoots until the plant begins to wither in parts or completely.

Aphids usually congregate on the underside of the leaves, preferably young, tender ones, as well as on young green shoots. Because of the secretion of honeydew, an invasion of aphids is frequently followed by sooty mould. In addition, aphids often bring with them dangerous viral diseases. This can be prevented by a well-balanced fertiliser without too nitrogen. If you are dealing with a mild attack, you can just remove the affected parts or wipe them with soapy water. A cold water nettle decoction, sprayed undiluted on the plants, is also very effective. In cases of more severe attacks, a pesticide that will not damage useful insects such as green lacewings and ladybirds should be used.

Scale insects: These tend to attack conifers and deciduous shrubs, fruit trees and fruit bushes. They often attack container-grown plants over-wintering indoors, especially citrus plants. The flat or rounded, yellow to brownish insects sit motionless on the branches and leaves. Their secretion of honeydew often leads to sooty mould. In mild cases, you can remove scale insects by hand or with a toothbrush. In more severe cases, you can spray the plant with a product containing mineral oil and repeat the operation several times. The scale insects will suffocate under the film of oil. However, this should not be done too frequently because the leaves would become too sticky. If the plants are grown in a greenhouse, you can buy parasitic wasps in specialist nurseries that will prove very useful in controlling the pest.

Woolly aphids: These aphids covered in tufts of waxy, white, woolly excretions gather on the underside of leaves, leaf stalks, shoots and more especially in the leaf axils. Unlike scale insects they move about but are just as troublesome. The secretion of honeydew is frequently followed by sooty mould. The leaves become sticky and shiny and the needles of conifers turn yellow and drop. They are treated in the same way as scale insects.

> **Tip:** Tender houseplants and container-grown plants should not over-winter in an excessively warm room, since that would enable aphids to multiply.

Red spider mites: The sucking action of the red spider mites, which only measure 1/50th of an inch, results in a fine mottling of the leaves which then discolor and die off. Pelargoniums affected by red spider mites display a "cork-like" mottling of the leaves. Red spider mites sit on the underside of the leaves and will attack a wide range of plants ranging from houseplants to fruit trees. Another indication of their presence is white gossamer-like agglomerations in the leaf axils and on the underside of the leaves.

Red spider mites are more prone to attack in dry, warm weather, which encourages their propagation. That is why excessively dry air should be avoided. One should encourage important rivals in the shape of predatory mites and bugs. Only in severe cases should you use a pesticide – of a kind that will not harm useful insects – such as a potash-soap based preparation.

Whiteflies: These winged insects are covered in a white powder and their fixed larvae sit on the undersides of leaves, where they lay their numerous eggs. The adult insects will immediately fly away if touched. Their sucking causes yellow spots on the leaves which finally dry up and drop. The secretion of honeydew also leads to fungus. Whiteflies prefer certain plants, which include fuchsias, verbenas and abutilons.

It is possible to reduce the risk of whiteflies by using a fertilizer that does not contain high levels of nitrogen so that the plant tissues do not become too soft and therefore vulnerable. Whiteflies mainly occur in plants over-wintering indoors. This is why it is important to hang up pesticide-impregnated sheets in the room to control possible pests, ventilate the whole area and if necessary introduce parasitic wasps. It the attack is very serious, use a pesticide that does not harm useful insects as soon as you notice the severity of the attack.

Thrips: These wingless larvae and adult insects leave fine silvery flecks on the leaves and petals that become discolored. The leaves become deformed, dry up and die. In the end the whole plant becomes stunted. The insects often suck the leaves and petals from the underside and occur more especially in damp weather and high air humidity. Predatory mites and bugs and green lacewings are natural enemies of thrips.

Check regularly to assess the seriousness of the attack. Mild attacks can be treated by the introduction of parasitic wasps, which can be bought in specialised garden centers. Pesticides should only be used in a serious attack and only of a kind that will not harm useful insects. In a very serious attacks, it is best to get rid of the whole plant. Ideally the affected parts should be burnt. They must not be thrown on the compost because thrips can over-winter in the soil as well in the discarded affected parts.

Weevils: Weevils have a flat body with a triangular shield between the forewings. The forewings lie flat on the body and, unlike beetles, their horny front overlaps. They are green to brownish and are very quick with their long legs. Their sucking causes yellow flecks on the leaves that later turn brown and die. The leaves are full of holes. Weevils also attack rosebuds and young shoots which become deformed. If they become troublesome, you can use a potash soap solution that will not harm useful insects. This best done in the morning when the insects are still unable to fly because of the low temperatures. You should also introduce natural enemies such predatory insects and birds.

Leaf miners: These pests are widespread. The females lay their eggs directly into the leaf where the larvae then develop undisturbed. Many species pupate there. The larvae eat the leaves, leaving behind clearly visible white blotches caused by their tunnelling through them and leaving excrement behind. If the attack is quite mild, just remove the affected leaves. If the attack is more serious use an ordinary pesticide that will not harm useful insects.

Fickle midge larvae: The larvae live in the soil and damage the roots and base of plants. If you touch the plant you will see small black midges – measuring about 1/10th of an inch long – suddenly fly away. The plants should be kept as dry as possible. A layer of sand on the surface of the pots will prevent the laying of eggs and is fatal to the larvae. Pesticide-impregnated sheets will help to prevent attacks while the introduction of parasitic wasps will be beneficial in the case of a mild attack.

Vegetable flies: The group of vegetable flies is very large but the damage they do is always the same. Whether carrot flies, cabbage flies, bean flies – the female maggots always tunnel through the fruit, leaves and often the roots, which causes the leaves to turn yellow and wither. Sometimes the entire plant is affected and dies. Carrots taste bitter when affected. To lay their eggs in late April or early May, flies prefer warm places sheltered from the wind. You can trick them and get round this dangerous period by sowing early or late varieties, or growing the seedlings indoors for the first few weeks. Insect nets are an effective physical barrier. But in the event of an attack it is important to replace the soil completely because carrot flies can over-winter in the soil and move onto other plants such as parsley.

Beetles: Beetles eat the leaves and buds of plants, leaving just the veins behind. The small white larvae eat the roots that leads to the withering and weakening of the plant. You can catch the wingless, nocturnal beetles only in the evening because they remain in the soil during the day. Larvae and beetles also over-winter in the soil. To get rid of larvae, you can introduce parasitic round-worms in spring and autumn. They can be ordered in specialist garden centers and used in roof gardens, containers and window boxes. But the best prevention is clean soil. Frequent victims are rhododendrons and yews, herbaceous perennials and strawberries, as well as vines and houseplants such as cyclamens.

Slugs and snails: Slugs and snails eat fruit and leaves, especially young, tender plant tissue. They can often completely defoliate plants in the course of one night. It is only in rainy weather that they come out during the day. They leave behind distinctive silvery slimy trails. However, gardeners are as inventive to combat these pests as the slugs are troublesome. Their methods include catching the snails, protecting the plants by surrounding them with a protective ring of sawdust or sand, putting up traps such as bowls of beer and special slug protection barriers. It is helpful to make sure there are no hiding-places for the slugs or snails, to avoid excessive dampness, and to create spaces for natural enemies such as birds, hedgehogs, frogs and toads. If this does not help, you can sprinkle slug pellets around the plants, but remember that these pellets are poisonous to pets.

Caterpillars: The green caterpillars of the great and small winter moths cause a lot of damage to leaves and young shoots of deciduous plants and trees in spring. Young leaves are spun together in the process.

Butterfly caterpillars are easily identified by their five pairs of legs and typical shape of the back while the great winter moth caterpillar has striking white side stripes. Make use of natural enemies such as parasitic wasps because a couple of titmice can consume up to 66 lb of caterpillars to feed their young. Sticky bands placed around the trunk in autumn will catch the flightless females on their way to laying their eggs at the top of the tree. Hornbeams, oaks and fruit trees are particularly vulnerable.

Stem and bulb eelworms: Typical indications of the presence of eelworms are stunted growth and swollen leaves and base. In phloxes the roundworms eat the leaves so that only the central vein of the leaf remains. Affected parts of the plant should be removed. An open position will help prevent infestation by eelworms.

Mixed cultivation and a pause in cultivation will also help. Weeds are often host-plants to eelworms and should therefore be removed to prevent new infestation. Besides herbaceous perennials, eelworms also attack bulbs (tulips, narcissi, crocuses) and summer flowering plants (pinks and carnations).

Leafhoppers: Like larvae, the fully grown insects cause white blotches on the top side of the leaf, very similar to those caused by the red spider mites. In fact, leafhoppers and red spider mites are often both present on the same plant but they are easy to distinguish from each other. The yellow-green leafhopper jumps away when you touch the part of the plant on which it is sitting after shedding its skin; indeed it leaves behind its very striking white skin. A striking feature of the leafhopper is the slimy foam on the shoots in which the larvae can feed undisturbed. They propagate particularly strongly during warm dry weather.

A well-ventilated position and the application of a fertiliser low in nitrogen can help prevent leafhopper attacks. Spraying with a cold decoction of nettles can be helpful in mild cases. In more severe cases you should repeatedly spray the undersides of the leaves with a standard pesticide against sucking insects that will not harm useful insects.

Plant diseases

Grey mould (Botrytis): This typical fungal disease causes brown, rotting blotches on the leaves and flowers, sometimes even affecting the stems. In fruits grey mould causes rotting of the fruit with grey areas that taste very mouldy. The disease becomes much worse in warm damp weather. Put the plants in an airy, well-ventilated place where they are not crowded by other plants so that they can dry out quickly after the rain. Trees and shrubs should be thinned, while for plants where the fruit is near the ground such as strawberries, a layer of mulch around the base of the plant is recommended. Avoid fertilisers with a high nitrogen content because this makes the plant tissue soft and as a result more vulnerable to grey mould. Dead parts of plants affected by botrytis on which the fungus can over-winter are sources of infection and should be removed immediately. If you want to use a chemical product during the flowering period, make sure it is not harmful to bees.

Rust: In spring spot-like fungal spores, yellow to rust-brown depending on the pathogen, develop on the underside of the leaves. These spores turn a darkish color in autumn. Meanwhile, yellow spots develop on the upper side of the leaf. The leaves dry out and become stunted. Make sure that the air is not too humid and the leaves are not constantly wet. The use of a fertiliser with a high nitrogen content also encourages the development of rust. The parts of the plant that are covered with spores must be removed and destroyed immediately because they harbour the rust fungus. The latter survive by passing from one plant to another. All infected plants should be removed as they are sources of infection. If your plants are repeatedly infected, find out from your garden center which plants could be the culprits. Horsetail and parsley fern extracts will have a toning effect on the plant and will also help prevent mildew attacks.

Seedling blight, root rot and stem rot: These can be caused by several different kinds of fungus, but the symptoms are always the same. The fungus easily penetrates unprotected young tissue or it enters the plant through wounds, so both seedlings and established plants are vulnerable. Roots and stems turn brown, the roots rot, the plant collapses and finally withers. The appearance of Pythium root rot and Phytophthora blight is the result of a location that is too wet, resulting for example from compacted earth on which water frequently stands. It is therefore worth making sure that all soil is water-permeable, and in the greenhouse the humidity should be not too high. Affected plants must be removed and destroyed. Sensitive seedlings can be treated by watering with a standard captan or other similar preparation.

Wilt: This infection invades in the usual way through wounds and it first withers the leaves on the shoots, which become dried up and remain hanging. In some cases whole shoots perish. The plants grow only weakly and eventually collapse. If an affected shoot is cut open, the tissues are discolored brown. The roots are not affected. The only option is to remove the attacked plants and destroy them. Asters in particular are prone to Verticillium wilt but there are many varieties that are resistant or immune.

Particular attention should be paid to hygiene in all operations with plants, especially clean vessels and sterile soil. Sclerotinia disease affects many varieties of plants; the fungus has black resting bodies that can over-winter in the soil for many years, and then infect diseased tissue, appearing in stems or roots as a white fluffy mass. It is therefore important to replace the soil completely after an attack. Wilt also frequently affects beans, cucumbers and tomatoes, but there are varieties that are resistant to it.

Powdery mildew: The typical characteristic of this widely dispersed fungus is the appearance of a white powdery coating that mainly covers the leaves, calyxes and young, soft shoots, and in the case of fruit trees, the flowers and fruit. The leaves go brown, curl and dry up.

The fungus multiplies especially quickly in muggy weather, particularly on warm sunny days with nightly dew formation. Therefore an airy location is recommended, with plants not too close together. Feeding with a balanced fertilizer, not too rich in nitrogen, is also helpful. Treating with a decoction of stinging nettles is also effective in preventing the onset of the mildew, as is horsetail tea. Choose the best resistant species that are widely available. With plants that are several years old, all affected parts of the plant must be cut back carefully as far as the healthy wood. In the case of a strong attack, a sulphur-based preparation can provide a remedy.

Downy mildew: The symptoms are similar to powdery mildew although it is caused by different viruses. It is characteristically observed in the leaf veins, which depending on the virus may be turned a bright red-violet color (in the case of roses). The undersides of the leaves show patches of white to brownish spores.

The fungus also attacks fruits and tubers; grapes change color to a bluish-brown hue and dry out. The spread of the fungus is promoted by cool, moist weather. Therefore plants should be planted far enough apart for them to dry off well. Since the fungus often spends the winter on diseased leaves and other affected tissue, it is best to remove and destroy any plants that have suffered. As a preventative measure, it is important to provide the greenhouse with good ventilation. Ask in a specialist nursery or garden center about resistant species, of brassicas and lettuces for example.

Brown rot and leaf rot: This illness is caused by the fungus *Phytophthora infestans* and attacks potato and tomato plants and fruit trees. It appears predominantly with wet weather, becoming more threatening from July onwards, and its symptoms are brownish-black stains on leaves and fruits. The fruit becomes hard and inedible. It can be prevented by selecting resistant varieties as well as by applying a decoction of stinging nettle that increases the plant's resistance. Covering the fruit with aluminium foil not only raises the temperature, encouraging the ripening of the fruits, but also protects them from infection by free-flying fungus spores. Horsetail tea is helpful in treating plants that have already been attacked. Use fresh compost each season.

Viral diseases: Viruses cause very varied symptoms of damage. These range from interference with growth to mosaic mottling of leaves and speckling of flowers, and to deformation of leaves, flowers, fruits, shoots and roots until all of the plant tissue is attacked. Viruses are frequently linked to a particular plant species. Important countermeasures include controlling carriers of viruses such as aphids, mites and leafhoppers; destroying affected plants and weeds; choosing healthy plants that are certified virus free, or even virus-resistant strains; and being meticulous about hygiene when propagating from cuttings, by disinfecting tools and containers.

Bacterial diseases: Like viruses, bacterial diseases can cause a number of different symptoms of damage. These include leaf staining, canker, bacterial fire, slime formation, over stem rot and root rot and wilt.

The bacterial disease fireblight is a Notifiable Disease and must be reported to the authorities if encountered. First the flowers and then the leaves of infected shoots become brownish-black. They look as if they are have been burned as they hang from the branches. With high humidity, slime develops and drips from the affected branches, carrying the bacteria with it, so they may infect other plants. The plants most frequently affected are from the *Rosaceae* family, such as apple, pear and pyracantha. There are no chemical means of fighting bacterial diseases, especially fireblight. Plants that are suffering from any of them and any suspicious plants nearby should be removed immediately and destroyed.

A secluded spot. If pests and diseases get the upper hand, nothing interferes more with enjoying the flowers and plants on your balcony or terrace.

Index